Decentralization in Health Care

The European Observatory on Health Systems and Policies is a partnership between the World Health Organization Regional Office for Europe, the Governments of Belgium, Finland, Greece, Norway, Slovenia, Spain and Sweden, the Veneto Region of Italy, the European Investment Bank, the Open Society Institute, the World Bank, CRP-Santé Luxembourg, the London School of Economics and Political Science, and the London School of Hygiene & Tropical Medicine.

European Observatory on Health Systems and Policies Series
Edited by Josep Figueras, Martin McKee, Elias Mossialos and Richard B. Saltman

Decentralization in Health Care

Strategies and outcomes

Edited by

Richard B. Saltman, Vaida Bankauskaite and Karsten Vrangbæk

Open University Press

Open University Press
McGraw-Hill Education
McGraw-Hill House
Shoppenhangers Road
Maidenhead
Berkshire
England
SL6 2QL
email: enquiries@openup.co.uk
world wide web: www.openup.co.uk
and Two Penn Plaza, New York, NY 10121–2289, USA

First published 2007

A catalogue record of this book is available from the British Library

ISBN 0 335 21925 X (pb) 0 335 21926 8 (hb)
ISBN 978 0 335 21925 4 (pb) 978 0 335 21926 1 (hb)

Library of Congress Cataloging-in-Publication Data
CIP data has been applied for

Typeset by RefineCatch Limited, Bungay, Suffolk
Printed in the UK by Bell & Bain Ltd, Glasgow

The McGraw-Hill Companies

European Observatory on Health Systems and Policies Series

The European Observatory on Health Systems and Policies is a unique project that builds on the commitment of all its partners to improving health care systems:

- World Health Organization Regional Office for Europe
- Government of Belgium
- Government of Finland
- Government of Greece
- Government of Norway
- Government of Slovenia
- Government of Spain
- Government of Sweden
- Veneto Region of Italy
- European Investment Bank
- Open Society Institute
- World Bank
- CRP-Santé Luxembourg
- London School of Economics and Political Science
- London School of Hygiene & Tropical Medicine

The series

The volumes in this series focus on key issues for health policy-making in Europe. Each study explores the conceptual background, outcomes and lessons learned about the development of more equitable, more efficient and more effective health systems in Europe. With this focus, the series seeks to contribute to the evolution of a more evidence-based approach to policy formulation in the health sector.

These studies will be important to all those involved in formulating or evaluating national health care policies and, in particular, will be of use to health policy-makers and advisers, who are under increasing pressure to rationalize the structure and funding of their health systems. Academics and students in the field of health policy will also find this series valuable in seeking to understand better the complex choices that confront the health systems of Europe.

The Observatory supports and promotes evidence-based health policy-making through comprehensive and rigorous analysis of the dynamics of health care systems in Europe.

Series Editors

Josep Figueras is the Director of the European Observatory on Health Systems and Policies, and Head of the European Centre for Health Policy, World Health Organization Regional Office for Europe.

Martin McKee is Head of Research Policy and Head of the London Hub of the European Observatory on Health Systems and Policies. He is Professor of European Public Health at the London School of Hygiene & Tropical Medicine as well as a co-director of the School's European Centre on Health of Societies in Transition.

Elias Mossialos is the Co-director of the European Observatory on Health Systems and Policies. He is Brian Abel-Smith Professor in Health Policy, Department of Social Policy, London School of Economics and Political Science and Director of LSE Health.

Richard B. Saltman is Associate Head of Research Policy and Head of the Atlanta Hub of the European Observatory on Health Systems and Policies. He is Professor of Health Policy and Management at the Rollins School of Public Health, Emory University in Atlanta, Georgia.

European Observatory on Health Systems and Policies Series

Series Editors: Josep Figueras, Martin McKee, Elias Mossialos and Richard B. Saltman

Published titles

Primary care in the driver's seat
Richard B. Saltman, Ana Rico and Wienke Boerma (eds)

Human resources for health in Europe
Carl-Ardy Dubois, Martin McKee and Ellen Nolte (eds)

Health policy and European Union enlargement
Martin McKee, Laura MacLehose and Ellen Nolte (eds)

Regulating entrepreneurial behaviour in European health care systems
Richard B. Saltman, Reinhard Busse and Elias Mossialos (eds)

Social health insurance systems in western Europe
Richard B. Saltman, Reinhard Busse and Josep Figueras (eds)

Health care in central Asia
Martin McKee, Judith Healy and Jane Falkingham (eds)

Hospitals in a changing Europe
Martin McKee and Judith Healy (eds)

Funding health care: options for Europe
Elias Mossialos, Anna Dixon, Josep Figueras and Joe Kutzin (eds)

Regulating pharmaceuticals in Europe: striving for efficiency, equity and quality
Elias Mossialos, Monique Mrazek and Tom Walley (eds)

Purchasing to improve health systems performance
Josep Figueras, Ray Robinson and Elke Jakubowski (eds)

Mental health policy and practice across Europe
Martin Knapp, David McDaid, Elias Mossialos and Graham Thornicroft (eds)

Contents

Acknowledgements

This study benefited greatly from generous contributions by numerous individuals and organizations. The editors are indebted to our chapter authors, whose willingness to share their knowledge and experience was essential to the success of the project. We also are grateful to the external reviewers who provided extensive comments on an early version of the manuscript: John C. Langenbrunner, Charles Normand, Lluis Bohígas Santasusagna, Hans Stein, Jon Magnussen, Yannick Lucas, George France, Rafael Bengoa, and the policy experts who participated in the authors' workshop: Martin McKee and Mikko Vienonen. The expertise of these two groups was critical in helping unravel the complexities of such a multi-faceted topic. Additionally, we would like to thank Luigi Bertinato and the Veneto Region for their elegant hosting of the authors' workshop, and for their efforts to facilitate the intellectual aspects of this project.

The overall project was co-ordinated by Vaida Bankauskaite. Research and editorial support were expertly provided by Hans Dubois of the Observatory/Madrid hub, with additional typing and manuscript preparation by Charlotte Brandigi in Atlanta. Coordination with Open University Press/McGraw-Hill Education on the delivery and production process was provided by Giovanna Ceroni.

List of tables

List of boxes

List of figures

List of contributors

Sarah Atkinson is a Reader in the School of Environment and Development, University of Manchester, United Kingdom.

Rifat Atun is Professor of International Health Management and Director of the Centre for Health Management at Tanaka Business School, Imperial College London, United Kingdom.

Runo Axelsson is Professor of Health Management at the Nordic School of Public Health in Göteborg, Sweden.

Vaida Bankauskaite is Scientific Project Officer at the European Commission and previously worked as a Research Fellow at the European Observatory on Health Systems and Policies.

Luigi Bertinato is Director of the International Health and Social Affairs Office at the Department of Health and Social Services of the Veneto Region in Venice, Italy.

Paula Blomqvist is Researcher at the National Institute for Working Life (ALI) and the Government Department at the University of Uppsala, Sweden.

Lluis Bohígas Santasusagna is Adviser to the Department of Health of the Government of Catalonia in Barcelona, Spain.

Silvia Boni is Senior Project Manager at Formez, Training and Study Centre, in Rome, Italy.

António Correia de Campos is Minister of Health, Ministry of Health in Lisbon, Portugal.

Kirill Danishevski is Associate Professor at the Moscow Medical Sechenow Academy in Moscow, Russian Federation.

Raisa B. Deber is Professor in the Department of Health Policy, Management and Evaluation, University of Toronto, Canada.

Hans F.W. Dubois is a PhD student at Bocconi University/CERGAS, Milan, Italy. This work was conducted when he was a Research Officer at the European Observatory on Health Systems and Policies in Madrid, Spain.

Unto Häkkinen is Research Professor at STAKES, Centre for Health Economics (CHESS) in Helsinki, Finland.

Oddvar Kaarbøe is Research Fellow in the Programme for Health Economics, Department of Economics, University of Bergen, Norway.

Juha Kinnunen is Professor and Dean of the Department of Health Policy and Management, University of Kuopio, Finland.

Meri Koivusalo is Senior Researcher at STAKES in Helsinki, Finland.

Akiko Maeda is Lead Health Specialist in the Human Development Department, Europe and Central Asia Region, the World Bank in Washington, DC, USA.

Jon Magnussen is Professor in the Department of Public Health and Community Medicine at the Norwegian University of Science and Technology in Trondheim, Norway.

Franca Maino is Assistant Professor in the Department of Labour and Welfare Studies, State University of Milan, Italy.

Gregory P. Marchildon holds a Canada Research Chair in Public Policy and Economic History and is Professor in the Graduate School of Public Policy, University of Regina, Canada.

Péter Mihályi is Professor in the Economics Department, Central European University in Budapest, Hungary.

Katarina Østergren is Associate Professor at the Norwegian School of Economics and Business Administration in Bergen, Norway.

José R. Repullo-Labrador is Director and Professor in the Health Planning and Economics Department of the National School of Public Health (ENS) in Madrid, Spain.

Richard B. Saltman is Professor of Health Policy and Management at the Rollins School of Public Health, Emory University in Atlanta, USA, and a Research Director of the European Observatory on Health Systems and Policies.

Paula Santana is Professor in the Department of Geography, University of Coimbra, Portugal.

Sergey Shishkin is Research Director at the Independent Institute for Social Policy, Moscow, Russian Federation.

Peter C. Smith is Professor at the Centre for Health Economics and the Department of Economics and Related Studies, University of York, United Kingdom.

Fabrizio Tediosi is Research Officer at the Swiss Centre for International Health, Swiss Tropical Institute in Basel, Switzerland. This work was conducted when he was a Research Officer at the Observatory of Health Economics, Regional Health Agency of Tuscany in Florence, Italy.

Theodore H. Tulchinsky is Associate Professor at the Braun School of Public Health, Hebrew University-Hadassah in Jerusalem, Israel.

Rosa María Urbanos Garrido is a Lecturer at the School of Economics, University Complutense of Madrid, Spain.

Karsten Vrangbæk is Associate Professor in the Department of Political Science, University of Copenhagen, Denmark.

Kaspar Wyss is Senior Researcher and Project Manager at the Swiss Centre for International Health, Swiss Tropical Institute in Basel, Switzerland.

Series editors' introduction

European national policy-makers broadly agree on the core objectives that their health care systems should pursue. The list is strikingly straightforward: universal access for all citizens, effective care for better health outcomes, efficient use of resources, high-quality services and responsiveness to patient concerns. It is a formula that resonates across the political spectrum and which, in various, sometimes inventive, configurations, has played a role in most recent European national election campaigns.

Yet this clear consensus can only be observed at the abstract policy level. Once decision-makers seek to translate their objectives into the nuts and bolts of health system organization, common principles rapidly devolve into divergent, occasionally contradictory, approaches. This is, of course, not a new phenomenon in the health sector. Different nations, with different histories, cultures and political experiences, have long since constructed quite different institutional arrangements for funding and delivering health care services.

The diversity of health system configurations that has developed in response to broadly common objectives leads quite naturally to questions about the advantages and disadvantages inherent in different arrangements, and which approach is "better" or even "best" given a particular context and set of policy priorities. These concerns have intensified over the last decade as policy-makers have sought to improve health system performance through what has become a Europe-wide wave of health system reforms. The search for comparative advantage has triggered – in health policy as in clinical medicine – increased attention to its knowledge base, and to the possibility of overcoming at least part of existing institutional divergence through more evidence-based health policy-making.

The volumes published in the European Observatory on Health Systems and Policies series are intended to provide precisely this kind of cross-national health policy analysis. Drawing on an extensive network of experts and policy-makers working in a variety of academic and administrative capacities, these studies seek to synthesize the available evidence on key health sector topics using a systematic methodology. Each volume explores the conceptual background, outcomes and lessons learned about the development of more equitable, more efficient and more effective health care systems in Europe. With this focus, the series seeks to contribute to the evolution of a more evidence-based approach to policy formulation in the health sector. While remaining sensitive to cultural, social and normative differences among countries, the studies explore a range of policy alternatives available for future decision-making. By examining closely both the advantages and disadvantages of different policy approaches, these volumes fulfil central mandates of the Observatory: to serve as a bridge between pure academic research and the needs of policy-makers, and to stimulate the development of strategic responses suited to the real political world in which health sector reform must be implemented.

The European Observatory on Health Systems and Policies is a partnership that brings together three international agencies, seven national governments, a region of Italy, three research institutions and an international non-governmental organization. The partners are as follows: the World Health Organization Regional Office for Europe, which provides the Observatory secretariat; the governments of Belgium, Finland, Greece, Norway, Slovenia, Spain and Sweden; the Veneto Region; the European Investment Bank; the Open Society Institute; the World Bank; CRP-Santé Luxembourg; the London School of Economics and Political Science and the London School of Hygiene & Tropical Medicine.

In addition to the analytical and cross-national comparative studies published in this Open University Press series, the Observatory produces Health Systems in Transition (HiTs) profiles for a wide range of countries, the journal *EuroHealth* and the policy bulletin *EuroObserver*. Further information about Observatory publications and activities can be found on its website, www.euro.who.int/observatory.

Josep Figueras, Martin McKee, Elias Mossialos and Richard B. Saltman

Introduction: the question of decentralization

Richard B. Saltman, Vaida Bankauskaite and Karsten Vrangbæk

The logic of decentralization is based on an intrinsically powerful idea. It is, simply stated, that smaller organizations, properly structured and steered, are inherently more agile and accountable than are larger organizations. In a world where large organizations control wide swaths of both public and private sector activity, the possibility of establishing more locally operated, locally responsible institutions, holds out great attraction. Even Max Weber, the turn-of-the-twentieth-century German sociologist who first formulated the key attributes of the bureaucratic model, and who himself reluctantly concluded that bureaucracy was inevitable in human organization, still yearned for the fruits of decentralization. "The only alternative to bureaucracy," he wrote, "is a return to small-scale organization" (Weber 1947).

Given the strength of this idea, it is not surprising that national and regional policy-makers in many countries across Europe have introduced decentralization strategies. In a restructuring process that has accelerated since the Second World War, the institutional landscape – particularly in the health sector – now incorporates an extraordinary range and variety of decentralized operating and managerial arrangements.

It is precisely this broad range and scope of decentralization, however, that make analysis of this concept difficult. The single, seemingly simple character of decentralization, when probed more deeply, opens up into a broad array of concepts, objectives, and consequences. Far from being a unitary, clearly defined concept, decentralization breaks apart into a kaleidoscope of different, sometimes contradictory definitions, each hallowed in its own theoretical and, often, practical context. As Chapter 2 explores, once one moves beyond Rondinelli's (1983) traditional public administration formula of devolution, deconcentration, delegation, and privatization, one finds that Europe contains a large number of political, economic, organizational, and legal variants of decentralization, each supported by its own specific logic. Decentralized bodies range from otherwise distinct countries containing millions of people (the United Kingdom) to tiny hamlets with only several hundred residents (Finland, Norway). Moreover, the health-related powers of these decentralized bodies run the gamut from nearly independent decision-making (regions in Spain) to serving as little more than administrative paper-processors for the national government (provinces in Finland). The decentralized bodies themselves may be publicly operated institutions (tax-funded countries), not-for-profit private bodies (sickness funds in social health insurance countries), or profit-making companies listed on the stock exchange (insurers in Switzerland). There are, further, additional variants of decentralization at work in central Europe and among the Former Soviet Republics, again reflecting a broad range that extends from county and municipality-based hospitals in Hungary to decentralized *akim* in Kazakhstan and all-but-independent *oblasts* in parts of the Russian Federation.

Viewed at a European level, decentralization in practice represents many things to many people, all buttressed by seemingly logical claims about the short- and long-term advantages of adopting a decentralization-based strategy. No doubt, one major reason for the concept's attractiveness to so many different decision-makers is its malleability, enabling it to simultaneously fit so many specific national and local agendas.

Such a wide variety of institutional forms, however, raises a number of unresolved questions about the core characteristics of decentralization, as well as the ability of those characteristics to accommodate key aspects of modern health care. Regarding core characteristics, for example, a central issue is whether decentralized units are primarily political entities (run according to democratic rules), administrative entities (run according to managerial precepts), or fiscal entities (run primarily as financial bodies) (Saltman and Bankauskaite 2006). As administrative and/or fiscal entities, are decentralized units more efficient than centralized units (as some economists suggest) or less efficient (as other economists contend)? Regarding the ability to accommodate key aspects of modern systems, are decentralized units more sensitive to equity issues (the democratic argument) or less sensitive (the tyranny of the majority argument)? Are decentralized units better or worse at providing integrated care for chronically ill and/or elderly patients? Do smaller decentralized units have adequate knowledge and managerial capacity to organize, and adequate resources to pay for, essential new technology for both clinical and information systems? On all these questions, as considered in more detail in Chapter 1, the available literature can best be described as equivocal.

More immediately, in the current period, there has been a small but growing number of countries that appear to be retreating from key tenets of decentralization and are, instead, re-centralizing important health system functions. In the Nordic countries, in 2002 Norway recentralized operating authority from 19 elected county councils into state hands, then allocated it to 6 new, appointed regional boards. Moreover, health sector financing in Norway has remained a national not a regional responsibility. Similarly, the Danish national government in 2006 recentralized both operating and financing responsibility away from its 14 elected county councils, dismantling these bodies to give operating authority to 5 new regional entities, while making the financing of health care an exclusive function of the state. Further, Sweden and Finland also are contemplating restructuring their health care systems, along similar if somewhat less dramatic lines. The new Nordic policy picture is thus one in which countries that had placed decentralization at the core of their health sector strategies now are reworking key elements of that prior strategy.

One can also observe important elements of recentralization in several central European countries. In both Poland and Slovakia, the previously regionalized sickness fund structure has now been pulled back into a single national organization, enabling it to be more directly supervised by national ministries of health and finance.

This recent upsurge in countries that are, in effect, reversing the trend and beginning to recentralize key functions within their health systems, raises new and fundamental questions about the overall strategy of decentralization in the health sector. Is the period of decentralization in European health systems coming to an end? Are the demands of introducing new technologies, of improving administrative efficiencies, of a renewed concern regarding cross-regional equity, or perhaps some combination of all these factors, generating pressures that can only be adequately addressed by larger organizational units? Is the local democracy argument now being supplanted by the economic efficiency argument? How in this context does one understand the upsurge in discussion about and, to a lesser degree, adoption of privatization in European health systems? Ultimately, will countries that are still assiduously decentralizing (Italy, Spain) find that the structural cycle has turned and that they, too, will need to consider recentralizing key functions?

Exploring these and other related questions is the central objective of this volume. Drawing on a series of commissioned chapters that marshal the available evidence and reviewing practical implementation-based as well as theoretically-based knowledge, this volume seeks to throw new light on the current and likely future role of decentralization, recentralization, and privatization in European health systems.

In meeting this objective, the study's editors chose not to impose one exclusive definition of decentralization on contributing authors. We felt that such an arbitrary definition would become a conceptual straitjacket, tying our expert contributors to only one of what, as already noted, are multiple different understandings across Europe of what decentralization encompasses. Instead, we adopted an umbrella approach, enabling contributors to define and use decentralization in their chapters as they felt best fit the aspect they were addressing and, not incidentally, the particular country experiences they were describing. In our own writing in Part I, however, we draw upon the various definitions of our contributors to generate a broadly comprehensive definition which is laid out in detail in Chapter 3, and utilized in the other chapters in Part I. The result of this editorial approach is that there is one specific definition of decentralization in Part I, but a variety of different, sometimes more, sometimes less, congruent definitions utilized in the commissioned chapters in Part II. Rather than creating confusion, we feel this approach enables readers to experience for themselves the complexity of the definitional question in Part II, while still being able to rely on a consistent approach in Part I.

The first five chapters that together make up Part I seek to give policy-makers and academic analysts a comprehensive yet consistent view into the complexities of understanding decentralization in the European health sector. Chapter 1 reviews the dilemmas raised by traditional views of decentralization. Drawing on the political, administrative and economic literatures, the chapter lays out the advantages and disadvantages of these standard arguments.

Chapter 2 maps practical country experience with decentralization, illustrating several of the analytic categories subsequently discussed in Chapter 3. Here the range of types, categories, and powers of decentralized bodies across Europe can be explored in considerable detail. One can also observe some of the difficulties that are created by attempting to conduct consistent comparative analysis regarding decentralization, as well as the wealth of options that the current European experience presents for future consideration by policy-makers.

Chapter 3 sets out a broad consistent definition of decentralization, drawing on the multiple approaches contained within the contributed chapters in Part II. The chapter goes on to explore decentralization from a variety of different analytic approaches, utilizing a multi-dimensional framework to measure and compare the type, degree and content of different approaches to decentralization.

Chapter 4 digs more deeply into the background factors that lead governments to adopt particular decentralization-related decisions. Drawing upon relevant political science and organization theory perspectives, the chapter applies a three-part analytic framework based on performance, legitimacy and self-interest. This tripartite framework results in a range of insights regarding the multiple layers of expectations that drive decentralization-related decisions.

The final chapter in Part I, Chapter 5, considers the policy-making lessons that can be derived from the multiple analytic perspectives found in Chapters 1–4. It also integrates some of the observations made in the commissioned chapters in Part II into a practical framework of policy options that national decision-makers will find useful both in Europe and beyond western Europe. The chapter concludes that decentralization and recentralization are intrinsically linked, and that the central issue for policy-makers is to find a balance between these two forces that fits their national values and context. Moreover, the chapter suggests that this balance is not permanent, but rather needs to be regularly revisited and re-adjusted.

In Part II, the volume delves more deeply into the impact of decentralization on a number of important health policy issues. These commissioned papers range across normative, organizational, and operational topics, exploring both academic and practical evidence on questions that influence contemporary national decision-making.

Chapter 6 (Atkinson) provides a view of research into decentralization and health systems from a cultural/organizational perspective. In it, both health systems and decentralization are understood to be organic in nature, characterized by a set of complex bi-polar dimensions (rational-symbolic, unitary-conflictual, static-dynamic, structure-actor, and individual-collective). The central policy lesson is one of inter-connectedness and complexity, admonishing policy-makers not to view decentralization as only a bolt-on administrative mechanism.

Chapter 7 (Magnussen et al.) examines the economic dimensions of decentralization. It observes that there are large variations in how decentralization has been applied to fiscal policy, and finds that "soft budgeting" is prominent in at least some of these health systems. More broadly, the chapter questions whether allowing different local districts to vary spending may in practice lower rather than increase overall welfare, mirroring earlier debates noted in Chapters 1 and 2.

Chapter 8 (Maino et al.) probes the political implications of decentralization. It explores the impact of decentralization and recentralization on the relationship between different levels of government, concentrating on the State/Region relationship. Reaching a similar conclusion to Chapter 11 (see below), Maino et al. link decentralization with diverging levels of performance among the different regions, and thus, triggering a movement toward recentralization.

The focus of Chapter 9 (Axelsson et al.) is the managerial dimensions of decentralization. The authors observe that decentralization has resulted in increased training of managers, which is viewed positively. They also note, however, that decentralization has in some countries brought increased administrative costs and greater bureaucracy. The chapter concludes that existing evidence is insufficient to support claims that decentralization generates more efficiency in health system management.

Chapter 10 (Kinnunen et al.) examines the impact of decentralization on clinical activities in health systems. The authors note that a multitude of factors can influence clinical outcomes, with decentralization being only one element among them. They conclude that the available evidence does not provide a broad or consistent picture. While the impact of decentralization appears to be only weakly correlated to health status, it does appear to influence more short-term issues such as service delivery and human resource issues. The chapter concludes by suggesting that a mix of decentralized and centralized elements may be the most effective approach.

In Chapter 11 (Koivusalo et al.) the focus is on the impact of decentralization on equity. Here the evidence is not particularly positive. Among other observations, the chapter notes that experience suggests that the local autonomy that accompanies decentralization can generate greater variation between local areas and may not always be "conducive to social rights" of vulnerable groups. The authors further note that increased freedom for providers has sometimes resulted in increased inequities in access to care. The chapter concludes that decentralization strategies need to be accompanied by effective regulatory measures, imposed by the central level, in such areas as standard-setting, performance criteria and cross-subsidization across population and area groups.

Chapter 12 (Smith and Häkkinen) explores the demand for information in decentralized health systems. It observes that, by its very nature, decentralization requires more rather than less information, since more administrative units require system management data. The chapter concludes that information formation needs to be divided between those that are top-down as against those that are bottom-up in nature, and that require appropriately structured information strategies as a result.

In Chapter 13, (Østergren et al.), the spotlight returns to the process of implementation. The authors note that recent experience suggests that implementation can best be characterized as an "arena of struggle" between central and local levels of government. The chapter lays out several criteria by which to explain the relative degree of difficulty of implementing decentralization in different national contexts. Among the criteria they propose are political legitimacy, time frame, and managerial competence (including adequate information).

Finally, Chapter 14 (Atun) addresses the role that privatization can play in the adoption of decentralization strategies. In particular, it explores the range of changes that have taken place across western, central and eastern Europe with regard to privatization. It first lays out a four-part conceptual model of privatization, ranging from full privatization (what it terms a narrow view based on transfer of capital) to increasingly expansive notions that include hybrid organizations, public–private partnership, and the adoption of private sector managerial mechanisms within public sector institutions. In documenting the practical extent to which each of these degrees of privatization have been adopted across Europe, it would appear that full privatization is more frequent in central Europe, and in sub-sections such as primary care (along with dentistry and pharmacies) where entrepreneurialism has been common in a number of western European countries for some decades (Saltman et al. 2002). Most interestingly, the evidence that the chapter copiously cites demonstrates that the greatest volume of innovation and development has been in the expansive middle ground between purely public and purely private forms of organization.

Each of the chapters in Part II raises relevant policy issues to consider, ranging from the organic character of decentralized health systems to issues of efficiency, equity, clinical performance, information processing, and the range and scope of privatization. Moreover, each chapter buttresses its observations with a number of specific case studies, providing insights into the broader context within which the observed activities occurred. In so doing, each of the chapters in Part II makes a valuable contribution to the potential lessons for future policy-making.

References

Rondinelli, D.A. (1983) Decentralization in developing countries, Staff Working Paper 581. Washington, DC, World Bank.

Saltman, R.B. and Bankauskaite, V. (2006) Conceptualizing decentralization in European health systems: a functional perspective. *Health Economics, Policy and Law*, **1**(2): 127–47.

Saltman, R.B., Busse, R. and Mossialos, E. (eds) (2002) *Regulating entrepreneurial behaviour in European health care systems*. Buckingham, Open University Press.

Weber, M. (1947) *The theory of social and economic organization*. New York, Oxford University Press.

Part one

Strategic dimensions

chapter one

Central issues in the decentralization debate

Vaida Bankauskaite and Richard B. Saltman

Introduction

Decentralization is a difficult concept to pin down. Different scholars view it through a variety of diverse, often inconsistent, sometimes overtly contradictory, analytic lenses. This divergence is compounded by differences between those writing about decentralization as it applies in the field of public administration generally, in contrast to those seeking to apply decentralization specifically to the health sector. A range of additional questions arise when one seeks to assess the actual outcomes of decentralization on pressing policy issues within health systems – its impact on the capacity to provide long-term care, for example, or to construct integrated care networks. It thus appears that decentralization covers the full range of possible judgements, with what seem to be broadly positive outcomes to some authors or in certain contexts, becoming broadly negative to other authors or in other contexts.

This chapter catalogues the multiple dilemmas involved in attempting to assess both the structure and function of decentralization in health care systems. After first reviewing the complexities involved in defining and measuring decentralization, it explores the multi-faceted political and financial contradictions that inhere within decentralization. Subsequently, the chapter reviews key questions about the ability of decentralization to achieve the outcomes that have been attributed to it. Supporting these discussions, the chapter cites both scholarly commentary and recent experience in real-world (mostly European) cases.

Defining decentralization

Decentralization has been defined and understood in multiple ways. Although typically defined in public planning, management and decision-making as the transfer of authority and power from higher to lower levels of government or from national to subnational levels (Rondinelli 1983; Collins and Green 1994; Mills 1994), it frequently has different characteristics for different writers. For example, decentralization has often been evaluated according to Rondinelli's (1983) four-part classification of delegation, de-concentration, devolution and privatization. *Delegation* transfers responsibility to a lower organizational level, *de-concentration* to a lower administrative level, *devolution* implies transferring authority to a lower political level and *privatization* takes place when tasks are transferred from public into private ownership. However, there is little agreement in the literature with regard to what these concepts actually entail.

As one example, including *de-concentration* as a form of decentralization has triggered dissenting opinions from researchers who believe de-concentration is not a type of decentralization at all. In their view, de-concentration does not require any decentralization of power since it usually does not provide the opportunity to exercise substantial local discretion in decision-making. Therefore, they argue it should not be regarded as a form of decentralization (Fesler 1968).

Other researchers do not consider *devolution* and *privatization* to be legitimate forms of decentralization. Sherwood (1969) argues that *devolution* is a concept quite separate from decentralization, in that it implies the divestment of functions by the central government and the creation of units of governance not in the direct control of central authority. He contends that devolution embodies a concept of separateness. He and others argue that decentralization and devolution are different phenomena: they use "decentralization" to describe an intra-organizational pattern of power relationships while devolution describes an inter-organizational pattern (Sherwood 1969).

Whether to include *privatization* as a type of decentralization also has generated disputes. Collins and Green (1994) contend that, since decentralization involves the transfer of authority, functions, and/or resources from the centre to the periphery, while privatization involves a transfer from the public sector to the private sector, they are different concepts. A different, alternative perspective identifies commonalities between both public and private sectors and suggests shifting focus from confrontation between the two sectors towards common issues of governmental regulation, financial incentives and planning tools (Mills 1994; Mackintosh 1999). Chapter 14 reviews recent empirical experience with privatization in European health systems.

Beyond decentralization's lack of clarity, several health sector reforms have been labelled "decentralization" when it is not clear that the term applies. For example, the shift of acute services from hospitals to home care has been termed decentralization (Wasem 1997). Since this reform did not entail a shift in the structure of power or authority, however, it may not have been appropriate to use the term this way.

Further, decentralization may be both a state and a process, with each dimension requiring a distinct approach. Decentralization as a state can itself involve two different measures, i.e. level and degree. With regard to level, decentralization may occur at system or organizational level. Mintzberg (1979) defined the latter as a distribution of power over the decisions made inside an organization. Different combinations of different degrees of decentralization at system or organization levels may exist. These reflections suggest the importance of defining decentralization explicitly, so as to identify whether one is speaking about process or state, and to specify the degree and level of decentralization.

Measuring decentralization

As a complex multilevel phenomenon, encompassing a number of political, fiscal and administrative dimensions, decentralization also is difficult to measure. At least three challenges exist in terms of assessing decentralization: (1) measuring decentralization (both state and process); (2) measuring the outcomes of decentralization in health care; and (3) comparing decentralization between countries.

Despite the number of theoretical frameworks for decentralization, few measure the scope and extent of decentralization. Rondinelli's frequently applied public administration framework, for example, does not measure degree of decentralization. Since decentralization and centralization represent two ends of a single continuum, the question of degree is an important one. Bossert's (1998) concept of decision space integrates both horizontal and vertical decentralization and is intended to measure the degree of decentralization. This approach, however, does not consider decentralization as a process.

The lack of analytic criteria is a key reason for difficulty in determining the outcome of decentralization. The challenges involve identifying dependent and independent variables and then demonstrating the appropriate associations between them. It is difficult to quantify dimensions such as responsibility, autonomy, power and accountability. The process of identifying independent variables is equally complex. The most common independent variables for decentralization have been fiscal ones, such as local spending as a proportion of national spending. However, fiscal indicators can often be misleading measures of power and authority.

Conversely, qualitative research has become increasingly popular with the recognition that quantitative methods can seldom address questions concerning implementation (see e.g. Pope and Mays 1995). Other scholars argue that it is difficult to obtain new insights using qualitative methods since they only gather data to answer an initial research question and suggest using anthropological methods to provide evidence on the context of social processes (Lambert and McKevitt 2002).

Comparative analysis can draw broad generalizations about the generic character of the policy process. However, comparisons of health care policies often spark intense debates as to the appropriate methodology. Smith (1985) argues, for example, that cross-national comparisons are difficult because the delegation of power occurs in such different contexts and takes such different forms. He suggests that time-series analysis tracking changes might produce less ambiguous results than cross-sectional analysis comparing degrees of decentralization across countries (Smith 1985). Gershberg et al. (1998) recommend describing the distribution of powers and responsibilities across different levels of government with particular attention given to policy development.

Politics, values and decentralization

Beyond definition and measurement, decentralization necessarily has both political and financial dimensions. In each of these areas, expectations and assessments differ widely depending upon the orientation of the analyst, adding to the question marks already noted.

In the political arena, decentralization can take on numerous dimensions. There is, first, the structural issue: how decentralization influences and is influenced by existing institutions of government in a given country. A second dimension reflects where those institutions come from, e.g. the values that led to and sustain a particular set of governmental institutions. Together, these factors are sometimes referred to as the "context" within which decentralization is undertaken. While there is a wide range of opinions about how to characterize different institutional arrangements, and what the likely impact of different forms of decentralization might be on these institutions and also on the outcomes obtained, the one point on which nearly all politically-oriented commentators agree is that – to quote an often-used phrase – "context matters".

A further set of issues on the interface between decentralization and governmental institutions can be termed steering questions. These involve such areas as regulatory structure, framework laws, and intra-country negotiation procedures.

All these political dimensions – institutional structure, social and cultural values, and governance mechanisms such as regulatory and negotiating arrangements – come to bear on the likely impact that decentralization may have within a particular health care system. This section briefly reviews differing perspectives on how to assess these political pressures, along with differing expectations for the outcomes that, as a result, decentralization can achieve.

The role of context is a key theme of this volume. Several chapters stress the impact of contextual factors on the outcomes obtained through health care decentralization. As a central component of context, the role of politics cannot be overestimated. Since decentralization involves the distribution and sharing of power and political control, it unavoidably has a strongly political dimension. In the world of politics and policy, moreover, institutions play a central role. Neo-institutional arguments contend that the role of institutions is crucial in shaping political behaviour (March and Olsen 1989). One well-known study, utilizing empirical evidence on 36 countries from 1945–1996, lends support to these arguments by suggesting that institutional configuration affects policy performance of political regimes (Lijphart 1999).

Rather differently, other scholars have insisted on the importance of adding a political economy perspective to assessments of decentralization. For example, Wolman (1990) argued that, since intergovernmental decentralization is often driven as much as by political and constitutional necessities as by economics, a political economic perspective is required. Mackintosh (1999) also has advocated a political economy approach to decentralization.

Another element of politics and decentralization concerns the concept of public participation. This is often seen as a central element for local responsiveness and allocative efficiency. However, several studies suggest that public participation may only create a limited degree of representation due to weak formal structures (Abelson et al. 1995). These studies imply that, despite frequent statements about the benefits of lay participation, public participation may not lead to more representative decision-making.

Following a different logical line, Tiebout (1956) argues that one driving force for decentralization is people moving from areas they do not like to other areas where their needs are better addressed, e.g. "voting with their feet". Yet others contend that, in practice, the needs of people in one area are not really so different from those in other areas (Salmon 1987).

Moving to the context within which institutions sit, a number of authors have drawn attention to the way in which restructuring processes may be "culturally embedded" – that is, influenced by broader social and cultural traditions within particular regions and nations (Clegg 1990). The concept of "values" has become a recognized element in policy analysis, as reflected in WHO publications (WHO 1996; Saltman and Figueras 1997). Yet research into the definition, operationalization and application of this notion of values remains underdeveloped. One Canadian study found that, despite widespread recognition of the importance of values, decision-makers and stakeholders in health policy often disagree fundamentally over the content of these values (Giacomini et al. 2004).

Turning to the mechanisms of institutional behaviour, regulatory parameters also are part of a governance process. In Chapter 12, Smith and Häkkinen note that the number of regulatory instructions would be expected to be low in highly decentralized systems due to weaker central efforts to influence local decisions. In Sweden, which has a long tradition of decentralization, the health system is now governed by "framework" laws and general principles provided at the national level, and only in a few instances do detailed directives still exist. As a result, different county councils have considerable freedom to develop the pattern of health services within their jurisdictions (Calltorp 1999).

The structure of regulation also reflects and reinforces the existing configuration of institutional incentives. It has been argued that the appropriate degree of decentralization depends upon which level of government will have the most incentives to bring about the desired outcomes (Cremer et al. 1996). However, incentives for local government levels are not always the main priority for central government. In the Russian Federation, revenue sharing between regional and local governments gives local governments little incentive to be efficient since change in any one local government's revenue is offset by changes in shared revenue. This results in a variety of less-than-optimal outcomes from the existing decentralized institutional structure (Dethier 2000).

An example of the complexity of relying upon negotiation as a steering mechanism in decentralized health systems comes from Spain, where, since 2003, regions and the central government are expected to negotiate differences in an inter-territorial council through formalized mutual adjustments.

This council consists of national and regional representatives and possesses coordination, cooperation, planning and evaluation functions. Unfortunately, there has been little evidence to date that the council functions effectively in practice (Fidalgo et al. 2004).

As these examples suggest, governance mechanisms confront numerous challenges in decentralized systems. Tensions occur at a variety of different levels within these health care systems. Tensions between the national and local levels arise when local levels need more financial resources and are unable to satisfy what they see as unnecessarily high standards from central government. Problems may also occur if local governments lack discretion or capacities in policy implementation to satisfy local preferences. A frequent cause of tension between different local governments is the unwillingness of richer local governments to help fund services from poorer regions. This problem is particularly noticeable in Canada, Italy and Spain.

One more aspect worth mentioning regarding steering issues is accountability. If central government is to monitor performance and ensure equal standards, transparency and accountability mechanisms need to be in place. Paradoxically, sub-national units with financial discretion are not always enthusiastic about being accountable to central government, which can complicate the mission of central government in decentralized settings.

Financing and decentralization

Financial decentralization – which some economists persist in terming "fiscal federalism" even in unitary parliamentary states (Saltman and Bankauskaite 2006) – can be defined as the division of taxing and expenditure functions among different levels of government. This has been a hotly debated issue in many western European countries. There are also a number of controversies in economic theory regarding the best way to finance intergovernmental levels. The most intense discussions refer to the rights of local governments to levy taxes, e.g. fiscal decentralization. Oates's theorem (1972), for example, contends that it will always be more efficient for local government to provide a good within its respective jurisdictions than for a central government to provide that good across several local authorities.

In a number of countries, central government transfers have been the main source of revenue for local authorities. This situation may result in several dilemmas. First, central contributions contradict the notion of local accountability. Second, high levels of decentralization will necessarily create high levels of "grant dependency", particularly when there are unconditional grants from higher levels of government that do not limit the discretion of the lower-level recipient. Further, a main principle of public finance argues that in order to ensure accountability, purchasing and taxing authority should be in the same institutional hands. Rathin (1999) has argued that decentralized governments might seek to raise revenues that would add to, rather than substitute for, the central tax burden. In these circumstances, decentralized provision could potentially be more expensive than centralized provision.

The structure of intergovernmental fiscal relations in a country is not only based on principles of public finance but also reflects specific contextual factors. For example, sub-national government in one country may have very low grant dependence (e.g. raise nearly all revenues from local sources), but may also do very little (be responsible for few functions or have low levels of expenditure) (Wolman 1990). Does this administrative unit, thereby, possess a higher degree of decentralization than one with high dependency on grants from national government, but high level of responsibility for health services?

Another issue here is cross-subsidies. Decentralization has the potential to increase inequalities, therefore, cross-subsidies are often introduced among a country's different regions. However, decentralization that incorporates cross-subsidies may reduce local discretion to develop innovative programmes. The redistribution of resources also can create political tensions between winners (administrative units receiving funds) and losers (administrative units paying these funds).

A further factor here concerns the European Union's concept of subsidiarity. According to this standard, the overarching goal in determining intergovernmental relations should be to push responsibility for service provision to the lowest level possible to promote participatory democracy and achieve efficiency gains from matching services to citizen preferences. From this concept has sprung much of the impetus for giving sub-national government more direct responsibility for service provision, and thereby reinforced the need for fiscal decentralization to fund those services.

Outcomes and decentralization

The evidence regarding the ability of decentralization to achieve its objectives is complex and ambiguous (see Table 1.1). There are several likely explanations for this result, including decentralization's complicated character, the strong role of context, and a lack of clarity regarding the definition and measurement of the concept.

Among positive reported outcomes of decentralization are the capacity to innovate within county councils, improved efficiency, a more patient-oriented system and enhanced cost-consciousness (Bergman 1998); higher regional and local authority accountability (Jommi and Fattore 2003); stimulation of broader change regarding work organization and working time (Arrowsmith and Sisson 2002); and better implementation of health care strategies based on need (Jervis and Plowden 2003). However, a number of studies reported negative or ambiguous effects from health care decentralization, inequity being the most frequent concern (Collins and Green 1994; Koivusalo 1999; Jommi and Fattore 2003).

A notably different impact can be discerned in the post-communist countries of central and eastern Europe, which face different challenges from those in western Europe. A number of post-communist countries sought to decentralize the financing of their health systems in addition to the provision of services. Along with economic difficulties, poor planning of decentralization resulted in negative outcomes in some countries. In the Russian Federation and Ukraine, for example, multilayered health care systems now have fragmented responsibilities. Decentralization of financing in Ukraine led to increasing inequalities

Table 1.1 Objectives, rationale and controversies of health decentralization

Objectives	*Rationale*	*Issues and controversies*
To improve technical efficiency	Through fewer levels of bureaucracy and greater cost consciousness at the local level Through separation of purchasers and provider functions in market-type relations	May require certain contextual conditions to achieve it Incentives are needed for managers Market-type relations may lead to some negative outcomes
To increase allocative efficiency	Through better matching of public services to local preferences Through improved patient responsiveness	Increased inequalities among administrative units Tensions between central and local governments and between different local governments
To empower local governments	Through more active local participation Through improved capacities of local administration	Concept of local participation is not completely clear The needs of local governments may still be perceived as local needs
To increase the innovation of service delivery	Through experimentation and adaptation to local conditions Through increased autonomy of local governments and institutions	Increased inequalities
To increase accountability	Through public participation Transformation of the role of the central government	Concept of public participation is not completely clear Accountability needs to be clearly defined in terms of who is accountable for what and to whom
To increase quality of health services	Through integration of health services and improved information systems Through improved access to health care services for vulnerable groups	
To increase equity	Through allocating resources according to local needs Through enabling local organizations to better meet the needs of particular groups Through distribution of resources towards marginalized regions and groups (through cross-subsidy mechanisms)	Reduces local autonomy Decentralization may improve some equity measures but may worsen others

between wealthy and poor areas. Latvia experienced significant problems when funding for health care services through local government budgets resulted in widely differing amounts of health expenditure per inhabitant between regions.

One interesting question is how well decentralization can address newly emerging health care needs in Europe. Two related issues of particular interest to policy-makers in Europe are long-term care and integrated networks. A third issue is improving access to mental health services.

Several countries have employed decentralization strategies to address their long-term care needs, mainly through the consolidation of administrative functions. In predominantly tax-funded Nordic countries (Denmark, Norway and Sweden), responsibility for planning, organizing, delivering and financing long-term care has been decentralized to municipal level. The aim of this strategy has been to achieve closer intersectoral cooperation between social and home care services through allocation of responsibility to the lowest level of governance. The largest part of social services in Denmark and Sweden is financed by local taxes while in the Netherlands, a predominantly social health insurance country, responsibility for long-term care has been pooled through regional "care offices" in order to simplify programme administration at the level closest to care recipients and to ensure appropriate resources to meet regional needs (De Roo et al. 2004).

Integrated care is another challenge for European health care systems. It involves integration between different health system levels or between different sectors, such as social and health care. Several commentators view the concept of decentralization as essential to the development of effective integrated care services (Frossard et al. 2004). For example, the 1999 reform in Scotland introduced local health care cooperatives (LHCC). LHCC are primary care organizations defined by geographical area and consist of GPs, community nurses, and other health and social care professionals which coordinate the delivery of services to assigned populations. Among their objectives was improvement of population health and the development of extended primary care teams (Simoens and Scott 2005). LHCC also are integral parts of Primary Care Trusts (PCTs) and are accountable to them. As decentralized structures, LHCC have considerable discretion in adopting governance arrangements suited to local circumstances (Woods 2001).

A number of countries in Europe employ decentralization strategies in dealing with mental health issues. Existing associations between the prevalence of mental disorders and geographical areas with specific risk factors imply that community-based interventions and programmes could be helpful. Good practice examples are available, e.g. in England, where some analysts believe that community-based mental health teams have had positive effects (Singh 2004). In addition, the integration of health and social care services in addressing mental health issues is important and here decentralization also can be useful.

In countries in transition, the agenda of important health sector challenges includes the increase in communicable diseases (notably HIV and tuberculosis), poor nutrition habits and high alcohol consumption. Tuberculosis is a major health problem in most countries of the former Soviet Union (McKee 2001). Some of these countries are also experiencing the world's fastest growing HIV/AIDS epidemic. In Ukraine, 1% of the adult population has HIV, which is the highest in Europe. It has been estimated that cumulative new cases of HIV in the Russian Federation may range from 4 to 19 million by 2025 (Eberstadt 2002). Public health interventions to tackle these epidemics may be more effective if they are community-based, making it possible to target marginalized and hard-to-reach population groups. This suggests that geographical (territorial) decentralization could contribute to an effective public health response.

Conclusion

This chapter has highlighted a number of problems in understanding the role of decentralization in health care systems. It suggests that these problems arise in part because decentralization is a multilevel concept that often is not well defined. The chapter then identified numerous problems involved in measuring decentralization and noted that the choice of the method depends on the specific question being asked. Additional dilemmas to do with the political and financial aspects of decentralization also were reviewed, and a variety of efforts to assess the outcomes that decentralization presents were explored. A brief list of key issues is presented in Table 1.2.

All these questions serve to demonstrate the complexities that have confronted

Table 1.2 Current issues in health care systems and examples of decentralization strategies to address them

Health care needs	*Examples of decentralization strategies*
To increase long-term care services	Responsibility for planning, financing, delivery and organization of long-term care decentralized to local health care level
To integrate care services	Responsibility for the set of services made under a single decision-making authority
To implement efficient public health interventions	Responsibility for interventions for hard to reach and high risk groups is transferred to local levels Community public health actions in high risk areas
To increase accountability	Responsibility for health care costs allocated to sub-national levels Unconditional block grants to local governments New forms of management of health care organizations
To increase efficiency	Innovative forms of organizing health provision and institutions Increased role of private sector (i.e. PPP, PFI, contracting out)
To improve mental health care services	Targeted community-based programmes in high risk areas

and continue to confront both policy-makers and scholars when they set out to review the role of decentralization in health systems. In response to these dilemmas, the subsequent chapters that follow in Part I set out an integrated comprehensive framework through which to understand and utilize the concept of decentralization in making policy for health care systems.

References

Abelson, J., Lomas, J., Eylees, J., Birch, S. and Veenstra, G. (1995) Does the community want devolved authority? Results of deliberative polling in Ontario. *Canadian Medical Association Journal*, **153**: 403–12.

Arrowsmith J., Sisson, K. (2002) Decentralization in the public sector: the case of the UK National Health Service. *Relations Industrielles*, **57**: 2. (Available at: http://www.erudit.org/revue/ri/2002/v57/n2/006784ar.html, accessed 17 July 2006.)

Bennett, R.J. (ed.) (1990) *Decentralization, local governments, and markets: towards a post-welfare agenda*. Oxford, Clarendon Press.

Bergman, S.E. (1998) Swedish models of health care reform: a review and assessment. *International Journal of Health Planning and Management*, **13**: 91–106.

Bossert, T. (1998) Analysing the decentralization of health systems in developing countries: decision space, innovation and performance. *Social Science and Medicine*, **47**: 1513–27.

Calltorp, J. (1999) Priority setting in health policy in Sweden and a comparison with Norway. *Health Policy*, **50**(1–2): 1–22.

Clegg, S.R. (1990) *Modern organizations: organization studies in the post-modern world*. London, Sage.

Collins, C. and Green, A. (1994) Decentralization and primary health care: some negative implications in developing countries. *International Journal of Health Services*, **24**: 459–75.

Cremer, J., Estache, A. and Seabright, P. (1996) Decentralizing public services: what can we learn from the theory of the firm? *Revue d'Economie Politique*, **106**: 37–60.

De Roo, A.A., Chambaud, L. and Güntert, B.J. (2004) Long-term care in social health insurance systems. In Saltman, R.B., Busse, R. and Figueras, J., eds, *Social health insurance systems in western Europe*. Maidenhead, Open University Press/McGraw-Hill.

Dethier, J-J. (ed.) (2000) *Governance, decentralization and reform in China, India and Russia*. Dordrecht, Kluwer Academic Publishers.

Eberstadt, N. (2002) The feature of AIDS: grim toll in Russia, India and China. *Foreign Affairs*, **81**(Nov/Dec): 22–45.

Fesler, J.W. (1968) Centralization and decentralization. In Sills, D.L., ed., *International encyclopedia of the social sciences*, vol. 2. New York, The Macmillan Company and The Free Press.

Fidalgo, J.M., Repullo, J.R., Alende, M.J. and Oteo, L.A. (2004) El acogedor "Estado del malestar" del Sistema de Salud. *El Pais*, 29 October.

Frossard, M., Genin, N., Guisset, M.J. and Villez, A. (2004) Providing integrated health and social care for older persons in France: an old idea with a great future. In Leichsenring, K. and Alaszewski, A.M., eds, *Providing integrated health and social care for older persons*. Aldershot: Ashgate.

Gershberg, A. (1998) Decentralization, recentralization and performance accountability: building an operationally useful framework for analysis. *Development Policy Review*, **16**: 405–31.

Giacomini, M., Hurley, J., Gold, I., Smith, P. and Abelson, J. (2004) The policy analysis of "values talk": lessons from Canadian health reform. *Health Policy*, **67**(1): 15–24.

Jervis, P. and Plowden, W. (2003) *The impact of political devolution on the UK's health services: final report of a project to monitor the impact of devolution on the United Kingdom's health services 1999–2002*. London, The Nuffield Trust.

Jommi, C. and Fattore, G. (2003) Regionalization and drugs cost-sharing in the Italian NHS. *Euro Observer*, **5**: 1–4.

Koivusalo, M. (1999) Decentralization and equity of healthcare provision in Finland. *British Medical Journal*, **318**: 1198–200.

Lambert, H. and McKevitt, C. (2002) Anthropology in health research: from qualitative methods to multidisciplinarity. *British Medical Journal*, **325**: 210–13.

Lijphart, A. (1999) *Patterns of democracy in thirty-six countries*. New Haven, CT, Yale University Press.

Mackintosh, M. (1999) Informal regulation: a conceptual framework and application to decentralized mixed health care systems. In Mackintosh, M. and Roy, R., eds, *Economic decentralization and public management reform*. Cheltenham, Edward Elgar.

March, J. and Olsen, J. (1989) *Rediscovering institutions: the organizational basis of politics*. New York, Free Press.

McKee, M. (2001) The health effects of the collapse of the Soviet Union. In Leon, D. and Walt, G., eds, *Poverty, inequality and health*. Oxford, Oxford University Press: 17–36.

Mills, A. (1994) Decentralization and accountability in the health sector from an international perspective: what are the choices? *Public Administration and Development*, **14**: 281–92.

Mintzberg, H. (1979) *The structuring of organizations: a synthesis of the research*. London, Prentice-Hall.

Oates, W.E. (1972) *Fiscal federalism*. New York, Harcourt Brace Jovanovitch.

Pope, C. and Mays, N. (1995) Qualitative research: reaching the parts other methods cannot reach: an introduction to qualitative methods in health and health services research. *British Medical Journal*, **311**: 42–5.

Rathin, R. (1999) Economic theories of decentralization: towards an alternative political economy approach. In Mackintosh, M. and Roy, R. eds, *Economic decentralization and public management reform*. Cheltenham, Edward Elgar.

Rondinelli, D.A. (1983) Decentralization in developing countries, Staff Working Paper 581. Washington, DC, World Bank.

Salmon, P. (1987) Decentralization as an incentive scheme. *Oxford Review of Economic Policy*, **3**: 24–43.

Saltman, R.B. and Bankauskaite, V. (2006) Conceptualizing decentralization in European health systems: a functional perspective. *Health Economics, Policy and Law*, **1**(2): 127–47.

Saltman, R.B. and Figueras, J. (eds) (1997) *European health care reform: analysis of current strategies*. Copenhagen: WHO Regional Office for Europe.

Sherwood, F.P. (1969) Devolution as a problem of organization strategy. In Dalan, R.T., ed., *Comparative urban research*. Beverly Hills, CA, Sage.

Simoens, S. and Scott, A. (2005) Voluntary or compulsory health care reform? The case of primary care organizations in Scotland. *Health Policy*, **72**(3): 351–8.

Singh, D. (2004) Community based team can transform mental health services, says report. *British Medical Journal*, **328**: 790.

Smith, B.C. (1985) *Decentralization: the territorial dimension of the state*. London, Allen & Unwin.

Tiebout, C.M. (1956) A pure theory of local expenditure. *Journal of Political Economy*, **64**: 416–24.

Wasem, J. (1997) A study on decentralizing from acute care to home care settings in Germany. *Health Policy*, **41**(suppl.): 109–29.

WHO (1996) *WHO policy statements: the Ljubljana Charter on reforming health care*. Copenhagen, WHO Regional Office for Europe.

Wolman, H. (1990) Decentralization: what it is and why we should care. In Bennett, R.J., ed., *Decentralization, local governments, and markets: towards a post-welfare agenda*. Oxford, Clarendon Press.

Woods, K.J. (2001) The development of integrated health care models in Scotland. *International Journal of Integrated Care* [serial online], 1(3) (http://www.ijic.org, accessed 15 April 2006).

chapter two

Patterns of decentralization across European health systems

Vaida Bankauskaite, Hans F.W. Dubois and Richard B. Saltman

Introduction

Among the key questions raised in this chapter regarding decentralization are: *what* powers are decentralized and *to whom* are these powers decentralized? Following on from these two questions, the focus here is to map the structures and responsibilities of decentralized health care systems in Europe. It should be noted that this picture of the administrative and government structure is necessarily a static one. A more dynamic view of decentralization, more consistent with actual country experience, can be found in Chapters 2 and 4.

Mapping the main characteristics of decentralized health care systems concentrates on laying out of two clusters of characteristics. The first includes the structure of government, the respective size of government levels, whether a government level is appointed or elected, and the right of the government level to raise taxes. The second cluster examines the specific health care functions that the different levels of government exercise.

Mapping the levels of government (structure)

Among the many factors related to the theoretically ideal form of decentralization, as well as to its actual form adopted in a particular country, is the number of sub-central government units along with their absolute and relative sizes (Litvak et al. 1998). Nevertheless, there seems to be no well-developed empirical evidence that clearly supports any existing theory about the significance of boundaries or local government size.

Table 2.1 presents the structure of the decentralized health care systems in selected European countries and Canada. The process of standardization of the structures for health care systems entails several challenges. First, countries use various names for different decentralized government levels, e.g. the level directly under the central government is called "*Provincies*" in the Netherlands, "*Comunidades Autónomas*" in Spain, "*Landsting*" in Sweden, "*Kantone*" in Switzerland, "*Countries*" in the United Kingdom, etc. In our analysis, for comparative purposes, the government level directly under the central government is called "region" and the level directly under these regions is called "district". The highest level of government is called "central government"[1] and the lowest is "local government". The national names for the government levels are included as well. Any additional levels of government included in Table 2.1 are called by the national name or/and a non-standardized English translation of it.

Second, some countries have areas with a special status which do not follow the typical national structure. Examples are the Açores and Madeira in Portugal, Åland in Finland, and the Danish cities of Copenhagen and Frederiksberg which have become unitary authorities, exercising the functions of both the *Amt* and *Kommun* level of government. Moreover, administrative structures may vary largely between the regions within the same country, e.g. three Swiss cantons (Appenzell, Basel and Unterwalden) are each divided into two half-cantons, and the Italian region Trentino-Alto Adige is divided into two highly autonomous provinces, while, for historical reasons, five Italian regions have a special statute (Friuli-Venezia Giulia, Sardegna, Sicilia, Trentino-Alto Adige and Valle d'Aosta). For Canada, all regional sub-divisions in Table 2.1 are called "Regional Health Authorities", while in fact the different regional entities have different structures (District Health Authorities/Health Boards/Health and Social Services Authorities). In the Canadian region of British Columbia, for example, the five geographic Regional Health Authorities are divided into 16 Health Service Delivery Areas.

Third, some countries have intermediate administrative levels or structures without specific functions allocated. Intermediate administrative levels may include associations of regions ("co-operation *Landsting*" in Sweden) and/or associations of local governments (*Gemeindeverbände* in Germany, *Circondari* in Italy). Hungary is sub-divided into seven regions which are aggregations of 2–4 lower-level governments, inspired by the EU Nomenclature of Territorial Units for Statistics (NUTS). These statistical-planning entities appear to be skeleton organizations, which might be assigned real powers, but that would require changes in the constitution and the election systems (Mihályi 2005). Also, three of the six German levels of government identified in Table 2.1 are administrative entities rather than levels of government: local, regional and central governments are most important for health care and for other sectors as well (Rosenbrock and Gerlinger 2004). Some of these powerless lower levels of government, such as *Sogne* in Denmark, have been omitted from Table 2.1.

Furthermore, the category "central government" in our analysis does not

Table 2.1 Number and size of levels of national government, whether appointed or elected, and tax-raising powers (2004)

Country	*Levels of government, including administrative health structures*	*Number*[1]	*Inhabitants per entity: average*[2] *(and approximate range) (× 1000)*	*Appointed/ Elected*	*Raising taxes*[3]
Canada	Central government	1	31 946	Elected	X
	Regions (*Provinces and Territories*)	13	2457 (28–11 874)	Elected	X
	Regional Health Authorities	91	351 (1–1783)	Appointed	
	Local governments	3715	9 (0.005–2481)	Elected	
Denmark	Central government	1	5384	Elected	X
	Regions (*Amter*)	13	414 (225–653)	Elected	X
	Local governments (*Kommune*)	272	20 (0.1–502)	Elected	X
Finland	Central government	1	5206	Elected	X
	Regions[4] (*Lääni*)	6	868 (26–2117)	Appointed	
	Districts (*Maakunta*)	20	260	Appointed	
	Hospital districts (*Sairaanhoitopiiri*)	21[5]	248 (70–800)	Appointed	
	Local governments (*Kunnat*)	444	12 (0.1–559)	Elected	X
France*[6]	Central government	1	59 630	Elected	X
	Regions (*Régions*)	22	2710 (260–10 952)	Elected	
	Regional Hospital Agencies (*Agence Régionale de l'Hospitalisation*)	22	2710 (260–10 952)	Appointed	
	Districts (*Départements*)	96	621 (74–2563)	Elected	
	Local governments (*Communes*)	36 679	2	Elected	
Germany*	Central government	1	82 537	Elected	X
	Regions (*Länder*)	16	5159 (661–18 080)	Elected	X
	Districts (*Regierungsbezirke*)	29	2846 (517–5245)	Appointed	
	Kreisfreie Städte and Landkreise	439	188 (36–1248)	Appointed	
	Ämter & Gemeindeverbände	1603	51 (1–106)	Appointed	
	Local governments (*Gemeinden / Städte*)	14 703	6 (0.004–152)	Elected	X
Hungary*	Central government	1	10 142	Elected	X
	Regions (*Régió*)	7	1445 (989–2825)	Appointed	
	Districts (*Megye and Megyei Varos*)[7]	20	507 (219–1105)	Elected	
	Local governments	3179	3 (0.02–1719)	Elected	
Italy	Central government	1	57 423	Elected	X
	Regions (*Regioni*)	20	2871 (121–9121)	Elected	X
	Hospital Trusts (*Aziende Ospedaliere*)	98	586	Appointed	
	Districts (*Province*)	100	574	Elected	
	Local Health Enterprises (*Aziende Sanitarie Locali*)[8]	197	293	Appointed	
	Health Districts (*Distretti Sanitari*)	843	68	Appointed	
	Local governments (*Comuni*)	8104	7	Elected	X
The Netherlands*	Central government	1	16 193	Elected	X
	Regionals (*Provincies*)	12	1349 (379–3452)	Elected	

	Local governments (*Gemeenten*)	489	33 (1–739)	Elected	
Norway	Central government	1	4552	Elected	X
	Health Regions (*Helse*)[9]	5	910 (600–1500)	Appointed	
	Regions (*Fylker*)	19	240 (73–522)	Appointed	X
	Local governments (*Kommuner*)	434	10 (0.2–522)	Elected	X
Poland*	Central government	1	38 219	Elected	X
	Regions (*Wojewodztwa*)	16	2389	Appointed	
	Districts (*Powiaty*)	373	102	Appointed	
	Local governments (*Gminy*)	2489	15	Elected	
Portugal	Central government	1	10 407	Elected	X
	Regions (*Comissões de Coordenação Regional*)	5	2081	Appointed	
	Districts (*Distritos and Regiões Autónomas*)	20	520	Elected	
	Local governments (*Concelhos*)[10]	308	34 (0.3–663)	Elected	
Russian Federation*	Central government	1	143 826	Elected	X
	Regions (*Oblasts, Krais,* Republics, Autonomous, Entities, Cities)	89	1616	Elected	
	Regional health authorities	89	1616	Appointed	
	Local governments (*Rayons,* Cities, Villages, Rural Administrations, Rural Settlements)	11 576[11]	12	Elected	X
Spain	Central government	1	41 551	Elected	X
	Regions (*Comunidades Autónomas*)	17[12]	2444 (287–7607)	Elected	X
	Districts (*Provincias*)	52	799 (68–6834)	Appointed	
	Local governments (*Municipios*)	8110	5 (0.001–3603)	Elected	
Sweden	Central government	1	8941	Elected	X
	Health Care Regions	6	1490	Appointed	
	Regions (*Landsting*)	21	426 (57–1839)	Elected	X
	Local governments (*Kommuner*)	290	31 (3–700)	Elected	
Switzerland*	Central government	1	7318	Elected	X
	Regions (*Kantone*)	26	281 (15–1182)	Elected[13]	X
	Districts (*Bezirke*)	181	40 (2–403)	Appointed	
	Local governments (*Gemeinden*)	2929	2	Elected	X
United Kingdom	Central government	1	59 554	Elected	X
	Regions (*Countries*)	4	See below	Elected	
	(1) Country government England	1	49 856	Elected	
	Strategic Health Authorities	28	1781	Appointed	
	NHS Trusts	176	283	Appointed	
	Primary Care Trusts	303	165	Appointed	
	Local governments (*Local Authorities/Unitary Authorities*)	355	140 (2–977)	Elected	
	(2) Country government Northern Ireland[14]	1	1703	Elected	
	Health and Social Services Boards	4	426 (281–666)	Appointed	

(Continued Overleaf)

Table 2.1 Continued

Country	*Levels of government, including administrative health structures*	*Number*[1]	*Inhabitants per entity: average*[2] *(and approximate range) (× 1000)*	*Appointed/ Elected*	*Raising taxes*[3]
	Health and Social Services Trusts	19	90	Appointed	
	District Councils	26	66 (16–277)	Elected	
	Local governments	582	3 (1–10)	Elected	
	(3) Country government Wales	1	2938	Elected	
	Local governments (*Unitary Authorities*)	21	140 (56–305)	Elected	
	Local Health Boards	21	140	Appointed	
	NHS Trusts	15	196	Appointed	
	(4) Country government Scotland	1	5057	Elected	
	Health Board Areas[15]	15	337	Appointed	
	Operating Divisions[16]	19	266	Appointed	
	Districts (*Council Areas*)	32	158 (19–578)	Elected	
	Local governments (*Wards*)	1 167	4 (1–10)	Elected	

Notes: *Country that finances health care costs largely by social health insurance (SHI) contributions.

[1] 2002 data for sickness funds.

[2] 1 January 2003 data for average population (July 2004 data for Canada, mid-2003 for Italy, Russian Federation and the UK).

[3] Most significant for health care.

[4] Including the autonomous Province of the Åland Islands.

[5] The semi-autonomous province of Ahvenanmaa, which forms its own hospital district, is included.

[6] Excluding the four overseas regions.

[7] 19 Counties (*megyek*) and 1 capital city (*fovaros*).

[8] They used to be called Local Health Units (*Unità Sanitarie Locali*), but most regions now call them Local Health Enterprises (*Aziende Sanitarie Locali*).

[9] Hospitals are run by Regional Health Enterprises.

[10] Based on geographical proximity rather than administrative areas. They are subdivided into *freguesias*. We decided to omit this lowest level of government because they have no real government.

[11] 2003 figure.

[12] Ceuta and Melilla are *Ciudades Autónomas*. Their health management of Spain's two small overseas territories is the responsibility of the regional government of Madrid.

[13] The cantons Appenzell, Glarus and Unterwalden do not hold elections and vote, but have a so-called *Landsgemeinde*, an outdoor assembly of all its citizens. The attendees raise their hands to show if they agree with or a particular request or not.

[14] Data for wards is for May 2003; other census data: 2001.

[15] Excluding special health boards.

[16] Formerly known as NHS Trusts. Restructuring from April 2004 resulted in NHS Trusts being abolished and replaced with operating divisions within NHS Boards. The reason there are now fewer operating divisions than NHS Trusts is that some NHS Boards decided to operate as single systems without operating divisions.

Sources: Boni (2005), Central Statistical Office (2005), Committee of the Regions (2004), Federal Statistics Office (2005), Federal Statistics Office Germany (2005), Government Statistical Service (2005), Hungarian Central Statistics Office (2005), ISTAT (2005), Longo (2001), National Institute for Statistics and Economic Studies (2005), National Statistics (2005), National Statistics Institute (2005), National Statistics Institute Portugal (2005), Northern Ireland Statistics and Research Agency (2005), OECD (2005), Statistics Canada (2005), Statistics Denmark (2005), Statistics Finland (2005), Statistics for Wales (2005), Statistics Netherlands (2005), Statistics Norway (2005), Statistics Sweden (2005), Swiss Federal Statistics Office (2005).

specify different ministries involved in health care policy-making. The distribution of authority within the central government ("split decision-making") reflects a situation in which several ministries have different responsibilities, for example, the ministry responsible for financing usually differs from the ministry responsible for public health matters (Kjellberg 1988).

The final observation refers to the accountability of different levels of governance. Even though it would seem to be logical for a lower level of government to be accountable to a higher level, this is not necessarily the case. For example, the main actors in the Swedish health system are *Landsting* (regions). Local governments have received significant responsibilities in health care recently, but they are not accountable for how they administer these responsibilities to *Landsting*.

In reviewing the data presented in Table 2.1, it is apparent that the number of levels of government varies considerably among European countries. According to some policy analysts, a two-tier system is best for the health sector: a lower-level authority should cover the largest area in which a sense of community exists and where citizens can participate, and a higher-level authority should cover the largest area to which it can deliver technical services (especially specialized hospital services) efficiently and which permits authorities to meet frequently (Mills 1994). This framework implies that countries should seek to combine two major objectives, local participation and efficiency, in how they organize a decentralized health care system.

Table 2.1 presents a diverse picture of decentralized structures in Europe. Countries have quite different governmental structures for the health sector, creating intermediate levels and allocating special rights to some regions, so that strict standardization of decentralized systems is not feasible. Moreover, a decentralized intergovernmental structure does not itself necessarily imply actual decentralization of decision-making responsibility. Whether the sub-central level plays a decision-making role in the health sector can only be determined after taking into account the functions and responsibilities allocated to them and investigating the consequent lines of accountability. These issues are discussed below. Nevertheless, the mapping of decentralized structures is an important exercise as it provides a framework for further analysis.

The size of administrative units

As mentioned earlier, scholars believe that the absolute and relative size of government units has an impact upon decentralization. In addition, factors such as the size and density of population, country size and homogeneity of population can also influence decentralized health care systems (Prud'homme 1995; Litvak et al. 1998; De Vries 2000; WHO 2004). However, it is not always clear how these factors affect decentralization. De Vries (2000), for example, demonstrated that a country's larger geographical size (rather than population size) is highly correlated to the percentage of elites in favour of local responsibility for the majority of policy areas. The important question for policy-makers here is whether there is some optimal size for administrative units. This review addresses this issue by examining government-generated catchment areas in terms of their average population size.

Mills (1994) suggests that a compromise "optimal" level is a geographically compact area of between 50 000 and 500 000 inhabitants, often a local government unit, which can provide comprehensive health service for most conditions. The data assembled here show that the size of local government units can vary greatly: from an average of just over 1600 inhabitants in France to 140 000 in England. The Canadian resort village of Etter's Beach in Saskatchewan, with its five inhabitants, is one of the smallest local governments.[2] The largest local government in a country usually coincides with the capital city (e.g. Budapest local government in Hungary or Copenhagen local government in Denmark). The size of regions in various countries varies considerably as well. For example, the average German region (*Land*) has a size approximately equal to that of the entire country of Denmark. This suggests that what is considered a decentralized structure in one country might be perceived as centralized in another.

In terms of efficiency, the level and size of the geographic unit should be appropriate to the health services to be managed. If the units do not have comprehensive health care responsibilities, there should be means to ensure that an efficient mix of services is provided, across all responsible agencies, which meet the needs of the population in the most cost-effective manner (Mills 1994). However, cause–effect questions remain unanswered, and the relationship between size and efficiency is not clear-cut. There appears to be no correlation between country size and the average size of its administrative sub-unit.

The dynamics of decentralized administrative structures

General administrative structures in many European countries date back several centuries. For example, the Swedish County Councils emerged in the mid-1800s and the French local government structure (*communes* and *départements*) dates from 1789, when Napoleon replaced large regions with smaller units. Nevertheless, the overall environment across Europe has been quite dynamic.

One key point is that the numerical structure at higher levels of governance is relatively constant. For example, in Italy, the latest change in the number of regions took place in 1963, when the region Abruzzi e Molise was split into two separate regions. Switzerland's youngest canton, Jura, was created in 1978 to separate two linguistic groups, and The Netherlands reclaimed land for an additional province from the sea (Flevoland), which was recognized as a twelfth province in 1986. At lower levels, changes are more frequent. Profound reforms of local government size and function have taken place in north-western Europe, for example, since the 1960s (Brans 1992). Denmark massively restructured its local governments in the years after the 1970 reform, amalgamating 1300 administrative units into 275 *kommune*. This reform was triggered by a general increase in tasks handled by the public sector and by the fact that the urban expansion of localities had extended across their boundaries (Ministry of the Interior and Health 2002). Smaller-scale, more incremental changes in the number of local governments are very common. Here, the recent trend is towards centralization. For example, in Finland, the number of local governments decreased from 444 in 2004 to 432 in 2005 due to mergers, and in Denmark five local governments merged in 2003 as the result of a referendum.

Mergers sometimes result from the bottom-up initiative, as, for example, in Italy where several new *province* have been formed out of local government associations (*circondari*) recently. A top-down approach regarding mergers is also possible. The French Government has been actively searching to merge local governments due to relatively small local government units, but has been facing local resistance. For the past few years local governments (*communes*) have been obliged to make associations among themselves in new administrative bodies called "*communautés de communes*". The Portuguese state adopted a law in 2003 to stimulate local governments to associate themselves, mainly according to population size, into three new types of government entities: *Grandes Áreas Metropolitanas, Comunidades Urbanas* or *Comunidades Intermunicipais* (Statoids 2005).

In the health sector, new levels of government have recently been created in some countries. Examples include the Regional Health Authorities that have been created in several Canadian provinces since 1989 and the eight Irish Health Boards that were set up in 1970 with the aim of transferring power from the local governments to a higher level of government because the central government had become the major health care funder and because of the financial complexity caused by increased inter-local-government hospital visits. In France, regions obtained authorities for transport, education and culture domains only in 1982 even though regions were created in 1955. In 1996, as a result of the Juppe Plan, some health functions were devolved to the regional level and new organizational structures were created, such as regional hospital agencies and regional unions of the health insurance funds. Empirical evidence shows that some countries have recentralized their administrative units in order to achieve efficiency in providing inpatient care. The benefits of stronger centralization for specialized care include improved quality of health care, better possibilities to analyse outcomes and increased medical excellence. Table 2.1 indicates that a number of countries have created organizational structures specifically for inpatient health care (e.g. Regional Hospital Agencies in France, Hospital Districts in Finland and Health Regions in Norway).

The merger of units has also occurred in sickness funds in social health insurance (SHI) countries. The number of sickness funds decreased practically everywhere in western Europe during the past two decades, except in Belgium, Israel and Luxembourg. Sometimes the government actively stimulated this decrease. In addition, there have been two other centralizing forces at play that cannot be derived from looking merely at the numbers: sickness funds have become daughter companies of large insurance concerns in The Netherlands and certain functions were transferred to national sickness fund unions in e.g. Luxembourg (1992), Poland (2003) and France (2004) (Busse et al. 2004; Commission des Comptes de la Sécurité Sociale 2004).

Appointed and elected levels of government

One argument in favour of decentralization is to bring government decisions "nearer to the people" and to encourage community involvement, i.e. to increase democracy (Ranson and Stuart 1994).[3] Tiebout (1956) argues that elected local governments have more opportunities and stronger incentives to accommodate local preferences, and to meet socio-economic and demographic challenges.

The definition of "elected" used in Table 2.1 can be controversial in some cases. Several government structures indicated in Table 2.1 as "appointed" are in fact elected by democratically elected bodies. For example, governments of Spanish *Provincias* are elected by local governments, which are in turn elected by popular vote. Similarly, the chief administrative officer of the Norwegian *Fylker* is appointed by the elected national government. In this mapping exercise, however, we only attach the label "elected" to governments that are directly elected by popular vote on the grounds that this approach best represents democracy according to the theoretical criteria cited above.

Most countries have a mixture of both elected and appointed levels of government for health care, but at least two levels of elected governments – central and local governments – are present in all countries. While governmental levels that are responsible for other matters as well as health care are mainly elected, government bodies and levels dealing specifically with health care are, as a rule, appointed. These specific health care bodies are mainly found in tax-funded countries and include hospital districts in Finland, health regions in Norway, Local Health Enterprises in Italy, as well as Regional Hospital Agencies in the largely SHI-funded French health care system. These appointed health care government levels are not necessarily less responsive to local needs, since they can still be accountable to elected governments. Furthermore, it is important to understand the functions and powers of these government levels.

The common characteristic for SHI countries[4] is that the governance unit for the SHI system is either appointed or selected by the constituent (not-for-profit-private) organizations in a particular sub-sector. Non-elected bodies typically perform functions such as collection of funds and reimbursement of services. When the insured have a free choice of sickness funds, though, it could be argued that there are some democratic forces at work which sickness funds need to accommodate in order to survive, since the insured population can punish sickness funds by changing funds when they are dissatisfied. Moreover, sickness fund boards are often at least partly elected by their membership (Saltman et al. 2004).

Taxation

In countries with different agencies for funding and providing health care services, the process by which funds are channelled from one to the other is of considerable importance (Bennett 1991; Figueras et al. 2005). In countries that are largely financed through SHI, raising funds is, to different degrees,[5] the responsibility of sickness funds. In predominantly tax-funded countries, raising health care funds is mainly the responsibility of different levels of government.

"Fiscal (de)centralization" is a term that emerged from the study of (de)centralization in sectors different from health care (e.g. Gramlich 1993; Wildasin 1997; Davoodi and Zou 1998) and was adapted in research that focuses on tax-based health care systems (e.g. Frank and Gaynor 1994).

Decentralization of taxation could trigger inter-regional tax competition and might thus reduce overall government income. Rodden (2002) showed that countries that apply fiscal decentralization seem to move closer to the overlapping, inter-twined multi-tiered state described by Scharpf et al. (1976) in which the finances of central and local governments are increasingly difficult to disentangle. In Rodden's sample of OECD countries, decentralization, when funded primarily by autonomous local taxation, is associated with a smaller public sector. When funded by revenue-sharing, grants or centrally regulated sub-central taxation, decentralization is associated with higher public spending. The design of the tax system and intergovernmental grants can have a large effect on local spending patterns (Wilde 1971; Gramlich 1977; Rubinfeld 1987; Ahmad 1997), but it is unclear what these effects imply. In practice, predominantly tax-funded health care systems can be divided into two types: (1) systems in which sub-central levels of government have a right to raise taxes (Denmark, Finland, Sweden); and (2) systems in which sub-central levels of government predominantly receive grants from the central government (Spain, the United Kingdom). Some argue that unconditional fiscal equalization grants are essential for an efficient (and equitable) fiscal federal system (Boadway and Flatters 1982), while others state that such transfers have adverse effects (Oakland 1994).

Financial autonomy is an essential aspect in assessing decentralized government structures, since the power of a level of government tends to be weakened by the absence of financial autonomy and the consequent financial pressure from other levels of government. Financial autonomy has two important aspects: (1) raising funds; and (2) spending funds. As Box 2.1 demonstrates, autonomy in raising funds involves more than simply the power of a certain level of government to raise taxes. Funds can also be raised by borrowing, so it is important to know whether a certain level of government can run deficits. Additional sources of government funds include private payments (user charges, private/SHI insurance). Furthermore, in order to fully assess the financial autonomy of a level of government, one should know whether the level of government can determine the tax rate and if it is autonomous in deciding what type of tax it can raise. Autonomy in determining the type of tax can have implications for equity as e.g. sales tax is generally less progressive than income and property tax. Some analysts suggest that the local public sector should be financed by user charges and "local" taxes such as property tax, regional government by consumption taxes, and central government by income tax (Musgrave 1983). On the spending side, there are also numerous questions that are essential in assessing a government's autonomy: how far does a higher level of government determine what type of health care services and to what geographical location the lower level should allocate funds; what part of the money raised is transferred to a higher level of government or to a solidarity fund, how spending patterns influence future allocation of funds,[6] etc. (see Box 2.1). The high number of financial variables implies difficulties in assessing the financial discretion of sub-national levels of government. This chapter only looks at a limited number of these variables.

Table 2.1 explores one key question concerning the collection of funds: can a particular level of government raise taxes that are relevant for health care? As just noted, this measure only partly reflects a level of government's financial

Box 2.1 Variables on financial discretion of sub-national government levels

Right of sub-national government levels to raise taxes.

Right to determine the tax rate and what type of taxes could be raised.

Ability of sub-national government to run deficits and to borrow money.

Right to raise and determine user-fees.

Percentage of raised funds transferred to a higher level of government or solidarity fund.

Type of grants allocated to sub-national levels (conditional or unconditional).

Percentage of the national and local funding of health care.

Right to finance health care services as local government prefers.

autonomy. Nevertheless, in practice, the power to raise taxes might be a second-order indicator of financial autonomy as levels of government that are allowed to raise taxes often have higher autonomy concerning the other variables mentioned above than levels of government that are not allowed to raise their own taxes. One could further argue that, in addition to collecting and spending funds, a third aspect of financial autonomy is ownership of health sector institutions. This aspect will be discussed separately below.

The concept of authority to raise taxes has some additional limitations. It does not reflect the complex picture of the fund-raising structure within each country, which can in turn vary dramatically among countries. Table 2.2 illustrates the complexity and the dynamics of fund-raising by the Swedish regions that accounted for 92% of total health expenditure in 2003. These data from Sweden are presented as an example chosen due to its availability, as it can be difficult to obtain these data.

Table 2.1 also does not reflect the magnitude of the share of health care funds raised by each particular level of government. While, for example, Swedish regions not only spend, but also raise the major share of health care funds (Table 2.2), the Spanish *Comunidades Autónomas* are indicated as able to raise taxes related to health care, but in fact the only tax which they can raise (earmarked to health care) is a supplement of the petrol tax, and, as of 2005, only a few *Comunidades Autónomas* have used this right. Furthermore, even with a national tax, lower levels of government might have some fiscal power. The Scottish Parliament, for example, has the power to vary the rate of the national tax that should apply in Scotland (up to 2005, this has not happened yet, though).

Several final observations can be made from the information presented in Table 2.1. First, while appointed government levels often have health care functions, generally, the right to raise taxes is limited to elected levels of government. Second, there did not appear to be any correlation between the rights of sub-central levels of government to raise taxes and country size. Third, the

Table 2.2 Funding sources for health care in Sweden, 1993 and 2003

	Funding sources for the sector of County Councils (%)	
	1993	*2003*
Tax revenues	70.7	72.2
National insurance	4.2	12.8[1]
State subsidies	8.5	5.5
Payments from other principals	6.6	2.4[2]
Reimbursement for services rendered	3.7	2.7[2]
Other revenue	3.2	1.7
Patient fees	3.1	2.7

Notes:
[1] For medicine 9.8%.
[2] Excluding payments in the sector.

Source: Swedish Association of Local Authorities and Regions (2004)

biggest portion of taxes related to health care, or general taxes that might be used for health care, is generally raised at the central or regional level. In Nordic countries, local and regional governments have a major stake in raising taxes in this field. In Denmark, municipalities and counties spent a larger share (more than half) of total public expenditure than local governments in any of the other countries examined (Ministry of the Interior and Health 2002). In 2002, 56% of these funds were raised through taxes, while the remaining 44% were operating and investment income (26%), general and earmarked grants (10%), proportional refund grants (8%) and loans and repayments (1%). In other countries, sub-national governments usually have a much less crucial role, and if they have some stake in health care at all, funds are usually used for social and primary care.

Finally, when looking at the dynamics of fiscal decentralization, countries that devolved taxation power to a lower level of government rarely withdrew these functions, while they sometimes have withdrawn other powers related to health care. A good illustration of the latter case is the changing role of the Norwegian counties, which had been largely (never fully – consistent with the statement made earlier about power following money) responsible for management of specialized and secondary care since 1969. Never having been given the ability to raise health care-related taxes, their managerial responsibilities were withdrawn in 2002. Conversely, when the right to levy taxes has been decentralized, that authority has only rarely been recentralized. One of the few cases in which tax levying rights were recentralized occurred in Denmark in 2006 (thus not shown in Table 2.1) where the central government has now stopped the counties' taxation rights, and directed managerial responsibilities into a small number of new regional administrations.

Mapping responsibilities of government levels (functions)

This section of the chapter maps several major health care responsibilities in selected countries, including raising health care funds; contracting providers; identifying the ownership of secondary care; long-term care and primary care institutions and the status of general practitioners (GPs).[7] Since there is no agreement on what are the most suitable indicators for defining decentralized health care systems, we will first attempt to explain the choice of these specific measures.

Ownership, management and governance are proxies for institutional responsibilities; however, none of them is ideal. The government level that owns a certain health care institution might differ from the level that is responsible for its day-to-day management. Other variables, e.g. the responsibility for budget, strategic decisions and management, are important for decentralization as well. For example, in Norway, secondary care hospitals are owned by the central government, but run by regional health enterprises. In The Netherlands, long-term care institutions are privately owned, but running costs are paid by mandatory contributions, collected by the central government. Taking into consideration complexity and diversity across the countries, ownership would appear to be the best proxy for the government function with regard to health care institutions.

The variable "raises health care funds", included in Table 2.3, refers only to the level on which the major share of funds is raised. For example, in most SHI countries, the central government often raises additional funds that are allocated to health care (e.g. to subsidize insurance for the less well-off as in France). A second financial indicator is also included, indicating the government level that contracts with health care providers.

An additional criterion included in Table 2.3 is the status of GPs. Combining theoretical frameworks from Øvretveit (2003) and Saltman (2003), GPs can be employed by a public (state/non-state) or private (for-profit/non-profit) entity, and be either salaried or self-employed. In Table 2.3, we examine only whether GPs are private or not. This is an unfortunate if necessary simplification. For example, in The Netherlands in January 2004, 90.4% of GPs were self-employed, while the remaining 9.6% worked for these self-employed GPs as salaried employees, thus all of them are formally private GPs (NIVEL 2004).

A further challenge of this mapping exercise arises in comparative perspective. Since several non- and semi-governmental entities have important health care powers, some of these are also included here (e.g. private sickness funds). However, many other non- and semi-governmental organizations with health care functions are excluded (physician associations, non-government quality inspectorates, etc.). Furthermore, health care functions can differ considerably among entities that all fall within the same level of government. For example, the Swedish local authority of Gotland has the responsibility and tasks normally associated with a *Landsting*. In Canada, British Columbia and Prince Edward Island are the only regions with a Provincial Health Service Authority, providing respectively specialized services and secondary/acute care. The labels attached to certain entities can also create confusion. For example, the Scottish "Health

Table 2.3 Levels and respective responsibilities in health care in selected countries in Europe and Canada (2004)

Country	*Levels*[1]	*Health care responsibilities*					
		Raises health care funds (public)	*Contracts hospitals*	*Owns secondary hospitals*	*Owns long-term care institutions*	*Owns primary care centres*	*Pays GPs*
Canada[2]	Central government						
	Regions (*Provinces and Territories*)	X	X				
	Regional Health Authorities			X	X	X[3]	
	Local governments				X		X
Denmark	Central government						
	Regions (*Amter*)	X	X	X		X	X
	Local governments (*Kommune*)				X		
	Private				X		
Germany	Central government						
	Regions (*Länder*)			X			
	Districts (*Regierungsbezirke*)						
	Kreisfreie Städte / Landkreise			X			
	Ämter / Gemeindeverbänder						
	Local governments (*Gemeinden / Städte*)			X	X		
	Sickness funds	X	X				
	Private			X	X	X	X
Hungary	Central government	X		X	X		
		X	X				
	Regions (Regional Health Councils)						
	Districts (*Megye and Megyei Jogú Város*)[4]			X	X		
	Local governments			X	X	X	
	Sickness funds						
	Private						X
The Netherlands	Central government						
	Regions (*Provincies*)						
	Local governments (*Gemeenten*)						
	Sickness funds	X[5]	X				
	Private			X	X	X	X
Norway	Central government	X		X			
	Health Regions (*Helse*)[6]			X			
	Regions (*Fylker*)						
	Local governments (*Kommuner*)	X	X		X	X	X
	Private						
Poland	Central government	X					
	Regions (*Wojewodztwa*)	X	X	X			
	Districs (*Powiaty*)			X		X	
	Local governments (*Gminy*)						
	Private						
	Sickness funds	X	X				

(Continued Overleaf)

Table 2.3 Continued

Country	*Levels*[1]	*Health care responsibilities*					
		Raises health care funds (public)	*Contracts hospitals*	*Owns secondary hospitals*	*Owns long-term care institutions*	*Owns primary care centres*	*Pays GPs*
Russian Federation	Central government	X	X				
	Regions (*Oblast*, Republic)	X	X				
	Local governments (Municipalities)	X	X	X	X	X	X
	Sickness funds	X	X				
	Private						
Sweden	Central government						
	Regions (*Landsting*)	X	X	X		X	X
	Local governments (*Kommun*)				X		
	Private						
Switzerland	Central government						
	Regions (*Kantone*)			X			
	Districts (*Bezirke*)						
	Local governments (*Gemeinden*)				X	X	
	Sickness funds	X	X				
	Private			X	X	X	X
United Kingdom	Central government	X					
	Regions (*Countries*)						
	Health Boards[7]		X	X		X	
	Local governments				X		
	Private				X	X	X

Notes: Thanks to Kai Mosebach (*Medizinische Hochschule Hannover*) for general comments on this table.

[1] Sickness funds are included because they are sometimes important fundraisers, contractors and health care institution owners. While some predominantly tax-based countries (such as Portugal) also have sickness funds, we excluded these as they are perceived to play a less important role in these countries. There are more public and private bodies that have important health care responsibilities (such as physician organizations), but taking into account the limited scope of the table and the variables chosen, we left them out. Sickness funds are taken as a separate category even though they can be public (AOKs in Germany) or private (Netherlands, partly Germany) and could thus sometimes fit into any of the other categories. They can be either non-profit (Germany, partly Netherlands) or for-profit (Switzerland, partly Netherlands). And in Germany the 17 regional sickness funds coincide with the *länder* (only in *Northrhein Westfalen* there are two regional sickness funds).

[2] There are few primary care centres in Canada. We refer to public health offices instead. In the relatively large province of Ontario almost all hospitals are private non-profit corporations and public health offices are owned by the government.

[3] There are few primary care centres as most primary care is delivered by private fee-for-service physicians. In the table we indicated information for public health offices that deliver public health, health promotion and prevention services. In Ontario these are ran by the regional ministry, not by the RHAs.

[4] 19 Counties (*megye*) and 1 capital city (*föváros*), 22 cities have the legal status of a *megye*.

[5] Flat-rate premiums are collected by the sickness funds, but income-dependent premiums are collected by the different companies who deposit this money in the General Health Insurance Fund.

Boards" might sound similar to Welsh local "Health Boards", but they differ substantially in their functions.

Finally, only the most common arrangements of health care institution ownership and the main actors are indicated. In Switzerland, for instance, some secondary hospitals are owned by the local governments (*Stadtspital*) or a local government group (*Bezirksspital*), but most are private or owned at the regional level. In Denmark, less than 1% of the hospital beds are privately owned and only the Danish GPs who decide not to sign the public system health care reimbursement agreement are fully private. The health configuration in the United Kingdom has been simplified given that organizational structures differ among its four constituent countries.

Table 2.3 suggests that providers usually are contracted by the sub-central entity that raises the major part of health care funds. In predominantly SHI countries, responsibility for contracting providers falls to the sickness funds.

Secondary care hospitals are most often owned by regional governments. They can also be owned by various regulatory bodies, such as Health Boards, Regional Health Authorities (RHA) and others. Concerns about managerial capability and efficiency are probably the main reasons why secondary care institutions are owned by a government level higher than local level. In general, the private ownership of secondary health care institutions is not common. The Netherlands is an exception to this situation, with the majority of secondary hospitals being privately owned through not-for-profit, often religious linked foundations. What is more common in terms of privatization (and is not reflected in Table 2.3) is outsourcing of services (e.g. cleaning or laboratory services) and private–public mixes (e.g. foundations, private–public partnerships and private finance initiatives). Recently some countries (e.g. Hungary) have been selling off secondary hospitals to the private sector (Hirs 2005). While ownership and/or management are sometimes in the hands of decentralized levels, these levels often have restrictions from "above", e.g. the few privatized Hungarian hospitals can be renationalized if there are clear signs of mismanagement. In Northern Ireland, the Health and Personal Service Trusts and Area Boards are managerially responsible for health care institutions and can even decide to sell buildings, but within strict limits established by the Northern Ireland Department of Health, Social Services and Public Safety, and only with its approval.

Ownership of primary care (PC) centres varies considerably among countries. These centres can be owned by RHAs or other appointed bodies (Canada,

---

[6] Hospitals are run by Regional Health Enterprises.

[7] Local Health Boards (Wales), Health Board Areas (Scotland), Health and Social Services Boards (northern Ireland) are all included, even though they often have very different functions. In northern Ireland the region does own some health care (e.g. long-term care) institutions.

Sources: Statoids (2005), and for Canada: Marchildon (2005), Fortin (2004), Shearer (2004); Denmark: Worm (2004); Germany: Mosebach (2005), Rosenbrock and Gerlinger (2004); Hungary: Mihályi (2005). Netherlands: NIVEL (2004), Hendriks (2005); Norway: Lian (2003), Manavado (2005); Russian Federation: Danishevski (2005); Sweden: Stenberg (2004); Switzerland: Furrer (2004); UK: Diabetes UK (2004), Morrish-Thomas (2005), NHS (2004), Scottish Executive (2004), Walshe et al. (2004), Dunne (2004), National Assembly for Wales (2004), Sweeney (2004), Laing & Buisson (2004), Smith (2005); Poland: Wieczorowska-Tobis and Rajska-Neumann (2006).

partly in the United Kingdom), regions (Denmark, Sweden), local government (Norway, Finland), or can be private, as is the case in many predominantly SHI-funded countries such as Germany, The Netherlands and Switzerland. The average size of administrative units does not seem to play the major role in arrangements for PC centres.

GPs are usually private or employed at the local level. Denmark (Copenhagen) and Sweden seem to be exceptions: here, PC physicians can be employed by a higher (regional) level with a relatively large catchment area of on average 414 000 and 426 000 inhabitants respectively.

Long-term care institutions are most often owned by local governments, in order to ensure better integration with social care services.

Conclusion

This chapter examines and compares the institutional infrastructure within decentralized health care systems. The main challenges of this comparison included identifying the most appropriate variables for assessing decentralized health care systems.

Despite considerable variation in terms of levels of government and their functions, several broader trends can be observed. Countries generally have more than the two levels of government that some health policy analysts have suggested as adequate. Nevertheless, most often only two or three of these levels have significant responsibilities in health care. The average size of the different levels varies widely and each country seems to have a unique design of its government units, but there are common features, such as the fact that the largest local government in a country usually coincides with a capital city, and that many countries have some regions with special status and arrangements. No relationship was observed between the country's population size and number of levels of government, average size of administrative units or responsibilities allocated to different levels. This may imply that, in practice, country size might matter less for decentralization than sometimes is suggested or, alternatively, that this exercise was not able to detect this correlation due to the limited number of indicators.

It did appear that the administrative structure in the different countries is dynamic in nature and that efficiency issues were a major driver for changes in government levels responsible for health care. Concerns about efficiency and also managerial capability regarding new clinical and information technologies appear to have led recently to incremental recentralization of administrative units at the local level as well as the establishment of new, regional administrative levels and bodies, especially for inpatient care.

Most countries have a mixture of both elected and appointed levels of government, but there are at least two levels of elected governments in all countries: the central and local government level. While elected government levels also have responsibilities in fields beyond health care, the bodies and levels created specifically for health care as a rule are appointed. While appointed levels may have significant responsibilities in health care, generally, the right to raise taxes is reserved for elected bodies. The major portion of taxes related to health care, or of general taxes that might be used for health care, is generally raised at the central or regional level, or by sickness funds in SHI systems. In some Nordic countries, however, local and regional governments have a major stake in raising taxes in this field. Countries that devolved taxation power to a lower level of government rarely cancel these powers subsequently, while this sometimes does happen in the case of decentralization of other powers related to health care.

Thöni (1999) argues that "Preferences for public goods and services in an area are very much dependent on the 'culture' of the area and factors such as language, religion, race and history do matter, and provide a good argument for decentralisation." It can be argued that decisions should be made on a level where government is responsive to such – culture-dependent – personal choice, has enough knowledge, and is efficient enough (Dahl 1970). All countries examined seem to have been searching for the appropriate level, for their specific circumstances, on which health care issues should be dealt with. However, the degree to which these structures are empowered, in terms and the level at which certain health care functions are performed, differs. There are arguments that suggest that a "Europe of Regions" on the one hand, and the centralized powers of the European Union on the other hand, can reduce national government leverage (Rodríguez-Pose 2002). Other policy analysts argue exactly the contrary, that the European Union seems to have reinforced central government power (Milward 2000).

Notes

1 It should be noted that countries such as France, Germany, Poland and Portugal have a constitutionally guaranteed division of power between the central government and "lower" levels of government (CSES 2004).

2 It is interesting to note that this, the smallest Canadian local government, has a mayor, two councillors and an administrator.

3 There are also researchers who argue the reverse and use the democracy argument in favour of centralization, pointing to relatively low local election turn-out rates (Goldsmith 1995). This might apply less to countries where voting is mandatory (Belgium, Luxembourg and parts of Italy) or for countries where election turn-out is relatively high (e.g. Denmark).

4 It should be noted that so-called SHI *countries* often do have a tax-component in their financing system and a substantial part of several tax-funded countries such as Greece and Portugal are funded through SHI contributions. Thus, it would be more correct to speak of SHI *systems*. See Saltman et al. (2004).

5 In The Netherlands, sickness funds do not collect wage-related contributions directly from the insured (as is common in other western European SHI countries), but the employers deduct the contribution from the wages and transfer it to the General Fund that redistributes it among the different sickness funds (nevertheless, sickness funds do directly charge fixed-rate premiums).

6 While there is formal autonomy, if allocation of funds by higher levels is dependent on historical expenditure on a certain service, there are incentives to opt for a certain expenditure pattern.

7 Boerma (2003) showed that tasks of primary care physicians differ greatly across Europe. This should be kept in mind when considering GPs in different European countries.

References

Ahmad, E. (1997) *Financing decentralized expenditures: an international comparison of grants*. Cheltenham, Edward Elgar Publishers.

Bennett, S. (1991) *The mystique of markets: public and private health care in developing countries*. Department of Public Health and Policy Publication No. 4. London, London School of Hygiene & Tropical Medicine.

Boadway, R. and Flatters, F.R. (1982) *Equalization in a federal state: an economic analysis*. Ottawa, Economic Council of Canada.

Boerma, W. (2003) *Profiles of general practice in Europe*. Utrecht, NIVEL.

Boni, S. (2005) Personal communication, Formez, 31 March.

Brans, M. (1992) Theories of local government reorganization: an empirical evaluation. *Public Administration*, **70**: 429–52.

Busse, R., Saltman, R.B. and Dubois, H.F.W. (2004) Organization and financing of social health insurance systems: current status and recent policy developments. In Saltman, R.B., Busse, R. and Figueras, J. eds, *Social health insurance systems in western Europe*. Maidenhead, Open University Press/McGraw-Hill.

Central Statistical Office (2005) Database (http://www.stat.gov.pl/, accessed 20 July 2006).

Commission des Comptes de la Sécurité Sociale (2004) *Tome I: Les comptes du régime général*. Paris, Commission des Comptes de la Sécurité Sociale.

Committee of the Regions (2004) Calendar of regional and local elections in the European Union: 2000–2009. Brussels: Committee of the Regions (http://www.cor.eu.int/Pesweb/pages/Whatsnew/general_interest/Calendar%20Regional%20Elections.pdf, accessed 2 February 2005).

CSES (2004) Database. Michigan: the comparative study of electoral systems. (www.cses.org, accessed 18 April 2006).

Dahl, R. (1970) *After the revolution*. New Haven, CT, Yale University Press.

Danishevski, K. (2005) Personal communication, Moscow Medical Sechenow Academy, 16 December.

Davoodi, H. and Zou, H. (1998) Fiscal (de)centralization and economic growth: a cross-country study. *Journal of Urban Economics*, **43**: 244–57.

De Vries, M. (2000) The rise and fall of decentralization: a comparative analysis of arguments and practices in European countries. *European Journal of Political Research*, **38**: 193–224.

Diabetes UK (2004) *Diabetes in Wales*. Cardiff, Diabetes UK. (http://www.diabetes.org.uk/cymru/english/inwales/nhsguide.htm, accessed 18 April).

Dunne, M. (2004) Personal communication, Health and Social Care Services in Northern Ireland, 14 October.

Federal Statistics Office (2005) Database (http://www.gks.ru/, accessed 20 July 2006).

Federal Statistics Office Germany (2005) Database (http://www.destatis.de/, accessed 20 July 2006).

Figueras, J., Robinson, R. and Jakubowski, E. (2005) Purchasing to improve health systems performance: drawing the lessons. In Figueras, J., Robinson, R. and Jakubowski, E., eds, *Purchasing to improve health systems performance*. Buckingham, Open University Press/McGraw-Hill.

Fortin, J. (2004) Personal communication, Health Canada, 1 April.

Frank, R.G. and Gaynor, M. (1994) Fiscal (de)centralization of public mental health care and the Robert Wood Johnson Foundation Program on Chronic Mental Illness. *The Millbank Quarterly*, **72**(1): 81–104.

Furrer, M-T. (2004) Personal communication, Swiss Federal Office of Public Health, 9 December.

Goldsmith, M. (1995) Autonomy and city limits. In Judge, D., Stoker, G. and Wolman, H., eds, *Theories of urban politics*. Thousand Oaks, CA, Sage.

Government Statistical Service (2005) Database (http://www.scotland.gov.uk/, accessed 20 July 2006).

Gramlich, E.M. (1977) Intergovernmental grants: a review of the empirical literature. In Oates, W.E., ed., *The political economy of fiscal federalism*. Lexington, MA, Lexington Press.

Gramlich, E.M. (1993) A policy-maker's guide to fiscal (de)centralization. *National Tax Journal*, **46**: 229–36.

Hendriks, R. (2005) Personal communication, 18 January.

Hirs, H. (2005) Privatisering in Hongarije: verkoop redt ziekenhuis van ondergang [Privatization in Hungary: sale saves hospital from downfall]. *Medisch Contact*, **60**: 240–2.

Hungarian Central Statistics Office (2005) Database (http://portal.ksh.hu/, accessed 20 July 2006).

ISTAT (2005) Database (http://www.istat.it/, accessed 20 July 2006).

Kjellberg, F. (1988) Local government and the welfare state: reorganization in Scandinavia. In Dente, B. and Kjellberg, F., eds, *The dynamics of institutional change: local government reorganization in western democracies*. London, Sage.

Laing & Buisson (2004) Company valuations skyrocket as Barchester wins Westminster. *Community Care Market News*, **11**(6): 1–2.

Lian, O.S. (2003) Convergence or divergence? Reforming primary care in Norway and Britain. *The Millbank Quarterly*, **81**(2): 305–30.

Litvak, J., Ahmad, J. and Bird, R. (1998) *Rethinking decentralization in developing countries*. IBRD (918). Washington, DC, World Bank.

Longo, F. (2001) *Federalismo e decentramento: proposte economico-aziendali per le riforme*. Milan, Egea.

Manavado, L. (2005) Personal communication, Norwegian Directorate for Health and Social Affairs, 15 February.

Marchildon, G. (2005) Personal communication, University of Regina, 15 February.

Mihályi, P. (2005) Personal communication, Central European University, January and December.

Mills, A. (1994) Decentralization and accountability in the health sector from an international perspective: what are the choices? *Public Administration and Development*, **14**: 281–92.

Milward, A.S. (2000) *The European rescue of the nation-state*. 2nd edn. London, Routledge.

Ministry of the Interior and Health (2002) *Municipalities and counties in Denmark: tasks and finance*. Copenhagen, Ministry of the Interior and Health (http://im.dk/publikationer/Municipalities/html/index.htm, accessed 16 February 2005).

Morrish-Thomas, C. (2005) Personal communication, 6 January.

Mosebach, K. (2005) Transforming the welfare state: continuity and change in social policy since 1998. In Beck, S., Klobes, F. and Scherrer, C., eds, *Surviving globalization? Perspectives for the German economic model*. Dordrecht, Springer.

Musgrave, R.A. (1983) Who should tax, where, and what? In McLure, C.E., ed., *Tax assignment in federal countries*. Canberra, Australian National University Press.

National Assembly for Wales (2004) Understanding the National Assembly (http://www.wales.gov.uk/nafw/understand-e.htm, accessed 17 April 2006).

National Institute for Statistics and Economic Studies (2005) Database (http://www.insee.fr/, accessed 21 July 2006).

National Statistics (2005) Database (http://www.statistics.gov.uk/, accessed 20 July 2006).

National Statistics Institute (2005) Database (http://www.ine.es/, accessed 20 July 2006).

National Statistics Institute Portugal (2005) Database (http://www.ine.pt/, accessed 20 July 2006).

Northern Ireland Statistics and Research Agency (2005) Database (http://www.nisra.gov.uk/, accessed 20 July 2006).

NHS (2004) NHS in England (http://www.nhs.uk/, accessed 17 April 2006).

NIVEL (2004) Cijfers uit de registratie van huisartsen (http://www.nivel.nl/pdf/cijfers-registratie-huisartsen-2004.pdf, accessed 11 July).

Oakland, W. (1994) Fiscal equalization: an empty box? *National Tax Journal* **44**(March): 199–209.

OECD (2005) *OECD health data 2005: a comparative analysis of 30 countries*. Paris, OECD.

Øvretveit, J. (2003) Nordic privatisation and private healthcare. *International Journal of Health Planning and Management*, **18**: 233–46.

Prud'homme, R. (1995) The dangers of decentralization. *The World Bank Research Observer*, **10**: 201–20.

Ranson, S. and Stuart, J. (1994) *Management for the public domain*. Basingstoke, Macmillan.

Rodden, J. (2002) Comparative federalism and decentralization: on meaning and measurement, unpublished paper, MIT.

Rodríguez-Pose, A. (2002) *The European Union: economy, society, and polity*. Oxford, Oxford University Press.

Rosenbrock, R. and Gerlinger, T. (2004) *Gesundheitspolitik: Eine systematische Einführung*. Bern, Verlag Hans Huber.

Rubinfeld, D. (1987) The economics of the local public sector. In Auerbach, A.J. and Feldstein, M. eds, *Handbook of public economics*, vol. 2. Amsterdam, North-Holland.

Saltman, R.B. (2003) Melting public-private boundaries in European health systems. *European Journal of Public Health*, **13**: 24–9.

Saltman, R.B., Busse, R. and Figueras, J. (2004) *Social health insurance systems in western Europe*. Maidenhead, Open University Press/McGraw-Hill.

Scharpf, H.J., Reissert, B. and Schnabel, F. (eds) (1976) *Politikverflechtung, Theorie und Empirie des kopperativen Föderalismus in der Bundesrepublik*. Kronberg, Ts.

Scottish Executive (2004) About us (http://www.show.scot.nhs.uk/sehd/about.htm, accessed 20 December 2004).

Shearer, R. (2004) Personal communication, Health Canada, 29 October.

Smith, P. (2005) Personal communication, University of York, 11 February.

Statistics Canada (2005) Database (http://www.statcan.ca/, accessed 20 July 2006).

Statistics Denmark (2005) Database (http://www.dst.dk/, accessed 20 July 2006).

Statistics Finland (2005) Database (http://www.stat.fi/, accessed 20 July 2006).

Statistics for Wales (2005) Database (http://new.wales.gov.uk/, accessed 20 July 2006).

Statistics Netherlands (2005) Database (http://www.cbs.nl/, accessed 20 July 2006).

Statistics Norway (2005) Database (http://www.ssb.no/, accessed 20 July 2006).

Statistics Sweden (2005) Database (http://www.scb.se/, accessed 20 July 2006).

Statoids (2005) Administrative divisions of countries ("Statoids") (http://www.statoids.com/, accessed on 17 April 2006).

Stenberg, J. (2004) Personal communication, *Sveriges Kommuner och Landsting*, 1 November.

Swedish Association of Local Authorities and Regions (2004) Database. Stockholm, The Swedish Association of Local Authorities and Regions (http://www.skl.se/artikel.asp?C=756&A=180, accessed 18 April 2006).

Sweeney, J. (2004) Personal communication, National Assembly for Wales, 27 October.

Swiss Federal Statistics Office (2005) Database (http://www.bfs.admin.ch/, accessed 20 July 2006).

Thöni, E. (1999) Fiscal federalism in Austria: facts and new developments. In Fossati, A. and Panella, G., eds, *Fiscal federalism in the European Union*. London, Routledge.

Tiebout, C.M. (1956) A pure theory of local expenditure. *Journal of Political Economy*, **64**: 416–24.

Walshe, K., Smith, J., Dixon, J., et al. (2004) Primary care trusts. *British Medical Journal*, **329**: 871–2.

WHO (2004) *WHO European Health for All database*. Copenhagen, WHO Regional Office for Europe, June.

Wieczorowska-Tobis, K. and Rajska-Neumann, A. (2006) Personal communication, 11 January.

Wildasin, D. (ed.) (1997) *Fiscal aspects of evolving federations*. Cambridge, Cambridge University Press.

Wilde, J.E. (1971) Grants-in-aid: the analytics of design and response. *National Tax Journal*, **24**: 143–55.

Worm, K. (2004) Personal communication, Ministry of the Interior and Health, 2 November.

chapter three

Towards a typology for decentralization in health care

Karsten Vrangbæk

Introduction

This chapter presents a conceptual framework for characterizing decentralization in health systems. The introductory section outlines the content of the chapter, highlighting the main points followed by a short introduction to the theoretical background for the chapter.

The second section contains a definition of decentralization and a conceptual framework for analysing decentralization processes and structures. The conceptual framework can be used for characterizing decentralization trends in individual systems, and as a starting point for comparisons and policy learning from other systems. However, a number of important issues must be considered. First, comparing decentralization trends in different systems raises the difficult issue of how to measure degrees of decentralization. This issue will be addressed in the third section where the possibilities for measurement are discussed and a multidimensional approach is suggested. Decentralization trends are often discussed at a general level. However, health systems include a number of different functions (delivery, financing, arranging/planning). Each of these functions may have different characteristics in terms of decentralization. This is the second important issue when applying the framework for comparative analysis. The fourth section addresses this and provides some general examples along with a simple framework for characterizing different functions of health care systems. Combination models and variability in decentralization characteristics for different functions are discussed. This section also emphasizes a third main point for comparative analysis, namely, that the actual functioning of different decentralization strategies depends on informal functioning, tradition, culture and coordination mechanisms across the health system. These points for comparative analysis are essential when attempting to draw policy lessons from decentralization trends in other countries. Finally, concluding remarks are made and we look ahead to the chapters that follow.

The conceptual framework presented in this chapter is based on the theoretical understanding that both formal and informal institutional arrangements matter as frameworks for decision-making in health care. Institutional structures assign responsibility and set boundaries for decision-making. They constitute the regulatory and normative infrastructure and thus the background for individual and collective action (March and Olsen 1989; Olsen and Peters 1996; Scharpf 1997). It is thus relevant to analyse developments in political and administrative authority structures including the degree of decentralization in order to get an idea of the arena for the health system actors, and the functioning of the system. Institutional arrangements are subject to change over time based on political and administrative decisions. The parliamentary system and practice, administrative traditions, norms and values regarding health care and the perception of health and disease all influence political decision-making, resulting in the institutional structure of health systems (Contandriopoulos et al. 1998). The mix of decentralization and centralization will thus be dependent on historical contingencies, institutional choices, traditions and values in each country. This means that universal claims of optimality are unlikely to withstand detailed scrutiny, although some lessons may be learned by comparisons across systems.

Formal institutional arrangements provide important input, but it is equally important to realize that the effect of formal institutional changes will depend on the administrative and organizational practices that emerge on the basis of such formal structures. This point is emphasized by implementation theorists (Pressman and Wildavsky 1973) and organization theorists who suggest that there may be a gap between the rhetoric of reforms and the practice that emerges (March and Olsen 1989; DiMaggio and Powell 1991; Brunsson and Olsen 1993). Effective analysis thus requires a framework that is sensitive to both formal and informal institutional elements and the development of linkages and coordination mechanisms between them in order to understand decentralization/centralization trends.

Concepts for characterizing decentralization and re-centralization[1]

Decentralization has been on the political agenda in many European health systems over the past decade. However, there are considerable differences in the meanings attributed to the term and divergent ideas about its defining characteristics (Hoggett 1996; Pollitt et al. 1998; Mackintosh and Roy 1999; Hunter et al. 1999; Hopkins 2002; Rhodes et al. 2003; Peckham et al. 2005; Pollitt 2005). In this chapter, a number of the complexities in characterizing decentralization trends in health care are discussed. It is argued that a comprehensive framework is needed to capture the complexities and paradoxes of real-life decentralization.

Based on a public administration perspective, the following definition of decentralization can be offered: *The transfer of formal responsibility and power to make decisions regarding the management, production, distribution and/or financing of health services, usually from a smaller to a larger number of geographically or organizationally separate actors.*

We will use this definition as our starting point. It consists of several elements. First,"Transfer of formal responsibility and power to make decisions" indicates that decentralization implies a shift in formal accountability and decision-making structures, usually from a smaller to a larger number of institutional actors either within the same organizational structure or at different organizational levels. Extending the framework of Cheema and Rondinelli (1983) and the discussions in Bossert (1998), the transfer can be within political levels (devolution), within administrative levels (deconcentration), from political to administrative levels (bureaucratization) or to relatively independent institutional levels (delegation/autonomization within the public sector). Finally, there can be transfer of responsibility to private actors (privatization).

Second, the term "usually" in the definition refers to the fact that decentralization also may be at a horizontal level or based on functional principles and thus not necessarily transferring authority to a larger number of actors (Mintzberg 1979; Boyne 1992; Pollitt 2005). Examples include the creation of semi-autonomous public agencies which involves transfer of power from central ministries to arm's-length central agencies. Other examples include internal shifts in decision competence from managerial staff to professionals or "street level bureaucrats" (Lipsky 1980).

Third, the definition includes the terms "responsibility" and "power". "Responsibility" is linked to decision-making and should be understood as formal responsibilities for making decisions, for which someone can be held accountable by representatives of citizens within the public sector (elected politicians or appointed bureaucrats) and/or health care consumers, management boards, shareholders, etc. within private sector organizations. Public authorities may delegate responsibility for certain functions to privately owned and managed organizations or network structures, as is commonly seen in SHI systems (Saltman et al. 2004). In such cases, there will usually be a dual responsibility structure where operating units answer to both private management boards and public or semi-public agencies via contracts or through a statutory grant of authority.

Somewhat differently, the degree of "power" is linked to the scope for decision-making, i.e. the range of decisions one can take, including the degree of discretion and the importance in terms of impact on producers and consumers of health services (see Bossert 1998, for a similar emphasis on "decision space"). The scope and level of discretion are determined by the specific institutional set-up including the legal framework and the norms and routines that develop in the system. It should be evident from this short discussion that neither "responsibility" nor "power" are absolute measures. They should be understood as relative terms to be analysed in specific contexts (see also the discussion in Peckham et al. 2005: 31).

Fourth, the term "health services" should be understood in a broad sense as products or services, where some degree of public involvement is considered necessary within a particular health system context. Decisions regarding health services may relate to arranging health care services, management, production, distribution and/or financing of public goods (and private services in SHI countries) (see below). This means that both high-level decisions regarding the structure and organization of health services and more ongoing production-related decisions might be decentralized.

It is apparent from our definition that decentralization can be analysed in both dynamic/process terms and static/structural terms. Throughout the book we will apply these different perspectives at different times. We will look at dynamic/process perspectives, such as the implementation and politics of decentralization processes, and structural perspectives in terms of the institutional arrangements and the functional arguments underpinning them. Our initial typology of decentralization is designed to deal with both dynamic and structural components of decentralization.

Table 3.1 illustrates the typology and thus the relationship between the concepts presented so far. Structural elements are presented in bold and dynamic in italics. Table 3.1 describes a simplified and ideal typical perspective, while actual processes and structures will often be characterized by lack of clarity, overlapping structures and combination models as illustrated in the rest of the volume. Nevertheless, it is useful as a conceptual starting point for characterizing the main features and development trends.

The structural dimensions listed on the vertical axis represent typical constructions of political/administrative levels ranging from the central/state level to group/individual level. These distinctions are commonly used and to some extent codified in national legislation. However, the exact combination, size and scope of influence vary significantly across countries, as illustrated in Chapter 2, moreover, national structures may contain combination models and exceptions.

The structural elements on the horizontal axis represent different institutional spheres. The first distinction is between political and administrative levels, where

Table 3.1 Structural and process dimensions of decentralization

Decision-making and responsibilities in health care functions				
	Political	**Administrative**	**Organizational**	**Private**
		→ *Bureaucratization*	→ *Delegation/ autonomization*	→ *Privatization*
Central/state	↓ *Devolution*	↓ *Deconcentration*	↓ *Public management delegation*	↓ *Management delegation*
Regional				
Local/municipal				
Organizational				
Group/individual				

Note: Structural dimensions in bold. *Process dimensions in italics.*

the political levels are characterized by indirect or direct democratic elections, while the administrative structures are appointed and subservient to the political level. The organizational level represents a further subdivision into organizations within the public hierarchical structure. This is where actual health system activities take place, e.g. within delivery organizations such as hospitals. The distinction between the administrative hierarchy and the producing organizations is a key component of many decentralization strategies in the public sector, particularly in the New Public Management (NPM) philosophy (Hood 1991; Pollitt and Bouckaert 2000).

Organizations within the public realm can be distinguished from fully private organizations, although recent decades have seen a number of quasi or combination models (Saltman and Von Otter 1992; Ham 1997; Preker and Harding 2003). Ownership, strategic control over entry and exit, and distribution of risk and profits are some of the parameters that can help define the continuum between public and private organizations.

Combining the two structural (vertical and horizontal) dimensions generates a grid of elements within which it is possible to identify a number of process/ dynamic decentralization types. Each of these will be discussed in turn.

Devolution (political decentralization) means decentralization to lower-level political authorities such as regions or municipalities. Examples include the devolution of power to Scotland, Wales and Northern Ireland in the United Kingdom and the devolution of powers to the regional and municipal authorities in Scandinavia. In principle, there may also be devolution to organizational-level elected boards as seen for schools and childcare in Scandinavia. However, this is uncommon in health care and would normally also be restricted to very specific functions. The last row in Table 3.1 has the heading group/individual. In terms of devolution, this indicates the possibility of extensive use of direct democracy, e.g. through town meetings or public referendums on health matters. Some examples of this can be found in the input to prioritization schemes such as the initial Oregon model in the United States, and in the use of referendums in Switzerland.

Political devolution may relate to all functional areas of health care (e.g. as described below in terms of financing, arranging and delivery). The degree of autonomy at decentralized levels can vary considerably, but it is hard to imagine a system that does not retain some regulatory and oversight capacity at the central level. In practice, there is often shared or mixed responsibility at central, regional and/or local levels so that the boundaries and scope for joint and individual decision-making will be subject to negotiation and change over time. This joint or mixed responsibility is a key feature of most public health care systems. At best, it provides flexibility and ability to adjust to changing contingencies. At worst, it leads to stalemate and unclear lines of responsibility. In most cases it is the arena for ongoing struggles over the distribution of political and administrative power.

Deconcentration refers to transfer of responsibility and power from a smaller number to a larger number of administrative actors within a formal administrative structure (vertical deconcentration) or from central management to other non-managerial groups such as health professionals (horizontal deconcentration) (see Mintzberg 1979, for an organizational theory treatment of horizontal decentralization). Typical examples of vertical deconcentration include the transfer of power from central authorities to local representatives of the central level, for example, to the Strategic Health Authorities in the United Kingdom. The local representatives may have a more or less comprehensive portfolio of functions both within and outside health care. The last row indicates that deconcentration may be to group level or somewhat differently to individual street-level bureaucrats within the public organization who require a large degree of de facto discretion over the implementation of services.

Bureaucratization refers to the transfer of responsibility and power from political levels to administrative levels. An example is the transfer of responsibility of health services from politically elected representatives to regional authorities controlled by appointed boards, as seen in the recent Norwegian reforms with the change from counties/*fylker* to regions. Another example would be the transfer of power from direct political control in ministries to various arm's-length agencies. Depending on the number of agencies, this could be understood as vertical or horizontal bureaucratization. Another term for such developments could be functional decentralization (Pollitt and Talbot 2004), since agencies may operate at central level but with more specifically defined functions than general ministries (e.g. medicines agencies, public health agencies).

Delegation and autonomization refer to the transfer of selected functions to more or less autonomous public organizational management. This is thus a further deconcentration of responsibilities but for limited functions and usually for specific periods of time and to organizational or network levels that are less directly controlled by the public hierarchical structure. Examples include the creation of semi-autonomous entities ("public enterprises") to arrange and deliver hospital care in Norway, the reliance on medical societies for elaboration of standards and guidelines and the creation of implementation networks including public and privately practising doctors, and patient organizations. Another example would be the role of sickness funds in negotiating budgets with hospitals in several SHI countries (Saltman et al. 2004).

Delegation and autonomization are often implemented through contracting, which is a general concept for a number of different types of more or less formalized relationships between public organizations or across public and private sector boundaries (Ham 1997; Preker and Harding 2003). Responsibility can be further delegated internally, e.g. to hospital departments through decentralized budgeting or to groups or individual street-level bureaucrats.

Privatization exists when responsibility for particular functions is transferred from public to private actors either permanently, e.g. through purchase or for particular time periods, e.g. through contracting. The concept of public–private partnerships is a variant that combines delegation and privatization in various forms (see Chapter 14). These mechanisms are predominantly used on the supply/provision side of health care systems.

Privatization (and delegation/autonomization) of health functions can in principle take place at all levels. National health delivery functions for parts of the population or for particular diagnosis groups as well as national distribution of drugs and supplies may be privatized. More commonly, privatization takes place through regional or local level contracts with management or delivery organizations. Examples include SHI system contracting with private delivery organizations or contracting in the Nordic countries. In privatized structures there may be more or less transfer of power to geographically or organizationally separate units.

The introduction of patient choice can be seen as a radical privatization of the demand function in health care. Although funding and delivery remain public, such schemes "privatize" decisions that can have significant aggregate impact on financial flows and delivery structures (see Vrangbæk and Beck 2004, for a Scandinavian example, and Burge et al. 2005, for an evaluation of the London choice project). In some cases, patient choice is extended to include both public and private facilities. This is the case in Denmark and Norway, and thus combines privatization of decision-making with a (slightly) greater role for private providers.

A different and more far-reaching example would be privatization of financing functions through greater reliance on user payment or voluntary private insurance (Mossialos and Thomson 2004). This may reduce the political and /or administrative responsibility for financing of health services to particular groups.

A general distinction can be made between decentralization with and without competition (Pollitt 2005). Competition is particularly relevant for the cases of delegation/autonomization and privatization. In both cases, there may be competition for contracts and thus the responsibility for delivering services, managing health needs or purchasing services (Figueras et al. 2005).

In cases of devolution, deconcentration and bureaucratization, it is common to have politically or administratively determined boundaries for the responsibilities of each unit. However, the combination of choice and activity-based payment may create situations where strategically acting public authorities seek to expand their responsibility scope at the expense of others (Vrangbæk and Beck 2004).

Devolution has a different and usually more comprehensive character than the other forms of decentralization. Arguments for devolution typically extend beyond functional claims and usually include considerations for democratic participation and legitimacy (see Chapters 4 and 6, also Saltman and Bankauskaite 2006). Devolution is usually comprehensive in the sense that it is often accompanied by decentralization of administrative responsibilities and tasks. Bureaucracies are created or enhanced to support decentralized authorities and management functions become tied to the decentralized decision process.

The issue of network-based governance forms (Kickert et al. 1997; Pierre 2000; Newman 2003; Thompson 2003) is somewhat problematic for typologies of decentralization. In the above, we have discussed the potential of delegation/ autonomization to network structures that are characterized by more or less formalized collaboration across organizational boundaries. There are at least two problems with this in practice. First, responsibility and accountability tend to be somewhat blurred in network structures. It thus becomes unclear exactly to whom decision responsibility is decentralized and how the public can hold them responsible. Second, networks may include central and decentralized public actors as well as private actors. It is also possible that they can consist entirely of private actors, e.g. in managed care networks with vertically integrated functions. This opens a new set of issues on how to differentiate between different combinations of public and private. In this instance, then, privatization becomes a problematic category.

In principle, the typology set out here provides a framework for describing all types of decentralization within health care. In practice, it will usually be necessary to supplement by more detailed descriptions of particular cases in order to capture variations, combinations and dynamic processes of how interaction develops within the formal frame. It is particularly relevant to consider how to supplement the description of the categories with elements that are better suited to capture the complexities of SHI systems (see Saltman et al. 2004, for an extended description of SHI systems). Saltman and Dubois (2005) identify a number of recent institutional developments in SHI systems that can serve as examples. The first sets of changes relate to the financing function such as Austria's "health platform" and Switzerland's proposal to allow selective contracting by sickness funds. The Austrian "health platforms" represent a stronger role for public planning and purchasing at the regional and federal levels, while private sickness funds lose autonomy in terms of contracting, and sickness fund-owned hospitals become dependent on gaining public contracts. In terms of the above framework, this represents a bureaucratization, albeit from a different starting point than discussed above, and a horizontal autonomization of hospital management in terms of their contracting status. The Swiss reform entails a constraint on patient choice and thus a restriction on privatized demand at the individual level. However, the private sickness funds gain more autonomy to develop their business concept through selective contracting, i.e. expanded privatization at the organizational level.

Other important developments in SHI countries include the introduction of mandatory gate-keeping in France and "standard" insurance in The Netherlands and possibly Germany. Gate-keeping is a reduction in consumer choice and thus a restriction on privatized demand at the individual level. Standard insurance packages and mandatory enrolment involve a reconfiguration of the autonomy for sickness funds as they lose the capacity to define their preferred care package and, in the German proposal, their ability to differentiate premiums. It also entails a limitation in choice for wealthy citizens in The Netherlands, although a choice between private and public sickness funds is created. Generally speaking, the SHI system reforms involve changes in the configuration between the important institutional players of sickness funds, federal and regional authorities, hospitals (private and public) and citizens. In many cases, the changes aim to control expenditures, often by introducing regulatory restrictions for citizens, sickness funds or hospitals, i.e. a strengthening of the state's political and administrative power that is centralized not decentralized in character.

The use of conceptual frameworks such as this for cross-national comparisons raises the difficult issue of how to measure the degree of decentralization in health systems. The first step may be to characterize structural features and dynamic decentralization processes. The next step may be an attempt to measure the degree of decentralization related to these characterizations. The concepts of autonomy and decision-making discretion are particularly important for such assessments.

Is it possible to measure and compare the degree of decentralization in health care systems?

A number of scholars have addressed the issue of how to measure the degree of decentralization (see Peckham et al. 2005). The typical starting point is measures of economic importance such as total spending at the local level as a percentage of all social spending (Oates 1972) or the percentage of financing raised at decentralized levels compared to central levels. These measures may reflect the best available quantitative data, but both are problematic in failing to account for the relative level of autonomy in determining how funds are allocated and the discretion regarding level and composition of financing. More institutional and qualitative descriptions are thus needed to supplement the picture. This leads to difficult issues of how to define and compare such concepts as "power", "autonomy" and "discretion" that are embedded in national system characteristics (see also Bossert 1998). One possible solution is to combine several different measures while remaining sensitive to the interpretive character of some dimensions.

Building on the work of Swedish social scientist Lennart Lundquist (1972[2] and 1992) the following variables would appear relevant in the assessment of the degree of decentralization:

- *Geography and socio-demographics* are two different ways of measuring size and resources. The assumption is that the level of potential autonomy varies with size and socio-economic composition. Larger and more resourceful decentralized units will have more potential for autonomous administration, *ceteris paribus*.
- *Political decision structure* refers to the formal structures for decision-making, the possibilities of citizens' participation and the degree of openness and transparency. Generally, it can be argued that the level of autonomy is a function of the organization for involvement of citizens and organized interests in decision-making. More scope for involvement means more decentralization. Traditionally this means that smaller units with easy access to political forums and relatively few voters per representative can be seen as more decentralized than larger units. However, new representational forms and demographic patterns can change the picture (electronic access and more mobile citizens).
- *Functions and economic importance* refer to the portfolio of different tasks and the relative importance of these tasks. Importance can be measured in percentage of total public expenditure or in terms of symbolic importance for the voting population. In health care it is useful to make a further distinction between delivery, financing and regulatory functions (arranging/organizing, control, oversight, etc.) (see below). A large portfolio of relatively important tasks at decentralized levels tends to increase the degree of autonomy and thus the level of decentralization.
- *Steering* refers to the strength and composition of steering by the central political or administrative levels. In terms of strength, one can differentiate between direct steering, where goals and means are given, and indirect steering that is focused on the conditions for achieving particular purposes in

terms of organizational, budgetary and informational resources. Direct steering usually places tighter constraints on subordinate levels and thus amounts to less autonomy. One can further differentiate between specific steering (involving particular cases) and general steering aimed at all similar cases. A further variable is the degree of details in the steering. Thus, a number of detailed variables contribute to characterizing the steering of subordinate organizations. Generally, the more direct, specific and detailed the steering, the less autonomy for decentralized units. Steering may be implemented through a variety of different coordination mechanisms (e.g. rules, regulation, contracts, agreements and the monitoring and sanctioning of these instruments – see below).

- *Control* refers to the conscious attempts of the decision-maker to obtain information about the reliability of steering attempts and the rationality of the decision. One can differentiate between active and passive control, and between extensive and limited control. Amount and type of sanctions are another important variable.

Table 3.2 can be summarized as "what is the scope for decision-making at decentralized levels?; what are the resources?; what are the possible channels for influencing decision-making for citizens and users at the decentralized level?; what are the tasks and how important are they?; and, finally, how tightly are actions directed and controlled from higher levels?" As suggested above, comparisons of the degree of decentralization in health systems should be based on composite evaluations rather than one-dimensional quantitative measures

Table 3.2 Summary of decentralization variables

Decentralization variable	*Underlying parameters*	*Factors that provide more decentralized autonomy*
Geography and socio-demographics	Geographical area, socio-demographic development	More resources at the decentralized level
Organization of political processes	Structures for participation and inclusion at the decentralized level	More local democratic influence
Functions and economic weight	Number and importance of functions/tasks	Greater percentage of total public expenditure. More strategically important tasks
Steering	Strength and composition of steering instruments from the central political or administrative levels	More imprecise/broad, general and indirect steering
Control	Strength and composition of control instruments from the central political or administrative levels	Less intensive and more passive control. Limited sanctions and limited credibility of control/sanctions

(such as the percentage of health expenditures at various levels). Apart from general data issues, this also raises the question of how to assign weights to different parameters in qualitatively different health system contexts. This can only be addressed in each individual study.

Up to this point we have mainly discussed decentralization as a system-level concept. However, actual health systems are comprised of several different functions that may not display the same characteristics in terms of their degree of decentralization and thus the distribution of actual decision-making power. The following section pursues this point further.

What is being decentralized? Distinguishing between different functions in health care systems

The framework presented in the above can be applied to different functional areas of health care services. Indeed, there may be different degrees of decentralization for different functions. A simple framework for distinguishing functional areas could include the health system functions of arranging, financing and delivery of services (see Bossert 1998, for a slightly different typology). Table 3.3 provides examples illustrating the different possibilities.

Responsibility for *arranging, planning* and *facilitating* includes the system-level organization and facilitation by setting the regulatory institutional framework for the system. This entails decisions on the actors involved e.g. through licensing and regulation, decisions on the rules for interaction such as rules for contracting, rules for coordination, surveillance and control of access, quality and service levels and decisions regarding general incentives and sanctioning mechanisms. Some degree of this responsibility will probably always be maintained at a central level, but varying levels of authority can be transferred to decentralized political or administrative units. Both public integrated and social health insurance countries usually rely on combinations of central and decentralized authority to arrange health care services. In theory, it is possible to have the responsibility for organizing health care decentralized to institutional level within a public hierarchy, to network structures of public and/or private actors or to market mechanisms. In most countries this would give rise to concerns about equity and system robustness.

Financing of health services can take place though taxation, public insurance, private insurance or private out-of-pocket payment. Both taxation and public insurance can take place at the central level or can be decentralized to regional or local political authorities. A number of countries, e.g. the Nordic countries, have traditionally financed welfare services and, to varying degrees, health care through combinations of local, regional and national level taxes. Private financing can exist in a variety of forms (employee insurance, personal insurance, self-pay) and can be more or less regulated by public authorities at various levels. Combinations of public and private financing are found in most health systems including SHI systems and the US market-based system. Responsibility for the financing functions may be spread across several different public sector levels.

Delivery management concerns the practical and production-related decisions of services which may be further subdivided into primary, secondary and tertiary

Table 3.3 Governance structures: examples of institutional forms for different health service functions

	Arranging/planning/ facilitating	*Financing (revenue collection)*	*Delivery (ownership, distribution of risk and profit, "decision room" regarding organization, technology and processes)*
Central ↑ ↓ Decentralized	National planning system Formal national assignment of rights and obligations Centralized agreements Regional planning and networking Local/municipal planning and networking Market interaction Individual choice of insurance or treatment facility	National taxation (general or health-specific) Mandatory contribution to national sickness fund Regional taxation Mandatory contribution to regional level sickness fund Local/municipal taxation Mandatory contribution to local sickness fund Voluntary contribution to sickness fund/ insurance company Out-of-pocket payment to providers	National health system State ownership and control Regional ownership and control Local/municipal ownership and control Private organizations having contracts with public authorities or sickness funds (the internal structure of such organizations/ networks may be more or less centralized) Private independent service delivery

Note: Table 3.3 provides broad examples. Many other organizational forms and combinations exist in European health systems.

care or into prevention, treatment, diagnoses and follow-up/rehabilitation. Each involves decisions on production levels, technology and practices for the different functional areas. They also entail decisions on the composition of the workforce and the organization of work processes.

The responsibility for such decisions can be maintained at a central level through comprehensive planning and control systems. In some countries these decisions have been devolved to political or administrative authorities at lower levels in order to take advantage of local knowledge. It may also be delegated to private not-for-profit or for-profit hospital organizations, particularly in SHI and market-based systems where financing and delivery may be more or less closely integrated via contracts, networks or direct ownership.

Responsibility for delivery decisions may be delegated further to more or less autonomous delivery organizations such as hospitals. Private actors may be included via contracts or as independent market-based actors. The degree of autonomy of such organizations can vary as described above.

A main point of the matrix in Table 3.1 is to show that several different combination models are possible. Responsibility for arranging/organizing core institutional features may be maintained at a central level while operational and/or financial responsibility is decentralized to lower political and administrative levels (as in the United Kingdom). Financing responsibility and power may be located at the central level while operational responsibility is decentralized (e.g. Norway).

Delivery and arrangement responsibility may be closely connected in public integrated Beveridge systems. To some extent, they can be seen as broad headlines on a sliding scale where the exact division of labour can be highly variable and subject to negotiation. Social health insurance (SHI) systems such as Germany and The Netherlands represent a complex structure in the sense that arranging responsibility is shared between public authorities at national and regional levels. Financing is also a shared responsibility in SHI systems where relatively autonomous sickness funds act within a negotiated framework of rules and agreements between public and private actors. Delivery is in the hands of a diverse set of public and private (mostly not-for-profit) hospital organizations in negotiated collaboration with sickness funds. A number of decisions are thus made in negotiations across levels and in collaboration between public and private actors (Saltman et al. 2004).

The wide range of combination models raises the issue of advantages and disadvantages of particular arrangements. Several political scientists have argued that it is important to maintain financing and organizing responsibilities at the same level in order to ensure accountability for decision-making, as decision-makers will then be responsible for service level, management and financing via taxation. Politically elected decision-makers will thus periodically have to face their voters' judgement of their ability to balance tax levels and service provision. This type of argumentation resonates with the "fiscal federalism" debate in economic theory, which also points to the benefits of combining financing (taxation) and management responsibilities (Oates 1998; Rattsø 1998; also Chapter 7).

Other political scientists, particularly in the New Public Management tradition, emphasize the potential benefits of separating political decision-making from operational management in order to create greater scope for entrepreneurial behaviour at the management level and to limit the potential for "interference" from politicians (Saltman et al. 2002; Hughes 2003).

Pressures for reconfiguration of governance structures may arise from perceptions that the underlying conditions for both "optimal treatment areas" and "optimal democratic spaces" have changed and may be out of alignment. The arguments build on the idea that advances in medical technology combined with the introduction of free choice of hospitals make it more optimal to create larger administrative and delivery units. Similarly, it is argued that new labour market and socio-demographic structures have created a potential/need for larger democratic spaces (Strukturkommissionen 2004).

More sophisticated and systematic analysis of combination models is needed to make the decentralization debate more precise and thus more useful to policy-makers. Another issue that must be taken into consideration when attempting to draw policy lessons from comparative analyses of decentralization trends is the importance of informal functioning, tradition, culture and coordination systems.

Informal functioning, tradition and culture, and overlapping coordination systems

In order to understand the functioning of decentralization processes, one must be sensitive to the informal functioning of the system and the real level of autonomy provided in the various organizational systems. Informal structures will develop through ongoing struggles within the system. They will depend on historically developed conditions as well as actor interests, power and negotiation skills between central and regional/local authorities or between managers and political principals.

The issue of informal functioning can be approached by looking at formal and informal coordination mechanisms that influence the rules of the game and the interaction between the different institutional actors. Formal responsibility may be decentralized, but if this takes place within a setting of tight requirements in terms of national standards, the real level of autonomy will be limited. A central part of the analysis of decentralization is thus to describe the various types of coordination mechanisms applied inside the health system. Such coordination mechanisms provide linkages between the different subsystems, filling out the detailed process dimensions of how devolution, deconcentration, delegation, bureaucratization and privatization play out in real life.

The following represents a list of possible mechanisms for coordination based on public administration and organization theory literature (Mintzberg 1979; Harmon and Mayer 1986):

- *Rules and regulation*: Stating formal responsibilities, the range of formal autonomy and choice, and the framework for how interaction is to take place:
- *Negotiated agreements and contracts*: Ongoing negotiations on performance and division of work.
- *Standardization of output/results*: Creating uniform measures of performance and impetus for comparing service delivery and coordinating efforts within the production chain.
- *Standardization of work processes*: In order to increase transparency and synchronize expectations.
- *Standardization of knowledge and training*: Synchronize expectations and create a common platform for communication.
- *Shared information*: Create a common platform for communication; increase transparency.
- *Standardization of norms and culture*: For example, through recruitment, education.

The functioning of these measures will depend on the historically developed context in each individual system, subject to interpretation and negotiation between the involved actors over time (Pressman and Wildavsky 1973). This helps explain observed variability when adopting seemingly similar measures in different systems. It also re-emphasizes the need for caution (already noted in Chapter 2) in comparing structural features across different systems.

The informal practices that develop in response to structural changes will thus be dependent on the cultural and normative setting of each health care system (March and Olsen 1989; Altenstetter 1999). Traditional attitudes towards collaboration, trust, choice, learning, etc. all play important roles in the development of interactive patterns between the various actors in health systems. Culture can be perceived as a filter of values and cognitive schemes that influence the interpretation and implementation of new measures.

Adding to the complexity is that most health care systems consist of overlapping governance systems for decisions about administrative and economic issues, on one hand, and medical and professional issues, on the other (see also the discussion on functional issues above). Economic and administrative functions may be decentralized while medical control functions, development of practice standards, decisions on location of specialties, etc. are centralized. In practice, these are multidimensional systems with varying degrees of decentralization and interrelated governance structures.

Many real-life reforms contain elements of simultaneous decentralization and (re)centralization. Some functions such as oversight, setting standards, setting general economic targets, etc. may be centralized while operational control is decentralized to lower political, administrative or organizational levels. The processes of decentralization may also give rise to demands for more centralized control of standards for quality and equity across geographical areas. Performance-based payment systems and extensive use of contracting tend to create a political demand for more central control of the general framework and the results. This tendency can also be observed in the general public administration literature (Hoggett 1996).

These concerns further emphasize the need to be careful about defining the functions addressed in the decentralization debate, and the need to be sensitive to informal functions within formal structural arrangements.

Comparisons and historical starting points

When doing comparisons across countries, one needs to be sensitive to the different starting points for health systems in terms of formal and informal structures. A simple illustration of the point is the very different sizes of units in different countries (see Chapter 2). The following list illustrates some of the possible formal levels in the discussion of decentralization in health care:

- the European Union
- the nation state
- a separate country within a state (Scotland)
- a regional state (German *Länder*)

- regions (Swedish counties)
- local (municipalities)
- an institution (hospitals or treatment networks)
- a citizen/individual (citizen/patient and informal grass-root networks).

These levels are not applicable in all cases, and the sizes of each type will vary considerably between country systems (e.g. a county in Denmark covers between 45 000 and 625 000 inhabitants while regions in the United Kingdom or Italy can include several millions).

This means that is important to know the system's structural features and its functions in order to assess the degree of change. Changes that look like they follow an incremental path in some systems may be interpreted as breaking points or paradigm shifts in other systems (Hall 1993; Thelen 1999). Understanding historical developments is thus an important prerequisite for assessing the accumulated effect of change processes including incremental and decentralized changes, and for judging when they amount to a qualitatively new regime at the system level.

The distinction between unitary states such as Britain and the Nordic countries and federal states such as Germany or the United States may be a useful starting point for the discussion of historically developed structures (Saltman and Bankauskaite 2006). However, more detailed descriptions of institutional developments within the sector are necessary. This could lead to distinctions between Beveridge-type systems (NHS) and Bismarck (SHI) systems or between public integrated, public contract and market-based systems (OECD 1992). None of these distinctions are perfect, but each can be seen as short-hand for more complex underlying practices and a starting point for further analysis.

Conclusion

The chapter suggests that structural and process dimensions can be analysed by applying the conceptual framework presented on p. 47. However, to use this framework for cross-national comparisons, one needs to be sensitive to the structural, historical and culturally contingent features of each health system. One must also be sensitive to the wide variety of combination models of different functions in health systems. The degree of decentralization can be measured by applying a multidimensional framework that emphasizes autonomy, discretion and decision-making power as the key variables.

Building conceptual frames is always a balance between comprehensiveness and specificity. Any framework is a simplified representation of the complex reality. It is also a social construct that may postulate order where the reality may be a collection of messy and disconnected entities and processes. A social construct focuses attention on some elements and viewpoints while ignoring others. There may thus be legitimately diverging perceptions and views when applying the framework.

This chapter has sought to sketch out the dimensions that can create a platform for informed debate about structural and dynamic elements of decentralization in the complex and changing field of health care. Although it is a rather comprehensive framework, it is still an incomplete "image" of the possible landscape. The chapters that follow provide additional "images" and a number of empirical examples to illustrate and test the usefulness of the conceptual ideas presented.

Notes

1 (Re)centralization can be seen as the opposite of decentralization. Henceforth in this chapter the term decentralization will be used to illustrate both de- and (re)centralization.
2 Lundquist only deals with political decentralization and the variables presented here are most relevant for the concepts of devolution and deconcentration in Table 3.1.

References

Altenstetter, C. (1999) From solidarity to market competition? Values, structure, and strategy in German health policy, 1883–1997. In Powell, F.D. and Wessen, A.F., eds, *Health care systems in transition: an international perspective*. Thousand Oaks, CA, Sage, pp. 47–88.

Bossert, T. (1998) Analyzing the decentralization of health systems in developing countries: decision space, innovation and performance. *Social Science and Medicine*, **47**(10): 1513–27.

Boyne, G. (1992) Local government structure and performance: lessons from America? *Public Administration*, **70**(Autumn): 333–57.

Brunsson, N. and Olsen, J.P. (eds) (1993) *The reforming organization*. Oslo, Fakbokforlaget.

Burge, P., Devlin, N., Appleby, J., Rohr, C. and Grant, J. (2005) London Patient Choice Project Evaluation: a model of patients' choices of hospital from stated and revealed preference choice data. Available for download only. TR–230-DOH. (http://www.rand.org/pubs/technical_reports/TR230/, accessed 23 May).

Cheema, G. and Rondinelli, D. (1983) *Decentralization and development*. Newbury Park, CA, Sage.

Contandriopoulos, A-P., Lauristin, M. and Leibovich, E. (1998) Values, norms and the reform of health care systems. In Saltman, R.B., Figueras, J. and Sakellarides, C., eds, *Critical challenges for health care reform in Europe*. Buckingham, Open University Press.

DiMaggio, P.J. and Powell, W.W. (1991) *The new institutionalism in organizational analysis*. Chicago, University of Chicago Press.

Figueras, J., Robinson, R. and Jakubowski, E. (eds) (2005) *Purchasing to improve health systems performance*. Buckingham, Open University Press/McGraw-Hill.

Hall, P. (1993) Policy paradigms, social learning, and the state: the case of economic policy-making in Britain. *Comparative Politics* **25**(3): 275–96.

Ham, C. (ed.) (1997) *Health care reform: learning from international experience*. Buckingham, Open University Press.

Harmon, M.M. and Mayer, R.T. (1986) *Organization theory for public administration*. Boston, Little, Brown.

Hoggett, P. (1996) New modes of control in the public service. *Public Administration*, **74**(1): 9–32.

Hood, C. (1991) A public management for all seasons? *Public Administration*, **69**(1): 3–19.

Hopkins, J. (2002) *Devolution in context: regional, federal and devolved government in the European Union*. London and Sydney, Cavendish Publishing Limited.

Hughes, O.E. (2003) *Public management and administration: an introduction*. New York, Palgrave.

Hunter, D., Vienonen, M. and Wlodarczyk, W.C. (1999) Optimal balance of centralized and decentralized management. In Saltman, R.B., Figueras, J. and Sakellarides, C., eds, *Critical challenges for health care reform in Europe*. Buckingham and Philadelphia, Open University Press.

Kickert, W.J.M., Klijn, E.H. and Koppenjahn, J.F.M. (eds) (1997) *Managing complex networks: strategies for the public sector*. London, Sage.

Lipsky, M. (1980) *Street-level bureaucracy: dilemmas of the individual in public services*. New York, Russell Sage Foundation.

Lundquist, L. (1972) *Means and goals of political decentralization*. Lund, Studentlitteratur.

Lundquist, L. (1992) *Förvaltning, stat och samhälle*. Lund, Studentlitteratur.

Mackintosh, M. and Roy, R. (1999) *Economic decentralization and public management reform*. Cheltenham, Edward Elgar.

March, J.G. and Olsen, J.P. (1989) *Rediscovering institutions*. New York, The Free Press.

Mintzberg, H. (1979) *The structuring of organizations*. Engelwood Cliffs, NJ, Prentice Hall.

Mossialos, E. and Thomson, S. (2004) *Voluntary health insurance in the European Union*. Copenhagen, European Observatory on Health Systems and Practice.

Newman, J. (2003) *Modernising governance: New Labour, policy and society*. London, Sage.

Oates, W.E. (1972) *Fiscal federalism*. New York, Harcourt Brace Jovanovitch.

Oates, W.E. (ed.) (1998) *The economics of fiscal federalism and local finance*. Cheltenham, Edward Elgar.

OECD (1992) *The reform of health care systems: a comparative analysis of seven OECD countries*. Paris, OECD.

Olsen, J.P. and Peters, B.G. (eds) (1996) *Learning from experience: experiential learning in administrative reforms in eight democracies*. Oslo, Scandinavian University Press.

Peckham, S., Exworthy, M., Powell, M. and Greener, I. (2005) Decentralisation as an organisational model for health care in England. Report to NCCSDO (http://www.sdo.lshtm.ac.uk, accessed 24 May 2006).

Pierre, J. (ed.) (2000) *Debating governance: authority, steering and democracy*. Oxford, Oxford University Press.

Pollitt, C. (2005) Decentralization. In Ferlie, E., Lynn, L. and Pollitt, C., eds, *The Oxford handbook of public management*. Oxford, Oxford University Press.

Pollitt, C., Birchall, J. and Putnam, K. (1998) *Decentralising public service management*. Houndsmills and London, Macmillan.

Pollitt, C. and Bouckaert, G. (2000) *Public management reform: a comparative analysis*. Oxford, Oxford University Press.

Pollitt, C. and Talbot, C. (eds) (2004) *Unbundled government*. London, Taylor and Francis.

Preker, A.S. and Harding, A. (eds) (2003) *Innovations in health service delivery: the corporatization of public hospitals*. Washington, DC, World Bank.

Pressman, J.L. and Wildavsky, A. (1973) *Implementation: how great expectations in Washington are dashed in Oakland*. Berkeley, CA, University of California Press.

Rattsø, J. (ed.) (1998) *Fiscal federalism and state-local finance: the Scandinavian perspective*. Cheltenham, Edward Elgar.

Rhodes, R.A.W., Carmichael, P., McMillan, J. and Massey, A. (2003) *Decentralising the Civil Service: from unitary state to differentiated polity in the United Kingdom*. Buckingham, Open University Press.

Saltman, R.B. and Bankauskaite, V. (2006) Conceptualizing decentralization in European health systems: a functional perspective. *Health Economics, Policy and Law*, **1**(2): 127–47.

Saltman, R.B. and Dubois, H.F.W. (2005) Current reform proposals in social health insurance countries. *Eurohealth*, **11**(1): 10–13.

Saltman, R.B. and Von Otter, C. (1992) *Planned markets and public competition: strategic reform in Northern European health systems*. Buckingham, Open University Press.

Saltman, R.B., Busse, R. and Figueras, J. (eds) (2004) *Social health insurance systems in western Europe*. Buckingham, Open University Press.

Saltman, R.B., Busse, R. and Mossialos, E. (eds) (2002) *Regulating entrepreneurial behaviour in European health care systems*. Buckingham, Open University Press.

Scharpf, F. (1997) *Games real actors play: actor-centered institutionalism in policy research*. Boulder, CO, Westview Press.

Strukturkommissionen (2004) Report by the Danish Commission on structural change: Betænkning nr. 1434. Copenhagen, Strukturkommissionen, January.

Thelen, K. (1999) Historical institutionalism in comparative politics. *Annual Review of Political Science*, **2**: 369–404.

Thompson, G.F. (2003) *Between hierarchies and markets: the logic and limits of network forms of organization*. Oxford, Oxford University Press.

Vrangbæk, K. and Bech, M. (2004) County level responses to the introduction of DRG rates for "extended choice" hospital patients in Denmark. *Health Policy*, **67**(1): 25–37.

chapter four

Key factors in assessing decentralization and recentralization in health systems

Karsten Vrangbæk

Introduction

Decentralization is often presented as a "magic bullet" that can address a wide variety of different problems in health systems. This chapter explores the driving forces behind decentralization and the arguments that are often presented for and against its use. The main aim is to catalogue the range of potential pressures that can lead to decentralization and thus create a better platform to understand how and why decentralization occurs. The chapter draws on arguments from public administration, political science and organizational theory, as well as discussions elsewhere in this volume, particularly Chapters 3, 6 and 7.

From a theoretical perspective, there are three conceptual categories of driving forces that help explain the extensive reliance of health systems on decentralization policies: (1) performance issues; (2) legitimacy issues; and (3) self-interest issues. The first category (performance issues) reflects an image of health systems as organisms that can readily be adjusted to new contingencies by policy analysts and decision-makers (Morgan 1986; also Chapter 6). In this view, decentralization reforms are instrumental in both design and impact. Moreover, thorough analysis can lead to consensus on one best solution in terms of structural choices for health care reforms.

The second perspective focuses on legitimacy. It is related to the image of organizations as embodying a particular social culture (Morgan 1986; also Chapter 6). It can also be traced to the social science tradition of German sociologist Max Weber (Weber 1964). In this view, organizations are embedded in broader cultures consisting of values, norms and interpretational schemes. Shared values and norms are important for the level of mutual trust in the system and the ability to rely on traditions and routines. Legitimacy and cultural fit are important factors for decision-makers at all organizational levels in order to build support and facilitate change (March and Olsen 1989). Further, signalling a particular value position may be equally as important for gaining legitimacy as the actual change. Symbolic acts are thus valuable and all reform decisions include symbolic messages in addition to substantive performance-related claims. In this view, decentralization reforms may at least be partially driven by changes in value structure or by more or less conscious attempts to gain legitimacy by adjusting to value perceptions in various settings and countries.

The third perspective (self-interest) focuses on personal and institutional aggrandizement and material interests as a driving force. It reflects an image of health care organizations as political systems within which conflict rather than unity is the normal condition (Morgan 1986; also Chapter 6). Key issues relate to the dynamics of who controls and exploits discretionary space under different institutional arrangements; who has power (Lukes 1974; also Chapter 6); and where the important veto points are in the decision processes (Pressman and Wildavsky 1973; also Chapter 6). Behind these issues is the basic question of who gains and loses power and resources when institutional arrangements change. In this perspective, decentralization may be explained as a conscious attempt by some actors to change the institutional structure in a direction that will benefit them.

Elements of all three types of "drivers" for decentralization can usually be observed at the same time in any particular case or context. Legitimacy and self-interest are particularly important in political and administrative decision processes while functionally based performance arguments are important in all phases of decision processes. The chapter will discuss each perspective separately.

Performance-related arguments for decentralization

As noted above, performance issues are connected to an image of health systems as organisms that can readily be modified in response to new contingencies by policy analysts and decision-makers (Morgan 1986; also Chapter 6). A range of different kinds of performance issues may come into play. We will first consider positive performance related arguments that favour taking decentralization decisions. Subsequently we will review a parallel set of performance-related arguments that militate against decentralization. We can usefully distinguish among input-, throughput- and output-related performance arguments (Donabedian 1985).

Input-related performance arguments in favour of decentralization can be found in both organization and political theory. Organization theory arguments concentrate on improvements in term of input factors to health care delivery such as finances, personnel, technology, etc. Political theories focus somewhat differently on taxation and inputs to the political decision processes in terms of participation, voting, etc.

A main argument in political theory is that decentralization may bring benefits by providing closer linkages between decision-makers and users (Baldersheim and Rose 2000; Peters and Wright 1998). The case of financial inputs (taxation or other politically mandated contributions) can be taken as an example. It is often argued that decentralized structures provide improved possibilities for transparent and acceptable linkages between preferences and financial burdens. There are several contentions behind this. First, the political/administrative argument that decision-makers are closer to, and in more frequent contact with, the population in decentralized units and thus have a better chance of becoming aware of population needs and preferences. The possibilities for participation and voicing opinions will provide opportunities for citizens to give input to political decision processes in health care, and will thus generate a better match of preferences and service/taxation levels as well as other benefits such as greater awareness of cost and benefits.

Second, the decentralized units have the ability to offer differentiated service and financing (taxation) levels, enabling citizens to move to areas with tax/service combinations that fit their preferences (the Tiebout effect). In political terms, this means that citizens "vote with their feet" by using the "exit" option with regards to particular health services (Hirschman 1970).

These arguments comprise the core of what is known as "fiscal federalism" in the political economy literature (Oates 1998; Ratts 1998; see also Chapter 7). As stated in Chapter 7, the prerequisite for the fiscal federalism argument is that people have consistent preferences and are willing and able to make active choices to pursue these preferences. In particular, it is assumed that people are willing to move residence in order to seek the best tax/service combinations. Another assumption is that the decentralized units in fact choose different taxation/service combinations. This may not be the case in practice due to homogeneous preferences or pressure from the central level based on equity concerns.

Throughput or *process-related* performance arguments are found in both organization theory and political theory. Organizational arguments relate to issues of control and accountability, staff motivation, coordination across units, patient flow and resource utilization.

It is well known in organizational theory that coordination difficulties increase with size. Large centralized units will have a higher tendency to rely on formal coordination measures via standardization of input and procedures, while smaller decentralized units are more flexible in terms of ad hoc coordination (Mintzberg 1979). Organization theory thus points to a number of possible benefits of decentralized decision-making. First, it may facilitate the use of knowledge and experience accumulated by local staff. Second, it may improve flexibility and adaptability in the organization. Third, it may motivate employees and stimulates entrepreneurship. Fourth, it may strengthen feelings of responsibility among employees (Jacobsen and Thorsvik 2002).

Extending these arguments to public (health) organizations, it can be argued that internal coordination is easier in decentralized units where administrative hierarchies are less elaborate and several functional areas may be located within the same structure. Locating different services within decentralized structures may lead to improved communication. An example would be joint administration of primary care, rehabilitation and social services. This may lead to better coordination of patient flows and more timely and flexible utilization of services where local knowledge and experience are utilized.

From a steering perspective, it has been argued that smaller and more decentralized units create better possibilities for controlling performance and holding staff accountable. Motivation may also be higher as employees feel more closely related to the population being treated and the (local) organizations running the treatment facility.

The political discussion of process-related benefits of decentralization can be traced back to Adam Smith and John Stuart Mill (Pollitt 2005). Mill makes a particularly strong argument in his *Principles of Political Economy* of 1848. He argues that decentralized democratic structures could provide essential breeding grounds for active and informed participation as well as a countervailing force against central bureaucracy (Mill 2004). Participatory decision processes within decentralized units are thus seen as a value in their own right and as a way for citizens to become knowledgeable and active in political issues generally (Peters and Wright 1998; Baldersheim and Rose 2000; Mill 2004).

Decentralization policies may also provide efficiency advantages in terms of reducing the risk of bottlenecks at the central level, thus increasing the overall throughput capacity of the system. Using an analogy from computer science, decentralization enables parallel processing at decentralized levels as opposed to serial processing at the central level. By decentralizing implementation decisions, centralized authorities gain more resources to concentrate on strategic planning for the health care system (Hughes 2003). Decentralization may thus bring a more optimal division of labour into the political decision process.

Parallel processing also opens up the possibilities for local experimentation and learning across units (Baldersheim and Rose 2000; Mouritsen and Svara 2002). The ongoing efforts of creating locally responsive and efficient solutions may create new organizational solutions that can be exported to other parts of the health care system. Decentralized systems thus may have a higher capacity for innovation.

Further, it has been argued that decentralization creates better conditions for implementation of centrally designed policy initiatives. The possibility for local adjustment and the detailed knowledge of needs and conditions in the local area may create more efficient and flexible interpretation of general initiatives (see Chapter 13). The parallel structure may thus ensure a higher throughput of more detailed implementation decisions (Baumgartner and Jones 1993). Of course, it could also be argued that strong decentralized units provide multiple arenas for possible resistance against centralized initiatives.

The positive view of this phenomenon is that process performance may be enhanced by the fact that decentralization creates a countervailing power to central decision-making, thus providing a situation of checks and balance, which will reduce the risk of uninformed and unrealistic policies from the central level. A related argument is that decentralization in some instances may provide opportunities to bypass incompetence or corruption at the central level.

Output-related performance concerns the ability to deliver satisfactory results on various goals specified for health systems. Typical goal formulations for health systems involve economic, quality and service parameters as well as concerns for equity and fairness.

Decentralization may be linked to improvement of output performance by enhancing both input and throughput performance as described above. A better division of labour in decision-making and the creation of room for experimentation and learning may enhance potential output due to the flexibility to focus on service and quality dimensions. Involving citizens and "street-level bureaucrats" (health professionals) more in decision-making tends to create greater awareness and better motivation, which may reflect positively on performance. Accountability and responsiveness may increase by creating a shorter distance between users and decision-makers. These positive effects will, of course, be dependent upon the actual implementation and the specific choices in given contexts.

Such general arguments about linkages between decentralization and output performance are also reflected in the New Public Management (NPM) tradition (Hood 1991; Pollitt and Bouckaert 2000; Hughes 2003). It is argued that managers should be empowered to make managerial decisions with less interference from political actors. This increase in autonomous room for decision-making is expected to strengthen the entrepreneurial spirit and encourage more careful evaluation of cost and benefits, particularly if it is combined with stronger incentives, e.g. through the creation of quasi-market conditions or other measures for strengthening the demand function. Such changes are also thought to enhance the attention to service and quality dimensions.

Thus far, this section has identified a number of arguments favouring decentralization based on performance considerations. We have looked at input-, throughput- and output-related performance arguments, having drawn on organization theory, political theory and public administration. Decentralization was linked to performance issues and the quest for improving performance on various dimensions. In this sense, decentralization can be seen as a structural response to a number of different development trends and challenges in health care. Decentralization is perceived as a potential remedy for problems caused by such diverse factors as changes in socio-demographics, macroeconomic and state financing conditions, medical technology and costs, changes in preferences and expectations, globalization and international collaboration. The underlying drivers for performance-based decentralization may thus be external shocks, gradually evolving challenges, internal tensions, and/or shifts in technological and knowledge level.

Recognizing the diversity of these underlying factors suggests that structural solutions such as decentralization are unlikely to provide adequate answers to all these challenges in one swoop. Rather, decentralization should be understood more as an attempt to facilitate the gradual handling of a variety of different issues by changing the playing ground and rules of the game. The structural frame must be filled in by actors in the health field. We thus need to be cautious about faith in decentralization as a quick solution for all contingencies. Furthermore, the literature indicates that decentralization may have its own inherent problems, suggesting that we face a trade-off situation in which the task is to find an optimal mix of central and decentralized management at any particular point in time. The following two sections present arguments against decentralization and provide an overview of the arguments presented so far.

Performance-related arguments against decentralization and for centralization

The claims of performance benefits related to decentralization are not unanimous. Depending on the specific historical and ideological context, one can also find performance-based arguments favouring centralization. Organizational theory includes arguments that centralization can: (1) provide clearer steering signals; (2) facilitate standardization of processes and products; and thus (3) improve predictability in organizational practice (Mintzberg 1979; Jacobsen and Thorsvik 2002).

The main disadvantages of decentralization according to organization theory are: (1) the risk of sub-optimality as decentralized entities focus on their own performance rather than the entire organization; (2) lack of coordinated steering impulses; (3) inappropriate diversity in practices and standards especially in personnel management; and (4) reduced comparability and predictability at the system level (Jacobsen and Thorsvik 2002).

In terms of health services, spreading decision capacity to several decentralized units may create problems in coordination across these units. Planning of investments and development of treatment facilities may thus become less than optimal. It may also become more difficult to impose common standards and create transparency if steering ambitions from the central level are met with opposition by strong decentralized units.

The political interpretation of such arguments frequently focus on the risk that decentralization can create inequality across administrative areas. Accepting local differences is an inherent although not always explicit consequence of decentralization and a requirement for a number of listed benefits (adjusting to local needs, local level experimentation, etc.). When equity problems occur, they often give rise to public or political pressure for standardization and equalization across units. In order to achieve this, a certain amount of (re)centralization of political and administrative power may become necessary. Recentralizing can provide better possibilities for setting standards and holding delivery organizations accountable to uniform principles. It may also strengthen the capacity for planning and coordinating service levels across the system. A relevant example is the introduction of new technology and investment in new equipment. There is an obvious risk of over-investment and poor or inappropriate utilization if decision-making is decentralized without some mechanism for coordination.

Coordination problems in decentralized systems and the risk of duplication of services are thus major arguments for centralizing some degree of power. Other arguments for centralization relate to possible disadvantages of small scale, including the limited capacity to handle complex problems, the risk of capture by strong interest groups such as local industry, and the problems of externalities and shared resources where the actions of one political/administrative unit negatively affects another. All these arguments may lead to (re)centralization policies (Baldersheim and Rose 2000; De Vries 2000).

Comparing functionally based arguments for and against decentralization

Table 4.1 summarizes the main arguments for and against decentralization. Most have already been presented in the text, although a few arguments are new.

One important conclusion from this apparently conflicting set of arguments is that context and historical situation matter, both for the argumentation as well as for the functioning of decentralization. Different situations call for different structural responses and the specific historical, social and cultural trajectory is a factor in building arguments and driving the process (see also Chapter 3 for this point). The merits of specific arguments have to be weighed against concrete cases. This suggests scepticism about the likelihood of determining benefits and drawbacks of different structural choices once and for all. The national context and history, the bureaucratic and civil society infrastructure and capacity, the political institutions and the broader value base in society will all influence the appropriateness of various structural choices in particular circumstances.

This assessment of relative merits of decentralization can be further informed by drawing on organization theory. Organization theorists often argue that the optimal mix of centralized and decentralized control is dependent on a number of variables such as the types of tasks performed (simple or complex; heterogeneous and indeterminate or homogeneous and predictable), the technology used (well known or evolving), the knowledge level and capacity of staff (well educated and autonomous or inflexible and narrowly focused) and finally the type of environment, which may require more or less flexibility of the organization (degree of uncertainty and dependency) (e.g. Woodward 1965; Pfeffer and Salancik 1978; Mintzberg 1979; Williamson 1985; Scott 1992).

Translated into health services, this could indicate that the optimal level of decentralization is likely to vary across the different sub-functions. For example, planned surgery that may be parcelled into groups of fairly homogeneous procedures with well-known technology may be more suitable for standardization, formalization and thus centralization than acute medicine, geriatrics, psychiatry or primary care, which typically entail more uncertain environments (in terms of social factors, epidemics, etc.), heterogeneous contacts and a range of diagnostic, therapeutic and follow-up services.

In general, there seem to be ongoing tensions in health care between concerns for specialization, volume and flexibility. Medical technology developments in some instances point to a need for centralization in order to support a higher degree of specialization. This can, for example, be seen in the case of sophisticated scanners, which are expensive and cannot be purchased for all units. In addition, there are a limited number of specialized personnel, who need a relatively high volume of procedures to maintain their skills. On the other hand, as particular technologies become more common and their prices fall, there will be opportunities for decentralizing services that were previously only performed at highly specialized units. Some technologies such as tele-medicine

Table 4.1 Performance-based arguments for and against decentralization

	For decentralization	*Against decentralization*
Input	Proximity between decision-makers and population provides better match between service/ payment levels and needs/ preferences. This means better utilization of resources and more satisfied users Decentralization creates differentiation and thus possibilities for exiting to units with preferred service level and payment combinations Recruitment of human resource input becomes more efficient as decentralized knowledge can be utilized to hire the right persons. Staff may be more motivated in smaller units where they feel that they can have a real impact	Decentralization may lead to inequality in financing of health systems Risk of political capture by strong industry or interest groups is greater in decentralized units Harder for minority groups to gain formal representation in local democracies Exit is not a real option as employment and accommodation options are limited It may be difficult to attract qualified personnel to remote areas Centralized planning creates more uniform standards
Throughput	Decentralization improves control and accountability, staff motivation, coordination across units, patient flow and resource utilization Decentralization creates opportunities for local adjustment and experimentation with organizational solutions that may spread to other units though systematized learning processes Decentralization creates a countervailing power to poor decision-making at the central level	Decentralization reduces equity and fairness as service and quality will differ across decentralized units depending on local capacity and choices Coordination and optimal patient flows across units require a strong hand from the central level Learning across units will not take place without centralized collection of information and control of performance The central level must retain power to force decentralized units to adopt the best solutions and implement centrally decided plans
Output	Decentralization improves input and throughput performance and thus creates better conditions for meeting the objectives of productivity, efficiency and effectiveness, quality, service and expenditure control	Decentralization weakens coordination and creates situations of duplication of services Drawbacks of small-scale production will reduce efficiency and quality in some cases Externalities from the decisions of one unit may negatively affect the performance of other units, e.g. competing for input factors such as personnel and patients

and computer-assisted surgery also increase the opportunities for decentralization as the decentralized units can draw on specialized knowledge when needed.

Most policy initiatives will include one or more of the performance-related arguments for decentralization presented above. However, policies are likely to be driven by other factors in addition to purely instrumental concerns. Concerns for legitimacy and the pursuit of individual and institutional interests are important additional elements in the decision-making calculus. In practice, decentralization will usually take place in political settings where it is difficult to find objective grounds for evaluating performance claims. It is therefore particularly important to be aware of the two issues of legitimacy and self-interest when assessing and developing decentralization/centralization policies.

Legitimacy concerns

Legitimacy issues constitutes the second category of potential drivers for decentralization/centralization. In the political science literature, the focus on legitimacy can be traced back to Weber and Lowi. The main issue is how to ensure acceptance of the state's legitimate use of power, e.g. in the allocation of resources and rights (Weber 1964; Lowi 1979; Rothstein 1998). This perspective can be further elaborated by insights from organization theory, which emphasizes that organizations (and health systems) are embedded in broader cultures consisting of values, norms and interpretational schemes (Morgan 1986; March and Olsen 1989; also Chapter 6). Legitimacy and cultural fit are important for decision-makers at all organizational levels in order to build support and facilitate change processes (March and Olsen 1989). Policy-makers are dependent upon their ability to persuade and win support for various policies by important actors. Connecting to cultural notions and shared conceptual images will improve their likelihood of success (Majone 1989; Stone 1998). From this analytical perspective, decentralization can be understood as a general concept that represents a positively valued shared image in Western cultural settings at this point in time (Pollitt 2005). Introducing decentralization policies may thus partially be driven by more or less conscious quests for legitimacy. It is possible to distinguish between input, process and output legitimacy. These categories reflect the performance dimensions described in the above but focus on perceptions among actors rather than performance *per se*.

Input legitimacy refers to acceptance of decisions based on citizen's ability to provide input to political decision-making. The relevant questions concern accessibility to democratic processes, proximity to elected officials, fairness in democratic procedures, etc. If health systems are perceived to fail on such dimensions, there may be a risk of diminished support. Decentralization is often presented as a potential solution to such problems as it brings decision-making closer to the local population and creates easier access for citizens and interest groups to political decision-makers. This may enhance satisfaction and acceptance in the community and thus may have a positive impact on all parts of the policy process.

Process legitimacy refers to control, trust, accountability and transparency of choices. On the one hand, it is often argued that smaller units with decision-making closer to the public are more transparent and easier to hold accountable. The population may find it easier to understand and control processes at local levels rather than in large centralized bureaucracies. On the other hand, it may be more costly to develop efficient monitoring and reporting systems in a decentralized setting. There is a risk of duplication of effort in building quality assurance systems, patient records or clinical databases. It may thus become more costly and perhaps also more difficult for both authorities and the public to compare across decentralized units, so the citizens may have less opportunity for critical assessment. A combination of decentralized decision units that are embedded in and supported by centralized standards and evaluation of performance may be the solution to this dilemma.

Output legitimacy refers to acceptance of results by relevant actors (patients, professionals, politicians, etc.) in terms of performance, service level, quality, equity across units, etc. Decentralization has been presented as a way to improve performance on such dimensions, or at least give the appearance of political action to address performance issues. Managing output legitimacy is made difficult by the fact that changes in socio-demographic structures, rising levels of income and education, etc. tend to affect general perception patterns. The population is likely to expect ever increasing service levels. Decentralization policies may be a way to shift attention (along with responsibilities) and signal responsiveness to such increasing demands.

A related issue is how to maintain legitimacy in the process of introducing reforms. It is well known that populations often have strong attachments to their historically developed national, regional or local solutions. Decentralization/centralization policies must take this into account in order to be considered legitimate.

The quest for legitimacy and the cultural embeddedness of policy-making can lead to the systematic spread of particular ideas that are able to win support from different relevant actor groups. In a situation of uncertainty about policy means, there may be a tendency for policy-makers to import ideas and to imitate organizational forms that appear successful in other public or private organizations or in other countries. This can lead to waves of concurrent adaptation of similar ideas in many different locations at the same time (DiMaggio and Powell 1991). In such cases, the symbolic value of a policy weighs at least as heavily as the perceived performance benefits. The mere signalling of intent to adopt solutions that are generally seen as proper and suitable in the current period of time may be more important than following through on implementation and effects (March and Olsen 1989). This could help explain some of the flawed decentralization attempts illustrated elsewhere in this book, since adaptation can become disconnected from analysis of the prerequisites and contextual situation.

Decentralization may thus be linked to more or less conscious attempts at building input, process or output legitimacy. Issues of legitimacy and acceptance seem particularly important in health policy for a number of reasons. First, the information asymmetry between professionals and both politicians/administrators and citizens/patients creates a strong need for trust in this sector. Accountability and control systems can be established to some extent, but at the core there will always be a reliance on professional judgement. This places a strong focus on popular acceptance of policy decisions both at the individual level and at systemic or aggregate levels. This is further reinforced by the fact that treatment often has profound and immediate impact on people's lives, and the fact that health care constitutes a large item on most national budgets. In organizational terms, there is often a high degree of uncertainty regarding the merits of different solutions. This may lead to a bigger role for imitative trend following than in other sectors.

Decentralization can be seen as part of a general policy trend in recent years tied to legitimacy issues. This does not mean that performance arguments are necessarily invalid, or that decentralization may not serve useful purposes. However, it suggests that there may be other driving forces than performance claims, and it emphasizes the link between decentralization and the current cultural and normative context for health policy-making (Morgan 1986; March and Olsen 1989; DiMaggio and Powell 1991. See also Chapter 6). One extreme consequence might be that decentralization becomes an "empty bucket" that is filled with different specific policy meanings in particular settings. National and local interpretations transform the meaning into different structural forms ranging from political devolution to creation of autonomous and business-like management units (Pollitt 2005). In such cases, the concept of decentralization may become so diversified that it resembles an empty but symbolically useful label that may serve a variety of political purposes. This leads us to the third potential driver for decentralization.

Self-interest as motivation for decentralization

Individual and institutional self-interest is the third key concept for explaining decentralization choices. In this view, health policy should be seen as an ongoing struggle for power and influence among individual and collective actors operating within institutional structures that provide both constraints and opportunities (Scharpf 1997; Peters 1998). Institutions define decision processes, participation and roles and they influence strategic options for the actors. Actors that feel particularly constrained in a centralized setting may attempt to promote policies of decentralization and vice versa. Examples could be political parties with strong representation at the local level or doctors associations that prefer to deal with a number of decentralized agencies rather than one powerful central negotiator.

A further reason for promoting structural change could be strategic attempts to weaken the strongholds of other actors (Schattschneider 1965) or eliminate veto points (Pressman and Wildavsky 1973). An example could be a health minister who perceives the parliamentary opposition or the central administration as barriers to particular policies. Decentralization may create new possibilities for alliances with political and administrative actors at other levels.

Decentralization may also be driven by long-term strategic considerations for promoting particular policy paths by changing institutional structures and the rules of the game. Decentralization could, for instance, be introduced as a first step towards privatization or a first step towards breaking the power of national interest organizations.

The key issues in this perspective thus relate to the dynamics of who controls and exploits discretionary space under different institutional arrangements; who has power (Lukes 1974; also Chapter 6); and where the veto points are in the decision and implementation processes (Pressman and Wildavsky 1973; also Chapter 6). Behind these issues is the basic question of who gains and loses power and resources by changing institutional arrangements, as this is usually an important explanatory variable for understanding different actors and their attempts to influence political decision-making. It is obvious that decentralization tends to give more power to decentralized authorities and administrators. Depending on the form of decentralization (see Chapter 3), it may also provide openings for management staff and private actors. Central authorities will usually lose power unless decentralization is combined with legislative measures to strengthen oversight and intervention capacity. We can thus imagine a number of different combinations. The analysis of such issues can help in understanding the motivation behind decentralization initiatives and improve the development of realistic implementation strategies.

Combining all three perspectives in assessing decentralization policies

As stated above, most decentralization initiatives will be driven by a combination of functional/performance-related concerns, legitimacy issues and self-interest. Health politicians will most likely be concerned with both legitimacy and functional issues, while the underlying drivers for their ambitions are likely to also include personal satisfaction, popularity and power. Health administrators are likely to have a similar combination of functionalist, legitimacy and individualist motives. Two implications of this should be highlighted. First, policy analysts should be sensitive to the possibility of different concurrent driving forces and use multidimensional analysis perspectives. Such multidimensional analysis is an important prerequisite for successful planning of decentralization policies. This book provides various tools for undertaking such multidimensional analysis (e.g. Chapters 3 and 6). Second, the outcome of the process may end up being less than optimal as seen from a purely functional system perspective. Pursuing legitimacy, individual and institutional self-interest may lead to compromises and decision processes that focus on what is possible (and legitimate) in a constrained political and administrative environment, rather than what is optimal from a purely system performance perspective. Indeed, there may be conflicting views of what would be optimal at the system level. Compromise solutions are an inherent and natural part of democratic processes, and can be regarded as steps along the way rather than end states. It is thus important to maintain an openness to evaluate and reconsider the effects of decentralization policies at regular intervals.

Similarly, it is important to be aware that not all policy designs are implemented as planned. This means performance-based or legitimacy-based expectations may not be met, and that adjustments may be needed along the way. Attention to implementation issues and evaluation of policies are thus important parts of the policy process, making performance, legitimacy and self-interest factors important in the implementation phase as well as in the planning and decision phases.

A further factor to consider is that decentralization policies in health care may be coincidental by-products of other policy changes. Policy is designed and administrative structures are changed for a number of reasons other than health system functionality. Decentralization may simply be part of larger administrative reform packages or it may be the result of national administrative crisis or adjustments to international developments such as the EU focus on regional governance units. Functional concerns in other sector areas may not coincide with the demands in health care, since the technology and interaction with users vary considerably across sectors. In such instances, the task for health policy-makers would be to optimize results within the constraints set by external reform processes.

The three types of driving forces presented in this chapter provide a framework for examining the multiple motivations that can lie behind different decentralization policies. They can thus be useful in analysing developing trends and explaining the various phases of decentralization policies observed in individual countries. Analysing such themes can lead to a more informed discussion about the pros and cons of decentralization and recentralization as health policy strategies.

References

Baldersheim, H. and Rose, L.E. (2000) *Det kommunale laboratorium. Teoretiske perspektiver på lokal politikk og organisering* [The municipal laboratory: theoretical perspectives on local politics and organization]. Oslo, Fakbokforlaget.

Baumgartner, F.R. and Jones, B. (1993) *Agendas and instability in American politics*. Chicago, University of Chicago Press.

De Vries, M. (2000) The rise and fall of decentralization: a comparative analysis of arguments and practices in European countries. *European Journal of Political Research*, **38**(2): 193–224.

DiMaggio, P.J. and Powell, W.W. (1991) *The new institutionalism in organizational analysis*. Chicago, University of Chicago Press.

Donabedian, A. (1985) *The methods and findings of quality assessment and monitoring*. Ann Arbor, MI, Health Administration Press.

Hirschman, A.O. (1970) *Exit, voice and loyalty: responses to decline in firms, organizations, and states*. Cambridge, MA, Harvard University Press.

Hood, C. (1991) A public management for all seasons? *Public Administration*, **69**(1): 3–19.

Hughes, O.E. (2003) *Public management and administration: an introduction*. New York, Palgrave.

Jacobsen, D.I. and Thorsvik, J. (2002) *Hvordan organisationer fungerer: indføring i organisation og ledelse* [How organizations work: an introduction to organization and management]. Copenhagen, Hans Reitzel.

Lowi, T. (1979) *The end of liberalism*. 2nd edn. New York, W.W. Norton.

Lukes, S. (1974) *Power: a radical view*. London, Macmillan.

Majone, G. (1989) *Evidence, argument and persuasion in the policy process*. New Haven, CT, Yale University Press.

March, J.G. and Olsen, J.P. (1989) *Rediscovering institutions*. New York, The Free Press.

Mill, J.S. (2004) *Principles of political economy*. Amherst, MA, Prometheus Books.

Mintzberg, H. (1979) *The structuring of organizations*. Engelwood Cliffs, NJ, Prentice Hall.
Morgan, G. (1986) *Images of organization*. Newbury Park, CA: Sage.
Mouritsen, P.E. and Svara, J. (2002) *Leadership at the apex: politicians and administrators in Western local governments*. Pittsburgh, PA, Pittsburgh University Press.
Oates, W.E. (ed.) (1998) *The economics of fiscal federalism and local finance*. Cheltenham, Edward Elgar.
Peters, B.G. (1998) Political institutions, old and new. In Goodin, R. and Klingeman, H-D., eds, *A new handbook of political science*. Oxford and New York, Oxford University Press.
Peters, B.G. and Wright, V. (1998) Public policy and administration, old and new. In Goodin, R.E. and Klingeman, H-D., eds, *A new handbook of political science*. Oxford, Oxford University Press.
Pfeffer, J. and Salancik, G.R. (1978) *The external control of organizations: a resource dependence perspective*. New York, Harper & Row.
Pollitt, C. (2005) Decentralization. In Ferlie, E., Lynn, L. and Pollitt, C., eds, *The Oxford handbook of public management*. Oxford, Oxford University Press.
Pollitt, C. and Bouckaert, G. (2000) *Public management reform: a comparative analysis*. New York, Oxford University Press.
Pressman, J.L. and Wildavsky, A. (1973) *Implementation: how great expectations in Washington are dashed in Oakland*. Berkeley, CA, University of California Press.
Ratts, J. (ed.) (1998) *Fiscal federalism and state-local finance: the Scandinavian perspective*. Cheltenham, Edward Elgar.
Rothstein, B. (1998) *Just institutions matter: the moral and political logic of the universal welfare state*. Cambridge, Cambridge University Press.
Scharpf, F. (1997) *Games real actors play: actor-centered institutionalism in policy research*. Boulder, CO, Westview Press.
Schattschneider, E.E. (1965) *The semisovereign people: a realist's view of democracy in America*. New York, Holt, Rinehart and Winston.
Scott, W.R. (1992) *Organizations: rational, natural and open systems*. 3rd edn. Englewood Cliffs, NJ, Prentice Hall.
Stone, D. (1998) *Policy paradox: the art of political decision-making*. New York, W.W. Norton.
Weber, M. (1964) *The theory of social and economic organization*. Trans. A.M. Henderson and T. Parsons. New York, The Free Press.
Williamson, O.E. (1985) *The economic institutions of capitalism*. New York, The Free Press.
Woodward, J. (1965) *Industrial organization: theory and practice*. Oxford, Oxford University Press.

chapter five

Drawing lessons for policy-making

Richard B. Saltman and Karsten Vrangbæk

Introduction

Decentralization has held an honoured place in the strategic thinking of European health policy-makers for many years. It has been an integral part of social health insurance systems from their formal beginnings in Germany in 1883, in the delegation of key decision-making responsibility to the not-for-profit private funding structures that lie at their heart (Saltman et al. 2004). Tax-funded health systems have also made decentralization central to their organizational structure. In the Nordic countries, operating responsibility for hospitals has been at regional level in Sweden since 1864 (Heidenheimer and Elvander 1980), followed after the Second World War by a swelling of additional Swedish as well as Danish, Norwegian, and Finnish decentralization initiatives. Moreover, in the Nordic Region, decentralization involved not only shifts from national to regional responsibility, but from regional to municipal roles as well. In Finland, for instance, hospitals are owned and partly funded by federations of municipalities. In southern and central Europe, similarly, starting in the 1980s in Spain and the 1990s in Italy and Poland, decentralization was adopted as a central organizational strategy in the health sector. In the United Kingdom, health-related decision-making has been decentralized to its four constituent countries (England, Scotland, Wales and Northern Ireland).

This strategic role for intra-country decentralization was further strengthened by the growth of the European Union. As the European Union grew in purview and competence, and as additional countries became members, an increasing number of decisions that had previously been taken by national governments were being taken at a supra-national level in Brussels. By decentralizing some of its remaining authority downward to (typically) regional governments, national governments sought to reinforce decision-making structures that were more closely associated with their citizenry's specific interests and culture – hence the popular 1980s phrase about a "Europe of Regions".

In the early 2000s, however, this uncritical adoption of decentralization has come under substantial scrutiny. In the Nordic Region – previously strong advocates of decentralization in the health sector – countries are adopting various types of recentralization. In January 2002, the Norwegian state took ownership and operating control of all hospitals away from the 19 elected county councils, and then vested management responsibility in five new, state-appointed regions. In January 2006, the Danish state took back financial responsibility for the hospital sector from 14 elected county councils, and from January 2007 hospital management will be handled by five newly designed regional governments. Moreover, the number of municipal governments in Denmark is being reduced from 275 to 100. In Sweden, there are strong expectations that the existing 21 county councils (already reduced from 26 in 1990) will be merged into six to eight large regional bodies. Both the Gothenburg and Malmö metropolitan areas have already formed a large new regional government. In Finland, there are heated debates about changing the future structure and responsibilities of both municipal governments (currently 470) and central hospital districts (currently 22).

Moreover, evidence of re-centralization can also be observed in central Europe. In 2003, Poland recentralized funding responsibility for the health sector, merging 16 regional insurance funds into one national body. Slovakia reduced the number of income funds from 13 in 1996 to five in 2004. Latvia reduced 32 territorial sickness funds in 1993 to eight regional sickness funds in 1998.

Even in large countries like Italy and Spain, where pressures to maintain administrative decentralization and extend decentralization are strong, fissures are opening up in the ability of regional governments to adequately match available funding to needed services, leading to tense relations with national governments that retain control over a large part of financial resources for the health sector.

From a policy-maker's perspective, these contradictory trends and counter-trends regarding decentralization are well mirrored in the available theory. As demonstrated in the early chapters of Part I, one can readily construct a strong intellectual argument both for and against decentralization. The existing economics, political science, sociology, organizational theory, and management literature, reviewed at length in Chapter 1, does not provide a compelling case either for or against decentralization. Similarly, the conceptual frameworks developed in Chapter 3, seeking to provide analytic criteria by which to assess and evaluate types and levels of decentralization, do not inherently lead to either positive or negative conclusions.

So what, then, is a policy-maker to think? Revisiting the questions raised in the Introduction, is decentralization a more democratic strategy, or not? Is it a more administratively effective strategy, or not? Is it a more financially efficient strategy, or not? How should one interpret the available evidence, and how then should more effective organizational strategies by focused? This chapter will consider each of these issues in turn.

Interpreting the evidence

Drawing together the wide range of issues and experiences discussed in the chapters in Part II with the theoretical frameworks reviewed in Part I leads to the following set of observations about the characteristics of decentralization as they currently present themselves within health care systems:

- Decentralization is not a "magic bullet", capable of solving all structural and policy dilemmas at a single stroke.
- There is no set model, no perfect or permanent solution that all countries should seek to adopt. Rather, there are multiple models of decentralization, each developed to fit the particular context and circumstances of an individual country. Advocates who are certain they have created a "perfect" model should be avoided.
- Decentralization in practice is neither unitary nor consistent across any given country's health sector. Typically, health systems in which some areas are decentralized will have other areas that have been centrally controlled or may be recentralized. Thus the practical question for policy-makers is the *mix* of decentralization and recentralization strategies in a given system and the balance between those strategies.
- Decentralization is not a static organizational attribute, but it reflects a permanent process of re-adjusting the mix, the balance between decentralizing and recentralizing forces in every health system. Any particular fixed equilibrium is fragile and will build up pressures internally that will contest the existing alignment, eventually forcing a re-alignment and an equally fragile new equilibrium.
- Adopting decentralization as a health system strategy is labour-intensive: it is hard to introduce, hard to maintain, and requires continual re-adjustment if it is to be successfully sustained over time.
- The recurring nature of the decentralization–recentralization cycle does not reflect how much experience a country has with decentralization. Nordic countries with decades of experience are just as susceptible to the same structural and organizational dilemmas as the recently independent countries in central and eastern Europe.
- Developing a decentralization strategy requires going beyond the all-purpose code words of "democracy", "efficiency", and "participation" to identify the real decision-making factors that have to be balanced. Since this balance ultimately is a political question, there are always trade-offs between these factors.
- The legitimacy of local government in the eyes of the population is dependent upon its ability to provide needed services. If decentralization impedes the delivery of those services, the result can be to delegitimize local democracy generally.
- There appear to be few, if any, links between decentralization and the evidence on specific policy outcomes. The chapters in Part II explore many of the anticipated links, but the only clear connection is a negative one: Koivasalu et al. in Chapter 11 find that decentralization appears to harm broad equity across the entire population, equity being defined as equal treatment of all citizens.

These observations add up to a simple but powerful conclusion. The decision to decentralize, together with the strategic mix of decentralized and centralized elements settled upon, is not so much an evidence-based decision as a political decision. Ultimately, a decentralization strategy is based upon the values, objectives, and preferences of the decision-makers, which will necessarily be context-dependent.

Strategies for policy-making

The complexity that surrounds the decentralization–recentralization debate can be confusing and misleading. It can make it difficult to pick apart and assess the various arguments that different proponents and opponents make. As the discussion in Chapter 1 suggests, different theorists use different definitions of decentralization and, drawing on different academic disciplines, often make conflicting and contradictory claims for their particular views. As the Introduction and several Part II chapters demonstrate, the evidence base among countries in Europe and beyond is similarly complex and contradictory. This situation leaves policy-makers in the uncomfortable position of not knowing which argument is correct or which model is most appropriate for their particular situation.

The lack of a clear model to follow should not be translated as meaning that decentralization is *per se* a bad strategy, or that countries – particularly larger countries with complicated funding and/or service delivery systems – should not pursue it. Nor should it be seen as providing intellectual justification for adopting a less sophisticated single-factor or otherwise over-simplified approach to the process of structural change in health system. Rather, by making policy-makers aware of the complexity involved in adopting decentralization-based approaches, these dilemmas and admonitions will hopefully encourage them to step back to consider the larger picture, and will serve to emphasize the importance of working simultaneously with the multiple different dimensions involved in designing and implementing a successful decentralized arrangement.

The essential element is to recognize that decentralization-related decisions need to be *regularly revisited and re-adjusted,* so as to maintain the fit of the particular mix adopted to the changing situation both organizationally (internally) and in the broader political, social and economic context (externally). If the central question for policy-makers is the mix of decentralized and centralized/recentralized components at any given point in time, the central policy challenge is to constantly ensure that the present structure adequately responds to evolving policy needs and objectives.

Once decision-makers acknowledge the complexity and contradictions in dealing with decentralization, it becomes easier to develop a strategy that fits the institutional and political context that it must work within. One valuable asset in this process is the set of analytical tools developed in Chapters 1, 3, and 4. Two of these tools can be particularly helpful. The first is to break decentralization up into the three functional components – political, administrative, and fiscal – and to evaluate the pros and cons of any proposed structural change in terms of its likely impact on these three areas of activity (see also

Saltman and Bankauskaite 2006). The second tool set, developed in Chapter 4, presents three key factors that can be used to evaluate a proposed decentralization strategy: performance, legitimacy, self-interest. Applying these analytical categories makes it possible to explore the likely future impact of a particular strategic initiative on the overall outcomes that the health system can achieve. It also can serve as a practical barometer to signal the types of implementation dilemmas that are likely to arise when putting a particular strategy into place.

The practical aspects of adopting this multi-dimensional, regular readjustment approach, and of using the two analytical tool sets, can be readily observed when one digs a bit deeper into the current health sector reform process noted at the beginning of this chapter. In the Nordic countries, for example, one can observe clear signs of political (Denmark, Norway) as well as fiscal (Denmark) recentralization. Similarly, one notes that administrative decentralization (although in larger regional units) remains broadly intact in these countries. Further, the impetus for both political and fiscal recentralization appears to revolve predominantly around performance (waiting lists; new technology) and legitimacy (equity) issues. In both Denmark and Norway, national governments have responded to pressures created by the changing external context. Socially, citizens are no longer willing to wait for elective procedures, and they blame national politicians for not "fixing the problem". Economically, the projected arrival of expensive new diagnostic and therapeutic technologies, including proton therapy and gene-based treatments such as bioengineered and (eventually) customized pharmaceuticals, indicate that larger catchment areas for service delivery units will be essential. As a result, in the new rebalancing of decentralization and recentralization that is underway in these countries, the previous predominance of local democracy has given up some ground to the need for larger, more administratively competent and more economically efficient service delivery units. In effect, the context has changed, requiring in turn that the balance between decentralized and centralized elements be revisited and re-adjusted.

Several additional points can be made about this issue of context. Countries like Denmark and Norway have relatively small populations, are relatively small geographically, and are economically affluent. Moreover, in all the Nordic countries, key interest groups (the third dimension of the performance/legitimacy/self-interest tool from Chapter 4) have a long tradition of moderating their claims in the collective interest (e.g. corporatism). Thus, structurally speaking, these Nordic countries have more latitude to respond to problems in the decentralization–recentralization mix and more cooperation from the various health sector actors in correcting those problems.

The process of decentralization raises quite different context questions in the countries of central and eastern Europe. Their historical situation means that they have had limited experience in designing their health systems, and they have an insufficient number of well-trained planning personnel. They are not particularly wealthy countries, and, further, the possibility of recentralization is a sensitive issue since it reminds citizens of the prior communist period. These countries may also face the dilemma that meaningful decentralization also may be constrained by corruption in regional and local level governments. This political, social, and economic context suggests that central and eastern

European countries may have additional dilemmas in dealing effectively with the complexities of decentralization.

Teasing out policy lessons

The wide disparity of objectives, expectations, and national configurations that have been attributed to decentralization complicate any effort to draw universal lessons from recent European experience. Extracting lessons is made even more problematic by the increasing divergence of national strategies, with intensifying decentralization in some countries (Italy, Spain) while a growing counter-trend of recentralization has begun (Poland) or taken substantial root (Denmark, Norway) in others. An additional confounding factor is the increasing "melting" of public–private boundaries and the creation of new public–private partnerships in ways that further muddy the analytic waters, particularly in central Europe. These multiple conflicting trends each appear to be strengthening a process which, coupled with increasing concerns about possible major structural reforms in several countries including Finland, Germany, potentially Sweden or Switzerland, suggests that generalizations about the direction that Europe as a whole is taking can only be made at the broadest level.

One major generalization would appear to be the fading character of decentralization as the "strategic cornerstone" for European health policy-making. In both tax-funded as well as social health insurance-funded systems, decentralization seems to have lost its status as the preferred organizational arrangement when a government seeks to enhance the performance of its health care system. Instead, decentralization is now recognized to be only one of several alternative possibilities, which indeed often needs to be balanced with a similar measure of centralization if it is to successfully achieve the objectives set for it. This shift in perception, while reflecting what has been true in practice for many years, nonetheless has a dramatic, if not radical, character. National governments appear to be removing key decision-making responsibilities from decentralized units and assuming them themselves, and/or their administrative units do so. In turn, this means that the basic assumption noted in Chapter 1 – that decentralization was an efficient, effective and more democratic strategy for decision-making – is now eroding. In its place, it would appear that decisions falling in two of the functional categories – e.g. political/policy-making and fiscal/budget-making – are being in varying degrees recentralized (Saltman and Bankauskaite 2006). Only administrative functions appear to be retaining a decentralized status.

The reasons for this strategic change of direction across European health systems are not as yet entirely clear. Certainly one key factor is the basic political reality that, when things go badly in a country's health care system – or, more precisely, are perceived by a substantial number of the population as no longer meeting their expectations – it is the national political level that receives the blame, and, consequently, national policy-makers feel they require the necessary levers or authority to resolve the problems that need to be addressed. These problems are seen to represent predominantly policy-related political matters (access, equity, quality) as well as the fiscal factors necessary to effect change. Additional elements in this policy mix are the capabilities that new information technology gives to central system actors to monitor and assess ongoing activity lower down in the health system, as well as the push from the rapid advance of medical technology toward more intensive, more expensive, and often more centralized diagnostic and therapeutic instrumentation.

A second apparent set of factors concerns the growing interaction of global and regional European economic issues. The impact of a globalizing economy has put considerable pressure on national policy-makers to restrain growth in health financing so as to help lower the relative cost of labour in a highly competitive international environment. Similarly, the introduction of the euro as a common currency across 12 countries (and the desire of a number of 2005 accession states to join the euro in the near future) have reinforced both the need to restrain public sector spending generally as well as the overall impact of the European single market on health system decision-making.

A third factor extends from concern about the imminent retirement of post-war workers (the so-called "Baby Boomers") and broader worries about the impact of an ageing population on health sector (as well as pension sector) expenditures. Although ageing in fact appears to be less significant an outcome influencing factor than previously thought, and governments do in practice have a range of potential policies that can be introduced to further blunt its effect (Saltman and Dubois 2005), policy-makers appear to believe that more centrally defined decision-making will be necessary to coordinate the political and fiscal response to this broad demographic challenge.

Conversely, it would appear that the administrative dimension of decentralization remains largely in place as a settled element of the broader picture. In Norway, where all ownership and management of hospitals was recentralized in 2002 into central government hands, the national government immediately decentralized administrative responsibility in two ways: to five newly created administrative units (the regions) and also, within those regions, to a series of entrepreneurially-based, semi-independently managed public firms (here, state enterprise) structures. Even when administrative elements were centralized, there was little interest on the part of central government to retain day-to-day managerial control – quite contrary to the observable pattern with both political and fiscal dimensions of decentralization.

Given this broad policy context and the range of factors at work within it, the kind of policy lessons that can be drawn from the wide range of experience in this volume is necessarily quite general. Ranging over the evidence and assessments provided about decentralization strategies in both Parts I and II, the following six policy lessons appear most prominent:

- *Means not ends.* Decentralization is a policy mechanism intended as an instrument to achieve a specific (or a set of specific) objectives such as efficiency, effectiveness, political democracy, etc. It is not a policy objective in and of itself. For a decentralization strategy to be successful, consequently, it should clearly specify the broader political, administrative or fiscal objective(s) it is designed to achieve.
- *Heterogeneously applied.* Decentralization is hardly ever applied as a uniform universal strategy that cuts across all categories of health sector activity. Rather, decentralization typically occurs in some health system sub-sectors

but not in others. This complex heterogeneous approach is particularly apparent with political issues: for instance, no European government has decentralized major aspects of national standard-setting or regulatory control.

- *Dynamic not static*. Decentralization strategies are not etched in stone. Approaches which no longer meet constantly evolving political, administrative or fiscal objectives as defined by policy-makers may need to be changed or eliminated. Recentralization has particularly reflected questioning about the ability of decentralization to achieve fiscal efficiency.
- *Context counts*. As part of an overall strategy of governance and government, decentralization occurs within a broader social and cultural context. How decentralization strategies translate into institutional structure and process decisions will necessarily reflect the composition, character, values and norms of the broader social system in which they must operate.
- *Regulation remains essential*. The concept of decentralization has little in common with geopolitical fragmentation. Allocating political, administrative or fiscal responsibility to lower levels of government (or outside the public sector) does not involve abandoning all central government standards or accountability. Well-designed regulation, particularly for equity and information distribution standards, is an essential element in successful local control (Saltman et al. 2002).
- *Outcomes vary*. Decentralization strategies appear to be most stable when they pursue administrative objectives. Conversely, decentralization appears to be increasingly volatile when targeted on political and, particularly, fiscal objectives. It may well be that changing technological, clinical, media, and popular conditions may limit or even eliminate effective fiscal decentralization in the short-to-medium-term future.

The most fundamental policy lesson is that decentralization is a learning process rather than a fixed managerial framework. It is permanently in flux, reflecting the constantly changing character of the organizational and managerial systems it is working within. If policy-makers approach the introduction of decentralization as only one stage in a permanent process of evolving managerial strategies, its potential as an effective instrument will increase considerably.

References

Heidenheimer, A. and Elvander, N. (eds) (1980) *The making of the Swedish health care system*. New York, St. Martins Press.

Saltman, R.B. and Bankauskaite, V. (2006) Conceptualizing decentralization in European health systems: a functional perspective. *Health Economics, Policy and Law*, **1**(2): 127–47.

Saltman, R.B. and Dubois, H.F.W. (2005) The impact of aging on health and long-term care services in Europe: a review of recent thinking. Report to ECA Unit, Human Development section, World Bank. Washington, DC, World Bank.

Saltman, R.B., Busse, R. and Mossialos, E. (eds) (2002) *Regulating entrepreneurial behaviour in European health care systems*. Buckingham, Open University Press.

Saltman, R.B., Busse, R. and Figueras, J. (eds) (2004) *Social health insurance systems in western Europe*. Buckingham, Open University Press/McGraw-Hill Education.

Part two

Assessing recent experience

chapter six

Approaches to studying decentralization in health systems

Sarah Atkinson

Decentralization is one of the commonest government policy measures found in the past 20 years. The very nature of its popularity, espoused across all colours of the political spectrum, indicates that this is a measure that holds different meaning for different people in terms of what it is and what it is for. Academic work interacts with the policy environment through two distinct bodies of research. On the one hand, political and economic theorists of fiscal federalism, since de Toqueville over a hundred years ago, adopt a normative perspective to determine what activities should be decentralized and which best kept under central control (Oates 1999). On the other hand, empirical approaches attempt to describe and compare the details of real experiences with decentralization in order to evaluate their success or otherwise according to defined goals.

The chapters in Part II fall largely into this second category and aim to capture this empirical nuts-and-bolts detail of decentralization experiences in health systems from the political, economic, clinical angles, and so forth. First, however, this chapter takes a step back from the detail of decentralization and reflects on how we, as researchers, using the policy-makers' research, construct meanings of decentralization and images of health systems through which to study its impact. The value of such reflection is that the assumptions we hold, often implicitly, about the nature of decentralization and health systems strongly influence the aspects of implementing decentralization that we choose to evaluate and therefore the policy conclusions we then draw. These reflections are presented in three sections: (1) rationales for decentralization that determine the desired outcomes and outputs; (2) definitions of decentralization that determine the formal framework of inputs; and (3) images of health systems that determine the aspects deemed relevant to explain impacts. The reflections presented in this chapter, while teasing out more abstract aspects of research design, nonetheless also belong in the second category of research work, based upon existing, empirical studies of decentralization in health systems rather than the normative theories on decentralization. The studies drawn upon include the collections on health reform in general by Ham (1997), Saltman and Figueras (1997) and Saltman et al. (1998) in Europe, on health system decentralization by Pollitt et al. (1998) within the UK and a special edition of the *British Medical Journal* (1 May 1999).[1]

Rationales for decentralization: the policy output and outcome

Decentralization has tended to be seen as a policy measure that is unquestionably desirable in its own right and a number of authors perceive the need to emphasize that decentralization should be seen only as a means to an end, not as an end in itself (Burns et al. 1994; Bossert 1998; UN 2000). At the same time, the restructuring of resource flows, management practices and auditing required even by a limited decentralization means that evaluation studies focused on the concrete details of impact obscure reflection on the underlying rationale. The observation that decentralization is attractive to a wide range of political positions indicates the range of rationales, official and unofficial, that may underpin the introduction of the measure.

Rationales can be distinguished into proximate and ultimate goals. Proximate goals involve greater consensus among decentralization's proponents and can involve both managerial and political goals (Smith 1985; Conyers 1986). Managerial goals are defined for the system's own outputs and outcomes and for which decentralization is argued to solve shortcomings; these invariably include variants on improved efficiency, effectiveness and equity (Mills et al. 1990; Thomason et al. 1991; Barnabas 1997; Bossert 1998; Hunter et al. 1998; Pollitt et al. 1998; UN 2000; Kähkönen and Lanyi 2001; Tountas et al. 2002). Broader political proximate goals showing at least superficial consensus involve relations with the population such as satisfaction, responsiveness, accountability and empowerment (Burns et al. 1994; Calnan et al. 1998; Hunter et al. 1998; Azfar et al. 1999; Atkinson et al. 2000; Kähkönen and Lanyi 2001; Collins et al. 2002; Atkinson and Haran 2004). The health system, however, does not exist in isolation (Ham 2001); an assessment of decentralization of a health system can be framed against the explicit or implicit ultimate goals of a wider political agenda. In particular, decentralization is variously seen as either part of an ideological shift from a predominantly public health system into a market-oriented one or as in tension with concurrent moves in this direction in the embedding political economy (Flynn 1993; Ham 1997; Calnan et al. 1998; Contandriopoulos et al. 1998; Birn et al. 2000; Laurell 2001).

An assessment of impact of whatever it is that decentralization has entailed in different contexts needs to relate to some, if not all, of these rationales. The majority of studies of health system decentralization assess the impact on the proximate goals, but there is increasing awareness of a wider shift taking place in the practice of governance and public policy of which the health system is necessarily a part (Burns et al. 1994; Ellison 1997; Ham 1997; Cole et al. 1999; Burns 2000).

Definitions of decentralization: the formal framework of inputs

Overview definitions of decentralization invariably emphasize the shifts in power and responsibilities between different scales in a government system. For example, "shift in power relationships and in the distribution of tasks between levels of government and the various stakeholders to be found at each level" (Hunter et al. 1998, p. 310).

Any decentralized system can be described by degree, pattern and pace (Willis et al. 1999). The descriptors used most commonly by researchers on health system decentralization to describe degree and pattern are provided by Rondinelli (Rondinelli 1981; Rondinelli and Cheema 1983): deconcentration; delegation; devolution; transfer to non-government organizations or privatization. A slightly more sophisticated variant is provided by Pollitt et al. (1998) using four dimensions of binary poles that overlap with Rondinelli's classification but also include some extra aspects. The four binary poles are:

political (elected) – administrative
internal (deconcentration) – devolution
competitive – non-competitive
vertical – horizontal

In practice, Rondinelli's typology has tended to be used to classify national systems, for example, the Ugandan and Zambian health systems have been classified as devolution and delegation respectively (Jeppson and Okuonzi 2000). In theory, both this typology and Pollitt et al.'s four dimensions could be applied to different scales and different functions to present a more complex definition of degree and pattern; the experience in most countries is a realignment of what is centralized and what is decentralized. For example, this kind of realignment following reforms in the UK during the 1990s has often been described as resulting in a hollowing-out of the system (Ham 1997; Pollitt et al. 1998). A description of the forms of degree and pattern in this way would feed empirically into the normative theorizations, and strengthen both the theoretical and experiential base of policy decisions.

A crucial aspect of decentralization, at least in its rhetoric, is the introduction of greater discretion over decision-making at different levels. This is an aspect that needs to be built explicitly into assessments of decentralization. Bossert (1998) proposes a simple, easily applicable and comparable approach by using a three-point Likert scale to describe the extent of the "decision-space" formally accorded to the decentralized scale over key functions. Defining which functions are key in assessments of decentralization is perhaps the more complicated element. The functions used by Bossert (1998) to measure decision-space and Jeppson and Okuonzi (2000) to compare two decentralized health systems are presented in Table 6.1 as examples of function lists used in practice. However, ideal lists may be constrained or redefined by what information is available.

Table 6.1 Comparison of functions assessed in two decentralization studies

Bossert (1998)	*Jeppson and Okuonzi (2000)*
	Type of decentralization: central level; intermediate level; district level
Finance: sources of revenue, allocation of expenditures; income from fees and contracts	Financial management User fees Planning and budgeting at district level Planning and budgeting at central level
Service organization: hospital autonomy; insurance plans; payment mechanisms; contracts with private providers; required programmes/norms	Hospital management Lower levels of health care Selection of the minimum package
Human resources: salaries; contracts; civil service	Staffing
Access rules: targeting	
Governance rules: facility boards; health offices; community participation	Role of MOH in appointment of Boards/ Committees NGOs and private sector Donor coordination

The third element, to describe decentralized systems by pace, has been less commonly addressed in studies of decentralization in health systems. Willis et al. (1999) define pace as the rate at which intergovernmental authorities are decentralized. Which functions are of interest is likely again to vary across studies. There is also no accepted and widely applied measure for pace; Willis et al. suggest a classification based on relative differences, something similar to Bossert and colleagues' three-point Likert scale for decision space (Bossert et al. 2000; 2003a; 2003b; Bossert and Beauvais 2002). Only a few studies of health system reforms have discussed aspects of pace as an important dimension, contrasting big bang or incremental approaches (Ham 1997). Again, the notion of pace can be applied not only to health system decentralization at the national scale but also at different scales and to different functions. The importance of sequencing different aspects of decentralization has been highlighted in case studies outside the health system (for example, the Russian Federation, Vardomsky and Rosenberg 2000). While this aspect of implementation has not been explored explicitly in health system decentralization to date, it is often implicit in discussions of whether appropriate capacities exist at sub-national scales.

Finally, in many countries the political move to decentralization is difficult to separate from discussions of increased democracy: an additional dimension to Pollitt et al.'s list based on polar oppositions could be the extent to which decentralization is managerial or democratic in its vision. A theme that emerges repeatedly is how different political conceptualizations of the population to be served by health care (patient, client, customer, citizen, and so forth) have implications for the policy strategy for including those populations into the running of the health system. Strategies for patient choice contrast strategies for citizen participation, echoing previous debates about the relative merits of exit compared with voice (Björkman 1985; Burns et al. 1994; Calnan et al. 1998; UN 2000; Kähkönen and Lanyi 2001).

With respect to these elements, the underlying assumptions are that a devolved degree and pattern with greater citizen control (although there are major differences of opinion of how to achieve this) are more likely to achieve both the managerial and political goals that decentralization is expected to deliver. However, experience has led to more sophisticated awareness that blanket decentralization is not always desirable. There does not seem to be any pre-set assumption with respect to pace, that is whether decentralization is implemented in a big bang or incremental manner. The importance of sequencing has been under-researched but intimations are that there may be something important to explore here. Thus, what pattern, to what degree, at what pace and in what order remain pertinent questions in the process of decentralized health system management.

The experiences of comparative studies indicate that the devil is in the detail; thus a vital additional question to those framed by Willis et al. (1999) should be, "In what contexts?". Unpicking the detail is what comparative studies of health systems' decentralization from different country contexts reflect. The task seems massive and there is a plethora of approaches to be taken.

Images of health systems: explaining impacts

The way in which our idea of what an organization comprises influences how we privilege particular aspects of organizational life in the research design and was demonstrated in Gareth Morgan's classic *Images of Organization* (1986). Morgan describes eight images or metaphors of organization that have been commonly used in organizational studies. Of these, three are found underpinning approaches to health systems and decentralization: organization as organism; organization as political system; organization as cultures. The majority of studies of decentralization in health systems fall into the organization as organism image, some of which are expanded with descriptive elements more typical of the organization as political system image. There are few falling entirely into the organization as cultures image, however, and this has been flagged up as offering a potentially interesting perspective to explore (Saltman and Figueras 1997; Contandriopoulos et al. 1998).

Organization as organism

The image of an organization as organism is a metaphor that underpins much modern organizational theory (Morgan 1986), including open systems (von Bertalanffy 1968) and contingency theories (Burns and Stalker 1961; Lawrence and Lorsch 1969). The image of an organism views strategy, structure, technology and human and managerial dimensions of organizations as sub-systems that need to be in balance. Importantly, the needs of the actors within the system are to be recognized and accommodated. The environment within which an organization is located is given prominence and organizational design can be flexible in response to features such as stability, certainty, resource abundance and dependence, competition, political, legal, technological, economic and social conditions.

This thinking underpins what may be termed the building block approach to health systems, as used in Roemer's (1991, 1993) comparative study of the world's health systems, or more modestly in Hurst's comparative models for health system financing in the European Union (OECD 1992). Similarly, the majority of contemporary studies of decentralization are frequently premised on the image of an organism. Thus, the core focus is to describe the formal structures introduced or altered by decentralization in terms of organizational arrangements, key functions and flows of resources, and the main aim is to try to link these structural changes to their impact on various defined aspects of system performance, including actor responses. The form of argumentation follows a logical-positivist approach seeking to establish, or at least hypothesize about, relationships of cause and effect. This may be done in a more discursive manner or in an explicitly cause-and-effect exploration. There may be debate about what constitutes the key functions and flows of resources: decentralization requires that explicit attention be given to the degree of decision-making ability built into the system at different scales (Mills et al. 1990; Acorn et al. 1997; Kokko et al. 1998; Reverte-Cejudo 1999; Almeida et al. 2000; Bossert et al. 2000, 2003a, 2003b; Arredondo and Parada 2001; Kähkönen and Lanyi 2001; Tountas et al. 2002).

A distinction may be drawn within the image of organization as organism between those approaches that interpret the behaviour of actors within the system as largely driven by individual interests and those that see behaviour as driven equally by norms or corporate cultures. In both cases, the structures of the system are key to influencing behaviour but have significantly different implications for policy-makers. Individual interests may be varied and complex but relatively responsive to organizational changes whereas organizational norms of behaviour can be entrenched and far more resistant to policy endeavours.

One main application of the variant based on responsiveness to individual incentives in health system decentralization is the principal–agent approach (Bossert 1998; Bossert and Beauvais 2002; Bossert et al. 2000, 2003a, 2003b). This approach contends that a discretionary space regarding behaviour always exists and particularly so within a decentralized system, and that consequently bureaucratic thinking in a command and control fashion is inappropriate. Instead, supervision, oversight and persuasion are needed by those mandating the system (the principal) over those who have to implement the system's daily functions (the agents). This framework focuses attention on different scales and intergovernmental relationships within the decentralized health system, the key role of health system personnel in implementing policy, and the intentional and perverse incentives that any given system structures may produce. There is, however, some question as to whether a principal–agent approach is easily applicable to decentralization. The core problem is who is defined as the principal and who is the agent. In the modelling applications of Poitevin (2000) and the framework used by Bossert (1998), decentralization is treated as a top-down policy, from the national government, in which sub-national units need to be encouraged to behave in accordance with the national policy aims. While some authors have, perhaps sceptically, claimed that most decentralization is initiated in a top-down manner (Esman and Uphoff 1984; Conyers 1986), there are three challenges to this principal–agent approach. First, since the ideology of decentralization posits that decision-making be decentralized to a sub-national scale with the national scale at most serving a regulation function and responsive support functions (Burns et al. 1994), the determination of who is really the principal immediately becomes unclear. Second, in numerous instances, sub-national units after decentralization have been seen to influence the national policy agenda (Sweden, Ham 1997; HIV/AIDS policy in South Africa, Steytler 2003). Third, a principal–agent approach assumes decentralization to have been initiated from the centre, which is clearly not the case in many countries, particularly large federated countries such as Brazil (Garman et al. 2001; Montero 2001) and Canada (Armstrong and Armstrong 1999), or in countries with a long history of local government such as the Scandinavian countries (Diderichsen 1999; Koivusalo 1999), Belgium and the Netherlands (Kelly 2000).

This image of organization as organism fits research concerned with the relative merits of deconcentration within the health system and devolution to local government (Jeppson and Okuonzi 2000), the extent and problems of continued dependency on the centre (Arredondo and Parada 2001), the ability of local governments and local health systems to manage (Illner 2000) and what aspects are appropriately decentralized and what are not (Hunter et al. 1998; Kähkönen and Lanyi 2001). A major concern with respect to the appropriate roles for national and local governments is the maintenance of equity between districts under systems that are extensively decentralized. Many studies have found decentralization increases inequalities in distribution of and access to health care (Diderichsen 1999; Koivusalo 1999; Leys 1999; Almeida et al. 2000; Birn et al. 2000; Laurell 2001; Fiedler and Suazo 2002).

However, while remaining a powerful, flexible and popular metaphor for researching organizational life, there are several drawbacks. Because the organism metaphor discusses an organization in the same terms as a natural or biological entity, there is a risk of seeing organizations as natural forms made up of inevitably interacting sub-systems and underplaying their social construction within society. Closely related to this is the emphasis on harmony and balance, resulting in a normative view that the healthy organization is one in which everyone works towards the same goals. Aspects of conflict within an organization are presented as abnormal or dysfunctional elements. Finally, critics have argued that the influence of external environmental factors may be given too much weight, de-emphasizing the potential that humans and organizations have to exercise control over that external environment.

The functionalist orientation of this perspective corresponds to the first set of "drivers" for decentralization policies identified in Chapter 4. The core question here is how best to construct the institutional structure in order to achieve particular aims.

Organization as political system

The image of an organization as political system addresses several criticisms of the organization as organism approach, in that conflict is viewed as the normal state rather than unity. The application of the political science literature to decentralized health systems gives prominence to relationships, especially relationships of power and vested interests, between actors and constituencies of actors within the system. Thus, weight is given to the actors in a system as the agents of change, to informal or non-system relationships within a system, and to the complexities in interactions through which implementation of policies come about. Many of the studies cited earlier that are built primarily on an image of organization as organism expand the static description of health system structures and the changes introduced with decentralization with case study material of the experiences and factors influencing the practice of health care delivery under the new form (Gonzalez-Block et al. 1989; Thomason et al. 1991; Kähkönen and Lanyi 2001; Tountas et al. 2002). This description of implementation and experiences almost always recognizes some aspects of the political relationships within the system and with agencies outside the system. However, these studies implicitly view policy definition and implementation as a largely technocratic activity (Shore and Wright 1997; Atkinson 2000) and react to the influence of informal and political relationships with evident irritation and frustration. Likewise, decentralization of necessity involves increasing the discretionary space for actors at lower levels in the system to interpret and implement health policies and practice. Studies based on variants of organization as organism treat this discretionary space as a problem, something that needs structures and incentives to control (Lee and Mills 1982; Hudson 1989). This is particularly explicit in the principal–agent approach. From a starting point of an image of an organization as a political system, the dynamics of who controls and exploits this discretionary space is essential to a health system. However, studies that start with an image of an organization as political and explore in more detail the relationships of power between the different constituent actors are far fewer. A major proponent of this approach has been Ham (1992, 1997, 2001; Ham et al. 1990).

Again, variants of the organization as political system differ in assumptions about what drives the behaviours of actors within the health system: constituencies as strictly interest groups; constituencies as influenced by their position and role within a system (Alford 1975; North and Peckham 2001); or constituencies influenced more by entrenched norms of behaviour (March and Olsen 1989; Pollitt et al. 1998; Coaffee and Healey 2003). The influence of professional cadres over policy definition and implementation is a theme of particular relevance to health systems, given the different professional associations of physicians, nurses and specialists (Illich 1977; Perkin 1989; Harrison and Pollitt 1994). An exploration of power is a key element in this perspective, requiring a conceptualization of what power is and how it may be studied. The three-fold definition by Lukes (1974) of overt, covert and latent power usefully maps onto those kinds of interactions that are often cited as of importance: bargaining and negotiation (more overt); the informal connections that enable string-pulling behind the scenes (covert); entrenched values of constituencies that even the actors themselves are unaware of (latent). A second concept that has proved useful in studies of decentralization is that of veto-points, points at which certain actors have particular potential for implementing, transforming, subverting or blocking policies (Pressman and Wildavsky 1973; Atkinson 1995). In Zambia, nurses in charge of health facilities (a health system version of street-level bureaucrats) were identified as a significant veto-point in the implementation of health reforms in a decentralizing system (Atkinson 1997). Medeiros (2002) identifies the critical role played by a local leader in the north-east of Brazil in introducing a different local culture in local health system management associated with noticeable improvement in health care provision. In this case, the formal structural position combined with an informal local power base and a more latent form of power based on values. Veto-points could prove a particularly useful addition to understanding the success or otherwise of intergovernmental relations both vertically and horizontally. Other studies have highlighted the roles of informal relationships inside and outside organizations, professional and other group cultures, and the political, economic, social and cultural contexts, in which any health system is embedded, repeatedly emerge as critical determinants of the form and behaviour of decentralized systems (Putnam 1993; Saltman 1997; Atkinson 2000, 2002; Atkinson et al. 2000; Araújo 2001; Ham 2001; Medeiros 2002; Atkinson and Haran 2004).

The political systems perspective parallels the "self-interest" motive identified in Chapter 4 as a potential driver in decentralization policies. In both cases, the focus is on conflict, power, negotiation and compromise. Unlike the functional (organism) metaphor, there is not an *a priori* assumption of being able to find a "best fit" solution.

Compared with the organization as organism image, the political system image offers greater conceptual richness with respect to human relationships, capturing some of the complexity of day-to-day practice within organizations and the varied interests that drive action. The findings of such studies are often frustrating to policy-makers, however, since the details of interactions are difficult to translate into straightforward policy guidelines or predictive models (Pollitt et al. 1998). The identification of where the key points and actors are in any system has clear policy implications for where capacity building resources might be targeted. The aspects of more informal power struggles are less clear in terms of easy policy measures but require engagement with conflict management in a pluralist setting.

Critiques of this approach have come from two different angles. On the one hand, more radical variants of the political system approach interpret interests as rooted far deeper in societal structures of class, gender and racial conflicts. In these versions, a pluralist management strategy is naïve or facile and organizations have to incorporate processes for structural representation through bodies such as trade unions. On the other hand, those pursuing a more unitary ideology of how an organization should function point out that adopting an approach that looks to interest group conflicts as the explanation for organizational behaviour runs the danger of seeing conspiracies and ulterior motives in every action, which in turn can result in increased politicization and a deterioration of trust and collective norms of behaviour (Morgan 1986).

Organization as cultures

The role of trust and collective norms of behaviour in organizations introduces the third of Morgan's images that has relevance for understanding approaches to decentralization in health systems. An image of organization as cultures rejects the assumption of a rational foundation, putting emphasis on symbolism and shared values or meanings as the bases on which those within the system enact their daily practices and thereby construct and reconstruct the structures and the environments of the organization (Morgan 1986). This perspective picks up research which has stressed the importance of changes in attitudes of actors within a system to take forward the tasks of a decentralized system (UN 2000) and brings together work in which the values of actors, both outside and inside the organization, are seen as central to policy definition (Wirt and Krug 2001), policy implementation (Burns et al. 1994; Illner 2000; Bossert and Beauvais 2002) and policy effects in changing values (Cole et al. 1999; Hambleton 2000; Kearns and Paddison 2000; Agranoff 2001). The particular standing of the health professions within health systems makes research on the cultures of these groups with respect to norms, values, informal and formal codes of practice central to studies of policy change such as decentralization; however, not much has been explored directly. This vision of a health system as primarily the expression of values is presented by Contandriopoulos et al. (1998) and by Saltman and Figueras (1997).

The organization as cultures metaphor can be applied to studies at different scales of the health system. Authors have demonstrated how national systems can only be understood as emerging as an integrated part of the whole society, imbued and defined by that society's values (Ham 1997, 2001; Saltman 1997). A necessary sequitur is that the implementation and effect of a major restructuring of such systems have to be designed, researched and interpreted within that context. While this may seem an obvious truism, most studies aiming to evaluate decentralization really only pay lip-service to researching the role of society's values in shaping health systems and health system decentralization; values are more likely to appear as identified problems in the conclusions rather than as an intrinsic definition of what a system is from the outset of the research.

Much the same remains true in exploring differences in performance between sub-national units. An exception is Putnam's (1993) high-profile analysis of differences in performance of local government in Italy that gave popularity to the concept of social capital. In its broadest sense, social capital means that the social bonds or associations between people can provide concrete advantages in many ways. Putnam argues that different local civic traditions and histories with respect to the existence of social organizations in which local government is embedded can account for observed differences in performance between the regions of Italy. While debate may exist over the details of this kind of analysis, a comparison of decentralized local health systems in north-east Brazil demonstrated similar influence of what the authors term political culture embedding and shaping the implementation of decentralization policy and local health system performance (Atkinson 2000; Atkinson et al. 2000; Atkinson and Haran 2004). This strand of research then tries to link the more complex notions of values and culture to the concrete, avowed aims of the health system at its various levels.

Contandriopoulos et al. (1998) present a bold attempt to tie down the sometimes imprecise notions of values and culture by detailing the elements in a dominant belief system. In their characterization, the health system is seen as a product of a dynamic equilibrium between tensions of differing values within society. They group these values around four "poles":

- over-riding values about the importance of equity, individual autonomy and efficiency;
- the definition of illness and health;
- the definition of roles and functions of those working in the health sector and allocation of public resources between different options;
- the methods of regulation, whether technocratic through command and control mechanisms, self-regulatory through professional practice or market-based through supply and demand in competing markets.

Health systems thus comprise norms, rules and practices rather than formal organization. This perspective would seem to offer a rich vein for future work on decentralization in health systems. The centrality given to values keeps the spotlight on the contextualized and constructed nature of the concepts current in health system debates. To a large extent, the approach of this chapter is located within this image of organization as cultures, starting with questions about the very rationales given for decentralization and its definitions. The broad categories defined here regarding group perspectives taken on health system decentralization similarly try to unpick the underpinning assumptions that researchers have taken when envisaging a system. Even the notion of levels commonly used within decentralized health systems (national, regional and district) are open to critical appraisal in that these kinds of political scales also do not exist independently of the society that creates them (Marston 2000; Brenner 2001; Bunnell and Coe 2001; Marston and Smith 2001). There has been almost no research on the ways in which governmental levels are produced, reproduced and challenged in health systems research, despite the centrality of these concepts to decentralization.

However, while research on decentralization in health systems has done little directly with this kind of approach, it has proved popular to managers and policy-makers across the wider organizational spectrum. In particular, the role of leadership and the creation of corporate cultures or consciousness have generated a swath of new management parlance including guru, logo, spin, and so forth. In this respect, policy and management responses to research insights are still built on a version of an organism metaphor in which the old set of sub-systems based on structures and functions have been replaced by a new set of sub-systems of units of culture – norms, rituals, beliefs, symbols, and so forth. This easy fix type of approach, while clearly appealing to management practitioners, badly misses at least two important aspects to the culture metaphor. First, cultures are not static systems but are created through lived experiences and as such are highly dynamic (Hall 1990, 1992). Second, there is a narrow line between building a positive corporate consciousness and ideological manipulation which is largely ignored in the literature but is not ignored by employees who may react, resent and resist attempts at such manipulation (Morgan 1986). Thus, despite a flourishing literature implying otherwise, creating or changing cultures is not easily amenable to quick fixes. The image of organization as cultures provides an important critique and insight into the nature of our health systems and decentralization, but again is less clearly translated into policy strategies.

The culture metaphor corresponds to a number of the points made in the identification of legitimacy as a main driver for decentralization policies in Chapter 4. In both cases, there is a focus on cultural beliefs and culturally based acceptance as core concepts for understanding policy developments. Adherence to commonly accepted norms and procedures creates legitimacy, so that decentralization may be seen as a more or less conscious attempt to signal such adherence.

Approaches to studying decentralization in health systems

The chapter has demonstrated the variation in the ways we can envisage what decentralization is for, what decentralization comprises and how we might understand its impact on a health system. The importance of taking a critical eye to how we ourselves construct the meanings of decentralization becomes evident when comparing the possible approaches and the different considerations they explore. As Morgan states, "a way of seeing is a way of not seeing" (1986: 73); how we view decentralization not only drives us to privilege particular aspects and concerns but also shuts our minds to aspects that might be equally important. Table 6.2 presents a highly simplified indication of the different kinds of policy direction that different approaches to studying decentralization in health systems can provoke.

Combining and expanding our approaches is perhaps more straightforward with respect to defining the rationales for decentralization and the dimensions for describing decentralization forms. The differing emphases in identifying rationales for decentralization can be arranged into a hierarchy of meanings, with relatively narrowly focused managerial goals nested within political health system goals in turn nested within the wider national or international political

Table 6.2 Schematic indication of approaches and policy focus

Rationales	*Dimensions*	*Image*	*Policy focus*
Managerial	Degree, pattern and pace	Organism	Structures, incentives
Political proximate	Democratization, participation	Political system	Conflict management, representation
Political ultimate	Political and historical contexts	Political system and cultures	Capacity, leadership, symbolism Wider social and political critique

agenda. However, health systems research often presents managerial goals of efficiency, efficacy, and so forth, as if they were the only rationales. The combination of managerial goals, or even proximate political goals with respect to improving relationships and responsiveness to the population to be served, draws on an image of organization as organism that focuses on getting the structures right to balance the different sub-systems and thus treats decentralization as a largely technological exercise, views the health system as primarily a static entity in equilibrium within itself and with its environment, and understands actors within the system as relatively passive responders to system incentives. While undoubtedly a useful approach to exploring the nuts-and-bolts details of what is done and whether it works in managerial terms, which is a major concern of policy-makers within the health system, this approach can obscure the political and cultural environments in which any such policy measure is embedded and can distract researchers and policy-makers alike from a more politically informed critique.

Similarly, identifying a range of dimensions which are useful to describe what measures decentralization has actually comprised in any given situation is also more straightforward. The appeal in this chapter is to move beyond the rather static typology drawn from Rondinelli to the use of a more detailed set of bipolar dimensions to be applied at both national and sub-national scales.

The greatest challenge comes in designing a research approach that can incorporate recognition of the various contributions that different images have to offer. An easy resolution or combination approach is unlikely since the three images are built on a number of apparently fundamental oppositions with respect to our understanding of a health system, including:

rational – symbolic
unitary – conflictual
static – dynamic
structure focus – actor focus
individual focus – collective focus
more bounded – more permeable
technological – political

It may well be that any approach to studying decentralization in health systems can only capture a part of the whole – the topic is too huge to cover every aspect of health system decentralization at a depth sufficient to give useful insights. This chapter thus concludes with an argument not for attempting the impossible in trying to combine all aspects into each study but rather for an explicit recognition of the image through which decentralization in a health system is being researched, together with an explicit recognition of what is, of necessity, being omitted.

Note

1 Studies were identified by two procedures: (1) search for "decentralization" on the databases Geobase (1997–), Medline (1996–), Social Sciences Index (1998–) and in the University of Manchester catalogue; and (2) search through volumes of the past

five years of leading public health journals – *Health Policy, International Journal of Health Planning and Management, International Journal of Health Services, European Journal of Public Health, Health Policy and Planning, Social Science and Medicine, Journal of Health Economics, British Medical Journal* – and government-oriented journals for more general considerations of decentralization – *Urban Studies, Publius, Environment and Planning, Progress in Human Geography.*

References

Acorn, S., Ratner, P.A. and Crawford, M. (1997) Decentralization as a determinant of autonomy, job satisfaction and organizational commitment among nurse managers. *Nursing Research,* **46**(1): 52–8.

Agranoff, R. (2001) Managing within the matrix: do collaborative intergovernmental relations exist? *Publius,* **31**(2): 31–56.

Alford, R.R. (1975) *Health care politics*. Chicago, University of Chicago Press.

Almeida, C., Travassos, C., Porto, S. and Labra, M.E. (2000) Health sector reform in Brazil: a case study of inequity. *International Journal of Health Services,* **30**(1): 129–62.

Araújo, J.L. (2001) Health sector reform in Brazil, 1995–1998: a health policy analysis of a developing country system. PhD thesis, Nuffield Institute for Health, University of Leeds.

Armstrong, P. and Armstrong, H. (1999) Decentralised health care in Canada. *British Medical Journal,* **318**(1 May): 1201–4.

Arredondo, A. and Parada, I. (2001) Financing indicators for health care decentralization in Latin America: information and suggestions for health planning. *International Journal of Health Planning and Management,* **16**: 259–76.

Atkinson, S. (1995) Restructuring health care: tracking the decentralization debate. *Progress in Human Geography,* **19**(4): 486–503.

Atkinson, S. (1997) From vision to reality: implementing health reforms in Lusaka, Zambia. *Journal for International Development,* **9**(4): 631–9.

Atkinson, S. (2000) Decentralization in practice: tales from Northeast Brazil. In Able, C. and Lloyd-Sherlock, P. eds, *Health care reform and poverty in Latin America*. London, Institute of Latin American Studies.

Atkinson, S. (2002) Political cultures, health systems and health policy. *Social Science and Medicine,* **55**: 113–24.

Atkinson, S. and Haran, D. (2004) Back to basics: does decentralization improve health system performance? Evidence from Ceará State, Northeast Brazil. *Bulletin of WHO: International Journal of Public Health,* **82**(11): 822–7.

Atkinson, S., Medeiros, R.L.R., Oliveira, P.H.L. and de Almeida, R.D. (2000) Going down to the local: incorporating social organisation and political culture into assessments of decentralised health care. *Social Science and Medicine,* **51**: 619–36.

Azfar, O., Kähkönen, S., Lanyi, A., Meagher, P. and Rutherford, D. (1999) *Decentralization, governance and public services: the impact of institutional arrangements. A review of the literature*. IRIS Center, University of Maryland, College Park.

Barnabas, G.A. (1997) *Local government, equity and primary health care in Ethiopia*. PhD thesis, University of London.

Birn, A-E., Zimmerman, S. and Garfield, R. (2000) To decentralize or not to decentralize, is that the question? Nicaraguan health policy under structural adjustment in the 1990s. *International Journal of Health Services,* **30**(1): 111–28.

Björkman, J.W. (1985) Comparative European and American experiences with representation, participation and decentralization. *Comparative Politics,* **17**(4): 399–420.

Bossert, T. (1998) Analyzing the decentralization of health systems in developing countries:

decision space, innovation and performance. *Social Science and Medicine*, **47**(10): 1513–27.

Bossert, T. and Beauvais, J.C. (2002) Decentralization of health systems in Ghana, Zambia, Uganda and the Philippines: a comparative analysis of decision space. *Health Policy and Planning*, **17**(1): 14–31.

Bossert, T., Larrañaga, O., Meir, F.R. (2000) Decentralization of health systems in Latin America. *Pan American Journal of Public Health*, **8**(1/2): 84–92.

Bossert, T., Larrañaga, O., Giedion, U., Arbelaez, J.J. and Bowser, D.M. (2003a) Decentralization and equity of resource allocation: evidence from Colombia and Chile. *Bulletin of WHO*, **81**(2): 95–100.

Bossert, T., Chitah, M.B., Bowser, D. (2003b) Decentralization in Zambia: resource allocation and district performance. *Health Policy and Planning*, **18**(4): 357–69.

Brenner, N. (2001) The limits to scale? Methodological reflections on scalar structuration. *Progress in Human Geography*, 25(4): 591–614.

Bunnell, T.G. and Coe, N.M. (2001) Spaces and scales of innovation. *Progress in Human Geography*, **25**(4): 569–89.

Burns, D. (2000) Can local democracy survive government? *Urban Studies*, **37**(5–6): 963–73.

Burns, D., Hambleton, R. and Hoggett, P. (1994) *The politics of decentralization: revitalising local democracy*. Basingstoke, Macmillan.

Burns, T. and Stalker, G.M. (1961) *The management of innovation*. London, Tavistock.

Calnan, M., Halik, J. and Sabbat, J. (1998) Citizen participation and patient choice in health reform. In Saltman, R.B., Figueras, J. and Sakellarides, C. eds, *Critical challenges for health care reform in Europe*. Buckingham, Open University Press.

Coaffee, J. and Healey, P. (2003) "My voice: my place": tracking transformation in urban governance. *Urban Studies*, **40**(10): 1979–99.

Cole, R.L., Hissong, R.V. and Arvidson, E. (1999) Devolution: where's the revolution? *Publius*, **29**(4): 99–114.

Collins, C.D., Omar, M. and Tarin, E. (2002) Decentralization, health care and policy process in the Punjab, Pakistan in the 1990s. *International Journal of Health Planning and Management*, **17**: 123–46.

Contandriopoulos, A-P., Lauristin, M. and Leibovich, E. (1998) Values, norms and the reform of health care systems. In Saltman, R.B., Figueras, J. and Sakellarides, C., eds, *Critical challenges for health care reform in Europe*. Buckingham, Open University Press.

Conyers, D. (1986) Decentralization and development: a framework for analysis. *Community Development Journal*, **21**: 88–100.

Diderichsen, F. (1999) Devolution in Swedish health care. *British Medical Journal*, **318**(1 May): 1156–7.

Ellison, N. (1997) Towards a new social politics: citizenship and reflexivity in late modernity. *Sociology*, **31**: 697–717.

Esman, M.J. and Uphoff, N. (1984) *Local organizations: intermediaries in rural development*. Ithaca, NY, Cornell University Press.

Fiedler, J.L. and Suazo, J. (2002) Ministry of Health user fees, equity and decentralization: lessons from Honduras. *Health Policy and Planning*, **17**(4): 362–77.

Flynn, R. (1993) Restructuring health systems: a comparative analysis of England and the Netherlands. In Hill, M.J., ed., *New agendas in the study of the policy process*. New York, Harvester Wheatsheaf.

Garman, C., Haggard, S. and Willis, E. (2001) Fiscal decentralization: a political theory with Latin American cases. *World Politics*, **53**: 207–36.

Gonzalez-Block, M., Layva, R., Zapata, O., Loewe, R. and Alagón, J. (1989) Health services decentralization in Mexico: formulation, implementation and results of policy. *Health Policy and Planning*, **4**: 301–15.

Hall, S. (1990) Cultural identity and diaspora. In Rutherford, J., ed, *Identity*. London, Lawrence and Wishart.

Hall, S. (1992) The question of cultural identity. In Hall, S., Held, D. and McGrew, T., eds, *Modernity and its futures*. Cambridge: Polity Press.

Ham, C. (1992) *Health policy in Britain*, 3rd edn. Basingstoke, Macmillan.

Ham, C. (ed.) (1997) *Health care reform: learning from international experience*. Buckingham, Open University Press.

Ham, C. (2001) Values and health policy: the case of Singapore. *Journal of Health Politics, Policy and Law*, **26**(4): 739–45.

Ham, C., Robinson, R. and Benzeval, M. (eds) (1990) *Health check: health care reforms in an international context*. London, King's Fund Institute.

Hambleton, R. (2000) Modernising political management in local government. *Urban Studies*, **37**(5–6): 931–50.

Harrison, S. and Pollitt, C. (1994) *Controlling health professionals*. Buckingham, Open University Press.

Hudson, B. (1989) Michael Lipsky and street level bureaucracy: a neglected perspective. In Hill, M.J., ed., (1993) *The policy process: a reader*. Hemel Hempstead, Harvester Wheatsheaf.

Hunter, D.J., Vienonen, M. and Wlodarczyk, W.C. (1998) Optimal balance of centralized and decentralized management. In Saltman, R.B., Figueras, J. and Sakellarides, C. eds, *Critical challenges for health care reform in Europe*. Buckingham, Open University Press.

Illich, I. (1977) *Disabling professions*. London, Marion Boyars.

Illner, M. (2000) Decentralization reforms in Central and Eastern Europe and the CIS after 1989: aims, problems and solutions. In UN ed., *decentralization: conditions for success. Lessons from Central and Eastern Europe and the Commonwealth of Independent States*. ST/ESA/PAD/SER.E/7, pp. 23–38. New York, UN Economic and Social Affairs.

Jeppson, A. and Okuonzi, S.A. (2000) Vertical or holistic decentralization of the health sector? Experiences from Zambia and Uganda. *International Journal of Health Planning and Management*, **15**: 273–89.

Kähkönen, S. and Lanyi, A. (2001) Decentralization and governance: does decentralization improve public service delivery? *World Bank Prem Notes* No. 55, June.

Kearns, A. and Paddison, R. (2000) New challenges for urban governance. *Urban Studies*, **37**(5–6): 845–50.

Kelly, M. (2000) Decentralization in the European Union. In UN, ed., *decentralization: conditions for success. Lessons from Central and Eastern Europe and the Commonwealth of Independent States*. ST/ESA/PAD/SER.E/7, pp. 49–55. New York, UN Economic and Social Affairs.

Koivusalo, M. (1999) decentralization and equity of healthcare provision in Finland. *British Medical Journal*, **318**(1 May): 1198–200.

Kokko, S., Hava, P., Ortun, V. and Leppo, K. (1998) The role of the state in health reform. In Saltman, R.B., Figueras, J. and Sakellarides, C., eds, *Critical challenges for health care reform in Europe*. Buckingham, Open University Press.

Laurell, A.C. (2001) Health reform in Mexico: the promotion of inequality. *International Journal Health Services*, **31**(2): 291–321.

Lawrence, P.R. and Lorsch, J.W. (1969) *Developing organizations*. Reading, MA, Addison-Wesley.

Lee, K. and Mills, A. (1982) *Policy-making and planning in the health sector*. Beckenham, Croom Helm.

Leys, C. (1999) The NHS after devolution. *British Medical Journal*, **318**: 1155–6.

Lukes, S. (1974) *Power: a radical view*. New York, Russell Sage.

March, J. and Olsen, J. (1989) *Rediscovering institutions: the institutional basis of politics*. London, Free Press.

Marston, S.A. (2000) The social construction of scale. *Progress in Human Geography*, **24**(2): 219–42.

Marston, S.A. and Smith, N. (2001) States, scales and households: limits to scale thinking? A response to Brenner. *Progress in Human Geography*, **25**(4): 615–19.

Medeiros, R.L.R. (2002) Locating policy: health reforms in Brazil. PhD thesis, University of Manchester.

Mills, A., Vaughan, J.P., Smith, D.L. and Tabibzadeh, I. (eds) (1990) *Health system decentralization: concepts, issues and country experiences*. Geneva, WHO.

Montero, A.P. (2001) After decentralization: patterns of intergovernmental conflict in Argentina, Brazil, Spain and Mexico. *Publius*, **31**(4): 43–64.

Morgan, G. (1986) *Images of organization*. Newbury Park, CA, Sage.

North, N. and Peckham, S. (2001) Analysing structural interests in primary care groups. *Social Policy and Administration*, **35**(4): 426–40.

Oates, W.E. (1999) An essay on fiscal federalism. *Journal of Economic Literature*, **37**(3): 1120–49.

OECD (1992) *The reform of health care: a comparative analysis of seven OECD countries*. Paris, OECD.

Perkin, H. (1989) *The rise of professional society: England since 1880*. London, Routledge.

Poitevin, M. (2000) Can the theory of incentives explain decentralization? *Canadian Journal of Economics*, **33**(4): 878–906.

Pollitt, C., Birchall, J. and Putman, K. (1998) *Decentralising public service management*. Basingstoke, Macmillan.

Pressman, J. and Wildavsky, A. (1973) *Implementation: how great expectations in Washington are dashed in Oakland*. Berkeley, CA, University of California Press.

Putnam, R.D. (1993) *Making democracy work: civic traditions in modern Italy*. Princeton, NJ, Princeton University Press.

Reverte-Cejudo, D. (1999) Devolving health services to Spain's autonomous regions. *British Medical Journal*, **318**: 1204–5.

Roemer, M.I. (1991) *National health systems of the world* vol. I: *the countries*. Oxford, Oxford University Press.

Roemer, M.I. (1993) *National health systems of the world* vol. II: *the issues*. Oxford, Oxford University Press.

Rondinelli, D. (1981) Government decentralization in a comparative perspective: theory and practice in developing countries. *International Review of Administrative Sciences*, **47**: 133–45.

Rondinelli, D. and Cheema, G.S. (1983) Implementing decentralization policies: an introduction. In Cheema, G.S. and Rondinelli, D., eds, *Decentralization and development: policy implementation in developing countries*. Beverly Hills, CA, Sage.

Saltman, R.B. (1997) The context for health reform in the United Kingdom, Sweden, Germany and the United States. *Health Policy*, **41**(suppl.): 9–26.

Saltman, R.B. and Figueras, J. (eds) (1997) *European health care reform: analysis of current strategies*. WHO Regional Publications, European Series No. 72. Copenhagen, WHO.

Saltman, R.B., Figueras, J. and Sakellarides, C. (eds) (1998) *Critical challenges for health care reform in Europe*. Buckingham, Open University Press.

Shore, C. and Wright, S. (1997) Policy: a new field of anthropology. In Shore, C. and Wright, S., eds, *Anthropology of policy*. London, Routledge.

Smith, D.C. (1985) *Decentralization: the territorial dimension of the state*. London, Allen and Unwin.

Steytler, N. (2003) Federal homogeneity from the bottom up: provincial shaping of national HIV/AIDS policy in South Africa. *Publius*, **33**(1): 59–74.

Thomason, J.A., Newbrander, W.C. and Kohlemainen-Aitken, R.L. (eds) (1991) *Decentralization in a developing country: the experience of Papua New Guinea and its health service*.

Pacific Research Monograph 25. Canberra, National Centre for Development Studies, the Australian University.

Tountas, Y., Karnaki, P. and Pavi, E. (2002) Reforming the reform: the Greek national health system in transition. *Health Policy*, **62**(1): 15–29.

UN (2000) *Decentralization: conditions for success. Lessons from Central and Eastern Europe and the Commonwealth of Independent States*. ST/ESA/PAD/SER.E/7. New York, UN Economic and Social Affairs.

Vardomsky, L.B. and Rosenberg, D.J. (2000) Interdependence and the balance between centralization and decentralization of financial resources in Russia. In UN, ed., *decentralization: conditions for success. Lessons from Central and Eastern Europe and the Commonwealth of Independent States*. ST/ESA/PAD/SER.E/7, pp. 68–74. New York, UN Economic and Social Affairs.

von Bertalanffy, L. (1968) *General systems theory: foundations, development, applications*. New York, Braziller.

Willis, E., Garman, C. and Haggard, S. (1999) The politics of decentralization in Latin America. *Latin American Research Review*, **34**(1): 7–56.

Wirt, F.M. and Krug, S. (2001) National and state cultural influences on principals' administration of local schools. *Publius*, **31**(2): 81–100.

chapter seven

Effects of decentralization and recentralization on economic dimensions of health systems

Jon Magnussen, Fabrizio Tediosi and Péter Mihályi

Introduction

In broad terms, the economic goals of a health system include control over total costs, allocative efficiency and technical efficiency. To reach these goals, policy-makers are concerned with (among other things) the structure and organization of the demand and supply side and the links between these. Public stewardship is the common feature of most health systems, but there is no consensus and indeed little in the way of systematic empirical evidence as to how one most appropriately ought to (de-)centralize policy-making powers. In this context, we now set out to discuss the effect of decentralization on the economic concepts of health systems.

A multitude of policy instruments are used to reach the goals attached to the economic dimensions of the health care system. Not all will fit under the heading of decentralization (or recentralization), and they are applied in different forms, with different degrees of rigour and in different mixes across the wide variety of health systems. It is therefore not surprising that there are few analyses of the specific effects of decentralization (or recentralization) as a policy tool on the economic aspects of health care systems. Instead, we must try to extract such effects from more generalized analyses of health systems (reforms) or from analyses of specific policy initiatives. Obviously, reforms must be seen as a part of a political process that includes more than the health sector, a point that is relevant when comparing the relative merits of decentralization (or recentralization) across Europe. Also the effects of similar forms of decentralization must be expected to differ between different forms of health care systems, e.g. depending on the form of interaction between the demand and supply side. This makes it difficult to separate the effects of the policy instrument (either decentralization or recentralization) from the effects of a changing cultural, economic and political environment as well as from the effects of different initial organizational environments.

The term decentralization is generally used to describe a transfer of financial and/or policy powers from a central to a less central authority. As such, it links to economic theory through the framework of *fiscal federalism*. Briefly defined, fiscal federalism deals with the vertical structure of the public sector, and in particular how different levels financially relate to another (Oates 1999). The core argument is that public goods that are consumed locally should also be produced locally. Thus, decentralization is believed to lead to increased welfare by allowing local authorities to act in accordance with local preferences and local cost structures. Adjusting to local preferences ensures allocative efficiency, adjusting to local cost structures ensures cost efficiency. It should be noted, however, that these arguments are only valid if preferences, as well as the cost of producing services, vary between different areas. Thus, it is possible to argue that the need for health services is a "non-spatial" variable, and that allowing the consumption of health services between areas to vary with local (income-related) preferences, will lower rather than increase welfare.[1] What we observe in practice is that many health systems try to accommodate this by limiting the types of decisions that are decentralized and/or by formulating a centralized "national health policy", often with the intention of providing a minimum level of services to all citizens. Again, from an empirical point of view, this makes the concept of decentralization more fuzzy and its effects more difficult to assess.

Another theoretical entry into the concept of decentralization is New Institutional Economics (NIE) (see, e.g. Williamson 1998). The economics of institutions can be analysed on three levels; *institutional environment, governance* and *resource allocation and employment*. Designing health systems includes what Williamson refers to the problem of "getting the institutional environment right". In this one found the policy, judiciary and bureaucracy of government as well as the laws regulating property rights. Once set, the institutional environment tends to remain stable over a long[2] period of time. On a lower level, the challenge is the structure of governance. This is also where transaction cost economics is most prominent. How does one align governance structures so that it fits the institutional environment *and* provides a satisfactory environment in terms of number and costs of transactions? Within the context of decentralization, is there a trade-off between the transfer of power to local authorities and the size of transaction costs? Finally, outside the core of the NIE, but still obviously relevant, is the problem of "getting the marginal conditions right". How does one allocate resources? What does the incentive structure look like? How does one construct contracts that "close" the gap created by informational asymmetries, etc.? Such informational asymmetries may be present both between central and local authorities, and between purchasers and providers. Furthermore, the traditional agency problem between purchasers and providers will not be independent of the degree of decentralization on the demand side (i.e. the scope for soft budgeting (Kornai et al. 2003)). Again economic theory has a lot to offer, mainly from the agency literature.

It is fair to say that the bulk of empirical work on economic effects of health systems reform in general, and decentralization in particular, has been done with few explicit references to transaction cost economics or fiscal federalism. As Oates (1999) notes, there is generally not much evidence on the relationship between fiscal decentralization and economic performance, and the few references given are not related to health care. Also, both NIE and transaction costs economics are mostly applied to the private sector. Agency theory, on the other hand, is widely applied to analyses of economic aspects of health care, though mainly in relation to the design of optimal financial contracts (see e.g. Newhouse (1996) for a survey of this).

The title of this chapter points in the direction of a survey of the effects of decentralization/recentralization *as a specific policy instrument* on the economic aspects of the health care sector. Decentralization is, however, not a precise instrument but rather a broad concept (as illustrated in Chapter 3). Within it there lies a plethora of models that are likely to have different implications for the performance of health systems. Several issues come to mind:

- *The number and type of agents to whom power is transferred.* With the central government as the baseline, decentralization will typically imply that power is transferred to regions, counties, districts or municipalities. In this case, local public authorities will typically have responsibility over a number of public services; thus making priority setting between these a major policy issue. The development of primary care trusts in the United Kingdom and regional health enterprises in Norway are, however, examples of decentralization of the responsibility for a specific service to organizations outside the day-to-day political control of local authorities.
- *The degree of financial discretion of the local authorities.* Decentralization implies the transfer of power, and the next issue is thus if this includes the power of the local authority to determine its own income base. At one end of the scale, income is fixed and follows from the allocation of a total budget between a number of local authorities. On the other end of that scale, local authorities are in full control over their own income base, either by deciding local tax rates, by user fees or by a combination of these. Norway and the United Kingdom are examples of the first model, Denmark, Italy and Sweden are examples of (attempts) at the second.
- *The relationship between local authorities.* Decentralization may be carried out by a partitioning of the market, e.g. by geographical boundaries or types of enrollees. Strict partitioning will generally lead to little competition, or competition may be subtle, as in the form of the Tiebout effect. However, introducing consumer choice into partitioned markets will generally lead to an altogether different and competitive environment.
- *The types of decisions that are decentralized (and those that are not).* Decentralization is defined as transfer of power, but not all powers are always transferred. Thus local authorities may be in charge of the purchasing of a set of services that is decided by detailed national health policy, or they may themselves freely decide what type of services are to be provided. Also, while purchasing

power is decentralized, capacity decisions may remain the responsibility of central authorities.

- *The organization and selection of health care providers.* Are local authorities both purchasers and providers? If not, are local authorities free to contract with any health care supplier or are they limited to a set of local suppliers? And, can suppliers contract with any purchaser? In other words, to what extent is the health care market one of concentration on the demand and/or supply side? Finally, can providers freely choose the services they wish to provide and the scale of their operation?
- *The flexibility and type of contracts used between purchasers and providers.* Some health care systems still use cost-based remuneration for several types of services, others use global budgets, and others again use more refined prospective payment systems. While the freedom to develop individual contracts is related to the type of powers that are decentralized, the way purchasers and providers interact is sufficiently important to warrant the inclusion of this as a separate factor.

Again, the point here is that decentralization cannot be analysed as one, clearly defined policy instrument, thus a formal analysis of its economic implications should be specific in describing the form and to what extent it is taking place. Unfortunately empirical evidence of the effects of (combinations of) the issues described here is scarce. Primarily this is because of a lack of analyses that specifically focus on decentralization as the policy instruments and the economic effects as the endpoint. This limits the possibility to draw solid conclusions about "the economic consequences of decentralization". We therefore choose to focus on some of the reforms that have been implemented in European health systems and that have included one or more of the issues that are described above. Thus, our aim is not to provide an all-inclusive overview of economic consequences of decentralization efforts, but rather to highlight some of the most prominent effects that can be seen. In this context it is also useful to discuss demand side issues separately from supply side issues.[3]

Demand side organization

There are two main issues related to the demand side: the organization of the immediate purchasing agents (number, type, discretion) and the links (control, type of decisions) between purchasing agencies and the ultimate agent responsible for the production of health care services. Within tax-funded systems, the choice has typically been to either devolve power to a few large[4] (region, county) or to many smaller (district, municipality) local authorities. Fiscal federalism arguments would pull in the direction of smaller purchasing agencies where decisions presumably would be in line with local preferences (Oates 1972). There are, however, also arguments in favour of larger agencies. Most tax-funded systems tend to limit the financial discretion of the local authorities, making them recipients of centrally distributed funds. These funds are allocated based on formulas taking into account factors presumed to influence the demand for services, i.e. they are based on a notion of the evening out of risks. Generally this will be more difficult the smaller the local authority, thus in order to reduce the financial vulnerability of local authorities they need to be of a certain size.[5]

A crucial question in decentralized systems is how to handle the potential problem of fiscal irresponsibility and soft central budget constraints (Kornai et al. 2003). On *a priori* grounds, it is difficult to determine whether soft budgeting is a likely result of decentralization or whether it is more likely to be a problem in centralized systems. Two conflicting arguments can be put forward. On the one hand, a model with many small units increases the distance from the central to the local government. Thus it might be easier for the central government to commit to hard budgets and "wash their hands" of local economic problems. On the other hand, small agencies may view themselves as less restricted by budgets, simply because they know that deficits will be small compared to the total health care budget. Also problems with asymmetric information may be greater in the case of many smaller agencies, thus reinforcing agency problems. Finally, we note that some countries lately have chosen to delegate responsibility to purchasing organizations outside the day-to-day political control of local authorities. Examples are the Norwegian regional health enterprises and the UK primary care trusts. This is an interesting development because it suggests that although some degree of decentralization is preferred, delegation rather than devolution is believed best to capture local efficiency gains and local preferences as well as the need for budget control.

A striking feature of health care systems is the diversity of solutions that are chosen to deal with seemingly similar challenges. Within the framework of institutional economics, this may be understood as differences in institutional arrangements that arise from differences in customs and norms, i.e. what Williamson (1998) terms embeddedness. Yet there also are differences between countries that are otherwise believed to be quite similar. A good illustration is the Nordic countries. These countries have cultural similarities, close political bonds and are of a roughly similar size.[6] All countries have decentralized provision of public goods based on logic taken from fiscal federalism, but they have nevertheless chosen quite different approaches to the issues described above. Finland devolves the responsibility for health services to municipalities. Sweden and Denmark have also a model of devolution but choose county councils as their preferred level.[7] Norway, like Finland, devolves the responsibility for primary care to municipalities, but treats specialized health care differently, and has recently transferred the responsibility for specialist care from 19 counties to five regions while also replacing devolution with delegation (from a political to an administrative level). Finally, while local authorities in Denmark, Finland and Sweden (in theory) have financial discretion with a right to locally set tax rates; this is not the case for Norway where tax rates are centrally defined.[8]

Regrettably, there are no studies that focus on how these differences in otherwise quite similar countries affect the economic dimensions of the health care system. Kristiansen and Møller-Pedersen (2000) conclude that the Nordic countries seem to devote similar amounts of resources to their system measured as share of GDP. OECD data, however, show that in 2001 Finland, Sweden and Denmark spent 63%, 78% and 85% of the Norwegian level, when spending is measured in PPP$ (OECD 2002). With the exception of Finland, annual growth rates are quite similar, but again how this relates to the degree and type of decentralization, however, is at best unclear. In addition to different solutions, countries also seem to move in opposite directions, some decentralizing, some recentralizing. To illustrate this we can look more closely at two countries – one which has recentralized (Norway) and one which has decentralized (Italy).

Norway – recentralizing the demand side

Although there is still limited empirical evidence on the effects of recentralization, the Norwegian reform process can serve as a good illustration of how difficult an application of fiscal federalism to the health care sector is in practice. The Norwegian system was designed in 1980 as a system where 19 counties were given the responsibility for education, part of road infrastructure, and health. The counties' income came partly from taxes (with fixed rates) and partly from matching grants from the central government. Initially the matching grant was centrally distributed between the three tasks of the counties, but from 1986 no specifications were made on the priorities between different types of services. This was thus a model in the spirit of fiscal federalism, albeit without the freedom for counties to generate their own income. In the 15 years that followed, however, the central government regained more and more control over the specialist health care. This was done partly by imposing an increased number of regulations on the counties[9] (Magnussen 1998) before the decision eventually was made to recentralize the responsibility for specialized care to the central government from 2002. While since 2002 there have been five regional health enterprises, what we now see is that devolution has been replaced by delegation and the county level has been replaced by the regional level. In a world of decentralization initiatives, what triggered this recentralization?

First, we note that the Norwegian model was characterized by (at least) two principal–agent relationships. The central government served as the principal and the counties as agents in the question of financing of county services. With centrally determined tax rates, counties also had little financial discretion. Counties, on the other hand, served as principals and hospitals as agents in the specific financing of health services. In this situation there were two main strategies that the counties could pursue: enforce strict hospital contracts or aim for soft budgeting from central authorities. In other words, how the counties chose to act as principals in relation to their hospitals would depend on how they chose to act as agents in relation to the central authorities. What happened in Norway was that hospitals systematically entered into a modus of soft budgeting with the counties which was then passed on by the counties to the central government (Carlsen 1994, 1995). Thus, the decentralized model did not work satisfactorily either from a cost containment perspective or from an efficiency perspective. Moreover, central political authorities, rather than looking at variations between counties as the result of variations in local preferences, increasingly looked upon these differentials as an undesirable feature of the system. Thus the main assumption behind fiscal federalism did not seem to hold for the health care sector. Finally, counties did seem to enter into competition for services, creating unnecessary duplication of services and reducing technical efficiency (Magnussen and Mobley 1999). Thus, neither from the perspective of cost containment, nor allocative or technical efficiency was the previous hospital system perceived as satisfactory. The solution chosen in 2002 was to reduce local autonomy, reinforce the role of central planning and reduce the incentives for soft budgeting by a transfer of ownership to the central government. It is still not clear whether the reform has been a success. The first two years after the reform, however, were characterized by (a seeming) growth in efficiency while the effect on total costs has been uncertain.

Italy – decentralizing the demand side

A second and seemingly different example of how decentralization can affect the economic dimensions of health care systems is Italy. Italian regions now have fiscal autonomy, and can increase local taxation to supplement national monies that fund regional health services. They can also set user charges for drugs prescriptions (which were removed from the national level by the 2001 budget law), reimburse delisted drugs, and reimburse health care services that are not included in the nationally defined benefit package. In the past few years Italian regions have used this opportunity widely, e.g. some of them increased tax rates to cover health care costs, other regions introduced user charges for drug prescriptions, while several increased both tax rates and introduced user charges for drug prescriptions.

Counter-intuitively, the central government has recentralized several activities, e.g. setting a national cap on drugs expenditure (13% on total health expenditure), attempting to define regulations of health care manager contracts at national level and imposing a resource allocation formula, and, through a provision of the 2003 budget law, blocking the possibility of increasing local taxation to cover public spending.

Another interesting development in the Italian health system is the increasing role of regional centralization, mainly concentrated on economic and financial aspects, driven by a compelling need to contain the growth of health care expenditure. This may reflect the fact that, in recent years, regions with more centralized expenditure control – those still relying more on regional planning – have been able to contain costs better than those relying more on quasi-market mechanisms and where private sector providers have higher market shares (Turati 2003). As a result, the use of centralized regional measures to contain expenditure growth is increasing. Many regions are seeking to contain expenditure and increase efficiency through recentralization at a regional or sub-regional level of some functions, such as purchasing drugs and goods (e.g. Tuscany), and setting reimbursement caps – on each provider – for inpatients' specialist care (e.g. Lombardy). Furthermore, regional governments are continuously revising the institutional structure of their health care services, with a trend towards the reintegration between local health enterprises (LHE) and independent hospitals, searching for synergies, eliminating duplication, and giving more power to stakeholders such as municipalities or the not-for-profit sector (Anessi Pessina and Cantù 2003).

The Italian case also provides an opportunity to explore the issue of soft budget constraints in decentralized health care systems, suggesting that if the national government cannot commit not to bail out additional expenditure at the local level, then local governments' budget constraint may become "soft". In Italy, there is a continuous confrontation between the national and regional governments on health expenditure levels and resource allocation formulae. On the one hand, regions claim that the national government intentionally under-finances them for the provision of health services which are mandated by constitutional law. On the other, the national government claims that regions overspend, and do not use resources efficiently. In the Italian experience, it has become common for the national government to make ex-post interventions to finance the past health deficits of regions.

The analysis of Italian public health expenditure in the past decade seems to support the case for soft budget constraint in decentralized health care systems. In fact, at the beginning of the 1990s, public health expenditure was out of control, and regions spent around 25% more than their pre-determined budget on public health care. Since 1992, however, the growth of public health expenditure has decelerated, and in 1995 regional health deficits were entirely wiped out, although national government financing in real terms actually dropped in those same years. Afterwards, in 1997, the expenditure began to grow again, with regions once more accumulating large health deficits. A recent study (Bordignon and Turati 2003) explained these health expenditure dynamics, showing that financing by regions is influenced by a series of political variables that capture changes in bail out expectations, that this expected funding has a positive relationship with expenditure, even when the national government decreased financing to regions, and that regional governments on the same political side as national government receive more resources and support it by reducing expenditure.

While we shall be careful with generalizations based on only two countries, some observations can nevertheless be made from these two cases. First, we should note that the Italian region in many cases has a population similar to Norway. Thus, when we observe limitations in the fiscal autonomy of the regions and a tendency to recentralize within the region, this is a development similar to the one observed in Norway. Second, both the Norwegian and Italian cases support the notion of soft budgeting in decentralized models. Both the Norwegian and Italian systems are characterized by an initial optimism with regard to the possibilities of decentralization, followed by a gradual recentralization when the (harsh) fiscal realities becomes clear. Thus, an open question is whether the perils of soft budgeting in the health sector outweigh the potential benefits of increased productive efficiency. In order to discuss this, we must also consider the supply side.

Supply side organization

In our context, decentralization mainly implies the transfer (devolution or delegation) of purchasing power and is therefore most relevant for the discussion of demand side issues. As discussed, the economic effects of decentralization will, however, depend on the relationship between the demand and supply side and on the degree of market concentration on the supply side. Thus it is relevant also to look at decentralization from the point of view of the supply side. In the literature, the discussion of this issue falls broadly into three categories. The first focuses on differences in aggregate spending and aggregate health expenditures. The second focuses on the (possible) effects of quasi-market solutions such as purchaser–provider splits and internal markets. The third focuses on the effects of different payment systems (contracts) on the efficiency of health services production.

Analysis of aggregate health spending is often done by using a framework introduced by Hurst (OECD 1992). Rather than use decentralization as an explanatory variable, this framework focuses on the interaction between the demand and supply side and differentiates between three types of systems: (1) public reimbursement systems; (2) public contract systems; and (3) public integrated systems. Thus, public reimbursement systems are systems where a public agency reimburses (private or public) health care providers (as in the United States or Switzerland), public contract systems are systems where a public agency contracts with providers (as in Germany or the Netherlands) and public integrated systems are systems where public agencies own the providers (the United Kingdom and the Nordic countries). This literature is undetermined with respect to effects on total costs. Hurst (OECD 1992) suggests that public integrated systems are most successful in controlling costs, while Gerdtham et al. (1998) argue that public reimbursement systems have a lower growth in costs. Gerdtham and Löthgren (2001) also find indications that public integrated systems have the lowest level of efficiency. Somewhat surprisingly, however, these analyses have not attempted to analyse the effects of decentralization on the demand side on growth in health care spending. On the contrary, Oxley and MacFarland (1994) specifically state that restricting health care spending is likely to be most successful when initiatives are taken against the supply side.

In integrated systems, the same agency will control both the funding and the provision of services. In most tax-based systems, the idea of introducing markets into the health sector has been controversial. The idea of a purchaser–provider split arose from a New Public Management way of thinking about the public sector, and led to the concept of "quasi" or "internal" markets. Internal markets may be viewed as a part of a policy of decentralization in the sense that they not only split purchasers and providers, but also are implemented by creating (many) autonomous agencies on the supply side. The expectation that creating internal markets in which private and public service providers engage in a quasi or managed competition would improve efficiency gained momentum with the NHS reforms of the Thatcher government beginning in 1991. The creation of internal markets meant that health care providers compete with each other for contracts from either public tax-funded purchasers or from private or public insurers. The main idea is that this competition will enhance efficiency, which may come in the form of lower unit costs, of higher quality for the same cost, and/or changes in work processes, internal organization or hospital structure (scale and scope effects). We can illustrate this by looking at three countries where models that have split purchasers and providers have been prominent.

The United Kingdom – the internal market

The high profile use of internal markets was the UK model as it functioned in the period 1991–1997. While the UK reform received considerable interest, it was at the same time characterized by a shortage of hard empirical evidence. As Propper and Soderlund (1998, p. 187) wrote: "[T]he primary intention . . . was to improve the efficiency of health care providers through the means of competition. . . [but] remarkably little evaluation has taken place of whether this desired effect has occurred." This lack of evaluation can be attributed to the poor quality of data in the NHS (Enthoven 2000), but it is still remarkable that few efforts were made to assess the effect of the internal market on technical efficiency. One notable exception is Mandiakis et al. (1999), who analysed the change in efficiency in a sample of Scottish acute care hospitals. They found an overall growth in technical efficiency in this period of more than 10%, but it is not clear whether this was due to the reform or not. It can also be discussed to what extent the internal market really represented a decentralization. One of the reform's original proponents, Alain Enthoven (2000, p. 110) summed up his view as follows: "On a scale of zero to ten . . . the internal market got the NHS somewhere between two and three for a year or two and then fell back to more central control." Enthoven does not believe that the "abolishment" of the internal market that took place under the New Labour government represented a recentralization. As he points out, the three main features of the internal market remain: the purchaser–provider split, the Trust hospitals and the commissioning of specialist health care services from the GP level. In Enthoven's view, however, the UK internal market was never a "real" decentralization to begin with. He bases his argument on four factors: (1) the lack of political space at the sub-national level; (2) the poor quality of the data necessary to monitor cost and service developments; (3) the weak motivation of purchasers; and (4) the inability of providers to escape the harsh realities of a market (e.g. it creates winners and losers).

Sweden – the internal market

A second, relatively high profile experiment with internal markets for hospital services took place in Sweden at the beginning of the 1990s. The Swedish system resembles the UK NHS in certain key respects. Hospitals are predominantly public, although the responsibility for both primary and secondary care was decentralized to 26 elected county councils. A second fundamental difference was that Swedish county councils were technically free to set their own tax rates.[10] A third distinction was that the introduction of internal-market type reforms in Sweden did not arise out of a national strategy as in the United Kingdom, but came about rather as separate local county initiatives. The introduction of a purchaser–provider split, in some counties, also was accompanied by a move to a DRG-based financing system. An interesting feature of the Swedish reform is that the pre-existing decentralization of decision-making control to county councils meant that not all councils had to implement the internal market. Thus, some counties adopted a model with contracting through global budgets.

Gerdtham et al. (1999a, 1999b) conclude that counties that implemented a full purchaser–provider split had substantially higher levels of technical efficiency (9–13%). This adds to the view that the transfer of power to lower administrative levels may not have a substantial economic effect unless it is accompanied by a change in the incentives on the supply side. Harrison and Calltorp (2000), on the other hand, claim that increased efficiency reflected formidable political pressure to increase productivity, not because hospitals began to compete for contracts. They claim that purchaser–provider loyalty remained strong throughout the reform period. Others concluded that the price that had to be paid for higher efficiency was lack of cost control (Whitehead et al. 1997), who also noted that simultaneous policy changes at both national and regional level led to reform overload, and thereby hampered systematic evaluation. Finally, we note that by the end of the 1990s, the internal market was somewhat adjusted, leading to more direct political control and a higher degree of cooperation and recentralization.

Italy – purchaser–provider split

The third reform that should be mentioned is the Italian one. The Italian health service underwent reforms in the 1990s with major changes including deconcentration, quasi-market and managerialism, and a policy of devolution. As a consequence, Italian regions developed different organizational and funding models and, although most of them retained many features of the traditional cost reimbursement model, now there are 20 relatively different Regional Health Services. For instance, Lombardy opted for a purchaser–provider split, with LHEs acting mostly as purchasers with independent hospitals and accredited private professionals and organizations as providers. One of the most important changes introduced in the 1990s was the transformation of the biggest hospitals into independent providers, bearing full responsibility for their own budget, management and technical functioning, and paid according to a prospective per case DRG-based system.

In the past decade, the pressure to contain public health expenditure, combined with regionalization and the new DRG-based payment mechanism, fostered an increase in hospital productivity, as well as a reduction of both hospitalization rates and average length of stay. However, due to a general lack of reliable data, there is not clear-cut evidence of variation and determinants of hospital efficiency in the Italian health service. One of the key questions is whether independent hospitals and accredited private providers – both of which in the past few years gained market shares in many regions – performed better than hospitals integrated into LHEs. A few studies tried to measure hospital efficiency comparing independent hospitals with those still integrated in LHEs, mainly using Data Envelopment Analysis (DEA) to measure technical efficiency and regression analysis to estimate determinants of efficiency (Cellini et al. 2000; Giuffrida et al. 2000; Fabbri 2001). The results of these studies based only on technical efficiency scores show that the way hospitals are organized seems to affect efficiency – independent hospitals always show higher efficiency scores than integrated ones. However, these results are quite weak and might be difficult to interpret for two reasons. First, it is hard in this kind of study to define outputs – all the Italian studies used admissions adjusted by DRG weights without any proxy of care quality. Second, the new DRG-based prospective payment system introduced in Italy since 1995 affects independent hospitals more than those integrated into the LHEs, which in many regions in practice are often still reimbursed on a global budget basis.

In addition, the most recent and comprehensive study on hospital efficiency, which covered 95% of Italian hospitals using 1999 data, showed that independent hospitals had, on average, higher technical efficiency scores. However, after controlling for a proxy of the "social value" of hospitals – based on a hospital choice model to account for the importance of each provider in responding to the demand of the catchment area – the variability in efficiency scores between different types of providers tended to disappear (Fabbri 2003).

Another important issue is the role played by competition between providers on efficiency levels. A study that explored this issue – using the DEA technique and regression analysis – found that in the Italian health service, given the existing rules, competition does not enhance efficiency in a relevant way, concluding that: "The creation of competition through an enlargement of markets, increasing the number of hospitals or the presence of private hospitals has an insignificant, if not negative, impact on efficiency" (Cellini et al. 2000, p. 515).

Conclusion

In the Introduction we identified six aspects of decentralization, while noting that both the multitude of models chosen and the difficulties of separating decentralization from other policy measures make it difficult to draw specific conclusions about the effect of decentralization *per se*. Or as Møller-Pedersen (2002, p. 5) puts it: "Much has been written about actual and planned reforms and considerably less about implementation and (lack of) success." However, the discussion presented above makes it possible to make some points related to potential effects of decentralization strategies.

First, the variety in models in tax-based systems has not been investigated regarding the effect of different financing schemes, different purchasing agencies or reforms aimed at recentralization or decentralization. Thus, we can compare these systems with respect to total costs but we cannot say whether these differences are attributable to the level of decentralization. Fiscal federalism theory suggests that decentralized systems may perform better, but the large variations in the way fiscal federalism is practised suggest that there is a need for more hard evidence. However, soft budgeting seems to be a prominent feature of at least some of these systems.

Second, the creation of internal markets substantially increased efficiency in the Swedish system as did the change of payment system in the Norwegian and possibly the Italian systems. In the Norwegian case, however, the introduction of an open-ended payment system seems to have led to an uncontrolled growth in costs. Thus, evidence tells us that the links between the supply and the demand side will affect economic performance, but that there may be a trade-off between cost control and productive efficiency. This is, however, relevant not only for the design of payment systems and purchaser provider contracts but also for the structure of the demand side.

However, the main impression we are left with is that there is a notable lack of coherency between the different decentralization and recentralization initiatives, even when the health care systems are reasonably similar to begin with. Thus, it is somewhat of a paradox that there should be large differences between the Nordic countries, and also that the reform processes in these countries should take such different routes.

On a final note we return to Enthoven (2000) who points out that reforms which may look good on paper tend to be hampered by lack of political space, lack of sufficient data, lack of motivation and the general inability of the health care sector to escape the "harsh realities of the market". To some extent, this reflects both the differences in cultures and perception of the role of the health system between the US-based economists and European policy-makers. However, it is worthwhile asking whether the large differences in health policy also reflect that, while there is the will to signal change, there is not always a will to see the changes through.

Notes

1 This argument relates to health care as a publicly financed good. Thus, we are essentially talking about the decentralization of a basic benefit package.
2 Williamson suggests that the institutional environment tends to change every 10 to 100 years.
3 Although these obviously interact.
4 A trivial, but sometimes overlooked, point when making comparisons across countries is that the size of a region, county or district will vary substantially. Thus regions in large countries may well have the population of a small country.
5 Or, as in Finland, they need to merge into larger entities for the purpose of purchasing health care.
6 Iceland excluded.
7 At the time of writing there is an ongoing process in Denmark aimed at reducing the number of councils.
8 It must be said that the possibility to exploit differences in local taxes is not used to a large degree.
9 Increasingly, staffing and capacity decisions were being made by central authorities, national waiting time guarantees were implemented, the amount of earmarked "extra" funds increased etc.
10 From 1990 to 1994, exceptionally, the national government froze Swedish county tax rates as part of the country's preparation to enter the EU in 1995.

References

Anessi Pessina, E. and Cantù, E. (eds) (2003) *Rapporto OASI 2003*. Milan, EGEA, Università Bocconi.

Bordignon, M. and Turati, G. (2003) Bailing out expectations and health expenditure in Italy, CESifo Working Paper, no. 1026, September.

Carlsen, F. (1994) Hospital financing in Norway. *Health Policy*, **28**(2): 79–88.

Carlsen, F. (1995) Hvorfor rammefinansieringssystemet sviktet. *Norsk Statsvitenskapelig Tidsskrift*, **11**(2): 133–49.

Cellini, R., Pignataro, G. and Rizzo, I. (2000) Competition and efficiency in health care: an analysis of the Italian case. *International Tax and Public Finance*, **7**: 503–19.

Enthoven, A.C. (2000) In pursuit of an improving National Health Service. *Health Affairs*, **19**(3): 102–19.

Fabbri, D. (2001) Efficienza tecnica e produzione ospedaliera. *Economia Pubblica*, anno **XXXI**(1): 33–70.

Fabbri, D. (2003) L'efficienza degli ospedali pubblici in Italia. In Banca d'Italia, (ed.), *L'efficienza nei servizi pubblici*, Rome, Banca d'Italia.

Gerdtham, U-G. and Löthgren, M. (2001) Health systems effect on cost efficiency. *Applied Economics*, **33**: 643–7.

Gerdtham, U-G., Jönsson, B., MacFarlan, M. and Oxley, H. (1998) The determinants of health care expenditure in the OECD countries: a pooled analysis. In Zweifel, P., ed., *Health, the medical profession and regulation*. Dordrecht, Kluwer Academic Publishers.

Gerdtham, U-G., Löthgren, M., Tambour, M. and Rehnberg, C. (1999a) Internal markets and health care efficiency: a multiple stochastic frontier analysis. *Health Economics*, **8**: 151–64.

Gerdtham, U-G., Rehnberg, C. and Tambour, M. (1999b) The impact of internal markets on health care efficiency: evidence from health care reforms in Sweden. *Applied Economics*, **31**: 935–45.

Giuffrida, A., La Pecorella, F. and Pignataro, G. (2000) Organizzazione dell'assistenza ospedaliera: analisi dell'efficienza delle aziende ospedaliere e dei presidi ospedalieri. *Economia Pubblica*, **4**: 101–24.

Harrison, M.I. and Calltorp, J. (2000) The reorientation of market-oriented reforms in Swedish health care. *Health Policy*, **50**(3): 219–40.

Kornai, J., Maskin, E., and G., Roland (2003) Understanding the soft budget constraint. *Journal of Economic Literature*, **41**: 1095–136.

Kristiansen, I.S. and Møller-Pedersen, K. (2000) Helsevesenet i de Nordiske land – er likhetene større enn ulikhetene? *Tidsskrift for den Norske Lægeforening*, **120**: 2023–9.

Magnussen, J. (1998) Sykehussektoren på 90 tallet [The hospital sector in the 1990s]. NIS Rapport 1/1998. Oslo, Kommuneforlaget.

Magnussen, J. and Mobley, L.R. (1999) The impact of market environment on excess capacity and the cost of an empty hospital bed. *International Journal of the Economics of Business*, **6**: 383–98.

Mandiakis, N., Hollingsworth, B. and Thanassoulis, E. (1999) The impact of the internal market on hospital efficiency, productivity and service quality. *Health Care Management Science*, **2**(2): 75–85.

Møller-Pedersen, K. (2002) Reforming decentralized integrated health systems: Theory and the case of the Norwegian Reform. HERO Working Paper no 7. Oslo, Health Economics Research Programme, University of Oslo.

Newhouse, J.P. (1996) Reimbursing health plans and health providers: efficiency in production versus selection. *Journal of Economic Literature*, **34**(3): 1236–63.

Oates, W.E. (1972) *Fiscal federalism*. New York, Harcourt Brace Jovanovitch.

Oates, W.E. (1999) An essay on fiscal federalism. *Journal of Economic Literature*, **37**(3): 1120–49.

OECD (1992) *The reform of health care: a comparative analysis of seven OECD countries*. Paris, OECD.

OECD (2002) *Health data 2002: a comparative analysis of 30 countries*. Paris, OECD.

Oxley, H. and MacFarland, M. (1994) Health care reform: controlling spending and increasing efficiency, OECD working paper no. 149. Paris, OECD.

Propper, C. and Soderlund, N. (1998) Competition in the NHS internal market: an overview of its effects on hospital prices and costs. *Health Economics*, **7**: 187–97.

Turati, G. (2003) *Modelli regionali di Sanità. Rapporto per la Commissione Tecnica per la Spesa Pubblica*. Rome, Ministero dell'Economia e delle Finanze.

Whitehead, M., Gustafsson, R.Å. and Diderichsen, F. (1997) Why is Sweden rethinking its NHS-style reforms? *British Medical Journal*, **315**: 935–9.

Williamson, O. (1998) Transaction cost economics: how it works; where it is headed. *De Economist*, **146**(1): 23–58.

chapter eight

Effects of decentralization and recentralization on political dimensions of health systems

Franca Maino, Paula Blomqvist, Luigi Bertinato, Lluis Bohígas Santasusagna, Rosa María Urbanos Garrido and Sergey Shishkin

Introduction

This chapter examines the main health reforms which have, during the past 20 years, decentralized and more recently also recentralized the health system in four countries: Sweden, Italy, Spain, and the Russian Federation. It seeks to assess two main questions about the political character of recent health policy reforms. The first concerns the impact of health decentralization/recentralization on the relation between different levels of government and in particular between the central state and the *meso* level. The second question concerns the impact of decentralization on the organization and delivery of health care services, and whether decentralization has increased community involvement in decision-making in the health care sector.

Health politics between decentralization and recentralization: an analytical framework

Recent literature has pointed out two tendencies that characterized the European system of public policy from the 1990s onwards (Jeffery 1997; Keating and Loughlin 1997; Ferrera et al. 2000; Scharpf and Schmidt 2000): the "downwards" transfer of competencies and prerogatives from national governments to sub-national governments (either regional or local) and the "upwards" transfer of important competencies and decision-making prerogatives from national governments to European institutions. This double process has not been homogeneous between policy sectors or between member states.[1] However, in health care in the four countries discussed in this chapter, this transfer of decision-making prerogatives and competences from the central government to sub-national levels has been very important.

Health care policy represents an almost emblematic case of sub-national decentralization, even if contained within the framework of national (the internal stability pacts between the state and sub-national levels of governments) and supra-national (European Monetary Union (EMU) and the 1997 European Stability and Development Pact) arrangements. Following the literature on health care decentralization, one can distinguish three key types of decentralization: (1) deconcentration; (2) functional decentralization (or delegation); and (3) devolution (Mills 1990). While this division does not account for various overlaps, it is useful in understanding which types of decentralization have occurred in these four health care systems.

In many countries, the process of health care decentralization has accelerated following the health care reforms of the 1990s, which transferred administrative and organizational competencies from the state to sub-national levels and defined caps for the contribution to health care expenditure by the central level. The scope of these reforms has been to establish a more clear-cut separation of roles between different levels of government in the health sector and to decrease inequities between regions in expenditure and regional involvement in financing. In this respect it is useful to explore the role of regions within the governance of health care and the extent to which the developing role of regions might lead in the future to reinforcing the meso level of government.

The welfare state has become a major object of conflict between the nation-state and its sub-national levels, reflecting the fact that its redefinition – after the crisis of the 1970s – implies also the modification of traditional solidarity pools and, as a consequence, the identification of a new collective identity, coincident with the *meso* level. As Banting (1997) has pointed out, social programmes can help in mediating conflicts between the state and the regions and to strengthen central government against centrifugal forces based on territorial politics. However, the process can also work the other way round (Banting 1995; Bartolini 1999). If social programmes are planned, implemented, managed and financed at sub-national levels, they can become an instrument of strengthening regional and local communities and at the same time weakening the national community.

One can raise several questions which have to do with the impact of decentralization (and recentralization) and health politics. A typical starting point in political science is to investigate where and how decisions are made in order to determine "who gets what, when and how" and "who pays" in health care. Further it may be asked which types of decisions (formal and informal politics of planning, prioritization, delivery, financing and coordinating health services) are taken at what levels. To what extent do different types of decentralization (administrative and political) affect the scope for and organization of such decisions? What are the implications for different actors?

Decentralization also raises the issue of coordination and power sharing across levels and units. As Vrangbæk (2004) has pointed out, an important aspect is the issue of formal (and informal) coordination mechanisms that control the rules of the game and the interaction between different institutional actors. The point is that formal responsibility may be decentralized, but if this takes place within a setting of very tight requirements in terms of national standards, the real level of autonomy may be limited. A central task of the analysis of decentralization is thus to describe the various types of coordination mechanisms applied in the system. What types of mechanisms can be employed in order to coordinate political decision-making vertically (between levels) and horizontally (between sectors and parallel decentralized units)? Is there any reason to believe that, given particular contexts, some mechanisms/instruments are more appropriate than others?

Some theories would argue that the "real politics" of health care take place outside of the formal political arenas. For example, it may occur in corporatist arrangements and in the many day-to-day decisions of health delivery which are made by professionals and health departments close to the core activity of treating patients (and perhaps influenced by pharmaceutical companies, media and local patient advocacy groups). What is the relationship between such a perspective and perspectives focusing on more formal top-down decision-making? To what extent does change in the formal political/organizational structure affect the "real politics" of health care? Are decisions concerning clinical practice and technology taken at the same political levels as decisions regarding funding and organizing health services? To what extent are local decision-makers constrained by national agreements on salary and working conditions for professionals?

Such questions are important in a political science analysis, but cannot be fully answered within the format of this chapter. The chapter seeks to illustrate changes in the institutional structure underlying health politics by looking at developments in the four case countries. The case descriptions are used to draw out specific and general lessons regarding the changing conditions for health policy-making.

Many health systems (and also many recent health reforms) contain elements of both decentralization and recentralization. Functions such as setting general economic targets and setting standards are centralized while management and service delivery are decentralized to lower political, administrative or organizational levels. Also monitoring and evaluation are typically national governments' tasks (Saltman et al. 2002). In many cases, it is the process of decentralization itself that makes it necessary to strengthen the role of supervision from the state. Political decentralization, in fact, usually generates differentiation, which in turn can produce inequality in service provision (Bennett 1990; Maino 2001). In this respect, the literature has pointed out the importance of the stewardship function of the state in helping those regions that are unable to fund and/or administer affairs on their own.[2] In effect, the process of "health regionalization" simultaneously requires the development of new national responsibilities to protect regions that perform worse, and to ensure that individual citizens who live in those regions are not unduly harmed. Therefore, it is important to analyse the role of the state in the area of quality assurance and, in some countries, in the regulation of the public–private mix. The question is what national regulatory roles need to be sustained if the state is to maintain its stewardship responsibilities even if the health system is increasingly decentralized in financial terms and on a day-to-day operational basis for curative procedures. The state (and/or the EU level) can also have an important role with reference to life style prevention issues, which are very difficult to pursue at the regional level but which have a high health impact, such as public health measures (restrictions on smoking and cigarette sales, alcohol consumption, etc.) as well as dealing with epidemics (AIDS, obesity, etc.).

Finally, decentralization aims at making health care "closer to population needs" (Mills 1990). This approach argues that locally controlled politics better reflect the political will of the citizens and, therefore, better fit their health needs. It is closely linked with the subsidiarity argument, according to which decision-making should be pushed down to the lowest appropriate level. What makes a decision "closer to the needs of the patient/citizen"? Is there any relationship between more collective vs. market-based decision-making and the "closeness to the patient needs"?

Overall, then, it seems that the institutional platform for health politics is changing in many countries. This will have implications for political processes, participation and distribution of power. Of particular interest for this chapter are state–regional tensions (both in financial and political terms); to what extent the municipal/regional role is growing; and to what extent the management of provider institutions has been decentralized.

Sweden

The Swedish health care system is an example of a tax-based, NHS-type system with predominantly public provision, managed locally by 21 elected political assemblies (the county councils). During the 1980s and the 1990s, political and administrative power within this system was further decentralized, as the county councils became more autonomous in relation to the central government. In recent years, waiting lists and poor coordination between different health providers have led to a critical debate about the functioning of the system and the performance of the county councils. Since the late 1990s, the government has made several attempts to strengthen its control over the system, but, so far, these do not appear to have been very successful. In addition, some observers believe that the county councils are too small to efficiently provide all types of specialized care within their geographical areas.[3] As a result, Swedish health care today is characterized by on-going discussions about the future of the county councils and their degree of independence in relation to the central government.

The key political decision-making bodies within the Swedish health care system are the county councils, as they provide over 90% all health services within the system. The small share of health care provided by non-public actors (about 9%) is typically regulated and, to an overwhelming degree, financed by the county councils as well. The county councils are also the employers of most health care personnel in Sweden, including the vast majority of doctors. Although the central government formally retains the overriding political responsibility for ensuring that needed health services are available to all citizens, the actual task of providing the services (including dental care) has thus been delegated to the county councils.

The most important national legislation underpinning the system is the Health and Medical Services Act of 1982. This is, however, framework legislation, which means that it stipulates general objectives rather than regulates the system in detail. Thereby, it gives the county councils a large measure of freedom in organizing the provision of services. Having the right to levy local taxes to finance the services they provide, the county councils enjoy considerable financial autonomy from the central government as well. Additional financial contributions from the central government, making up about 20% of the system's total finances, are typically block grants, that is, non-earmarked.

In 1991, the Local Government Act further extended the already substantive political autonomy of the county councils, as it removed previous regulations regarding their internal organization and gave them the right to contract out service provision to non-public actors, including for-profit companies (Montin 1992). This led to locally initiated reforms in many county councils, the most common of which was the introduction of purchaser–provider split and widening of patient choice rights. Local reforms during the second half of the 1990s often also included elements of decentralization, such as making provider units more organizationally independent or delegating the purchasing of services to local boards (Anell 1996). During the same period, responsibility for long-term and home-based health care, and later also outpatient psychiatric services, was transferred from the county councils to the 290 municipalities, traditionally the providers of social services for the elderly and handicapped. This added a new set of actors to the health care system, whose jurisdictions and responsibilities are not always clearly separated from those of the county councils.

The main role of the central government in the highly decentralized Swedish system is to formulate the overriding political goals and values guiding it. The government can also propose more detailed regulations regarding matters of national interest, for instance, the rights of patients or prevention of contagious diseases. The government supervises the system through its expert agency, the National Board of Health and Welfare (*Socialstyrelsen*). One of the tasks of the Board is to collect data from the county councils to monitor their performance, evaluate policy outcomes and provide treatment guidelines and other kinds of medical information to health care providers.

It should be noted, furthermore, that, in practice, health policy in Sweden is often formulated through largely informal contacts between the main actors of the system, i.e. the government (represented by the Ministry of Social Affairs), the Board of Health and Welfare and the organization representing the county councils at the central level, the National Federation of County Councils (*Landstingsförbundet*). The predominantly cooperative and consensual nature of these relations may at least in part be attributed to the dominant position of the Social Democratic Party in post-war Swedish politics, which resulted in social democratic governance both at the central, regional and local political levels during most of this period.

A prominent goal behind the far-reaching decentralization of political power to the county councils in the 1980s and 1990s was to strengthen the democratic character of the health care system. Reformers sought to bring the decision-making process within the system closer to the population and create new opportunities for active community involvement. This was also an important motif behind the separation between provider and purchaser functions subsequently implemented in many county councils. By making local politicians the purchasers of health services, rather than general "system managers", their role as the elected representatives of citizens was believed to be more pronounced in relation to other actors within the system, such as civil servants and health providers. Above all, it was hoped that their democratic accountability would be enhanced. Free choice of care provider in combination with a "money follows the patient" system of reimbursement was another reform measure employed to empower health consumers and democratize the system further (Blomqvist 2002).

Did these reforms have the intended effects? Reform outcomes have generally been hard to measure, given the plurality and vagueness of the stated goals (which were also related to the value of economic efficiency), but evaluations suggest that community involvement in health policy-making has increased at least in some places. Patient organizations appear to have become more actively involved in trying to influence the processes of local health services purchasing. Other examples of community involvement include participation in health policy study groups and meetings with county council politicians (Bergman and Dahlbäck 2000). The introduction of health services purchasing has led to more active attempts on the part of policy-makers to establish local medical needs and preferences, for instance, through public surveys. In some county councils, like Östergötland, there have also been moderately successful attempts to involve the local community in priority-setting, for instance, through polls and discussion groups (Garpenby 2002). Among providers, the introduction of patient choice and performance-related payments has stimulated a new interest in measuring and evaluating patient satisfaction.

Patient choice of provider is probably the one reform measure that has received the most public attention. Patients now enjoy the right to choose providers freely at both primary and secondary care level and across county borders. So far, patient flows between county councils remain marginal, however, and suggest that bureaucratic hindrances prevail when people seek care outside the previous "catchment areas" of, for instance, individual hospitals. Recent research indicates that another reason for persistent low patient mobility may be related to the attitudes of medical professionals, whose role in informing patients about their right to provider choice in further treatment is crucial in implementing this part of the reform (Windblad-Spångberg 2003).

Whether political accountability within the system has increased as a result of the decentralization reforms is hard to determine. There are some indications that local politicians have become more directly involved in the planning and purchasing of health services, thus "taking back" some power from the civil servants (Bergman and Dahlbäck 2000). Political accountability within the system may also have been enhanced by a different factor, namely the increased media attention to health care issues in recent years, which has tended to expose local politicians to more public scrutiny. At the same time, the organization of health care provision has become more complex after the introduction of contracting and more "market-like" relations between actors within the system. The increasingly complex web of contracts between the county councils and a multitude of different providers tend to diffuse lines of accountability and make the system less transparent. This problem is further complicated by the recent transferral of responsibility for long-term care and outpatient psychiatric services from the county councils to the municipalities, a change that sometimes has left patients confused about who is responsible for providing various services.

At present, questions of central–local relations and the placing of responsibility for various health services are highly salient in Swedish politics. As stated above, the government has made some recent efforts to reassert its influence over developments within the system, both through legislation and negotiated agreements with the county councils. Evaluations imply, however, that governmental initiatives to influence policy priorities often fail (National Board of Health and Welfare 2004). Partly in response to what has come to be regarded as an overly complex system, with overlapping lines of jurisdiction between different public bodies, in 2003 the government appointed an investigative committee to review the overall structure of and division of responsibilities within the health care system (Ministry of Finance 2003).[4] Since then, several political interest groups, including the conservative (*Moderaterna*) and liberal (*Folkpartiet*) parties, the Swedish Medical Association (*Sveriges läkarförbund*), and the main union federation, the LO (*Landsorganisationen*) have openly advocated the abolition of the county councils. These recent political developments serve well to illustrate the fact that power struggles within the nearly all-public Swedish health care system often have constituted themselves along the lines of central–local relations.

Italy

Italy's health care system is a regionally-based national health service, providing universal coverage free of charge at the point of service. The national level is responsible for ensuring the general objectives and fundamental principles of the National Health Care Service. Regional governments, through regional health departments, are responsible for ensuring the delivery of a benefit package through a network of population-based health management organizations (local health firms) and public and private accredited hospitals (Ministry of Health of Italy and the WHO European Centre for Environment and Health 1999; Donatini et al. 2001).

The 1978 reform assigned an important role to municipalities which were in charge of governing the local health units. From the late 1980s, a series of reforms progressively shifted municipal powers to the regional level (Maino 2001). At the same time, legislation in the early 1990s (with particular reference to Legislative Decrees no. 502/1992 and no. 517/93) meant a significant transfer of power from the state to the regions, which in turn were granted the freedom to decide on how to spend their health care budget allocation, as well as how to organize the health care system within the framework of the National Health

Plan, in line with the essential levels of health care provision. Thanks to this twofold process, the role of the regional level of government was strengthened and regions became the crucial actors in the day-to-day management of the health care system.

During the 1990s, the NHS underwent also a process of *delegation* (the so-called "*aziendalizzazione*"). All local health units as well as large hospitals were transformed into autonomous bodies. The delegation process was based on a more general set of structural changes aimed at introducing managed competition among public and private (accredited) providers. A network of public and private health structures and providers began to emerge at the regional level, categorized as follows: (1) local health firms (ASLs or LHFs) that operate on a more territorial level, acting as both "providers" and "purchasers" of health care services, and responsible for the management of hospitals, districts and the GP networks; and (2) public hospital trusts (*Aziende Ospedaliere*, AO), which are "providers" of health care services only and include university teaching facilities, and national institutes for scientific research (IRCCS). Both local health firms and hospital trusts are governed by a general manager appointed by regional health departments based on qualifications and technical skills.

Under this new governance model, the local health firms and the public hospital trusts have been given greater financial and decision-making autonomy, and top management teams have acquired greater responsibility for the effective management of resources and the quality of services delivered. Consequently, a "market" approach has emerged within the Italian health care system as distinctions are made between the "purchaser" and the "provider" of health care, thereby engendering competition between public and private services, as well as among public services (Taroni 2000). Following the reforms of the 1990s, the organizational health models are not equal and predetermined, but they can be shaped according to local requirements. In fact, within nationally defined institutional obligations (normative, budgetary, safeguard of public service principles), the local health firms enjoy wide autonomy in their organizational arrangements. A major challenge for health enterprises has been to acquire the organizational and managerial skills needed to make such decisions, capacities traditionally lacking in the previous local health units.

Decentralization of the health service to the 20 Italian regions is linked to embracing the concept of fiscal federalism, as well as rationalization of the health care budget. The health reforms of the 1990s paved the way for political devolution, investing sub-national authorities with greater autonomy in planning, funding, organizing and delivering services to citizens. In the mid-1990s, a Permanent Conference of the Presidents of the Regions and of the Autonomous Provinces was set up to promote cooperation between the state, the regions, and the autonomous provinces.[5] The regions became models for a federalist state in the making, invested with greater responsibility for budget allocation as well as autonomy in making key decisions on how the health care system should be organized. The Permanent Conference led to conflicting roles for the state and the regions. Annual meetings generated tensions, given the different perceptions on the part of the state and on the part of the regions as regards the cost of managing the health care system. According to the state's view, the regions are entitled to their share allocation from the National Health Fund based on needs evaluations and analyses carried out at the central level. From a regional view, however, perceptions about the financing of the health care system differ widely: more often than not, the regions consider their budget allocation to be totally insufficient to meet the real costs of running their regional health care systems.

Negotiations taking place within the Permanent Conference paved the way for the signing on 3 August 2000 of the first Stability Agreement between the state and the regions, which set out unequivocal rules for health care system management. Most importantly, a platform was set up for ongoing political and technical negotiations between the state and the regions. Following the first state–regions agreement, other important agreements were signed on 8 August 2001 and more recently on 25 March 2005.

From the early 1990s, legislation changed regarding how the health service in Italy is financed. There has been a move from a centrally funded, tax-based system to a system financed by the 19 regions and two autonomous provinces (Trento and Bolzano). This has implied that tax contributions normally allocated to the National Health Fund have been re-distributed horizontally between the regions and decided on the basis of a common agreement, and not on the basis of the central power of a higher jurisdiction (Dirindin and Mazzaferro 1997). Moreover, the concept of accountability of the regions has been reinforced with the introduction of the Stability Agreements, whereby regions endeavour to streamline, cut costs, and reduce deficits.[6] Central government's concern with health supply was to be guaranteed by a system of national standards, set by the central government itself, which had to guide regional supply of health services. Failure to meet these standards by a region would lead to a loss of autonomy, in that the central government could force regions to spend money in the failing sector.

It was the Reform of the 5th Chapter of the Italian Constitution (November 2001) that really brought home to policy-makers the urgent need to define criteria to establish the "essential" levels of health care provision (ELHC). Under this reform, the state would guarantee exclusively the determination of the ELHC as regards civic and social rights, whereas areas pertaining to human health would fall within the legislative and concurrent authority of the regions. The process of estimating the ELHC in the regions presents challenges, especially when attempting to identify indicators capable of quantifying health care needs, be they human, technological, or structural.

It is also widely acknowledged that the Italian regions are faced with a reduction in the budget allocation to regional health services. An imbalance between resources allocated and real needs among the regions has also been witnessed, leading to the application of new prescription charges ("ticket") and to modifications of the surcharge on the personal income tax (IRPEF). The average budget (or quota) per capita (*quota capitaria di finanziamento*) represents the national mean value per person needed to finance the essential levels of health care. Given the existing regional economic imbalances, differences in demographic and health indicators are particularly marked in the Italian regions. Criteria have so far been selected according to the size of the resident population, to levels of consumption of goods and services, to age and sex, to death rates, and to contextual and epidemiological health indicators. Much cause for concern remains about the capacity of health care systems to guarantee citizens' equal rights of access to health care across the Italian regions, and to ensure greater homogeneity in the ELHC provision.

From this short review of the Italian case, it can be observed that the evolution of Italian health care policy has been characterized by a high degree of tension between the state and the regional governments. This tension has been only partly mitigated by the use of mechanisms of concerted action, which have led to several Stability Agreements between the state and the regions from 2000 to 2005. A second feature of the Italian health service has been the process of health regionalization, which has increased the role of the regional level *vis-à-vis* the central government. The process of health regionalization – combined with the introduction of mechanisms of competition through the "*Aziendalizzazione*" – has also helped to decentralize the management of provider institutions (LHFs and public hospital trusts).

Spain

Medical care in Spain is principally provided by the national health service, and fully financed by general taxation. The radical change from the previous social security system, basically financed by workers' and employers' contributions, to the present national health service, was shaped by the 1986 General Health Act. Today, the health service is completely decentralized and comprises 17 Regional Health Services, which plan for, manage, finance and provide public health care in the 17 autonomous communities (ACs) into which the country is divided. This process of decentralization was initiated in 1981 and it developed in two phases: from 1981 to 1994 health powers were devolved to seven historic regions; the second phase took place in 2002, when health care was transferred to the rest of the Spanish ACs (see the country profile in the Annexe details). It is important to note that decentralization of health care in Spain has not been specifically aimed at improving the health care sector, but it has been part of a global devolution process involving the whole public administration as a consequence of the political requests from autonomous communities. Devolution of health care is especially significant, however, if one takes into account that health care, on average, constitutes more than a third of the total budget managed by the regions.

The process of health care decentralization has produced some interesting effects on political dimensions that, in many senses, have been promoted by the approval of the Cohesion and Quality Law in May 2003. This new law modifies the previous model of coordination included in the General Health Act, which was based on the assignment of all coordination functions to the central government (as stated in the Spanish Constitution). The new model is now based on joint action of different levels of government. In addition, the Cohesion and Quality Law changes the composition and extends the functions of the inter-territorial council, as described later. However, pharmaceuticals regulation remains centralized. This fact has provoked the ACs to complain about being responsible for financing pharmaceutical expenditure (which represents more than 20% of the health care total), when the relevant decisions are taken by the Spanish Ministry of Health.

One of the effects of Spanish decentralization has been to promote the ability of the central state to reform institutions by learning from international experiences and from innovation processes based on regional experimentation (López Casasnovas and Rico 2003). Furthermore, decentralization has allowed innovations in management and health policy implemented in some Autonomous Communities to spread to other regions, through mechanisms of informal cooperation (which in some cases explains its limited extension). However, decentralization has also implied adequate competence among central and sub-central governments in the expansion of autonomy and budget, and it has had negative consequences on transparency and democratic legitimacy. Historically, the bilateral negotiations between the central state and each of the regions for budget allocation have been characterized by a total lack of transparency. This feature has also been present in the processes of devolution of health care powers to the Spanish regions.

The end of this process of devolution and the replacement of the health care financial model took place simultaneously. The new agreement, reached by the Spanish Fiscal and Financial Policy Council (FFPC), increases fiscal decentralization and incorporates health care funds into the block grants that the central state transfers to the autonomous communities. Although in the new model there are no specific funds for health care, an estimation of health care expenditure based on the year 1999 was used to calculate the amount of resources to be transferred to the regions. In such a context, any new benefit to be covered by the health service should be financed with extra funds, not included in the basket of resources initially transferred. This fact has created some tension between the central state and the regional governments. In December 2003, some ACs governed by socialist and nationalist parties left the meeting of the inter-territorial council (CISNS) – see country profile for more details – accusing the minister of not fulfilling the principle of "institutional loyalty", mainly because the Ministry of Health had promised the inclusion under public coverage of a new benefit without considering the financing that had to be provided by the ACs. In order to avoid this source of conflict between levels of government, a new Commission was created in 2004. This Commission will prepare technical reports, which will be submitted to the FFPC and the CISNS, on all those measures that might affect the financial equilibrium of the national health service. The members of the new Commission belong to several ministries, but there are no representatives from regional governments.

Similarly to the Italian case, and despite the significant increase in fiscal co-responsibility included in the new financing model, the Spanish regions continue to demand more resources from the state in order to cover their so-called "health care deficit". As a consequence of these regional demands, the first Conference of Presidents, held in October 2004, promoted a new commission, formed by representatives from central and regional governments, to conduct a detailed study of the determinants of health care expenditure. The study would serve to clarify responsibilities between the central state and the regional governments, as a prior step to solving the question "who must pay what and how".

The processes of negotiation and cooperation between the ACs and the central government are, from now on, a key element in order to avoid fragmentation and, as a consequence, undesirable inequalities. However, the change in the composition of the CISNS after the end of the devolution process (which implied a significant loss of power of the central state and a notable increase of the representation from regional governments)[7] might have the effect of introducing non-health political elements into the discussion of health policy issues, making more difficult the necessary agreements on the future development of the health service. The first two meetings of the CISNS after the elections to the national parliament were boycotted by the regions governed by the opposition party because they considered the issues on the official agenda not to be important enough. This kind of behaviour could be partially interpreted as a political message sent to the central government through the health policy arena, especially when one takes into account that the result of the March 2004 general election was clearly unexpected. One possible way to solve this problem could be to promote technical agreements between the central state and the ACs on some health care issues in order to facilitate those agreements with more political content. Likewise, the need for political agreement on health care including all the representative parties – similar to that reached in Spain in 1995 on retirement pensions (*Pacto de Toledo*) – may need to be considered.

Although health care decentralization in Spain has generated some conflicts, it has also promoted the development and modernization of the Spanish health service. This result is well perceived by the Spaniards. In fact, more than 50% of the population believe that decentralization has contributed to an increase in the ability of governments to better serve the needs and preferences of citizens (Rico and Pérez Nievas 2001). The devolution process has also increased the political visibility of responsibilities for each level of government. For example, many regional governments have recently developed specific regulations in order to guarantee the rights of users of health care services. As a consequence, a significant number of "health care ombudsmen" have appeared in Spain during the past two years, who have to present annual reports to health care authorities and, in some cases, to the regional parliaments. The role of this kind of figure is being reinforced and the number of users seeking to protect their rights is increasing every year. However, all the potential rights of users are not similarly developed or well extended. That is the case of patient choice of medical professionals in specialized care, which is quite restricted and has not been developed in most of the regions. This fact imposes serious limits on public competition and reduces the degree of democratization of the system.

When the process of (fiscal and political) decentralization is intensified, as in the Spanish case, the authority of citizens to claim responsibility tends to increase, as well as political accountability, given that powers are concentrated on a particular level of government. However, this situation varies across regions. A recent study has shown that citizens living in those regions that received fully devolved powers at a first stage are better informed about the level of government that is responsible for each policy, compared to those individuals living in the ordinary regions, who tend to be confused about how the powers are distributed between the central and the regional government (León Alfonso 2003). Decentralization may also generate increased accountability and bottom-up coordination, given that citizens may exert some pressure over regional governments in order to get similar levels of health services to those available in nearby regions. This will likely occur more often now, since all the autonomous communities have fully devolved health care powers.

The latest phase of the Spanish health care decentralization process has had a significant influence on the amount of salaries paid to health care professionals. During 2002, those regional governments that for the first time received health transfers at the beginning of that year signed agreements with the trade unions in order to equalize salaries with those paid by other regional health services previously transferred – and in some cases with those paid to other public employees in the same category. The consequence has been a remarkable increase in staff costs, and in some cases the new payments are clearly above those set by the first group of regions. Among recent central reforms that have taken place in the Spanish health service, one requires special mention: the establishment in December 2003 of a new legal framework that states the basic principles of human resource policy. The central government will design a common model for basic payments, but the competence to set the complementary allowances rests with regional governments. It allows regional health services to design specific incentive models for their health care professionals and opens the door to an emulation process with an uncertain result: possibly more efficient incentive mechanisms could spread to some parts of the health service, but it also may reinforce the power of the trade unions and force regional health services to increase salaries.

The devolution of health powers to the ten additional regions in January 2002 has obviously expanded political autonomy in Spain. This fact may have some positive effects on the ability of central government to coordinate the health service more effectively. It also might reinforce mechanisms of horizontal cooperation and clarify central government's coordination functions, given that the central government is no longer a direct provider of health care (López Casasnovas and Rico 2003). However, several important uncertainties remain, as has already been shown. The Spanish devolution process has finished so recently that, in practical terms, there has been no time to disentangle the functions assigned to each level of government in a precise way. This situation also explains why there have not been attempts to recentralize health care powers. The idea of introducing some elements of privatization is also unlikely, given the strong opposition against reduction of public health care benefits among the population. Some of the Spanish regions are, however, interested in achieving a higher degree of decentralization. Catalonia is now preparing a law which will enable the sharing of health care powers between the regional government and city councils (*Diario Médico* 2004). It remains to be seen if Catalonia, which has been a pioneering region in introducing health reforms, will be imitated by other autonomous communities.

The Russian Federation

After the disintegration of the Soviet Union in 1991, the health care system was decentralized. In fact, all three types of decentralization (devolution, delegation and deconcentration) took place (Tragakes and Lessof 2003). Initially, this decentralization was not a reform of health care *per se* but rather the consequence of the overall devolution of state governance from 1991 to 1992. The vertical administrative hierarchy of health care governing bodies was dissolved. Deconcentration took place through the partial transfer of rights to regulate and to monitor clinical standards from the Ministry of Health to regional authorities.

This political devolution had a significant impact on the implementation of the reform of health finance in the early 1990s. The introduction of Mandatory Health Insurance (MHI) was expected to replace the budget-based health care financing system by delegation to public MHI funds and private health insurers of the right to allocate funds among health care facilities (Chernichovsky et al. 1996). Due to the federal government's inability to enforce the adopted health insurance legislation, the reform was decentralized. Implementation of the MHI has been poorly controlled by federal authorities and depended solely on regional authorities' attitudes. Most regions retained the previous system of budget funding of medical facilities and restricted the role of MHI to an additional financing system to the budget one. Many regional authorities opposed the participation of private insurers in MHI in the regions. As a result, the transition has been incomplete and jeopardized (Sheiman 1997; Shishkin 1999). But at the same time some advanced regions (Samara, Kemerovo, Tver, Kaluga, Moscow *oblasts*, etc.) used the opportunities created by decentralization to implement innovative reforms including new health care financing models and structural changes in health care systems to provide a more effective and efficient use of available resources.

At present, the Russian Federation has a decentralized health care system including separate federal, regional and municipal systems and a mixed budget insurance system of public health care financing with different models in different regions. Devolution of government administration has given regions and municipalities the right to allocate funds from regional and local budgets for health care according to their own priorities. There have been some federal regulations that have been used as minimum standards, for example, universal salary rates for health care workers. But the majority of federal regulations have been used as a reference for regions and municipalities. Thus the Ministry of Health has insisted on structural transformation in the health care system, including the shift from inpatient care to outpatient care, the development of primary health care on the basis of general practitioners, etc. Regions formally have not argued against federal priorities but in fact they have realized them as far as federal priorities have been consistent with regional ones.

The strength of federal–regional tensions has been influenced by the measure of financial dependency of regions on the federal centre. The economically autonomous regions have realized their own health care policy, but most regions have received funds from the Ministry of Health to implement federal targeted health care programmes and subsidies from the Federal MHI Fund for implementation of the MHI national programme. Allocation of these funds and subsidies, as well as distribution of quotas for free treatment in federal clinics for patients from different regions, have been the main mechanisms used by the federal centre to coordinate the activities of regional health care systems. Economic dependency has been the basis for political dependency of regions on the federal centre. The regions have had to reach agreement on their health care programmes with the Ministry of Health. As an implementation tool, the tripartite agreements on the interaction between the Ministry of Health, the Federal MHI Fund and executive power bodies of the regions have been signed. The agreement has provided the above-mentioned federal resources and, in exchange, regions have agreed to conduct necessary structural transformations in their health care systems. However, the effectiveness of such mechanisms has remained low (Russian Federation 2001). Moreover, the restructuring of the health care system declared in federal programmes has been very slow overall in the country.

A similar situation developed in the relationship between regional and municipal authorities. In comparison with the federal centre, the regional health care administrative bodies have had more tools to influence municipal health care policies. Almost all municipalities have received subventions (transfers) from regional budgets to cover general deficits of local budgets. In spite of the fact that these subventions were allocated formally as lump sums, without being broken down according to different uses, the municipal health care administrative bodies had to reach agreement with the regional health care administrative body on the planned health care expenditures from municipal budgets. The latter has also used allocation of funds to implement federal and regional targeted health care programmes as a tool for coordinating the activity of municipal health care systems. Regional health governing bodies have usually also had opportunities to informally influence the appointment of heads of municipal health care governing bodies. These mechanisms have lost power and have not been sufficiently effective in inducing change thorough restructuring of municipal systems. Local authorities have resisted the closing of ineffective health care facilities and have often ignored the recommendations of regional bodies.

Regional authorities had limited ability to effectively influence the activity of those municipal health care systems, which were independent of inter-budgetary transfers and therefore have worked autonomously. These are usually based in regional centres or large towns in the region. Officially, they have coordinated their annual plans of activities with the regional health care authority; however, the latter have not had administrative management levers. The regional–municipal tensions have often reflected the sharp political tensions between the regional governor and mayors of regional capitals. In some cases municipal health care authorities have deliberately chosen their policy in opposition to regional policies.

During the 1990s, a partial recentralization of health care administration took place in some regions. Instead of the allocation of general subventions to municipal budgets, regional authorities have centralized funds for salary payments for municipal health care facilities staff and/or for drug provision of municipal health care systems. Besides coordination of health policies vertically between health system levels, horizontal coordination of decision-making has been a separate problem. In fact, health financing systems in most regions of the Russian Federation are highly disintegrated, with each component (budget financing system and MHI) operating under separate rules. Regional MHI Funds have been subordinated to the top level of regional government but have been administratively independent from the regional health care governing body.

In spite of the fact that the head of the latter has been a member of the board of the former, tensions between the policies of these actors have often taken place.

Decentralization has increased the disequilibrium among regions as far as the expenditure is concerned. The Gini index calculated on the base of per capita public expenditures on health care in the regions of the Russian Federation increased 2.5 times (from 0.103 to 0.254) in the period from 1990 to 1997 (Starodubov and Potapchik 2000). While the average per capita health care funding in the Russian Federation was 2 287 rubles ($75 per resident per year) in 2003, the indicator ranged from 1 023 rubles ($33) in the Republic of Ingushetia to 13 631 rubles ($445) in Chukotka Autonomous Territory.

The main political implications for health care actors have been the following:

- the increasing dependency of regional and municipal health care governing bodies on special interest groups (e.g. professions and pharmaceutical companies);
- increasing autonomy of public health care facilities in economic and clinical decisions making; strengthening of the political role of managers of public facilities, especially of big regional and municipal hospitals;
- a gap between the decisions regarding funding and organizing health services made at regional and municipal levels and decisions concerning clinical practice and technology made mainly at the facility level.

The experience of health care decentralization has shown that, in the political and cultural context of the Russian Federation, the dissolution of administrative mechanisms of vertical and horizontal coordination might be effectively compensated only by mechanisms of centralized allocation of resources or by the restoration of administrative dependency of those actors on others. Other mechanisms of policy coordination have worked poorly so far.

In recent years, attempts to recentralize state governance overall and the health care system in particular have been made, but more comprehensive restoration of either a national health service or an integrated health system in each region has not been on the political agenda. Redistribution of political power and public finance from the municipal to the regional level and from the regional level to the federal level took place due to tax reform (2000–2004), reform of local self-government (adoption of new federal law in 2003, implementation from 2006), and reform of regional governors election mechanism (since 2005). As a result, the political role of the federal and regional health care administrative bodies has strengthened, and the processes of recentralizing the MHI system have taken place.

The Federal Government has clearly expressed its wish to maintain and develop the MHI and to complete the transition from a tax-based health finance system to a health insurance system. The implementation of the scheme of co-financing MHI contributions for pensioners by the Federal Pension Fund started in 2003 in 18 pilot regions. The scheme is based on trilateral agreements and has assumed the accountability of the regional government and the regional MHI Fund to the pension fund for health care of pensioners. Since 2005, the share of MHI funds accumulated in the Federal MHI Fund and allocated among the regional MHI Funds increased. Options to reform the existing MHI system are being discussed. The federal level is expected to reinforce its role in administration of the national health care system by centralization of the MHI funds system.

Development of a strategic planning system at both the federal and regional levels is considered also a tool for strengthening vertical and horizontal coordination of health care policy. Joint participation of various governing and funding bodies in health care planning and implementation of jointly developed programmes using contract-based relations might contribute to better coordination of their policies.

Effects and perspectives of decentralization and recentralization on health politics

The four cases reviewed in this chapter have all involved a process of health care decentralization, particularly in the past two decades. Starting from the second half of the 1990s, some of them have also shown signs of recentralization in terms of a return to some forms of coordination from the centre. There are, of course, differences in the starting point, the extent and the dynamics of these processes in the countries considered. Moreover, decentralization and recentralization have had different effects on the political dimension of these countries' health care systems.

In Sweden, the health care system was strongly decentralized in its origins. The reforms implemented during the 1980s and 1990s were oriented towards decentralizing political power even more and making the county councils more autonomous. During the 1990s, market-oriented reforms introducing purchaser–providers splits and private contracting practices were also approved. By making politicians the purchasers of health services on behalf of citizens, the reforms aimed at strengthening their relationship with the local community and at increasing political accountability within the health system.

In Italy, the 2001 Constitutional Reform has so far been the last stage in an ongoing decentralization process which in less than a decade has modified the intergovernmental system and the relationships between national and sub-national levels of government, deeply affecting also the functioning of the health service. The 1992–1993 health reform started a process of health regionalization which in turn is leading to the development of 21 different regional health systems.

In Spain, the health service is now completely decentralized into 17 Regional Health Services. What characterizes the Spanish case is that the process of decentralization has developed in two steps: from 1981 to 1994 health care responsibilities were devolved only to seven regions, while from 2002 onwards health care has been transferred to the remaining ten autonomous communities. The 2002 reform, increasing fiscal decentralization, has led to an expansion of financial, fiscal and political autonomy of the regional level. However, the increase of regional power has been complemented by the introduction of a new law concerning some common rules that guarantee a certain minimum for all the regions in order to avoid inequalities across the country.

In the Russian Federation, the decentralization of health care services has been one of the major tasks implemented in the public sector, largely due to the demands for regions to be allowed greater autonomy and to an increasing sense that centralization was politically unsustainable. Therefore, the new government of the Russian Federation has taken numerous steps to decentralize the health system. In particular, the 1992 reform shifted the responsibility for health care provision and financing to the local level. This, in turn, has led local government bodies to vary the degree of financial support they make available to the health sector locally and to redefine the amount of the funding provided for hospitals and clinics within their boundaries. This has also increased the regional differences in the provision of health care services. The lack of coordination among centres of authority in the Russian Federation makes coordination of different levels of government a clear priority in the future.

To contain costs, to stimulate greater efficiency, and to pay more attention to the quality of service, in all four countries, measures were taken to separate purchasers and providers and to encourage elements of competition. The task of implementing and administering quasi-markets has been attributed to the *meso* level (counties, autonomous communities, regions). For example, in the case of Italy, regions obtained the right to organize the health systems, redistributing or centralizing the health firms, governing the accreditation mechanism for private structures and (in the case of richer regions) supplying services to citizens in addition to those ensured by the state within the national health service. National legislation has been limited to the definition of a broad frame of reference, within which each region is free to adopt the form of managed competition that is more consonant with its particular situation and with the preferences of its residents as expressed through their elected regional representatives.

Therefore, health decentralization and reforms introducing elements of managed competition within the health service have worked together leading to the strengthening of the sub-national levels of government *vis-à-vis* the central state. Moreover, as a consequence of the process of health decentralization and the introduction of market-oriented reforms, differences among health care services at the different units of the *meso* level have increased in all four countries. Due to the strengthening of the *meso* level and to the risk linked to regional differentiation, starting from the early 2000s, central government has sought to regain power *vis-à-vis* the sub-national level. In fact, in all four countries, one can find recent signs of recentralization, in the sense that the national government is trying to assume a larger role in health coordination and monitoring.

The importance of coordination and monitoring by the central level as well as collaboration among Member States is fostered at the level of the European Union, which aims to extend the "open method of coordination" to health care and long-term care (European Commission 2004b) and to support patient mobility within Member States (European Commission 2004a). These two Communications, adopted together by the Commission, represent an overall strategy to develop a shared vision for European health care systems. Although both processes are still in their infancy, one can expect that in the future they will contribute to redefining centre–periphery relations and, therefore, will have an impact on both processes of decentralization and recentralization.

Notes

1 Some countries opposed this process in some sectors (i.e. the British opting out of EMU) while the transfer of decision-making prerogatives and competence from the central level to sub-national levels has been very strong in countries such as Belgium, Italy and Spain.
2 One of the most crucial policy issues is to ensure equity of health funding within a given country. Especially in decentralized health care systems, central governments have introduced fiscally decentralized mechanisms, including some form of equalization payments in which less-well-off lower level governments receive additional funds either from central governments or from other sub-national governments.
3 The size of the county council areas varies between 60 000 and 1.8 million people.
4 The committee will present its final report in 2007.
5 This political body, invested with legislative powers, operates on the basis of a rotating mechanism whereby a single region assumes responsibility in each of the areas decentralized to the regions to coordinate activities of decentralization among the 20 regions.
6 The phrase "*chi sbaglia, paga*" ("you err, you pay") was readily coined by government ministers meaning that at every level of government – from central to regional, to provincial to municipal – there would be direct accountability for direct and indirect debts (Il Sole–24 Ore Sanità 2004).
7 Until 2002, there were the same number of members representing the central state and the ACs, given that health care powers remained centralized for ten of the 17 Spanish regions. From 2002 on, each AC is represented in the CISNS by one member, and the central state is represented only by the Minister of Health. It is also important to notice that Spain is half divided between regions governed by the Socialist Party – at the present time governing the country – and those governed by the Conservative Party. This fact makes it difficult to consolidate the new model based on cooperation and joint action of different levels of government.

References

Anell, A. (1996) *Decentralization and health systems change: the Swedish experience*. Lund, IHE.

Banting, K.G. (1995) The welfare state as statecraft: territorial policies and Canadian social policy. In Liebfried, S. and Pierson, P. eds, *European social policy between fragmentation and integration*. Washington, DC, Brookings Institution.

Banting, K.G. (1997) Federalismo, standard nazionali e integrazione politica: il caso del Canada. In AA. VV., *Regionalismo, federalismo, welfare state*. Milan, Giuffrè.

Bartolini, S. (1999) Political representation in loosely bounded territories between Europe and the nation-state, paper presented at the Conference on "Multi-Level Party Systems: Europeanisation and the Reshaping of National Political Representation", European University Institute, Florence, 16–18 December.

Bennett, R.J. (ed.) (1990) *Decentralization, local governments and markets*. Oxford, Clarendon Press.

Bergman, S-E. and Dahlbäck, U. (2000) *Sjukvård – en svårstyrd verksamhet*. Stockholm, Landstingsförbundet.

Blomqvist, P. (2002) Convergence and policy reforms: health care reforms in the Netherlands and Sweden in the 1990s, Dissertation, Department of Political Science, Columbia University, New York.

Chernichovsky, D., Barnum, H. and Potapchik, E. (1996) Health system reform in Russia: the finance and organization perspectives. *Economics of Transition*, **4**(1): 113–34.

Diario Médico (2004) El CatSalut camina ya hacia una descentralización total, 15 July.

Diridin, N. and Mazzaferro, C. (1997) Il finanziamento del Servizio Sanitario Nazionale. *Sanità Pubblica*, **3**: 267–82.

Donatini, A., Rico, A., D'Ambrosio, M.G. et al. (2001) *Health care systems in transition: Italy*. Copenhagen, European Observatory on Health Care Systems.

European Commission (2004a) *Communication from the Commission: follow-up to the high level reflection process on patient mobility and healthcare developments in the European Union*, COM (2004) 301 final. Brussels, European Commission.

European Commission (2004b) *Communication from the Commission: modernising social protection for the development of high-quality, accessible and sustainable health care and long-term care: support for the national strategies using the "open method of coordination"*, COM (2004) 304 final. Brussels, European Commission.

Ferrera, M., Hemerijck, A.C. and Rhodes, M. (2000) *The future of social Europe: recasting work and welfare in the new economy*. London, Frank Cass.

Garpenby, P. (2002) *Samtalsdemokrati och prioritering: utvärdering av ett försök med medborgaråd*, Report no. 3, Prioriteringscentrum, Landstinget i Östergötland, Linköping.

Il Sole-24 Ore Sanità (2004) *Il Federalismo scalda i motori*, VII, no. 19, p. 6.

Jeffery, J. (ed.) (1997) *The regional dimension of the European Union*. London, Frank Cass.

Keating, M. and Loughlin, J. (eds) (1997) *The political economy of regionalism*. London, Frank Cass.

Le Grand, J. and Bartlett, W. (1993) *Quasi-markets and social policy*. London, Macmillan.

León Alfonso, S. (2003) La descentralización fiscal y sanitaria en España. Unpublished paper.

López Casasnovas, G. and Rico, A. (2003) La descentralización, ¿parte del problema sanitario o de su solución? *Gaceta Sanitaria*, **17**(4): 319–26.

Maino, F. (2001) *La politica sanitaria*. Bologne: Il Mulino.

Mills, A. (ed.) (1990) *Health system decentralization: concepts, issues and country experience*. Geneva, World Health Organization.

Ministry of Finance (2003) *Kommittédirektiv*, Dir. no. 10, Stockholm.

Ministry of Health of Italy and the WHO European Centre for Environment and Health (1999) *Health in Italy in the 21st century*. Rome: Ministero della Sanità, Repubblica Italiana and World Health Organization, European Centre for Environment and Health.

Montin, S. (1992) Privatiseringsprocesser i kommunerna. *Statsvetenskaplig tidskrift*, **95**(1): 31–57.

National Board of Health and Welfare (2004) *Den nationella handlingsplanen. Årsrapport 2004*. Stockholm, Socialstyrelsen.

Rico, A. and Pérez Nievas, S. (2001) La satisfacción de los usuarios con la gestión autonómica de sus servicios de salud. In López Casasnovas, G. and Rico, A., eds, *Evaluación de las políticas de servicios sanitarios en el Estado de las Autonomías II*, Cataluña, Fundación BBV.

Russian Federation (2001) *Support to public health management: the EU Tacis Russia health care management project EDRUS 9702*. Moscow, Russian Federation.

Saltman, R.B., Busse, R. and Mossialos, E. (eds) (2002) *Regulating entrepreneurial behaviour in European health care systems*. Buckingham, Open University Press.

Scharpf, F.W. and Schmidt, V.A. (eds) (2000) *Welfare and work in the open economy*, vols 1 and 2. Oxford, Oxford University Press.

Sheiman, I. (1997) *From Beveridge to Bismark: health finance in the Russian Federation*. In Sheiber, G., ed., *Innovations in health care financing*. World Bank Discussion Paper no. 365. Washington, DC, World Bank.

Shishkin, S. (1999) *Problems of transition from tax-based system of health care finance to mandatory health insurance model in Russia*. *Croatian Medical Journal*, **40**(2): 195–201.

Starodubov, V. and Potapchik, E. (2000) The process of decentralization of administration and its impact on the health care system. The directions of improving health care administration system in a federal state (in Russian), *Vestnik OMS*, **3**: 15–23.

Taroni, F. (2000) Devolving responsibility for funding and delivering health care in Italy, *Euro Observer*, **2**(1): 1–2.

Tragakes, E. and Lessof, S. (2003) *Health care systems in transition: Russian Federation*. Copenhagen, European Observatory on Health Systems and Policies.

Vrangbæk, K. (2004) Decentralization and recentralization in Scandinavian health care, paper for EHPG Conference, London, 8–11 September.

Whitehead, M., Gustafsson, R.Å. and Diderichsen, F. (1997) Why is Sweden rethinking its NHS-style reforms? *British Medical Journal*, **315**: 935–9.

Winblad-Spångberg, U. (2003) Från beslut till verklighet. Valfrihetsreformer i svensk sjukvård, dissertation, Department of Public Health, Uppsala University, Uppsala.

chapter nine

Effects of decentralization on managerial dimensions of health systems

Runo Axelsson, Gregory P. Marchildon and José R. Repullo Labrador

Introduction

Decentralization has long been regarded as an important management strategy to improve the efficiency and effectiveness of health systems and health care institutions. In managerial terms, decentralization can be defined as a shift in the scaling of administrative decision-making. This shift goes from organizations that are responsible for larger populations or geographical areas and more expansive policy responsibilities to organizations responsible for smaller populations or geographical areas and less extensive policy responsibilities. Administrative decision-making encompasses decisions concerning the allocation and distribution of financial, human and physical resources as well as delegated policy powers. Indeed, empowerment through delegation is one of the most important dimensions of decentralization.

The reason behind shifts both upward (recentralization) and downward (decentralization) in the scale of administrative decision-making have been explored in the organization and management literature, particularly in the institutional approach to economics and organizational behaviour. One well-known argument in this literature emphasizes the logic behind centralized control within private sector firms. In this view, economies of scale achieved through the "visible hand" of management are the key reason why so much economic activity is organized hierarchically within firms rather than through the "invisible hand" of the market (Chandler 1962, 1990; Williamson 1975; Ouchi 1978). As Coase (1988) has pointed out, the main reason a firm exists is to reduce the cost of market-based transactions by internalizing decision-making through a single organization, in effect, replacing contractual arrangements with hierarchical decision-making. This perspective suggests that central control may be more efficient at the level of the individual firm.

More broadly, Williamson (1985: 2), contended that an analysis of transaction costs should examine the "comparative costs of planning, adapting, and monitoring task completion under alternative governance structures". For private businesses, this means comparing contractual arrangements in a market to hierarchical arrangements within a firm.

In most western European health care systems, however, the character of this market vs. firm debate changes from a private to a public sector issue. The majority of health care activities in these countries have been treated more as a social service than as a private business since the Second World War. This can be seen in the rising percentage of health care that has been financed through the public purse over the past six decades. This rise in public expenditures and public administration relative to private expenditures and private administration has been in large part a response to market failures in the delivery of health care. It has also been a response to values which see access to necessary health care as a human right and a basic entitlement of citizenship (Esping-Andersen 1990).

Within the public sector, there have been different, sometimes contradictory approaches to the question of decentralized decision-making. During the 1980s, health care reforms in many countries emphasized decentralized public arrangements as a means of raising productivity and improving patient satisfaction. From the beginning of the 1990s, however, public governance has been increasingly questioned, and in some countries health care reforms have been predicated on a different process of decentralization, that would replace public decentralized decision-making with varying degrees of market-based contractual arrangements. In this connection, the real or perceived bureaucratic failures of public health systems (both centralized and de-centralized) have been used as a rationale to introduce more market-oriented policies (Enthoven 1988; Saltman and von Otter 1995).

While market failure and citizenship entitlement are the main arguments used to justify public sector responsibility for the financing, administration and provision of health care services, these two factors alone cannot explain the varying degrees of centralization or decentralization found within different national health systems. We must also examine the managerial dimensions of health care organizations – in particular, the costs and benefits of bringing health care decision-making under the rubric of a single, large organization – as well as the larger political and historical context of the state in which these organizations operate.

The benefit of creating larger-scale health organizations include the reduction of transaction costs, in addition to the patient and consumer benefits achieved through integration of services across the health continuum. The bureaucratic costs associated with large-scale, hierarchically organized health care organizations can be deduced from the literature on bureaucratic failure, particularly Williamson (1975, 1985). The following list of potential costs is based on this literature, although the individual factors have been applied to public health care:

- the costs of managing an increasingly complex organization as the number and breadth of health service categories grow (the scope problem);
- the inability to monitor and assess the performance of various actors in the system, including middle to low-level managers, smaller health organizations, and individual health providers (the scale problem);
- the degree to which larger organizations, as opposed to smaller organizations or the market, "forgive" under-performance or deviation from organizational goals;
- the instrumental capacity of certain actors or institutions in the health system to subvert broad organizational goals to their own personal advantage;
- the tendency of large organizations to demand re-investment in the status quo (inertia through investment renewal biases).

Since the late 1990s, however, previously strong concerns about bureaucratic failures in health care organizations have been overshadowed in some countries by concerns about the fragmentation and inefficiencies that have been brought about by market competition and contractual management. As a result, more integrative organizational arrangements have been introduced. Such arrangements have been described in the literature of inter-organizational relations (Powell 1990; Alter and Hage 1993). According to this literature, there is a tendency towards horizontal integration among private as well as public organizations, which means that, instead of competing with each other, organizations tend to form networks, partnerships, coalitions or strategic alliances. This new issue of how to manage and sustain such "loosely coupled" systems while avoiding bureaucratic and market failures is now at the centre of health care reforms in many countries (Ferlie and Pettigrew 1996).

In addition to considerations of bureaucratic and market failure, the choice of governance structure in health care is also influenced by higher-level political movements, agreements and constitutional norms. Federalism, quasi-federalism and associated constitutions can have a dramatic impact on the framework within which administrative structures are established, refined and reformed. Such arrangements can encourage a significant degree of decentralization within the health system (Banting and Corbett 2002).

In Canada, for example, health policy and administration have been politically decentralized from the beginning, in part, the product of a constitution in which primary jurisdiction over health is assigned to the provinces rather than the federal government. This political "structure" has also influenced the decentralized nature of the administrative structures of public health care, most of which have been determined by the provinces. Moreover, the movement for greater political decentralization, led by Québec's drive for greater autonomy and (at times) secession, has increased the pressure for decentralization of health care. In Spain, the movement towards greater political autonomy for its regional governments (the 17 Autonomous Communities), led initially by nationalist claims in País Vasco and Cataluña, has also created a momentum for political decentralization to all regions. This movement has had a direct impact on the health system, which has been organized on a quasi-federalist basis since 2002.

At the same time that one can observe strong political and administrative pressures towards decentralization in public health care, there has also been an opposite policy push in a number of countries toward centralization, or in the case of countries with a past history of centralization, a recentralization of administrative decision-making. At the heart of this second, more recent trend is the desire to improve the cost efficiency and the continuity of care across a continuum of health services. In practice, this has translated into the coordination of different health institutions and providers. At the forefront of such changes are vertically integrated models of planning, purchasing and providing services with an increasing emphasis on primary health care (Marriott and Mable 1998). While some cost efficiencies have been achieved through horizontal integration of institutions – acute care hospitals in particular – the effort to ensure improved access to higher quality and more appropriate services has been mainly through a process of vertical integration. This integration has typically involved long-term institutional care, home care, mental health care, acute medical care, primary health care, public health and prevention services.

The current regionalization reforms in many of the OECD countries provide a possible meeting point between the two "conflicting" trends of decentralization and centralization. To the extent that governments delegate the function of resource allocation to smaller administrative units, they are decentralizing. To the extent that they transfer a policy mandate to such administrative units to coordinate the delivery of a broad range of services, they may be either decentralizing or centralizing. If the responsibility for such coordination originally lay with the delegating political authority, they are decentralizing, but if health organizations are being brought together through regionalization, they are centralizing or recentralizing depending on the history of these organizations.

The history of any country's health system is important since decentralization is often a movement away from the historical status quo. As Atkinson points out in Chapter 6, decentralization in many countries represents a realignment of what was already centralized or decentralized. The same is of course true also for recentralization. In Sweden, for example, significant administrative authority and responsibility for health care have long been at the level of the counties rather than the national government. The development of decentralization and centralization must therefore be regarded from this perspective. In Canada, the current regionalization reforms inside the provinces simultaneously involve decentralizing the funding allocation function and centralizing key management functions. In this case, the historical context is a highly decentralized health system. In contrast, Spain had a highly centralized health system until 1980, when there was increasing state involvement combined with an increasing decentralization to the regions.

Starting from an historical perspective, this chapter will compare the development of decentralization, recentralization and regionalization in the health systems of Sweden, Norway, Spain, France and Canada. First, the historical development in these countries will be described in terms of different administrative levels, the roles and responsibilities of actors at the different levels, and the allocation of resources between the different actors. Subsequently, the effects on the managerial dimensions of these health systems will be analysed in terms of administrative costs, managerial competence and efficiency, and the coordination and integration of different health and health-related services. The impact on both the macro level of the health system as a whole and on the micro level of the different health institutions will be examined.

The development of the health systems

Sweden and Norway

The health systems of the Nordic countries are often described as Beveridge systems, although they were developed long before Lord Beveridge proposed a National Health Service in the United Kingdom. Moreover, in contrast to the United Kingdom, there is a long tradition of decentralization in the health systems of the Nordic countries. In Sweden, however, decentralization was preceded by an initial centralization from the local to the regional level. In 1862, the county councils were established as a new political and administrative level, mainly to provide a broader financial and administrative base for the expanding somatic hospitals of the municipalities (Gustafsson 1989). After that, a number of responsibilities for planning, provision and financing of other health services were gradually decentralized from the national government to the county councils. In the words of Rondinelli (1981), there was a gradual "devolution" of authority in the Swedish health system from the national to the regional level.

This devolution reached a peak during the 1960s, when the national system of general practitioners and district nurses was transferred to the county councils, along with the state-owned mental hospitals. From 1967, the county councils were responsible for the administration and financing of all the different branches of health care. The aim of this development was to create an integrated system of health services at the regional level of the society. The nature of this system changed in 1992, however, when the responsibility for the care of the elderly was further decentralized from the county councils to the municipalities, in order to be better integrated with the municipal social services. In 1996, responsibilities for the disabled and long-term psychiatric care were also decentralized to the municipalities. Thus, during the 1990s, there was a further devolution of authority in the Swedish health system from the regional to the municipal level of society.

In spite of the gradual devolution of authority in the health system as a whole, there was an oscillation between centralization and decentralization at the institutional level (Axelsson 2000). From a traditional organization run by the medical profession, the county councils went through a long period of centralization starting in the 1960s, when they brought different branches of health care together into large district health authorities. There were usually three or four health authorities within each county council. At the beginning of the 1980s, however, there was growing criticism of the increasingly bureaucratic structures of the health authorities. As a result, a number of responsibilities related to financial and personnel administration were decentralized to clinical departments, health centres and other basic units. Following Rondinelli (1981), there was a "delegation" of administrative responsibilities to lower levels of the organization.

In the beginning of the 1990s, about half of the county councils went one step further and introduced an internal market, with separate organizations for purchasers and providers of health services. Since the county councils finance some two-thirds of their services from county taxes, they are also free to choose their own organization of these services. The county councils with internal markets established district boards of politicians, who were supposed to act as purchasers of health services on behalf of their population. The hospitals and the health centres within the districts became more or less independent providers of services in competition with other public or private providers. In some of the county councils, this purchaser–provider split was combined with granting the patients a free choice of family doctors and also a free choice of hospitals. This combination was problematic, however, since the patients did not always choose the doctors and the hospitals that the politicians had contracted (Diderichsen 1995).

Gradually, in most of the county councils with internal markets, competition has been replaced by increasing cooperation with longer contracts between purchasers and providers of health services. There has also been increasing cooperation and collaboration between the county councils and the municipalities in health-related services. In this connection, there has been the development of a new concept of local health care, with emphasis on horizontal integration and continuity of care (Anell 2004). At the same time, however, this development has been combined with mergers of hospitals and even mergers of county councils into larger regional councils. A parliamentary commission has also been appointed to suggest a new distribution of responsibilities between the state, the municipalities and the county councils. All these developments indicate increasing vertical integration and recentralization in the Swedish health care system, both at the macro level of the system as a whole and at the micro level of the different health institutions.

In Norway, the development of the health system has been generally similar to the development in Sweden. After the Second World War, there was gradual decentralization of responsibilities for administration, financing and delivery of health care from the national level to the regional and municipal levels. In contrast to the Swedish development, however, more responsibilities have been decentralized to the municipal level in Norway. Since 1967, the municipalities have been responsible for the planning, provision and financing of primary health care and care of the elderly, which has been largely integrated with the social services. In 1969, the administrative responsibility for hospitals, including psychiatric institutions and ambulance services, was decentralized from the national government to the county councils. The hospitals were still financed, however, by substantial block grants from the national government. Thus, there has been a gradual devolution of authority in the Norwegian health care system from the national to the regional and municipal levels, although the national government has kept financial responsibility for the hospitals.

This trend was reversed in 2002, when administrative responsibility for the hospitals was removed from the county councils and transferred to the national level. The main reasons for this recentralization were to improve the efficiency of the hospitals, to reduce the waiting lists for highly specialized care and to equalize the provision of health services across the different regions (Hagen and

Kaarbøe 2004). Ownership of the hospitals was recentralized to the national government, but at the same time the government also delegated the responsibility for the management of the hospitals to five state-owned health enterprises at the regional level, with around 50 subsidiary enterprises at the local level. The regional health enterprises are independent legal subjects with professional management boards. They are supposed to act as purchasers of health services from their own subsidiaries and also from private providers. These health enterprises are not organized as internal markets, however, but operate rather as divisionalized structures (Mintzberg 1993).

At the institutional level, the Norwegian organization of primary health care has been a part of municipal administration, which has a centralized bureaucratic structure although the different health stations are geographically dispersed. The hospitals have also been organized according to strict bureaucratic principles. During the past ten years, however, there has been increasing decentralization of management responsibilities within the hospitals (Kjekshus 2004). According to the recent hospital reform, the hospitals should be run in a more business-like fashion. This means, among other things, that the health enterprises should be able to make difficult structural decisions on mergers and closures of institutions without political interference. It remains to be seen, however, if this will be possible within the Norwegian system of public health. There are already some indications of interference from the Ministry of Health in the structural decisions of the health enterprises.

Spain and France

The health system in Spain was created in the 1940s. It was inspired by the Bismarck system of social insurance for the working population and conditioned by the state centralization and bureaucratic administrative tradition of that time. In contrast to other Bismarck countries, however, the Spanish social security system developed its own network of hospitals, ambulatory centres for specialists and ambulatory practices for general medicine (Fernández Cuenca 1998). Hospital doctors were contracted on salary and ambulatory doctors on a part-time basis through a mix of salary and capitation. The social security branch for health care was a huge bureaucratic organization with hierarchical power with regard to its own network and contractual or purchasing power with regard to other providers, particularly the public hospitals and services from the state, the provinces and other public entities. In this way, the social security system exerted a delegated authority over the health system on behalf of the state.

Democracy and the 1978 Spanish Constitution recognized the citizens' right to protection against the risks of ill health, addressing a more active and direct role of the state. This also brought a new political framework based on devolution of important competencies and functions to new political entities on the regional level called Autonomous Communities. In the General Health Act of 1986, the Spanish health system was formally redefined as a national health system of the Beveridge type. This system was going to be universal for the whole population, fully financed by taxation, and organized through the regional health services of the Autonomous Communities coordinating all public health services within their territory.

At the institutional level, there have also been a number of managerial reforms in the Spanish health system. In the 1980s, a dual management structure was introduced in the district health authorities, one for the coordination of specialized care and one for primary care. In the 1990s, a model of contractual management with a weak purchaser–provider split and annual negotiated contracts was introduced. There were also some pilot projects with limited self-governance of hospitals, health centres and primary health care teams (Rico 1998).

Since January 2002, the devolution process has been complete. The Autonomous Communities have new taxation powers to finance a set of decentralized services, mainly welfare services such as education, social services and health care. The national government is entitled to enact "basic" legislation, but not to influence the way in which the regions organize or provide their services. The distribution of responsibilities and legal competencies is not so clear, however, and many issues are referred to the Inter-territorial Council where national and regional representatives can negotiate decisions through mutual adjustments. After 2002, the national government perceived a need to assume a stronger stewardship role to guarantee the equity and homogeneity of the health system, and to prevent differences among the Autonomous Communities.[1] Nevertheless, the prospect of a more active role of the national government is unpopular and unlikely to succeed except where it can mobilize substantial resources to support initiatives and proposals.

In contrast to Spain, there is a radical and structural split between financing and provision of health services in France. The most important institution for the financing of health services is the sickness assurance, a branch of the social security system created in 1945. The sickness assurance is built on the Bismarck principles of social health insurance. It is an autonomous institution managed by the trade unions and the employers associations and financed through social security contributions. The insurance is organized in different schemes according to occupational affiliations. Currently the entire population is covered, since unemployed workers, relatives, dependants or retired people are also able to join and access the insurance system. Since 2000, there has been a law on universal medical coverage. Moreover, people with low income can be relieved of co-payments and reimbursement. The social security system exerts a delegated authority over these issues on behalf of the state.

Even though the social security system has a basic role in financing health services, the state has the role of stewardship and overseeing the functioning of the whole system. The state has also direct responsibility for running the network of public hospitals and managing other services related to public health, training, technological development and pharmaceuticals. The role of the state has been expanding in the 1990s due to a growing economic imbalance in the health system. It became particularly important after a constitutional amendment in 1996, which empowered the parliament to set health targets and financial structures for the whole social security system. This development has reinforced the role of the state in the health system, and it can be considered a process of centralization where the state assumes the responsibilities of the delegated agency of the social security system.

There is a lack of demand-side or supply-side constraints on consumers and providers in the French health system. The population has free access to health services and free choice of providers. Until 2006, the primary health care provider had no gatekeeper role in relation to specialists or hospitals. Private practitioners provide ambulatory services, and they are paid on a fee-for-service basis by the patients who are partially reimbursed later. The fees are collectively negotiated between the sickness assurance and the medical associations. The fee-for-service system in the ambulatory sector and private insurance against cost sharing (patient fees) has created an alliance against the third party payer, which has led to escalating health care costs. Currently the social security system is suffering a deep financial deficit, caused by diminishing contributions due to the current economic cycle and increasing expenditures. Health care costs are an important part of this imbalance (French Senate 2003).

From the mid-1970s to the mid-1990s, a number of different cost-containment policies were implemented in the French system of social security, for example, modifications of reimbursement rates, higher cost sharing for patients, and increased salary contributions (Lancry and Sandier 1999). Other policies have been developed in order to influence the providers of health services. Most inpatient care is provided by state-owned hospitals, which are almost completely financed by the sickness assurance. Since 1984, these public hospitals have been working on prospective global budgets, which have been reviewed annually in relation to national expenditure targets. There have also been other initiatives that include creating incentives for a gatekeeper role of the general practitioners, to coordinate providers in health care networks, and to promote technology assessment, quality assurance and clinical guidelines.

Another important development has been the increasing regionalization of hospital services. In 1996, regional hospital agencies (AHRs) were created for planning and coordination at the regional level, mainly overseeing the performance and expenditures of the public hospitals. Three years later, the AHRs were given a more active role also over private hospitals, where payments were changed to DRG adjustments. At the same time, regional boards of sickness funds were also established for regional coordination and management of health expenditure risks. This process of regionalization can be understood as an increasing state involvement in the health system as a whole. In the words of Rondinelli (1981), it may be regarded as a "de-concentration" that allows for a greater state influence at the regional level, especially on the hospital supply side but also on the coordination of health and social services. Nevertheless, up to now, the effectiveness of this regional strategy seems to be weak and the main stakeholders of the system tend to exercise a considerable influence at the national level.

Canada

Compared to other political federations in the world such as the United States, Germany, and Australia, Canada is relatively decentralized (Watts 1999). In addition, it is one of the few federations in the OECD that has witnessed a considerable shift in control over fiscal resources from the central government to the provinces in the post-war era (Marchildon 1995). Key provinces such as Quebec and Alberta have led the way in recent decades in the struggle for greater provincial autonomy, and less federal direction, in numerous areas of public policy including health care. However, while the federal government has retreated from some policy domains such as labour market training, it continues to play a broad directional role in health care, a role that that has been an important part of the history of the establishment of universal hospital and physician care in Canada.

Universal public hospital coverage, commonly known as hospitalization, was first introduced by the province of Saskatchewan in 1947 and it was eventually adopted by all provinces through a series of federal–provincial cost-sharing agreements. Federal legislation dating from 1957 provided the legal framework for these agreements. In 1962, Saskatchewan again led the way in introducing universal, pre-paid outpatient care. As in the case of hospitalization, federal cost sharing provided the requisite incentive to get all of the provinces to adopt the Saskatchewan model by the early 1970s. The broad national principles on medical care were enumerated in federal legislation in 1966. In 1984, the Canada Health Act replaced the previously separate Hospital and Medicare Acts. This legislation clarified the rules surrounding the imposition of user fees by physicians or health institutions. To encourage provinces to eliminate all such user fees, the legislation stipulated that federal transfers to the provinces would be reduced by an amount equivalent to the user fees charged in the individual provinces (Canada 2002; Maioni 2004).

Although provincial and territorial public health plans were originally established to replace private methods of payment for medically necessary hospital and physician services with universal public coverage, the role of the provincial governments has expanded considerably over time. By the 1970s, most provinces were providing an array of health and medical services that went far beyond the core of hospital and physician services stipulated in the Canada Health Act, including long-term residential care, continuing care and home care services as well as public coverage for prescription drugs.

Similarly, the federal government's role in health care has gone well beyond setting the national dimensions of medically necessary hospital and physician services through conditional transfers to the provinces. It funds and administers a national research infrastructure, numerous health promotion activities and initiatives, as well as extensive public health programming. In addition, it has extensive regulatory responsibilities in terms of patented prescription drugs as well as food and drug safety. Finally, the federal government is also responsible for providing direct health care services and benefits to designated populations including First Nations and Inuit peoples.

It should be noted, however, that the expansion of most public activities and coverage by both orders of government, while changing the payment system, had only a very limited impact on the managerial structure of health care in Canada. While hospitalization changed the terms of access to hospitals, provinces did not take control or ownership of hospitals. Instead, hospitals remained in the hands of non-governmental organizations or municipal agencies controlled by local community members. Similarly, the introduction of Medicare did not fundamentally change the managerial dimensions of the system. Based upon the historic "Saskatoon compromise" of 1962, the physicians remained a self-employed and self-regulating profession. They simply replaced their contractual fee-for-service relationships with individual patients and insurance companies with a contractual, fee-for-service relationship with the provincial governments. The only exception occurred in Quebec in the 1970s. In a pioneering initiative, that province introduced community health and service clinics that employed a large number of salaried doctors responsible for servicing the varied needs of disadvantaged populations (Béland 1999).

The managerial nature of the Canadian system has recently been changed by the introduction of a regionalized system in most provinces. By introducing regional health authorities (RHAs), which operate between the provincial governments on the one hand and the local health institutions and physicians on the other, the provinces have decentralized the responsibility for allocating resources. This means a deconcentration of responsibility from the provincial to the regional level. At the same time, however, the provinces have also created a new managerial function for the coordination and integration of health service delivery on a regional basis. This means a centralization of responsibility from the local to the regional level through a vertical integration of different health services. The origins of this bi-directional shift in the scaling of administrative decision-making are relatively recent.

As the costs of provincial health plans escalated through the 1980s, the sponsoring governments initiated a variety of studies, advisory committees and independent commissions of inquiry. Their task was to provide advice on how to constrain costs and improve the continuum of health services provided, paid for, or subsidized by the provinces and territories. Almost all the reports recommended the creation of geographically based RHAs that would be responsible for integrating different health services, providing prevention and promotion services, and actively moving the locus of health care, where appropriate, from higher-cost institutional facilities to lower-cost community-based care (Mhatre and Deber 1992). The reports also emphasized the advantages of local management and delivery, with health experts arguing that health care was "far too complex to be run effectively from provincial capitals" (Lewis 1997).

When combined with the perceived benefits of local governance including public participation through RHA boards, some of whose members could be elected, the arguments in favour of regionalization seemed unassailable. Starting in Quebec in the late 1980s, regionalization became the centre of reform efforts in nine of the ten provinces and in one of the territories. Beyond service integration, the aim of this regionalization was also to ensure that local organizations rather than provincial health departments made the appropriate decisions on the allocation of resources based upon an assessment of needs for health services within their respective geographic areas (Tuohy 1999).

Table 9.1 summarizes these regionalization reforms. From the beginning, there was no theory or model that provided guidance on the appropriate size of individual RHAs, and the number and size of individual regions have varied considerably from jurisdiction to jurisdiction. Moreover, most provinces have re-adjusted the number of RHAs at some point after the initial reform. The most extreme changes have occurred in the three far western provinces of British Columbia, Alberta and Saskatchewan, where health ministries concluded

Table 9.1 Regionalization in Canada's provinces and territories, 1989–2003

Province or Territory	*Total population (1000s)*	*Established – changed (year)*	*Number RHAs*	*Population size of RHAs (2003)*	*Services included*	*Funding allocation*
British Columbia	4156	1997 2001	52 5 (16)[1]	320 000 to 1 300 000	Acute, home, continuing, mental health, public and preventative care	Population needs-based funding model
Alberta	3134	1994 2003	17 9	66 156 to 1 085 496	Acute, home and continuing care, protection, promotion and prevention	Population needs-based funding model
Saskatchewan	1009	1992 2002	32 13	10 364 to 278 000	Acute, rehabilitative, home and long-term and community and ambulance services	Population needs-based funding model
Manitoba	1151	1997–98 2002	12 11	7000 to 646 733	Acute, home and long-term, community and mental health services, emergency response and transportation	Historical global budget
Quebec	7468	1989–92 2003–04	18	20 000 to 1 255 950	Acute, primary, rehabilitative, residential, extended and nursing care, mental health, child welfare and youth, alcoholism and drug addiction, and public health	Historical global budget

Nova Scotia	944	1996 2001	4 9	34 000 to 395 000	Acute, home and long-term care, mental health, public health and addiction services	Historical global budget
New Brunswick	756	1992 2002	8	50 000 to 200 000	Primary, secondary and some tertiary care, short- and long-term care, rehabilitative, public health, mental health and ambulance services	Historical global budget
Prince Edward Island	140	1993–94 2002	6 5	14 261 to 66 586	Acute, home and long-term care, community mental health, child and family services, dental, pharmacy, environmental and public health	Historical global budget
Newfoundland and Labrador	531	1994	6/4/2[2]	28 000 to 180 000	Addiction, child and youth, family and rehabilitative, and continuing care services, health protection and promotion, mental health/acute and long-term care/mix of above services	Historical global budget

(Continued Overleaf)

Table 9.1 Continued

Province or Territory	*Total Population (000s)*	*Established – changed (year)*	*Number RHAs*	*Population size of RHAs (2003)*	*Services included*	*Funding allocation*
Northwest Territories	41	1988–97 2002	7 8	2441 to 18 115	Acute, primary and continuing care, family, community, dental, addiction and rehabilitative services, mental health, child and youth services	Historical global budget

Notes: [1] British Columbia's original 52 health authorities were made up of 11 Regional Health Councils, 34 Community Health Councils and 7 Community Health Services Societies. In 2002, this was restructured into 5 Regional Health Authorities which administer a total of 16 Health Service Delivery Areas, as well as one provincial health authority responsible for province-wide services.

[2] In 1994, the government of Newfoundland introduced a parallel structure of institutional and community care through 6 Institutional Health Boards and 4 Health and Community Services Boards, as well as 2 Integrated Boards. In 2002, the government announced its intention to create a modified structure that would further integrate institutional and community care services but it has not yet been implemented.

Sources: Hurley (2004); Lewis and Kouri (2004); Provincial and Territorial Health Department Annual Reports; Statistics Canada population estimates, preliminary postcensal estimate for 1 January 2003, rounded off to nearest 100 000 by author: http://www.statcan.ca/Daily/English/030625/d030625e.htm.

shortly after introducing regionalization that the first RHAs were simply too small in terms of institutional and senior managerial capacity. The opposite occurred in Nova Scotia where the number of RHAs increased to focus on smaller geographic regions. Provinces continue to search for the optimal administrative size of RHAs, attempting to balance the efficiency and continuum of service gains from organizations with sufficient scale and scope on the one hand, with the bureaucratic costs associated with large-scale, hierarchically-organized organizations on the other.

Effects on managerial dimensions

Sweden and Norway

As mentioned earlier, the devolution of authority in the Swedish health system during the 1960s led to institutional centralization and increasing bureaucratization of the county councils. The expanding district health authorities were run by an increasing number of administrators. Between 1974 and 1981 there was a 68% increase in the number of administrators, while the total number of employees increased 48% during the same period (Lane and Westin 1983). This development has been cited as an example of the famous Parkinson's Law on the growth of bureaucracy (Parkinson 1957). The bureaucratization of the Swedish county councils started, however, from a very low level and the administrative costs of the county councils have never been more than 6–8% of the total costs (Federation of Swedish County Councils 2005).

The low administrative costs can be attributed to the fact that there have been very few economic transactions going on in the system. The resources of the county councils and their institutions have been allocated mainly through detailed annual budgets. During the delegation of administrative responsibilities in the 1980s, these detailed budgets were replaced by global budgets and management by objectives. During this period, the bureaucratization and the expansion of administrative costs were halted due to increasingly restrictive budget frames. Administrative costs increased, however, with the introduction of internal markets in the 1990s. In the county councils with internal markets, there have been an increasing number of economic transactions between purchasers and providers of health services, requiring an increasing number of administrators for contractual arrangements (Blomqvist 1996). In addition, a performance-based reimbursement system means that health professionals also have to spend more time on administrative tasks (Forsberg 2001).

There is an ongoing discussion in Sweden whether the increasing transaction costs are compensated by increasing efficiency in the management and delivery of health services. There were two main reasons for introducing internal markets into the county councils. One reason was to clarify the role of the county politicians as purchasers of health services on behalf of the population. The other reason was to improve the efficiency of the providers of health services through competition and contracting of services. For geographical reasons, however, there has not been very much competition between the providers of health services in Sweden. Instead, the main feature of the internal markets has been the increasing use of contractual management within the county councils. Therefore, the transaction costs of contracting have not replaced the administrative costs of the county council bureaucracies, but only been added to these costs. Whether there have been increases in efficiency to compensate for these increasing costs remains an open question (Hallin and Siverbo 2003).

In Norway, there has been some interest in market mechanisms during the past ten years, but internal markets have not been introduced in any of the county councils. Instead, the hospitals have continued to work with annual budgets. In 1997, however, a system of performance-based reimbursement was introduced in order to stimulate the efficiency and cost consciousness of the clinical departments. The new regional health enterprises have a global annual budget from the national government combined with detailed directives and regulations, and they purchase health services from their local subsidiaries or private providers. It is difficult to estimate the administrative costs, since most of these transactions are internal transactions. According to a recent analysis (Møller Pedersen 2002), there may be both decreases and increases in administration compared with the previous organization. On the other hand, as the five regional enterprises have taken over functions from 19 county councils, there must be more possibilities for administrative rationalizations.

In Sweden, managerial competence within the health system has increased with the delegation of administrative responsibilities within the health institutions. Since the beginning of the 1980s there has been extensive training of managers on all levels of the health system, particularly at the clinical level, to deal with their delegated responsibilities. As a result, there has been increasing interest in management development and also increasing competition among different health professionals for managerial positions. This investment in training and development has probably increased the efficiency of management in the Swedish health system, but to date there are no studies to support such a conclusion.

In Norway, the government has introduced a national programme for the development of managers and heads of department in connection with the implementation of the hospital reform. According to the reform proposals, there will be more focus on professional management in order to improve the efficiency of the hospitals. This means, among other things, increased emphasis on performance measurement and management control. Although the hospital reform has recently been implemented, there are already indications of increasing efficiency in the Norwegian hospitals. The waiting lists for specialized treatments have been reduced for a number of diagnoses (Slåttebrekk and Aarseth 2003).

Coordination and integration between health care and other sectors have been problematic in both Norway and Sweden. In Sweden, there had been a permanent game of cost shifting between the county councils and the municipalities. In 1992, with the shift in responsibility for elderly residential care to the municipalities, a contractual arrangement was introduced, requiring municipal authorities to reimburse the counties for patients who block hospital beds because they have not yet been moved from hospital to nursing homes. There have also been experiments with financial coordination between health care and related sectors, such as social services, social insurance and employment services (Hultberg et al. 2003). These experiments are based on horizontal rather than vertical integration between the different organizations involved. As mentioned before, however, there are also indications of a more vertical integration of health institutions in Sweden. A sitting parliamentary commission is expected to suggest an increase in national coordination of the health care system.

In Norway, there have always been close contacts between primary health care and social services, since they both belong to the municipalities; however, their collaboration with the hospitals has been more problematic (Kjekshus 2004). The Norwegian hospitals have had the same problems with "bed blockers" as the Swedish hospitals and it has been due to a lack of collaboration between the county councils and the municipalities. This lack of collaboration may become even more problematic with the new health enterprises because of increasing "cultural" differences between the municipalities and the enterprises in the way that they are organized and managed (Møller Pedersen 2002). One of the main issues for the hospital reform is how to create incentives and organizational arrangements to support more seamless care across different health and health-related institutions.

Spain and France

The process of decentralization in Spain can be regarded as the outcome of two vectors, one political and one managerial. The political vector has two components, one integrative and one disintegrative. The integrative component is the creation of a national health system, while the disintegrative component is the devolution of authority to the regions. The managerial vector has three different components. The first component is the centralization of health resources to the regional authorities as a consequence of the devolution. The second component is the integration of health services in a dual management structure, one for specialized care and one for primary care. The third component is the introduction of contractual management, which has had a slight disintegrative effect although the centrifugal trends have been offset by hierarchical coordination. A fourth component is also emerging. The idea of vertical integration is gaining momentum in several regions and models are being developed to include hospital care, primary care, mental health care, community care and social health services in the same management unit and in the same budget.

In the Spanish health system, administrative or transaction costs are not a burden. The providers are financed basically through budgeting, although the increasing use of contracting within the system has implied growing administrative costs. There are no good figures available on the administrative costs of the whole system, but the public hospitals had an average of executive managers per hospital that grew from 1.71 in 1973 to 10.82 in 1993. There has also been a slight increase of non-healthcare personnel from 0.69 per bed in 1995 to 0.72 per bed in 1998 (National Institute of Statistics 2005). The increasing number of administrators can partly be explained by the increasing number of economic transactions in the system of contractual management. On the other hand, contractual management in the 1990s has shown some efficiency increases, which have been achieved through application of modern management methods such as data envelopment analysis techniques (Gonzáles López-Valcarcel and Barber Pérez 1996).

The devolution to the regions has implied additional administrative costs but also a huge shift in the number of public employees from national to regional administration. Between 1996 and 2003, the national administration reduced its personnel by 73.8%, while the regional administration increased its personnel by 79% during the same period (Ministry of Public Administration 2005).

The regional authorities now appoint the managers of the health institutions. A common worry, however, is the amount of political influence in the appointments, which can lead to a loss of human managerial capital in every political cycle. In the 1980s, extensive training in health management was initiated, stimulated by the lack of skilled managers and the quick turnover of existing ones. In the 1990s, contractual management produced more information on the performance of the health institutions and services, providing also a more solid basis to evaluate the performance of managers. It is still not clear, however, whether more information on performance will limit political interference or improve the professional identity and career development of managers.

The modernization of public services is a major challenge in Spain. The managerial functions of the health authorities were organized according to the rules of the civil service, but there is now a trend towards increasing self-governance of organizations within the public sector. As mentioned before, some hospitals, health centres and primary health care teams have been given a limited amount of self-governance. There are also other agencies for activities such as public health, quality assurance, information, continuous training and health research, which have been given self-governing status to allow a more flexible and business-like functioning. Although it has been discussed at length, there is no evidence on the efficiency and quality of this pattern of delegation (Martín 2003). Nevertheless, it fits the context of the New Public Management movement (Hood 1991), and it has also had some influence on the French administration.

Retaining strong public support, the French health system has been ranked number one among OECD countries by the WHO (2000). Nevertheless, the French system faces severe financial and managerial problems. The administrative costs of the reimbursement part of the system have reached 10% of the total costs for the sickness assurance. There are 90 000 employees who manage and evaluate the reimbursement system for ambulatory health care (Lancry and Sandier 1999). Moreover, it is estimated that the financial deficit of the sickness assurance will reach 11 000 million EUR in 2004, and a recent official report has questioned the financial sustainability of the system (Haut Conseil pour l'avenir de l'Assurance Maladie 2004). Reforms are envisaged, however, to achieve a financial balance in 2007, and to set a growth rate aligned to the GDP. This means, among other things, that the sickness assurance will have to be transformed beyond a passive reimbursement system.

As mentioned before, the role of the state has been expanding due to the growing economic imbalance of the health system. The state has assumed an important stewardship role in relation to the sickness assurance and the health system as a whole. The Ministry of Health and Social Affairs is dealing with the main stakeholders at the central level, pushing ahead reforms aimed at reducing the economic imbalance of the system. On the periphery of the system, the state is also providing expertise for reform implementation through the civil servants dealing with the management of the public hospitals. The traditional structure of hospital management is based upon this body of hospital directors, providing the basic know-how for the new and more active role of the state.

The increasing regionalization is intended to play a key role in the reforms of the health system. The regional hospital agencies (RHAs) mentioned above represent a movement towards the deconcentration of the system that may eventually spread to the whole state administration. The integration and collaboration between the health sector and other related sectors also seem to be reinforced by the regionalization movement. In the past few years, there have been a number of regional conferences and regional health plans to further promote the regionalization of the system (Polton 2004).

Despite all these efforts, the prospects for reform are not particularly good. The French health system, like other systems based on social insurance, seems to closely follow the model of "path dependence". It is difficult to change the system and powerful coalitions are easily recruited against reform initiatives. There are a number of potential constituencies for such coalitions because of the large number of actors in the system, including the state, the trade unions, the business associations, the medical profession and other health professionals, many of whom have a major interest in retaining the status quo (Hassenteufel 1999).

Canada

At their core, the Canadian regionalization reforms involve both decentralization and centralization. The regional health authorities (RHAs) have been created as intermediate bodies between the provincial government, on the one hand, and individual health institutions and the health providers that cluster around them, on the other. In terms of financial, human resource and capital allocation decisions, as well as the delivery of services such as public health that had previously been delivered by provincial government departments, these reforms involve decentralization. To the extent that regionalization takes governance and decision-making out of the hands of individual hospitals, nursing homes and similar institutions, the reform has resulted in greater centralization. However, to the extent that the RHAs perform a coordinating or integrating function never before performed by any provincial or local organization, they are also introducing a new managerial dynamic to the health system.

In practice, regionalization has involved the migration of a significant number of provincial health department employees to the RHAs. And while providers in local hospitals and long-term care institutions have kept their jobs, regionalization has shuffled the deck for the senior management of these institutions. The most profound change, however, has been at the governance level since regionalization in most provinces has required the disbanding of numerous hospital and other institutional boards in favour of a single RHA board of directors. In Saskatchewan, for example, 127 hospital boards, 133 nursing home boards, 45 home care boards and 108 ambulance boards were disbanded in favour of 32 RHA boards, subsequently reduced to 13 RHA boards (Church and Barker 1998).

As can be seen in Table 9.1, all RHAs provide a combination of primary, secondary and tertiary services from hospitals to home care as well as prevention, promotion and public health services. However, prescription drug plans as well as physician remuneration are administered centrally by the provinces, largely for cost control reasons.

RHA funding comes entirely from provincial budgets. Unlike municipal governments or administrative units such as school boards, RHAs do not raise any revenues through taxation. The budget allocation to RHAs varies from province to province, but British Columbia, Alberta and Saskatchewan have all recently adopted population-based funding formulas that take into consideration various factors including the age/gender and socio-economic composition of the population and its health needs. While other provinces intend to eventually implement population needs-based funding formulae, they are currently relying on historical funding methodology although the annual updates are based upon varying methodologies (Hurley 2004). Theoretically, RHAs are responsible for allocating resources within their assigned budgets, but lack of budgetary authority for physicians and prescribed drugs may be hampering efforts to integrate institutional and community care within the regions (Lomas 1997).

With approximately 44% of all health expenditures being managed in single-payer public health insurance schemes, administrative costs in Canada are low relative to predominantly multi-payer health insurance systems such as the United States. In a recent comparison of the two countries using data for 1999, total health administration costs in Canada were estimated to be 16.7% of total health care expenditures, while total health administration costs in the United States amounted to 31% of total health care expenditures. The per capita costs of hospital and home care administration as well as the administrative costs of physicians are one-third less in Canada than in the United States largely because of the higher costs related to billing, contracting and marketing that are a requisite part of private insurance. This is reflected in the very low ratio of employees to enrollees in the provincial single-payer plans relative to American health insurers. The Saskatchewan and Ontario provincial health plans employ from 1.4 to 1.2 employees per 10 000 enrollees. This compares to a range of 13.7 employees to 31.2 employees per 10 000 enrollees in the larger US health insurance plans (Woolhandler et al. 2003).

Thus far, there has been no comprehensive study of the impact of regionalization on the administrative cost of public health care in Canada. The emergence of new regional health bureaucracies, along with the publicity associated with the salaries of some chief executives of RHAs, has helped to fuel a popular perception that administrative costs have been rising. To the extent that RHAs are employing managers previously employed by provincial health departments or individual hospitals or health facilities, there has been little change. To the extent that the RHAs are tasked with new and highly complex management responsibilities related to the coordination and integration of services across a broad health continuum, they must recruit, train and educate a new corps of senior managers at additional cost to a system undergoing major changes.

Indeed, the early regionalization reforms underestimated the extent to which the new management tasks assigned to the RHAs would exceed the existing stock of managerial knowledge and competence in the country. The RHA managers, many of whom had previously managed individual organizations such as hospitals or nursing homes, were now required to align a broad spectrum of health needs to a given set of physical, human and financial resources within a sizeable geographic space. They were required to integrate services across previously atomized health organizations, to increase service quality and efficiency through evidence-based best practices and performance measurements, and to reallocate more resources to prevention and health promotion. In retrospect, it now seems obvious that the reforms underestimated the task of educating and training a senior management cadre in such broad skills and knowledge.

While Ontario is an exception to these regionalization reforms in terms of hospital services, the province has regionalized home care and community-support services, which it funds on a population needs-based formula (Hurley 2004). The Ontario government has also emphasized service improvement and coordination of care through integrated health organizations as well as "district health councils" that are advisory to the government.

In terms of coordination and integration, the recent regionalization reforms have improved patient access to a fuller range of health and health care services by managerially linking previously separate health organizations and providers. Based upon limited observation, regionalization appears to have produced some improvements to the coordination and integration of health care. The degree to which regionalization has also improved health promotion is more questionable. The proximity of an RHA to pressure by both providers and patients may actually result in more resources being devoted to downstream "illness" care rather than upstream "wellness" promotion and education. In addition, regionalization has only rarely served to integrate health and social services. As a general rule, social services continue to be administered centrally by a dedicated provincial ministry with little or no connection to the health and health care services administered by the provinces, RHAs and individual health institutions. Even in Quebec, where a combined ministry of health and social services has been operating for decades, the two sets of services have not been fully, or even partially, integrated from an administrative or service delivery perspective.

Community empowerment was intended to be one of the great benefits of decentralizing provincial authority and responsibility. In fact, some RHAs have also experimented with innovative forms of public participation. Initially, three provinces made space for elected members on their RHA boards of directors with separate elections. Today, however, only Prince Edward Island has elected boards, although New Brunswick is about to introduce elected members to its RHA boards (Lewis and Kouri 2004). Even for the provinces that have had, or continue to have, more democratically selected RHA boards, public survey results and poor voter turnout rates indicate that Canadians see RHAs as artificially constructed administrative organizations with little or no democratic legitimacy (Abelson and Eyles 2004).

Conclusion

The development of the health systems in Canada, France, Norway, Spain and Sweden reflects the different social, economic and political developments of these countries. The health system in Spain has changed from an insurance-based Bismarck system to a tax-financed Beveridge system. The French health system seems to be moving in the same direction. The Nordic countries had Beveridge-like health systems long before Lord Beveridge, but they have been subject to increasing changes and experiments. The Canadian health system is based on public financing like a Beveridge system, although with private providers of health services. In all these countries, there has been increasing decentralization, although it has taken different forms and had different managerial effects.

In Sweden, there has been a decentralization of responsibilities for financing and provision of health services from the national to the regional level since the middle of the nineteenth century. Recently the responsibilities for the care of the elderly, the disabled and the long-term mentally ill have been further decentralized to the municipal level. Thus, there has been a gradual devolution of authority from the national level to the regional and the municipal level. Norway has had a similar devolution from the national to the regional and municipal level, but the responsibilities for the hospitals and the psychiatric institutions have recently been transferred back to the national level. Thus, there has been a recentralization of responsibilities to the national level, but at the same time also a delegation of these responsibilities to a number of state-owned regional health enterprises.

In Spain, and more recently also in France, there has been increasing state involvement in the health system. In Spain during the 1980s, the state took over the social security system and its network of health institutions and built up an integrated national health system. At the same time, there was devolution of authority from the state to the autonomous communities, leading to a regional quasi-federal framework of health finance and provision. This devolution has now lasted for more than 20 years. In France, there is still a structural split between the financing and provision of health services, built on the Bismarck principles of social insurance, but the state has increased its involvement in the health system because of concerns for the economic sustainability of the system. The ongoing regionalization in France is a deconcentration strategy that reflects the active role of the state. In Canada, there is also an ongoing process of regionalization, which means a deconcentration of responsibilities from the provincial level to the regional level, but at the same time also a centralization of health institutions from the local to the regional level.

There have been different managerial effects of decentralization as well as recentralization and regionalization in the different countries. In Sweden, there has been increasing bureaucratization at the institutional level as the decentralized health services have been concentrated to large district health authorities. The introduction of internal markets in some of the regional county councils with contractual relations between purchasers and providers has led to increasing transaction costs that have been added to the existing administrative costs in some of the county councils. The question is whether these transaction costs have been compensated by increasing efficiency in the management and delivery of health services. There are different opinions about that, but very little evidence to answer this question.

There are similar increases in administrative costs in Spain, mainly as an effect of contractual mechanisms employed at the regional level. At the same time, however, there are also some indications of efficiency increases due to the application of modern methods in contractual management. In France, the administrative costs for the sickness assurance have been rising, which may be due to transaction costs in connection with the billing and controlling of the reimbursement system. It is not clear what will be the effects of the ongoing process of regionalization, but there is an urgent need to cut administrative costs as well as other costs in the French health system. In Canada, there is a popular perception that administrative costs have been rising in connection with the regionalization reforms, but they may also be decreasing as numerous hospitals and other institutional boards have been disbanded in favour of regional health authorities. In Norway, policy-makers hope to see the same decrease in administrative costs as the regional health enterprises take over functions from the county councils.

In all these countries, there has been intensive training and development of managers in connection with the decentralization of authority and different responsibilities for the administration, financing and provision of health services. The effects on managerial competence and efficiency remain to be seen. There are indications, however, of improved coordination and integration between the health system and other sectors of society. In Sweden, there are a number of collaboration projects and, in Norway, there is a long tradition of close cooperation between primary care and social service. These are examples of horizontal integration in the form of networks or partnerships between different institutions. In Spain, the relationship between health care and other sectors has clearly benefited from the devolution to the autonomous communities and in France the intersectoral collaboration has been reinforced by regionalization reforms. In both these countries, regionalization has produced a horizontal rather than a vertical integration of health and health-related services. In Canada, regionalization has led to greater coordination between a myriad of institutional and community services, but mainly through a process of vertical integration and centralization.

The aim of this chapter has been to give a description and a comparative analysis of the effects of decentralization, recentralization and regionalization on managerial dimensions of the health systems of Canada, France, Norway, Spain and Sweden. Before ending this chapter, however, a final caveat is necessary. Although it may be relatively easy to describe and analyse changes in different managerial dimensions, it is almost impossible to know which changes are the effects of decentralization, recentralization and regionalization, and to isolate them from the effects of other changes in the different health systems. In Sweden, for example, there have been a number of simultaneous changes at the national and regional level during the past ten years, which have had different managerial effects. In fact, some researchers have talked about a "reform overload" that has seriously hampered systematic evaluation (Whitehead et al.

1997). The same is true also for the other countries studied in this chapter. Our analysis and conclusions should be seen in this light.

Note

1 Ley 16/2003, de 28 de Mayo, de cohesión y calidad del Sistema Nacional de Salud. Boletín Oficial del Estado, 29 May 2003; 128: 20567–88.

References

Abelson, J. and Eyles, J. (2004) Public participation and citizen governance in the Canadian health system. In Forest, P-G., Marchildon, G.P. and McIntosh T., eds, *Changing health care in Canada*. Toronto, University of Toronto Press.

Alter, C. and Hage, J. (1993) *Organizations working together: coordination in interorganizational networks*. Newbury Park, CA, Sage.

Anell, A. (2004) *Strukturer, resurser, drivkrafter – sjukvårdens förutsättningar*. Lund, Studentlitteratur.

Axelsson, R. (2000) The organizational pendulum: health care management in Sweden 1865–1998. *Scandinavian Journal of Public Health*, **28**: 47–53.

Banting, K.G. and Corbett, S. (2002) Health policy and federalism: an introduction. In Banting, K.G. and Corbett, S., eds, *Health policy and federalism: a comparative perspective on multi-level governance*. Montreal, McGill-Queen's University Press.

Béland, F. (1999) Preventative and primary care access systems: CLSCs as neighborhood and social service centers in Quebec. In Powell, F.D. and Wesson, A.F., eds, *Health care systems in transition: an international perspective*. Thousands Oaks, CA, Sage.

Blomqvist, P. (1996) Valfrihet, konkurrens och offentlig välfärdspolitik: går ekvationen ihop? In Anell, A. and Rosén P., eds, *Valfrihet och jämlikhet i vården*. Stockholm, SNS.

Canada (2002) *Building on values: the future of health care in Canada*. Saskatoon, Commission on the Future of Health Care in Canada.

Chandler, A.D. (1962) *Strategy and structure: chapters in the history of the American industrial enterprise*. Cambridge, MA, MIT Press.

Chandler, A.D. (1990) *Scale and scope: the dynamics of industrial capitalism*. Cambridge, MA, Harvard University Press.

Church, J. and Barker, P. (1998) Regionalization of health services in Canada: a critical perspective. *International Journal of Health Services*, **28**: 467–86.

Coase, R.H. (1988) *The firm, the market, and the law*. Chicago, University of Chicago Press.

Diderichsen, F. (1995) Market reforms in healthcare and sustainability of the welfare state: lessons from Sweden. *Health Policy*, **32**(2): 141–53.

Enthoven, A. (1988) *Theory and practice of managed competition in health care*. Amsterdam, Elsevier.

Esping-Andersen, G. (1990) *The three worlds of welfare capitalism*. Cambridge, Polity Press.

Federation of Swedish County Councils (2005) *Landstingsanställd personal*. Stockholm, Federation of Swedish County Councils (www.lf.se, accessed 17 July 2006).

Ferlie, E. and Pettigrew, A. (1996) Managing through networks: some issues and implications for the NHS. *British Journal of Management*, **7**: Special Issue, S81–S99.

Fernández Cuenca, R. (1998) Análisis de los servicios sanitarios. In Catalá, F. and De Manuel, E., eds, *Informe SESPAS 1998*. Granada, EASP-SESPAS, pp. 252–53.

Forsberg, E. (2001) Do financial incentives make a difference? A comparative study of the effects of performance-based reimbursement in Swedish health care. Dissertation, Uppsala University, Department of Public Health and Caring Sciences.

French Senate (2003) Rapport, séance, 18 June 2003, no. 358.

Gonzáles López-Valcarcel, B. and Barber Pérez, P. (1996) Changes in the efficiency of Spanish public hospitals after the introduction of program-contracts. *Investigaciones Economicas*, **20**: 377–402.

Gustafsson, R.Å. (1989) Origins of authority: the organization of medical care in Sweden. *International Journal of Health Services*, **19**: 121–33.

Hagen, T.P. and Kaarbøe, O.M. (2004) *The Norwegian hospital reform of 2002: central government takes over ownership of public hospitals*. Oslo, University of Oslo, Department of Health Management and Health Economics.

Hallin, B. and Siverbo, S. (2003) *Styrning och organisering inom hälso – och sjukvård*. Lund, Studentlitteratur.

Hassenteufel, P. (1999) How do insurance systems change? France and Germany in the 1990's. Conference paper W5/38. European Forum, Florence, 26–27 February.

Haut Conseil pour l'Avenir de l'Assurance Maladie (2004) *Rapport du Haut Conseil pour l'avenir de l'assurance maladie*. Paris, Haut Conseil pour l'Avenir de l'Assurance Maladie.

Hood, C. (1991) A public management for all seasons. *Public Administration*, **69**: 3–19.

Hultberg, E.L., Lönnroth, K. and Allebeck, P. (2003) Co-financing as a means to improve collaboration between primary health care, social insurance and social service in Sweden: a qualitative study of collaboration experiences among rehabilitation partners. *Health Policy*, **64**(2): 143–52.

Hurley, J. (2004) Regionalization and the allocation of healthcare resources to meet population health needs. *Healthcare Papers*, **5**: 34–9.

Kjekshus, L.E. (2004) Organizing for efficiency: a study of Norwegian somatic hospitals. Dissertation, University of Oslo, Department of Political Science.

Lancry, P.J. and Sandier, S. (1999) Rationing health care in France. *Health Policy*, **50**(1–2): 23–38.

Lane, J.E. and Westin, T. (1983) Landstingen och byråkratiseringen. *Ekonomisk Debatt*, **11**: 419–26.

Lewis, A.S. and Kouri, D. (2004) Regionalization: making sense of Canadian experience. *Healthcare Papers*, **5**(1): 12–31.

Lewis, S. (1997) Regionalization and devolution: transforming health, reshaping politics? HealNet Occasional Paper No. 2. Saskatoon, Health Services Utilization and Research Commission.

Lomas, J. (1997) Devolving authority for health care in Canada's provinces: 4. Emerging Issues and Prospects. *CMAJ*, **156**: 817–23.

Maioni, A. (2004) Roles and responsibilities in health care policy. In McIntosh, T., Forest, P.G. and Marchildon, G.P., eds, *The governance of health care in Canada*. Toronto, University of Toronto Press.

Marchildon, G.P. (1995) Fin de siècle Canada: the federal government in retreat. In McCarthy, P. and Jones, E., eds, *Disintegration or transformation: the crisis of the state in advanced industrial societies*. New York, St. Martin's Press.

Marriott, J. and Mable, A.L. (1998) Integrated models: international trends and implications for Canada. In National Forum on Health, ed., *Striking a balance: health care systems in Canada and elsewhere*. Ottawa, National Forum on Health.

Martín, J.J. (2003) Nuevas fórmulas de gestión en las organizaciones sanitarias. Working Paper 14/2003. Madrid, Fundación Alternativas.

Mhatre, S.L. and Deber, R.B. (1992) From equal access to health care to equitable access to health: a review of Canadian provincial health commissions and report. *International Journal of Health Services*, **22**: 645–68.

Ministry of Public Administration (2005) *Registro central de personal*. Madrid, Ministry of Public Administration (www.map.es, accessed 17 July 2006).

Mintzberg, H. (1993) *Structure in fives: designing effective organizations*. Englewood Cliffs, NJ, Prentice-Hall.

Møller Pedersen, K.M. (2002) Reforming decentralized integrated health care systems: theory and the case of the Norwegian reform. Health Economics Research Programme, Working Paper 2002:7. Oslo, University of Oslo.

National Institute of Statistics (2005) Estadística de indicadores hospitalarios y estadística de establecimientos sanitarios con régimen de internado (www.ine.es).

Ouchi, W.G. (1978) The transmission of control through organizational hierarchy. *Academy of Management Journal*, **21**: 248–63.

Parkinson, C.N. (1957) *Parkinson's law or the pursuit of progress*. London, John Murray.

Polton, D. (2004) Dêcentralisation des systèmes de santé, un êclairage international. *Revue Française des Affaires Sociales*, **4**: 267–300.

Powell, W.W. (1990) Neither market nor hierarchy: network forms of organization. *Research in Organizational Behavior*, **12**: 67–87.

Rico, A. (1998) *Descentralización y reforma sanitaria en España*. Madrid, Centro de Estudios Avanzados en Ciencias Sociales, Instituto Juan March.

Rondinelli, D. (1981) Government decentralization in comparative theory and practice in developing countries. *International Review of Administrative Sciences*, **47**: 133–45.

Saltman, R.B. and von Otter, C. (eds) (1995) *Implementing planned markets in health care*. Buckingham, Open University Press.

Slåttebrekk, O.V. and Aarseth, H.P. (2003) Aspects of Norwegian hospital reforms. *Eurohealth*, **9**: 14–17.

Tuohy, C.H. (1999) *Accidental logics: the dynamics of change in the health care arena in the United States, Britain, and Canada*. New York, Oxford University Press.

Watts, R. (1999) *Comparing federal systems*. Montreal, McGill-Queen's University Press.

Whitehead, M., Gustafsson, R.Å. and Diderichsen, F. (1997) Why is Sweden rethinking its NHS-style reforms? *British Medical Journal*, **315**: 935–9.

WHO (2000) *The world health report 2000*. Geneva, World Health Organization.

Williamson, O.E. (1975) *Markets and hierarchies: analysis and antitrust implications*. New York, Free Press.

Williamson, O.E. (1985) *The economic institutions of capitalism*. New York, Free Press.

Woolhandler, S., Campbell, T. and Himmelstein, D.U. (2003) Costs of health care administration in the United States and Canada. *New England Journal of Medicine*, **349**: 768–75.

chapter ten

Effects of decentralization on clinical dimensions of health systems

Juha Kinnunen, Kirill Danishevski, Raisa B. Deber and Theodore H. Tulchinsky

Introduction

This chapter examines available evidence relating decentralization and recentralization to improved health status, as indicated by process and outcome measures. Regrettably, the evidence is sparse and inconclusive. Health status is influenced by a wide variety of factors, only some of which relate to the organization of a health care system. Ascertaining the impact of health reforms thus requires both a conceptual framework that highlights what changes might be expected, and the existence of appropriate comparison cases that are otherwise similar but have not undergone the particular reforms. Not surprisingly, these requirements are rarely met. As emphasized in the EU competitiveness report 2004 (SEC 2004), "Evaluating performance in services, and the public sector in particular, is fraught with difficulties" (O'Mahony and Stevens 2002). Doing so for the health sector is more difficult than in other service sectors since both the system provision and the nature of the production process have a number of unique features. This chapter concentrates on recent decades, during which decentralization was a widely recommended health reform policy to reduce inequities and improve integration of services. However, we also provide some examples of long-standing decentralization because of constitutional allocation of health to provincial, state or local authorities. Other examples include cases where sudden political change resulted in dramatic "decentralization" of the former Soviet Union, followed by adoption of different approaches and differing achievements by some newly independent republics.

Conceptually, we try to identify mechanisms linking decentralization with behaviour of health care professions and users, programme performance and approaches to monitoring the outcome effects of decentralized health systems on health status. Although measures of expenditure are readily available, comparisons of aggregate health expenditure have been hampered by the lack of a theoretical basis for the determinants of health expenditure (Gerdtham and Jönsson 2000). While decentralization involves transfer of funds and responsibility, it is clear that central authorities' responsibility does not end with this process. However much political and economical decentralization is desired, there remains a major role for central guidance, standards and evaluation in the accountability process (Tulchinsky and Varavikova 1996). In short, it is important to clarify which dimensions of a health care system are being decentralized – how it is financed, how care is delivered, how it is planned, or how it is regulated. Models also vary as a function of the public–private mix in both financing and delivery (Bach 2000; PHR 2002; Berg and van der Grinten 2003; Deber 2004; Alexis 2005). Decentralization takes on very different meanings in Beveridge-style models (where delivery resides in the public sector), than in models relying upon private delivery.

Earlier chapters of this book have discussed forms and mechanisms of decentralization and recentralization, drawing on previous literature (Wolman 1990; Church and Barker 1998; Pollitt et al. 1998; Church and Noseworthy 1999; Bossert et al. 2000; Amara et al. 2003; Saltman and Bankauskaite 2004; Vrangbæk 2004). One key point, stressed in Chapter 4, is that the impacts of de-recentralization will differ depending on national contexts. The objectives may be the same, but the means and consequences may differ. Consider, for example, Germany's federal government and social insurance system with a strong role for private providers (both not-for-profit and for-profit), as compared with Sweden's regional government and taxation-based health system where delivery rests in the public sector. At regional, local and provider levels, the impacts and consequences of political, administrative and financial decentralization/recentralization procedures are complex combinations of interactive factors and the causal connections are unclear (Cheema and Rondinelli 1983; Collins et al. 1999; Byrkjeflot and Neby 2003).

The impact of decentralization and centralization on clinical processes and outcomes needs to be viewed as a multidimensional reality. Decentralization should be examined for such potential outcomes as its effect on participation of communities, whether it contributes to improved implementation of health programmes, and whether it leads to more effective allocation of resources. The impact on individual care services may be different from the impact on population health. Quality may be measured in terms of process, safety and outcome of care and prevention.

Evaluation of the health status of a population in a region and comparisons to determine effectiveness of a programme or policy require a broad set of measures including the demography, geography and socio-economic status of the population, the public health and health financing infrastructure, resources (such as hospital beds/1000 population and percentage of GDP per capita spent on health), process of care measures (such as utilization rates, PYLL), outcome measures of morbidity, mortality and functional or physiological indicators (such as DALYs, QALYs, anaemia rates), peer review (internal and external), knowledge, attitudes and practices (of consumers, providers and the population), and cost–benefit analysis (Tulchinsky 1982). While these are all important to the policy of reform in health care, few studies have been conducted which compare the impact of decentralization with these factors (Bankauskaite et al. 2004; Frank and Gaynor 2004; Litvack 2004). In this review, we examine the limited evidence available on this issue, recognizing that decentralization/recentralization may play only a small role in influencing clinical outcomes compared to these other, more fundamental factors.

Potential mechanisms and links between decentralization/recentralization and clinical dimensions

Specifying the possible links between decentralization/recentralization and clinical dimensions of health care must take into account that health care systems at regional and local levels are complex social and institutional entities (Pflanz and Schach 1976; Ellencweig 1992; Esping-Andersen 1997; Saltman and Figueras 1997). Health needs, expectations, utilization and outcomes of services are influenced by such factors outside the health care system *per se* as education, income, employment, genetic endowment, nutrition, environment (including air and water quality), accident prevention, housing, lifestyle and health awareness, and historical experiences (Lalonde 1974; Hastings Center Report 1996; Callahan 2002; Derose 2003). Advances in public health and medical care have played a major role in health gains globally, with much of the gain attributed to public health rather than clinical medical care services. The relative contribution of public health and clinical medicine since the Second World War is less easily defined, but both have played major roles in the reduction of major causes of death, including infectious and cardiovascular diseases. To the extent that decentralization/recentralization tends to focus primarily on clinical services to individuals, it is unlikely that such reforms would have a major impact on broader determinants of health.

Further, managing health care at local and institutional levels is a challenge requiring careful balancing of policy goals, as well as the tools needed (and available) to implement them. Often, contradictory incentives, disincentives and power games affect implementation and presumably explain some of the gap between policy and practice (Cheema and Rondinelli 1983; Chen 1990; Pollitt et al. 1998; Holm 2000; Martin and Singer 2003). Thus, overly simplistic conclusions about decentralization and clinical outcomes are to be avoided.

In Figure 10.1, some of the potential mechanisms between general decentralization factors and the clinical behaviour of professions and clients/patients have been identified. The basis of this integrated model is described elsewhere (see Kinnunen and Vuori 2005). The model emphasizes that changes (influenced by de-/recentralization mechanisms) in any part of the system have to be seen holistically. The basic horizontal tensions appear between humanism and equity vs. effectiveness. There are also vertical tensions between mechanisms and stability of structures versus organic flexibility of processes. For example, quality of care at the individual and organizational level (levels I and II) is dependent on strategy level choices (III) and system level factors (IV). Thus, the

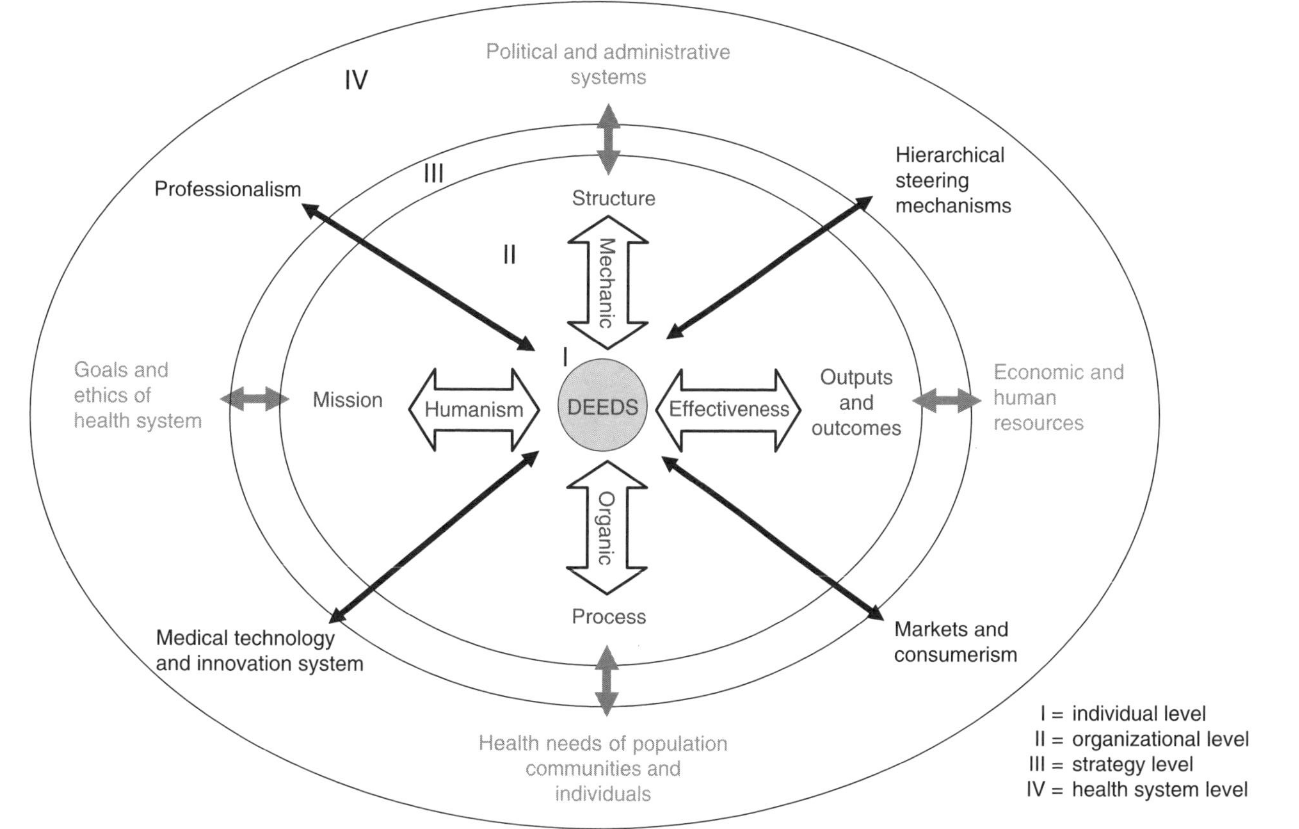

Figure 10.1 Potential impacts of decentralization/recentralization on clinical behaviour

Source: Kinnunen and Vuori (2005)

relationships between decentralization and clinical behaviour or outcomes are mostly indirect. Behaviour of physicians and nurses in a single hospital or in a primary health clinic may continue unchanged although financial and political responsibilities have decentralized from central to regional and local government. However, the distribution of those physicians and nurses, the incentive structures governing their reimbursement, and the way in which their services are organized and monitored may well be affected. At the micro level, health professionals may resist economic incentives if they are seen as conflicting with their professional oath and other professional commitments. Thus, a professional culture and collective actions of care-givers may sustain themselves despite management changes in working environments.

In contrast, financiers, managers and politicians, of necessity, place considerable emphasis on cost containment and efficiency, which means transition of the focus from individual-level issues to organization, community and population-level factors. However, in order to maintain public support, they are also highly vulnerable to accusations regarding problems with access, with waiting lists/wait times becoming a major policy/political issue in many countries, regardless of the actual implications for health outcomes (Ham and Robert 2003; Hurst and Siciliani 2003; Siciliani and Hurst 2003). In order to introduce changes at the health professional level, clear strategy, structural change, rewards and incentives should ideally be addressed in a coherent manner, although this is often easier said than done. In terms of policy analysis (Berndtson 1995; Parsons 1995; Hill and Hupe 2002), different steering mechanisms (such as reformulated policy goals, renewed legislation, economic incentives and disincentives, supply of services, market mechanisms) often have different impacts on the actions of institutions. As identified in Figure 10.1, contradictory contextual factors can affect the clinical processes and outcomes.

The interests and demands of patients or clients are also important in the clinical dimension of any health reform. Citizens in most industrialized countries have legal rights to appropriate health services through social financing schemes which give universal access to a defined bundle of "necessary" services. This, combined with increased individualistic values, the growing wealth of the population and improved awareness of health issues, makes the situation in future even more complex than it was in the past.

The rationale of decentralization is based on the idea that decision-makers are often able to change the behaviour (deeds/actions, levels I, II and III in Figure 10.1) of individuals and institutions, either directly (using command-and-control approaches) or indirectly (through manipulating incentives). Decentralizing reform is based on the assumption that increasing the local and regional responsibility for health issues will enable better involvement of local people in decision-making (democratic dimension), and better resource allocation, monitoring and management. The idea is that local decision-makers are the best judges of how given resources can be used to meet the health needs of their population, and, thus, that reasonable diversification across regions is acceptable. Centralizing reform assumes that certain interests and groups may have little power at the local level, and hence need to be protected through the imposition of national standards. In centralized health systems, policy decisions and resource allocations are accordingly based on national goals which may lead to overriding regional and local health priorities. Finding the balance between flexibility to meet local needs and equity to ensure national standards can be contentious. Additional complexity arises when economic disparities across regions lead to differential ability to pay for services. One common approach is redistribution of resources from richer to poorer jurisdictions. When national or sub-national bodies allocate resources to decentralized bodies, however, issues about accountability also arise.

Three case studies

This chapter focuses on countries in which decentralization reforms have been implemented for several years at regional and local levels. The Nordic countries, Canada and the Russian Federation were selected as examples. We describe and summarize research-based evidence available in the literature. The number of studies explicitly analysing this topic is limited; however, the clinical dimensions of de-recentralization are touched upon in many studies, at least implicitly. The publications reviewed do not cover the entire academic or policy debate on the topic but represent the main issues, allowing some useful conclusions.

Nordic cases

The Nordic countries, for the most part, employ both public financing and public delivery (Thorslund et al. 1997; Harrison and Calltorp 2000; Harrison 2004; Kolehmainen-Aitken 2005). Vrangbæk (2004) compares issues of decentralization in Denmark and Norway, exploring the driving forces in health care de-/recentralization in a manner relevant for the entire Nordic region. These studies concentrate on recent ongoing reforms and the impact of previously decentralized systems on clinical dimensions.

In Norway, after the reform in 2002, the central authorities were again responsible for strategic and overseeing functions (including health targets, budget allocations, determining rules for base financing, monitoring and follow-up). However, regional health authorities would have autonomy in planning and executing health services for their regional population. This means larger regional units and a greater degree of regional political autonomy than previously. At the institutional level, hospitals and other service providers act according to more independent rules and incentives. The role of the private sector has been limited in the Norwegian health care system, but the introduction of the principles of freedom of choice and "waiting time guarantee" (also applied in Sweden and Finland) has led to new challenges. More recently, Norway seems to be moving from the previous decentralized governance system towards a more centralized and semi-market-oriented model, based on national standards, activity-based payment and choice. There are, however, serious difficulties in delivering cost-efficient and equitable services to the citizens in the regions. Recruitment and selection of some health professionals in the system have been difficult in several regions for years.

In Denmark, health care is one major sector in broader reforms of the political-administrative structure of regions. Final policy decisions have not been made, but the plan is that primary and secondary health care will become the responsibility of the new regions, and municipalities are going to receive increased responsibility for prevention and health promotion. The central state level is to take on a stronger role in decisions on the placement of specialized treatment facilities.

What will be the consequences of these latest reforms for the clinical dimension? In structural and process terms, it is clear that both Denmark and Norway seem to be moving toward recentralization, in contrast to trends in some other European health care systems. From the clinical point of view, remarkable reform has been combined with the structural changes. Both countries' health systems are currently being reconfigured to accommodate individual choice, demands for greater flexibility, activity-based funding, demand for higher and more uniform standards of quality and service. This trend is similar in the entire Nordic region.

As mentioned, these latest reforms are new and not yet comprehensively implemented, so that monitoring of their impact on clinical dimension or system functionality is not yet available. Underlying the reform is the desire to achieve better control over increasing costs, as well as the increasing burden of patient flow because of universal access to the services, and unacceptably long waiting lists for non-emergency treatments.

Byrkjeflot and Neby (2003) discuss the decentralized path of Nordic health care reforms and compare the longer historical trends of de-recentralization in Norway, Sweden and Denmark. They conclude that the era of professional dominance, in which physicians were able to develop and sustain strong positions, continued up to 1960 in Scandinavia (Scott et al. 2000, see comparative statistics below). All the Nordic countries reduced their hospital bed supply (beds/1000 population) as part of their health reforms in the 1990s to address the crisis of unsustainable cost increases. Competition and other elements of the New Public Management, which means selective application of market mechanism in management, increased choices for empowered patients/clients/customers, at least to some degree, and made the hospitals semi-independent managed public firms. This trend has reduced the political position of the medical profession (Lane 2000; Rosén 2002).

The impact of decentralization/recentralization in the Finnish health care system has been analysed in a few academic studies (Niskanen 1997; Möttönen 1999; Tuorila 2000; Leskinen 2001; Korhonen 2005). In addition, several national evaluation projects were conducted by the Finnish Ministry of Social Affairs and Health (Viisainen et al. 2002; Ryynänen et al. 2004; STM 2004), mainly in the 1990s. During this decade, the Finnish health care system underwent significant changes triggered by severe economic recession at the beginning of the decade, with a marked reduction in acute care hospital bed supplies, stabilization of health expenditure increases and decentralization of management to the municipalities.

Leskinen (2001) analysed the "behaviour" of municipal decision-makers who wanted to reform institutional-oriented health care (including both somatic and psychiatric) towards a more ambulatory and home care orientation. The main findings from a clinical point of view were that decentralized political and administrative power led to remarkable downsizing, re-organizing, closure of hospitals, reduced patient access and utilization of services, but at the same time, continuous increase in life expectancy and reduced mortality from many disease groups. New managerial procedures (characterized by results and goal-oriented management) were adopted which increased cost containment. These were applied quite differently between municipalities and hospital districts, resulting in increasing geographic inequality regarding access to care. Waiting times were prolonged and the role of private or semi-public services was strengthened. One tendency in municipalities (which paid the bills of secondary and specialized health care) was to gain savings by reducing the length of stay in hospitals.

Contrary to the official goals of the decentralization,[1] the resources spent on specialized medical units actually increased steadily, mainly in the central hospitals. Cuts occurred in primary health care units (operated and owned by municipalities) and in some areas or specialities of medicine like psychiatry, preventive services and health promotion. In fact, secondary and tertiary care hospitals were winners in resource allocation. The number of physicians and nurses increased and annual costs in hospitals increased twice as fast as that in primary health care or in elderly care. It seems that the impact of decentralization in clinical terms was much stronger in primary and public health services than in specialized health care (except psychiatry). This trend was confirmed in several other studies (Valtonen and Martikainen 2001; Viisainen et al. 2002).

Korhonen (2005) studied the decentralization of dental services in Finland from 1970 to 2000. He demonstrates that after the decision-making and accountability were transferred from central (and regional) level to municipalities, variation of access and utilization increased substantially. Services for children (under 16 years) were perfectly organized and the dental health status of this population group was excellent around the country. In contrast, dental health of adults was not as good as should be expected, particularly considering the high number of dentists per capita (OECD 2004). Variation among municipalities increased and was related to local decision-making, particularly annual budgeting.

Gissler et al. (2000) report on all live births born in 1987 who were followed up until the age of 7. Statistically significant regional variations were found for all health indicators, not fully explained by variables such as maternal age and social class. These geographical variations indicate that regional equity in childhood health has not been achieved in Finland. Recently published studies confirm an increase in inequality in the Finnish health care system. Although access is universal and financially compensated, in reality, wealthier (and healthier) population groups utilize health services more than poorer groups. The gap in health status (mortality and morbidity) between the most educated and least educated (particularly male) groups is one of the largest in western Europe since the 1970s, despite targeting of health inequities as official health policy. It appears that the decentralization of financial, political and managerial means has increased rather than decreased the rich–poor gap in health status.

Based on the Finnish studies of the decentralized system, we can conclude the following:

- Municipalities appeared to be too small to provide sustainable quality services for local needs and achieve advantages of economies of scale. As a consequence, at the micro level, efficiency was worsening.
- Inequality in access and utilization of services increased between municipalities and is related to decentralization of health care to small units.
- Planning and development capacity and knowledge are scarce in local municipalities, especially regarding secondary levels of care.
- Municipalities' power position over hospitals is low, leading to transfer of human and economic resources from primary health services to specialized health care and from rural areas to urban regions.

Canada

Canada is a federal system, with a national government in Ottawa, and 13 subnational units (10 provinces, 3 sparsely populated northern territories). Because health care has been seen as under provincial jurisdiction, tensions have arisen as to the extent to which the federal government is entitled to set national standards. The resulting compromise, developed in stages since the 1940s, transfers funds from the federal government to the general revenues of each province to defray, in part, the costs of their insurance plans. These provincially administered plans offer universal coverage to all eligible residents for all "medically required" services offered in hospitals or by physicians, with no co-payments permitted by insured persons for insured services. The system is commonly referred to as "Medicare". Provinces are allowed, but not required, to insure other services. In consequence, about 70% of Canadian health expenditures come from public sector sources, with the public share ranging from about 99% of physician services and 90% of hospital services to about 1% of dental care (CIHI 2002, 2004a, 2004b). Services outside the Medicare definition (and hence not subject to the federal rules), including outpatient pharmaceuticals, dental care, etc., are largely privately financed, including a significant role for employment-based insurance.

In contrast to the United Kingdom and the Nordic countries, in Canada, almost all health care services other than the disease prevention/health promotion activities performed by "public health" units, regardless of source of funding, are privately delivered. The precise arrangements vary considerably both within and across provinces, generally reflecting historical patterns. Hospitals are largely not-for-profit organizations, including many which were set up by religious groups. Physicians, even those practising within hospitals, are predominantly independent for-profit small businesses, largely paid on a fee-for-service basis, with fee schedules negotiated between provincial medical associations and provincial governments. Although many provincial governments are seeking to reform primary care and encourage multi-disciplinary groups, such arrangements remain the exception rather than the rule.

The establishment of these provincial Medicare programmes addressed financing issues, and significantly reduced inter-provincial variations; a relatively high degree of health equity was achieved across the country (Tulchinsky and Varavikova 1996). However, it did not significantly alter how care was delivered.

Canada was not immune to the cost pressures that characterized most industrialized countries. A series of reviews at the federal and provincial levels in the 1980s produced a common set of recommendations (Mhatre and Deber 1992) including the need to reduce numbers of hospital beds and develop lower cost alternatives to hospital care, such as home care and long-term care, reform primary care, and emphasize health promotion and disease prevention. The federal government responded by restricting its transfers to the provinces. Provinces in turn responded by closing hospitals and hospital beds and otherwise attempting to control costs. The share of health expenditures devoted to hospitals fell from 44.7% of total health expenditures in 1975 to 30.1% by 2002.

In 1974, a broader approach to understanding the determinants of health was outlined by the federal government in a landmark public policy document, *A New Perspective on the Health of Canadians* (Lalonde 1974). This report described the Health Field Theory in which health status was attributed to four factors: genetic, lifestyle and environmental issues, as well as medical services. This recognition of the importance of health promotion and disease prevention has provoked considerable attention, initially concentrating upon changing personal lifestyle habits to decrease risk factors such as smoking, obesity, and physical inactivity, but over time also stressing broader social factors, including poverty and inequity (Evans et al. 1994). Not surprisingly, this emphasis on the health of populations has proved difficult to fully implement (although smoking rates have indeed decreased considerably). There is considerable regional variation in these lifestyle and environmental factors, leading to variations in health outcomes across the country (Health Council of Canada 2005; Statistics Canada 2005).

A series of pressures in the mid-1980s encouraged provincial governments to restructure care. All were under fiscal pressure, accentuated by the federal government's efforts to reduce its own deficit by curbing transfer payments. Technology was enabling care to shift outside hospitals to home and community; because of the definition of insured services under the Canada Health Act, this also had the potential to allow provincial governments to shift the responsibility for financing this care from public to private sources. At the same time, the Lalonde Report and the research it encouraged had led to recognition that improving health outcomes required attention to broader determinants of health, and a focus beyond the traditional physician and hospital services required by Medicare. There was a sense that organizing care in "silos" was allowing individuals to "slip through the cracks" and that restructuring care might both improve health outcomes and reduce costs.

Since the mid-1970s, the common mechanism suggested to achieve these aims had been regionalization. These reforms implied setting up a series of geographically-based intermediary organizations that would take responsibility for organizing and delivering a basket of defined services to a defined population. By 1989, the province of Quebec was ready to begin implementation. Over the next period of years, every province, except the sparsely populated northern territories followed suit (for information about the regional reforms, see http://www.regionalization.org/Regionalization/Reg_Prov_Overview_Table.html).

These regionalization models varied in the scope of services assigned to the regional authorities. All of the models included hospitals; none included physicians. All retained financial control at the provincial level; regional authorities were not given taxing authority. Budgetary allocations were a combination of targeted funding (particularly to protect potentially vulnerable services), population-based models, and historical budgets. Most provinces defined some services as "provincial programmes" outside the scope of the regional health authorities. Provinces varied in the extent to which such services as home care, public health, mental health and addictions, and social services were assigned to the regional authorities.

Although commonly referred to by provincial governments as "decentralization", and defended in the language of community empowerment, local organizations often saw things differently. For example, the former associate deputy minister for planning, evaluation and health in the Quebec Ministry of Health gave as the first reason for "decentralization" that "The ministry had to decide on each request sent in by over 900 health and social services institutions, over 1,500 community organizations, and a large number of professional groups" (LaMarche 1996). To the extent that power had rested with these organizations rather than with the provincial government, efforts to gather it under the auspices of the 18 new regional authorities were seen as centralization. Certainly, the abolition of individual hospital boards throughout the country was seen as a centralizing effort, and rural communities were particularly anxious. Similar reductions in the number of provider organizations occurred in all provinces.

It is important to recognize that "regionalization" was used to represent two separate (and often contradictory) trends: the establishment of regional health authorities, and the consolidation of clinical services into networks of centres of excellence (which did not always correspond with the subsequent regional boundaries). Indeed, to the extent that it is not compatible with referral patterns, regionalization may have accentuated urban–rural differences in access to care, and has evoked concern from rural physicians to the extent that it sites decision-making outside particular communities (Collins and Green 1994; Larsen-Soles 2005). Again, this is open to variation, since provinces have often designated services as "provincial programmes" and placed responsibility for funding them outside the regional authorities.

The models are not static; provinces continue to fine tune them. Some provinces are abolishing regional authorities (e.g., Prince Edward Island), while the "hold out" province of Ontario is replacing its advisory District Health Councils with new bodies, Local Health Integration Networks, with the potential of evolving into regional authorities with funding responsibilities. Nor, however, have they accomplished most of their desired goals. Evaluation is now beginning. One recent special issue of *Healthcare Papers* (Vol. 5, No. 1, 2004) concludes that there is little consensus on what regionalization is, little stability in how it operates, and many constraints on the ability of the authorities to act. For the most part, accountability has been slow to shift from provincial governments (Lewis and Khouri 2004). Further, regionalization has yet to shift the focus from sickness care to population health, and to improve service integration.

In consequence, the study of outcomes or "clinical effects" of decentralization are in the beginning stages. A 2002 national report found generally good health outcomes, but considerable regional variations – both within and across provinces (CIHI 2002). Regional authorities stated their intention to use this information to improve care, but again, evaluation is often lacking.

Further complicating evaluation of the clinical impact of regionalization in Canada is the close connection between implementation of regionalization and cost cutting, including reductions in hospital beds. Indeed, regional reforms have often been viewed as a form of "blame shifting" through which provincial governments attempted (with very limited success) to channel requests for resources towards regional boards. Making one-to-one connections between policies and outcomes is accordingly difficult, although in theory comparisons could be conducted between jurisdictions which have and have not regionalized. Conrad et al. are conducting one such analysis in the three Atlantic provinces, where a natural experiment resulted from the varying regionalization models used. For example, Nova Scotia left home care at the provincial level, New Brunswick integrated its acute home care ("Hospital in the Home") with the regional authorities, and Prince Edward Island integrated a fuller range of services, including both acute and chronic home care. Rather than encourage reallocation, however, budgetary allocations by the regional authorities across programmes remained remarkably static. Indeed, only Nova Scotia devoted significantly more resources to home care. Given the incremental changes, it thus appears unlikely that major impacts would be expected.

Although there have been no reports of deleterious effects on health status associated with the decentralization carried out in those Canadian provinces which did so, there is considerable unhappiness, particularly associated with perceived difficulties in obtaining access to care. Unsurprisingly, this is being met with additional efforts at structural change. One key variable is the extent to which these models adopt direct provision – in which the regional authorities own and operate facilities – as opposed to purchasing services.

Another ongoing issue is the role of citizen participation in managing the health authorities. Again, views have varied considerably, from initial optimism about using direct participation to mute provider voices, to recognition of the difficulties accompanying such efforts (Lomas et al. 1997; Lewis et al. 2001; Lomas 2001; Frankish et al. 2002). In practice, elected boards do not appear to have been fully successful; turnout tends to be low in elections, and the board members experience tension as to whether they are responsible to the province (who is paying the bills), the residents of their region, or the local providers. Lomas (2001) noted that reduction in the number of local boards may have decreased opportunities for citizen participation.

One summary of the impact on health outcomes of restructuring in six health regions in the provinces of Manitoba and British Columbia was reported. Penning et al. (2002, p. i) concluded that:

> Trends in access to and use of health services appear fairly consistent immediately before and after regionalization, suggesting declines in service, increasing intensity of care, and redirection of specific services. A shift of focus and resources toward a more social, community-based model of care remains to be achieved.

These researchers confirmed that the impact of other secular trends – particularly cost control and downsizing of hospitals – tended to swamp the impact of regionalization.

They call for "more stable and transparent provincial–RHA relationship, information and measures to better align resources to needs, increased regional-level system integration and changes to organizational culture and practice in the health system".

A series of commentaries concur that it is still too early to judge. Davis (2004) notes:

> Regionalization of healthcare is in its infancy. Systems necessary to support regionalization, which can only be established under a regionalized structure (e.g., information technology, procurement, human resources and service planning), are evolving. Given the size and complexity of the healthcare system, as we gain more experience with regionalization, the systems we need to support it will attain their potential, as will the managers of the system.

On the other hand, there is also a sense that the boundaries may not always have made sense, that regions may have been too small to be sustainable, that integration with primary care has been inadequate, and that the transaction costs, in some cases, may be excessive. The Canadian case thus highlights the importance of clarifying policy goals, and what impact they could conceivably have even under ideal situations. It also suggests that evaluation is difficult in the absence of comparable data. To date, improvements in health outcomes appear to be occurring within particular clinical conditions, within particular regions, rather than as a function of structural reforms *per se*.

The Russian Federation

Evidence to link decentralization with clinical care or health outcomes is very limited in the Russian Federation. Some small-scale studies undertaken recently can shed light on the effects decentralization has on clinical practices. There is some evidence to link outcomes with these practices, and hence indirectly with decentralization. However, it should be noted that the results give a mixed picture and should, therefore, be treated with caution.

The distribution of power has changed drastically in the Russian Federation. Prior to the collapse of Soviet Union, the whole state system was completely centralized. Throughout the 1990s, however, many of the central government functions were devolved to lower levels of the state. Even before he became president of an independent Russian Federation, Boris Yeltsin had urged the regions of the Russian Federation to "gobble up as much autonomy as you can handle" (Service 2002). This view was enshrined in the 1993 Constitution of the Russian Federation, which made the 89 regions "equal subjects", led by elected governments, within a federal structure. The devolution of powers inside the regions to local (e.g. municipal) governments received less attention; however, this process is crucial as most health care facilities are owned and largely funded by local governments. Together with the introduction of health insurance, the process of sharing power and responsibilities between the three layers meant that the federal government lost the levers to regulate the largest part of health care.

In over 70 years of a centralized state, however, the culture of self-governance and knowledge of strategic management skills had been all but lost at the local level. Lower levels of the system were not ready to run a complex network, nor to define or regulate clinical practices. Decentralization was piecemeal, with budgetary and other provisions still constraining badly needed change in organization, regulation and funding principles. At the same time, clinical care regulation was not stipulated within the general legislative provisions for publicly funded organizations, leaving more space for variation by locality or even by facility. Definition of practices and procedures of monitoring of quality clinical outcomes and of medical care had to undergo change while key powers were redistributed between tiers of the system.

Attempts to recentralize state authority, including over the health care system, were undertaken after Vladimir Putin succeeded Boris Yeltsin as president in 2000. However, given the massive scope of decentralization, it is very hard to re-establish control over what was once a rather integrated and cross-linked system. Clinical practice improvement is less politically sensitive as compared to changes in health care management structures, and therefore is among the issues closely looked at by central government in the process of health care reforms.

This review explores how changes in power distribution in the past 20 years have influenced the way in which practices have been shaped. It is largely based on research carried out in Tula region of the Russian Federation to explore determinants of obstetric practices in all 19 facilities that provide maternal care. Inevitably the study had a broader focus, exploring how the evidence is developed and perceived in the Russian Federation, and how it has changed over time, looking at the evolution of practice culture and clinical methods and linking it to outcomes. The study used a combination of methods, analysing outcomes in obstetric departments utilizing data on all births (over 11 000) in 2000 in the Tula region, followed by interviews with heads of the departments to explore variation in major practices and the reasons for variations in outcomes. The methodology is discussed in greater detail elsewhere for both quantitative (Danishevski et al. 2005) and qualitative (Danishevski et al. 2006a) methods.

Regulation of quality of care

The Soviet health care system was governed by a system of decrees or orders (*prikaz*) promulgated by the Ministry of Health. This system, usually referred to as administrative command, was mainly concerned with defining the funding, administrative and reporting aspects of the system, leaving the questions of treatment algorithms and clinical practices to the discretion of senior physicians at the departmental or facility level. Thus, contrary to the popular view among some commentators from the West, the ability of the Soviet Ministry of Health to determine clinical practice was actually quite limited.

During Soviet times as well as in today's Russian Federation, most of the decrees of the Ministry of Health labelled as "standards of practices" concern levels of staffing, organization, structural issues, frequency of visits and procedures, but otherwise say little about the content of care or the indications to intervene. Sometimes such decrees define a minimum and a maximum set of procedures the patient should receive, leaving considerable discretion to individual clinicians. There is still a presumption that, by virtue of the use of "approved" textbooks and curricula, the content of care would be uniform throughout the country (Denisov 2005). There are, however, few studies to assess whether this is the case, even though there was some anecdotal evidence of regional diversity of practices linked to views promulgated by senior physicians in individual medical universities or facilities. Research on quality of care during the Soviet period was also impossible, as this would have been considered ideologically unacceptable and is still nearly impossible due to closed corporatism and the behaviour of medics (Saverskiy 2005).

As noted earlier, the process of decentralization that followed the collapse of the USSR led to considerable changes[2] in the organization of health care delivery. Regional and district administrations assumed a much greater role in funding and managing health care facilities. The majority of health care was now delivered in facilities owned by local governments, although the decree (*prikaz*) issued by the Ministry of Health in Moscow still, officially, had legal authority. Especially after the introduction of a health insurance system in 1994 (following legislation passed in 1991[3]), regulations issued jointly by the Ministry and the Health Insurance Fund began to focus on the content of clinical care and were complemented by a new set of regulations issued by the Regional Health Insurance Funds. This took place in parallel with the introduction of medico-economic standards (MES, analogous to diagnostic related groups) and a basic minimum health care package that health care providers must deliver.

This increased focus on the content of clinical care has, however, faced some administrative obstacles. Despite the formal existence of a homogeneous set of funding mechanisms throughout the Russian Federation, in reality, the funding of care differs between regions, in part, reflecting the complexity and variable implementation of the 1994 health insurance system (Danishevski et al. 2006b). The Federal Health Insurance Fund collects a premium of around 6% of health insurance contributions to fund its role in providing oversight of the regional insurance funds as well as to redistribute some resources from rich to poor regions. The network of regional or territorial insurance funds obtains contributions from the tax authorities and from the Federal Fund, distributing finances through a series of privately owned insurance companies to health facilities. Direct support for general facilities owned by local governments comes from district revenues. In many localities, over half of the total health bill is paid from local budgets, limiting the influence of the Health Insurance Funds.

The changing structure of the health care delivery system, and in particular the often ambiguous lines of accountability in relation to clinical care, pose challenges for the traditional system of top-down management based on decrees. The lack of central guidance has not, however, been replaced by a process of local uptake of evidence-based practice. Although there is a Russian Cochrane Centre, and the key evidence-based medicine texts have been published in Russian, these do not seem to have been taken up widely. Furthermore, the highly centralized and hierarchical style of management and lack of research and critical reading skills are also likely to act as a disincentive to challenging traditional non-evidence based practices.

Macro-level decentralization and clinical care

Decentralization can influence whether effective medical practices are implemented, the scope of practice, their mix, how priorities are defined, and how funds are allocated. For instance, during the centralized period in Soviet times, there was a clear tendency to prioritize clinical disciplines depending on the specialty of the minister (Denisov 2005), which resulted in the development of both objectively needed activities and misallocation of resources to areas outside objective public health priorities. During the subsequent decentralized period, the Ministry has had less power to affect what was happening on other than national levels. Hence only the national excellence centres were developed by the ministers in their personal discipline, leaving the broad scope of activities of the health system at regional and local levels unchanged. Thus, while Minister E.I. Chazov or Professor I.N. Denisov were able to make cardiology and family medicine respectively a country-wide priority, U.L. Shevchenko in 2000–2004 was able only to establish a new excellence centre for cardiology, which he currently is heading, but not to influence the health system at large.

The early achievements of the Soviet health care system in ensuring virtually universal access to basic care of (at least in theory) uniform quality are largely attributed to the development of an extensive network of health care facilities under highly centralized control. Since the break-up of the Soviet Union, the scope for variation is thought to have increased. There are also numerous local, often donor-driven, initiatives.

Throughout the 1990s, decrees were promulgated that established norms for treatment of individual conditions. However, these applied primarily to health care paid for by regional health insurance funds while, in practice, much health care, especially in smaller local level facilities, continued to be funded mainly from municipal budgets, outside the health insurance system. A number of decrees on standards of care were issued by the Ministry of Health, setting out guidance on the management of typical conditions, yet it is not known whether this had any effect. Anecdotal evidence suggests that many central decrees never move beyond the regional health department and have little impact on clinical practice. Most of these decrees are vague in nature and do not define indications and contra-indications in order to avoid debates and any sort of responsibility. They rather describe sets of procedures which can be provided to patients as the minimum and as the maximum. No attempts were undertaken to ensure implementation of these, to control or to monitor whether these are adhered to. It was largely left to local physicians with high administrative positions to define care standards.

One element of the most recent reforms is the reimposition of centralized control. The 89 regions, which since 1993 had shared responsibility for health policy with the federal government, formed nine supra-regional economic groupings with no political or administrative power. In May 2000, Putin issued a decree replacing these groupings with seven federal regions.[4] He appointed his own representatives to lead them, giving them wide-ranging but poorly defined authority. Although formally the new regions had no responsibility for the health sector, the President's representatives soon appointed deputies to fill a perceived vacuum in relation to health and other policy areas. As a consequence, an unforeseen process of interregional coordination is now taking place in the health sector. So far, this new mechanism has not interfered with the content of services, beyond some cases which concern availability of resources rather than details of treatment or diagnostic methods.

Further restructuring took place on the federal level in parallel with the election of Vladimir Putin to a second term as president. The model inherited from the former USSR involved powerful ministries that combined policy-making with regulation and service delivery. The 13 former ministries, as well as various other central bodies, were abolished, and were replaced by five ministries that focus solely on policy development, with 17 regulatory bodies (referred to as "services") and 20 agencies responsible for the delivery of services. Thus, the Ministries of Health, Social Affairs, and Labour have been merged to create a new Ministry of Health and Social Development. The new ministry has been given an enhanced policy-making role, while losing many of its traditional functions, such as epidemiological surveillance and management of federal bodies, e.g. research and training institutes and tertiary referral facilities.[5] This at least in theory should enable the new ministry to play its regulatory role more effectively, and to influence policies concerning clinical practices. This would, of course, result in a recentralization of decision-making control in central government hands.

Micro-level decentralization and clinical care

The issues of decentralization at the micro level are seldom addressed. Russian health care is information-constrained and quite hierarchical. Hierarchy has an important role in an information-poor setting.

Throughout the Russian Federation, centralization of power within institutions or departments is a strategy used by senior staff to retain authority and maintain control. Integration of the administrative and scientific authority in addition to other power-concentrating methods (e.g. nominations of heads of department for extended terms) often blocks implementation of new scientifically proved clinical practices for the sake of the authority of senior medics.

Summing up the Russian Case

Despite the limited evidence linking decentralization at either the micro- or macro-organizational level directly to clinical outcomes, there are clear mechanisms as to how it can influence the definition of clinical practice, which can affect outcomes. The relationship is complex, multi-faceted and context-specific. Stating that decentralization would produce better or worse clinical outcomes would be overly simplistic; however, this case study suggests that the Russian Federation needs to reduce the micro-level hierarchy and to promote evidence-based practice, with leadership from the federal level.

Conclusion

The three case studies provide further support for the observations made in the introductory sections of the chapter. While structural decentralization can be linked to aspects of the broad practice conditions under which patients receive medical services, and while general issues of equity, access and quality can be affected in aggregate and/or indirect terms, it is difficult to connect specific decentralization or recentralization decisions to particular clinical outcomes. This lack of direct connection can be attributed to a series of factors:

- multiple policy changes introduced in simultaneous and/or overlapping timeframes, obscuring the impact of each separate initiative;
- widely differing definitions, size, and responsibilities of decentralized public units (as in Canada and the Russian Federation);
- overlapping responsibilities for key health sector decisions (e.g. funding services in the Russian Federation);
- the importance of individual physician practice patterns and of local management styles in determining specific clinical outcomes for individual patients;
- the weak association of structural characteristics of health care delivery systems with the overall health status observed on a population basis.

These factors combine to reinforce the conclusion that a firm link between decentralization and clinical outcomes is not only unclear in the currently available evidence, but that it may be very difficult to establish under any circumstances except at the most general and thus least valuable level.

Acknowledgements

Richard B. Saltman and Gwyn Bevan contributed to the chapter conclusion.

Notes

1 Constraint on cost increases in health expenditures, more efficiency in use of health resources, integration of different levels of health care such as hospitals with long-term care and home care, increased responsiveness in health decision-making to local community needs, increased emphasis on supportive care in the community for the ageing and those with chronic diseases and promotion of health as an important factor in community and individual health.

2 Government of Russian Federation, Local Governance Law, 6 July 1991, changed to #131 on 6 October 2003.

3 Government of the Russian Federation. Health Insurance Law, N 1499-1 of 28 June 1991.

4 Government of Russian Federation. Decree on "improving efficiency of Presidential administration to fulfil constitutional duties". N849, 13 May 2000. http://cmiki.-garant.ru/today/predst/.

5 Government of Russian Federation. Decree on issues of the Ministry of Health and Social Development N153 of 6 April 2004. Moscow: Russian Federation, 2004. http://www.edu.ru/legal/public/default.asp?no=12035032.

References

Alexis, O. (2005) *Is decentralization the key to achieving equity in health care in developing countries?* London, International Poverty and Health Network (http://www.iphn.org/obrey2.rtf, accessed 16 April 2006).

Amara, R., Cain, M., Bodenhorn, K., Cypress, D. and Dempsey, H. (2003) *Health and health care 2010: The forecast, the challenge.* Princeton, NJ, The Institute for the Future/Jossey-Bass.

Bach, S. (2000) Decentralization and privatization in municipal services: the case of health services. Working paper. Geneva, International Labour Office.

Bankauskaite, V., Saltman, R.B. and Vrangbæk, K. (2004) The role of decentralization on European health care systems. Report to IPPR, London.

Berg, M. and van der Grinten, T. (2003) The Netherlands. In Ham, C. and Glenn, R., eds, *Reasonable rationing: international experience of priority setting in health care. State of health.* Buckingham, Open University Press.

Berndtson, E. (1995) *Politiikka tieteenä. Johdatus valtio-opilliseen ajatteluun* [Introduction to politics as a science]. Valtionhallinnon kehittämiskeskus. Painatuskeskus Oy. 4. painos. Helsinki, painatuskeskus.

Bossert, T., Beauvais, J. and Bowser, D. (2000) *Decentralization of health systems: four country case studies.* Washington, DC, Partnerships for Health Reform.

Byrkjeflot, H. and Neby, S. (2003) *The decentralized path challenged? Nordic health care reforms in comparison.* Bergen, Stein Rokkan Centre for Social Studies, University of Bergen.

Callahan, D. (2002) Ends and means: the goals of health care. In Danis, M., Clancy, C. and Churchill, L.R., eds, *Ethical dimensions of health policy.* New York, Oxford University Press.

Cheema, G. and Rondinelli, D. (1983) *Decentralization and development.* Newbury Park, CA, Sage.

Chen, H-T. (1990) *Theory driven evaluations.* London, Sage.

CIHI (2002) *Health care in Canada.* Ottawa, Canadian Institute for Health Information.

CIHI (2004a) *Health care in Canada.* Ottawa, Canadian Institute for Health Information.

CIHI (2004b) *National health expenditure trends 1975–2004.* Ottawa, National Health Expenditure Database.

Church, J. and Barker, P. (1998) Regionalization of health services in Canada: a critical perspective. *International Journal of Health Services*, **28**: 467–86.

Church, J. and Noseworthy, T. (1999) Fiscal austerity through decentralization. In Drache, D. and Sullivan, T., eds, *Health reform: public success, private failure.* New York, Routledge.

Collins, C. and Green, A. (1994) Decentralization and primary health care: some negative implications in developing countries. *International Journal of Health Services*, **24**: 459–75.

Collins, C., Green, A. and Hunter, D. (1999) Health sector reform and the interpretation of policy context. *Health Policy*, **47**(1): 69–83.

Danishevski, K., Balabanova, D., McKee, M., Nolte, E., Schwalbe, N., Vasilieva, N. (2005) Inequalities in birth outcomes in Russia: evidence from Tula, Russia. *Paediatric and Perinatal Epidemiology*, **19**(5): 352–9.

Danishevski, K., Balabanova, D., McKee, M. and Atkinson, S. (2006a) The fragmentary federation: experiences with the decentralized health system in Russia. *Health Policy and Planning*, **21**(3): 183–94.

Danishevski, K., Balabanova, D., McKee, M. and Parkhurst, J. (2006b) Delivering babies in a time of transition: the changing pattern of maternal care in Tula, Russia. *Health Policy and Planning*, **21**(3): 195–205.

Davis, J. (2004) Let regionalization continue to evolve. *Healthcare Papers*, **5**: 50–4, 96–9.

Deber, R.B. (2004) Delivering health care: public, not-for-profit, or private? In Marchildon, G.P., McIntosh, T. and Forest, P.G., eds, *The fiscal sustainability of health care in Canada*. Toronto, University of Toronto Press.

Denisov, I.N. (2005) Personal Communication.

Derose, K.R. (2003) *Social capital: what is it good for? Exploring the relationship between community social structure and access to health care*. Los Angeles, University of California, Health Services.

Ellencweig, A.Y. (1992) *Analysing health systems: a modular approach*. Oxford, Oxford University Press.

Esping-Andersen, G. (ed.) (1997) *Welfare states in transition: national adaptations in global economics*. Cambridge, Polity Press.

Evans, R.G., Barer, M.L. and Marmor, T.R. (eds) (1994) *Why are some people healthy and others not?: the determinants of health of populations*. New York, Walter de Gruyter Inc.

Frank, R.G. and Gaynor, M. (2004) Fiscal decentralization of public mental health care and the Robert Wood Johnson Foundation Program on chronic mental illness. *The Millbank Quarterly*, **72**(1): 81–104.

Frankish, C.J., Kwan, B., Ratner, P.A., Higgins, J.W. and Larsen, C. (2002) Social and political factors influencing the functioning of regional health boards in British Columbia (Canada). *Health Policy*, **61**(2): 125–51.

Gerdtham, U-G. and Jönsson, B. (2000) International comparisons of health expenditure. In Gulyer, A.J. and Newhouse, J.P., eds, *Handbook of health economics*. North Holland, Elsevier.

Gissler, M., Keskimaki, I., Teperi, J., Jarvelin, M. and Hemminki E. (2000) Regional equity in childhood health: register-based follow-up of the Finnish 1987 birth cohort. *Health Place*, **Dec. 6**: 329–36.

Ham, C. and Robert, G. (eds) (2003) *Reasonable rationing: international experience of priority setting in health care. State of health*. Buckingham, Open University Press.

Harrison, M.I. (2004) *Implementing change in health systems: market reforms in the United Kingdom, Sweden and the Netherlands*. London, Sage.

Harrison, M.I. and Calltorp, J. (2000) The reorientation of market-oriented reforms in Swedish health care. *Health Policy*, **50**(3): 219–40.

Hastings Center Report (1996) The goals of medicine: setting new priorities. *Hastings Center Report*, **26**: 1–27.

Health Council of Canada (2005) *Health care renewal in Canada: accelerating change*. Toronto, Health Council of Canada.

Hill, M. and Hupe, P. (2002) *Implementing public policy*. London, Sage.

Holm, S. (2000) Developments in the Nordic countries – goodbye to the simple solutions. In Coulter, A. and Ham, C., eds, *The global challenge of health care reform*. Buckingham, Open University Press.

Hurst, J. and Siciliani, L. (2003) Tackling excessive waiting times for elective surgery: a comparison of policies in twelve OECD countries. OECD Health Working Papers No. 6. Paris, OECD.

Kinnunen, J. and Vuori, J. (2005) *Terveydenhuollon johtamiskulttuurin holistinen malli* [The holistic model for health management]. Teoksessa: Vuori J. (toim.) Terveys ja johtaminen. Terveyshallintotiede terveydenhuollon työyhteisössä. Helsinki, WSOY.

Kolehmainen-Aitken, R-L. (2005) Decentralization and human resources: implications and impact (www.moph.go.th/ops/hrdj/Hrdj_no3/hrdec1.html, accessed 16 April 2006).

Korhonen, H. (2005) *Tietojärjestelmät suun terveydenhuollon ohjauksessa ja johtamisessa Suomessa, 1972–2001* [Information systems in the steering and management of oral health care in Finland]. Kuopion yliopiston julkaisuja E. Kuopion yliopisto, Yhteiskuntatieteet 127.

Lalonde, M. (1974) *A new perspective on the health of Canadians: a working document.* Ottawa, Information Canada.

LaMarche, P.A. (1996) Quebec. In: Dorland, J.L. and Davis, S.M. eds., *How many roads . . . ? Proceedings of the Queen's CMA conference on regionalization and decentralization in health care.* Kingston, Queen's University School of Policy Studies, 120.

Lane, J-E. (2000) *The public sector: concepts, models and approaches.* 3rd edn. London, Sage.

Larsen-Soles, T.M. (2005) A strategic plan for eliminating rural hospital services through the process of regionalization. *Canadian Journal of Rural Medicine,* **10**(2): 107–8.

Leskinen, H. (2001) *Kunta vastuuseen. Sosiaali-ja terveydenhuollon palvelurakennepolitiikan toimeenpano ja sen arviointi* [Municipalities and their responsibilities. Social affairs and health care: Execution and evaluation of the service structure policy]. Acta-väitöskirjasarja 1/2001. Helsinki, Suomen kuntaliitto.

Lewis, S. and Khouri, D. (2004) Regionalization: making sense of the Canadian experience. *Healthcare Papers,* **5**: 12–31.

Lewis, S.J., Khouri, D., Estabrooks, C.A. et al. (2001) Devolution to democratic health authorities in Saskatchewan: an interim report. *CMAJ,* **164**: 343–7.

Litvack, J. (2004) Decentralization and health care (http://www.ciesin.org/decentralization/English/Issues/Health.html, accessed 16 April 2006).

Lomas, J. (2001) Past concerns and future roles for regional health boards. *CMAJ,* **164**: 356–7.

Lomas, J., Woods, J. and Veenstra, G. (1997) Devolving authority for health care in Canada's provinces: 1. An introduction to the issues. *CMAJ,* **156**: 371–7.

Martin, D. and Singer, P. (2003) Canada. In Ham, C. and Robert, G., eds, *Reasonable rationing: international experience of priority setting in health care. State of health.* Buckingham, Open University Press.

Mhatre, S.L. and Deber, R.B. (1992) From equal access to health care to equitable access to health: a review of Canadian provincial health commissions and reports. *International Journal of Health Services,* **22**: 645–68.

Möttönen, S. (1999) Kunnallisten palvelujen priorisoinnin ongelmallisuudesta. [Difficult preferencies in welfare services of municipality]. *Hallinnon Tutkimus,* **1**: 93–9.

Niskanen, J. (1997) Markkinaohjautuvuuden vaikutus arvoihin julkisessa sairaanhoidossa. *Acta Wasaensia* No. 56, Hallintotiede 3, Vaasa, Universitas Wasaensis.

OECD (2004) *OECD health data 2004: a comparative analysis of 30 countries.* Paris, OECD.

O'Mahony, M. and Stevens, P. (2002) Measuring performance in the provision of the public services: a review, mimeo. London, National Institute of Economic and Social Research.

Parsons, W. (1995) *Public policy: an introduction to the theory and practice of policy analysis.* Cambridge, Cambridge University Press.

Penning, M.J., Roos, L.L., Chappell, N.L., Roos, N.P. and Lin, G. (2002) *Healthcare restructuring and community-based care: a longitudinal study.* Ottawa, Canadian Health Services Research Foundation (http://www.chsrf.ca/final_research/ogc/pdf/penning_final.pdf, accessed 18 July 2006).

Pflanz, M. and Schach, E. (1976) Cross-national sociomedical research concepts, methods, practice: a seminar convened by the Akademie für Sozialmedizin.

PHR (2002) *Decentralization and health system reform, no. 1.* Bethesda, Partners for Health Reformplus.

Pollitt, C., Birchall, J. and Putman, K. (1998) *Decentralizing public service management.* London, Macmillan.

Rosén, P. (2002) *Attitudes to prioritization in health services: the views of citizens, patients, health care politicians, personnel, and administrators.* Göteborg, Nordic School of Public Health.

Ryynänen, O-P., Kinnunen, J., Myllykangas, M., Lammintakanen, J. and Kuusi, O. (2004)

Tulevaisuusvaliokunta teknologian arviointeja 20. Suomen terveydenhuollon tulevaisuudet. Skenaariot ja strategiat palvelujärjestelmän turvaamiseksi. Esiselvitys. [The future of Finnish health care. Strategies and scenarios to secure health care services in Finland in the future]. Eduskunnan kanslian julkaisu 8/2004. Helsinki, Eduskunta.

Saltman, R.B. and Bankauskaite, V. (2004) Implementing decentralization in European health care systems: searching for policy lessons. Paper presented at European Health Policy Group session at 5th European Conference of Health Economists, London School of Economics, 8–11 September.

Saltman, R.B. and Figueras, J. (1997) European health care reform: analysis of current strategies. WHO Regional Publications, European series, No. 72. Copenhagen, WHO Regional Office for Europe.

Saverskiy, A.M. (2005) Personal communication, 25 August.

Scott, W.R., Martin, R., Peter, J.M. and Carol, A.C. (2000) *Institutional change and healthcare organizations: from professional dominance to manager care*. Chicago, Chicago University Press.

SEC (2004) European competitiveness report 2004. Competitiveness and benchmarking. Commission staff Working Document 1397. Brussels, European Commission.

Service, R. (2002) *Russia: experiment with a people*. London, Macmillan.

Siciliani, L. and Hurst, J. (2003) Explaining waiting times variations for elective surgery across OECD countries. OECD Health Working Papers No. 7. Paris, OECD.

Statistics Canada (2005) *Health indicators* (http://www.statistique-canada.org/, accessed 18 July 2006).

STM (2004) *Terveyskeskus toimivaksi: kansallisen terveydenhuollon hankkeen kenttäkierroksen raportti 2004* [Effective health centre: report on field visits with the National Health Care Project 2004 in Finland]. STM selvityksiä 2004:13. Helsinki, STM.

Thorslund, M., Bergmark, Å. and Parker, M.G. (1997) Difficult decisions on care and services for elderly people: the dilemma of setting priorities in the welfare state. *Scandinavian Journal of Social Welfare*, **6**: 197–206.

Tulchinsky, T.H. (1982) Evaluation of personal health services: a review with applications for Israel. *Israeli Journal of Medical Sciences*, **18**: 197–209.

Tulchinsky, T.H. and Varavikova, E.A. (1996) Addressing the epidemiologic transition in the former Soviet Union: strategies for health system and public health reform in Russia. *American Journal of Public Health*, **86**: 313–20.

Tuorila, H. (2000) *Potilaskuluttaja terveysmarkkinoilla. Yksityisten terveydenhuoltopalvelusten käyttäjien oikeuksien toteutuminen lääkäriasemien asiakaspalvelussa* [Patient consumers on health care markets]. *Acta Universitatis Tamperensis* 746. Tampere, Tampereen yliopistopaino Oy Juvenes Print.

Valtonen, H. and Martikainen, J. (2001) Kuntien sosiaali: ja terveystoimen menojen jakauma ja jakauman muutokset vuosina 1975–1998. Kuopion yliopiston selvityksiä. E. Yhteiskuntatieteet 24. [The distribution of the health and social care expenditures in the Finnish municipalities and the change of this distribution in 1975–1998]. Kuopio University Occasional Reports. E. Social Sciences 24.

Viisainen, K., Koskinen-Saalasti, U., Perälä, M-L., Kinnunen, J. and Teperi, J. (2002) Terveydenhuolto 2000-luvulle: hankkeen alueellisen toimeenpanon arviointi [Health care into the 21st century: an assessment of the regional implementation of the project]. STM, Selvityksiä 2002:8. Helsinki, STM.

Vrangbæk, K. (2004) Decentralization and recentralization in Scandinavian health care. Paper presented at EHPG Conference, London, 8–11 September.

Wolman, H. (1990) Decentralization: what it is and why we should care, in R. Bennett, ed., *Decentralization, local governments, and markets: towards post-welfare agenda*. Oxford, Clarendon Press.

chapter eleven

Effects of decentralization and recentralization on equity dimensions of health systems

Meri Koivusalo, Kaspar Wyss and Paula Santana

Equity dimensions of decentralization

This chapter reviews the relationship between decentralization and the equity dimensions of health systems, in the context of public policies. The first section examines how equity is defined and how it is understood. The second section discusses the framework of decentralization as part of public policies, while the third explores how policy interests and politics relate to decentralization and its equity dimensions. Since the process of decentralization is dependent on a broader framework of policies and political context, it is not useful to try to assess the impact of decentralization on equity without taking into account the context in which that interaction takes place. The evidence on decentralization and equity is also necessarily dependent on three matters. First, to what extent equity was and has been a concern in a less decentralized model of health system; second, to what extent actual decentralization has taken place; and third, the political context in which decentralization takes place. The fourth section of the chapter draws together existing experiences concerning the context of equity as well as raising particular aspects of decentralization in three countries: Finland, Portugal and Switzerland. A concluding section assesses these experiences and summarizes the key issues for further consideration.

Equity, as defined in the context of the general egalitarian principles of health systems refers to receiving treatment according to need and the financing of health care according to ability to pay. This might not be the most sophisticated definition, but is useful in setting the principles and grounds which are understandable in the context of medicine, public policies and different ethical frameworks (see e.g. Wagstaff and Van Doorslaer 1993; Culyer 2001; Hurley 2001). This understanding of equity is rooted in an implicit understanding of the concepts of horizontal and vertical equity. Horizontal equity requires like issues to be treated in the same way, for example, people with the same problem will get the same treatment and people who are affluent will pay as much as the rest. Vertical equity requires that dissimilar issues should be treated in a dissimilar way, in proportion to the differences between them, so that greater needs should receive greater attention. For example, more resources should be allocated to major health problems in comparison to minor health problems and that poorer should pay proportionally less than more affluent. In addition, equity in this chapter is considered in the macro context of public policies and geographical equity rather than in terms of equity between individuals.

The equity dimension of health systems covers various aspects of health policies, including health services financing and organization as well as other health policy measures that focus on health protection and health promotion. Derived from the egalitarian principle, the first and foremost equity issue in most health systems is that of ensuring that access to health care is based on need, rather than geographical area or capacity to pay, and that quality of care does not differ between population groups, health conditions or geographical areas. Health systems also have distributive impacts, and one part of the equity dimension is the progressivity or regressivity of overall financing of the health care system. The equity dimension of health care systems is not merely to ensure services for the poor, but a more fundamental question of the overall principles of functioning in a given health system. Mackintosh (2001) has pointed out that ethical and redistributive commitments in health care are both a set of principles and an institutional construction in the form of a set of working understandings. Such commitments have to be constantly reconstructed in a market-dominated or market-pressured system.

Another important dimension of health systems and equity is that of health inequalities and inequalities in outcomes. In most European countries health inequalities are only partly defined by access to health services, tending to reflect social variation in eating and living habits as well as overall inequalities in a society. While it is possible to limit the focus on health inequalities or inequalities in health outcomes more directly to the functions of the health system or causes of morbidity and mortality, such as infant mortality, which are directly related to service provision, it is not possible to make an overall assessment of the equity dimension of a health system merely on the basis of health inequalities or inequalities in outcomes (see Box 11.1).

Equity in health systems does not imply homogenization, but – broadly interpreted – does imply that people should have access to the same quality of care if they have the same need, and that this should not become dependent on the area they live in. Also, equity aspects of decentralization need to cover its relation to measures and policies which may lead to more inequitable financing mechanisms of health care in general.

Box 11.1 Health inequalities

There has been continued theoretical and practical interest in health inequalities and in reducing health inequalities through reduction of inequalities in determinants of health in Europe (see e.g. Benzeval et al. 1995; Whitehead 1998; Marmot and Wilkinson 1999; Mackenbach and Bakker 2002, 2003). Poverty, social inequality and the lack of social cohesion can also be seen as part of the root causes of health inequalities, and as part of the background of inequalities in education, nutrition and diet, mobility and consumption of health-hazardous substances. In a more public health-oriented context, the equity dimension of health also covers the impact of other policies and policy choices on determinants of health and healthy living. Decisions made at a national or regional level can have a direct influence on what is done at a local and community level in a country. Social inequalities and inequalities in health and determinants of health need to be seen in the context of overall policies of different countries, public health policy priorities and production, and the reduction of poverty and vulnerability.

Framework of decentralization policies and equity

Decentralization in health systems takes place predominantly as part of particular overall public policies. Decentralization will thus have differential implications on equity depending on overall political priorities. This means in practice that the effect of decentralization and recentralization on equity is strongly related to the context in which these reforms are applied and the country's overall policies with respect to social equity and equity in health in particular.

Decentralization is often expected to result in efficiency gains, reduced costs of health care and increased equity (see Chapter 1), yet it is not clear to what extent this is often the case. If decentralization leads to the creation of an additional layer of administrative governance, it may also increase overall costs. In an ideal world with equal distribution of wealth and health, the equity dimensions of decentralization would be limited to those of population size covered and costs of providing services in different areas. It is known that services in remote and sparsely populated and/or hard to reach areas tend to cost more. This means that, even in an ideal world, some equity issues would be of importance in relation to decentralization, especially if decentralization of financing is involved.

In a world in which wealth and health are not distributed equally, decentralization is necessarily related to the structure of mechanisms for cross-subsidization between different areas and population groups. It is not uncommon for areas which are poorer to be also more sparsely populated and remote. This means that these areas may be disadvantaged in terms of both overall resources and costs of care. Decentralization of responsibilities of services' financing and provision without mechanisms of cross-subsidization will then have a direct negative impact on the equity dimension of health services. It is thus fair to say that without mechanisms for cross-subsidization, decentralization of financing will always be problematic to equity.

Decentralization of administration may also become problematic if local decision-making on how to use resources is left without guidance on citizen rights and local level responsibilities. Even if financing were to be distributed equitably, local decision-makers may choose to use resources in a way which could increase or decrease inequity in access to care. Inequalities between areas may also result from different capacities to use resources efficiently. Similarly, local priorities may be at odds with national policy priorities or given local responsibilities. This problem became important in Finland during the recession in the early 1990s and has also been present in recent Swedish debates about the need for constraints to limit the freedom of regional governments to privatize hospitals (Burgermeister 2004).

Inequities may further result if local governments are given more responsibilities for provision and financing of health care than resources, as this may lead to greater emphasis on local resource gathering through regressive financing and create pressures towards user cost-sharing. It is also likely that, even in a context in which cross-subsidization were to occur on the basis of population characteristics, the freedom of local governments to impose fees and allowing, for example, faster access to care through cost-sharing arrangements or subsidies for the use of private care, may quickly expand inequities. Table 11.1 presents some concerns, challenges and strengths in relation to different mechanisms of financing and provision of care.

The current emphasis on choice as part of health care reforms may also lead to problems in decentralized administration and financing as population-based estimates become more difficult to maintain. Choice also tends to benefit those who are more highly educated, who are usually healthier and more able to choose and gain access to health care elsewhere. Inequities may also become more prominent between different disease groups due to different capacities to choose and utilize services and if specialists remain mostly in urban centres.

The level of decentralization matters. The existence of sufficient risk pools are a core issue, as it is known that the costs of health care are heavily concentrated. This may not be a problem in regional decentralized units, but can be important in the context of smaller local decentralized units which may become unable to cover costs of hospital care if cross-subsidizing mechanisms are not sought.

The politics of decentralization and recentralization

Decentralization is not only a technical administrative device, but is often associated with particular politics and policy choices. It is also nothing particularly new. The history of health policy could be written as a history of balancing centrifugal and centripetal forces. This process can also be extended from global to local levels. At the international level, decentralization-oriented elements were already found in the primary care emphasis of the Alma Ata declaration and as part of health care reform policies (Koivusalo and Ollila 1997). Community development has been seen as an important avenue to

Table 11.1 Decentralization and equity concerns with different means of financing and provision of health services

Financing and provision	*Insurance*	*Tax-based*	*Voluntary measures*
Equity concerns	Distribution of providers difficult to regulate Benefit coverage may differ on geographic basis Decentralization may lead to increasing cost-sharing by users and higher premiums in poorer areas Cross-subsidization between insured important and requires regulation to avoid selection of patients	Distribution of salaried providers easier to regulate Quality and services provided may differ on geographic basis Decentralization may lead to incentives towards more cost-sharing by users Cross-subsidization on population-related basis may become compromised due to introduction of choice	Distribution of providers very difficult to regulate Voluntary private insurance provides incentives to cream skimming and tends to enhance inequities Decentralization may influence use and contribute to inequities within and between areas Cost-sharing by users taken often as granted Cross-subsidization difficult, risk of two-tiered services
Challenges	Cost containment Ensuring equal benefit coverage and access Ensuring risk pooling, avoiding selective policies Insurability of high risk population and ensuring full coverage of benefits for all	Maintaining quality Commercialization through contracting out Addressing choice of provider Ensuring access to costly or low-esteem health problems and minority groups	Division to markets and charitable services Sustainability of services Avoiding cream skimming and dependency on contracted services Commercialization or in non-profit services, strong mission influence
Strengths	Less vulnerable to variation in quality of services and under-provision Risk of politicization low	Cost containment and overall services governance simpler Political accountability for services	May be important in filling an existing gap in services Responds to consumerist demands

increase democratization and participation also in the context of health services, and decentralization has been seen positively by social activists and other advocacy groups.

Wilensky (1975) argued that the greater the authority of the central government, the higher the welfare state spending and the greater the programme emphasis on equity. Klein (2003) noted that, in the context of the NHS in the

United Kingdom, equity is one gravitational force pulling decision-making to the centre. Pierson (1994) has argued that accumulating empirical evidence suggests that fiscal federalism actually helps the retrenchment of the welfare state. Taroni (2003, pp. 144–5) has emphasized, in the Italian context, that:

> "From the perspective of the potential impact of fiscal devolution on national healthcare services, the current trend towards the devolution of powers to local governments looks more like an exercise in downloading, cost cutting and diffusing and deflecting blame than a bold new experiment in deliberative democracy and community empowerment."

The extent to which this can be verified in European societies remains open, but it is clear that the connection between social rights and resources is of great importance. The impact of decentralization on equity may also depend greatly on whether it takes place in the context of increasing or decreasing overall resources to health care, and what type of risk adjustment, cross-subsidization and performance requirements exist or accompany decentralization. The current practice in many countries of allocating resources to regions on the basis of national average relationships between population characteristics and use of health services may not be sufficient, due to remaining regional heterogeneity. Thus, while horizontal equity between regions is achieved, this does not necessarily ensure vertical equity (Sutton and Lock 2000). The capitation systems in most countries also are based not only on empirical models of health care expenditures, but also on ethical considerations of likely future needs as well as which needs to include (or exclude) from such models (Rice and Smith 2002).

The political context of decentralization is perhaps of most importance in low- and middle-income countries and the transitional economies of the former Soviet Union, but matters also to many European Union Member States. The importance of decentralization may also increase within European Union Member States as decentralization is brought in as a means to improve the effectiveness of health care systems in the context of future cooperation and the use of so-called open methods of coordination in the field of health services (European Commission 2004b).

As decentralization is often introduced as part of broader reform efforts, it is difficult to address the empirical impacts of decentralization independently from other policies that were implemented at the same time. When decentralization is pursued in the context of public sector reform with the aim of reducing administrative costs and improving effectiveness through a New Public Management (NPM) type of reform, it is not merely technical, but also represents a political preference for certain types of values over others, since NPM emerged in developed countries as a response to both ideological changes and fiscal crises (Jackson and Price 1994). This implies that, while decentralization is often emphasized, cost-cutting and privatization might in practice be the more clear-cut aims of the overall policies. Some commentators have suggested that the impact of health care reform has not been sufficiently balanced between the aims of equity and efficiency, and that the latter has dominated the agenda (Gilson 1998). This viewpoint is also reflected in a study on impacts of new public management reforms in low- and middle-income countries: "Several of the NPM reforms (such as user fees and potentially autonomous hospitals) would seem to exacerbate inequities. Reforms which build upon social solidarity, rather than undermine it, may receive wider support within countries" (Mills et al. 2001).

In many countries, accountability for health service provision has been decentralized, but decisions on the regulatory framework of competition, economic policies and trade in services are made more at national, European or even at global level. This has implications for decentralization as the status of services may change if they are contracted out at local level and not provided directly by the government.

Trade agreements and internal market regulations do not prohibit the aim of equity in access to health services, but do influence how this can be reached due to requirements for domestic regulation and other measures if health and hospital services are scheduled (Fidler 2003; Luff 2003). Several legal reviews of General Agreement on Trade in Services have shown that the public services exception is unlikely to cover contracted out services and commitments made by the sector will inevitably have implications for the financing and regulation of services (Fidler 2003; Krajewski 2003; Luff 2003). Pharmaceutical policies are another important part of health systems in which European and global regulatory frameworks are increasingly driven by commercial interests in comparison to public health concerns. This may lead to further increases in health care costs as well as limitations in cross-subsidization mechanisms at local and national levels.

Decentralization and equity – where is the evidence?

It may be useful to separate aspects of decentralization that can increase geographical inequities between areas and those that can increase inequities within a given geographical area or by a shift towards more regressive mechanisms of financing health care. For example, decentralization of financing may increase geographical inequalities if mechanisms for cross-subsidization are not sought, whereas opening up the scope for additional local financing and use of cost-sharing may increase inequities within geographic regions.

The nature and quality of evidence in terms of equity are strongly related to the process and context of decentralization and thus seeking solid evidence on causal relationships is bound to be problematic. Studies of regional variations in inequalities do not necessarily imply that these are associated with the process of decentralization or local decisions as such. On the other hand, decentralization may render different localities vulnerable to national policy decisions or the ways in which cross-subsidisation takes place may have implications for the regressivity of health system financing. The equity impact of decentralization is also related to the previous organization of health care before decentralization. It is known that centralized health systems can be very inequitable. It is also likely that equity issues will be felt differently in the context of increasing and decreasing resource allocation to health care.

The history and political context of decentralization are evident also in the three national case studies, which each raise a different point of concern. In Portugal, decentralization can be seen as means to address problems of centralized organization, whereas in the Nordic countries, health systems have been built on a broader tradition of local governance. The ultimate level of decentralization becomes an issue with respect to the Nordic countries, as these are rather small countries representing often smaller units than national or regional bodies in other countries. When decentralization has taken place, moreover, it can be more difficult to operate a publicly accountable health system, since autonomous sub-units give higher priority to their specific interests than to broader societal or national interests – which created a continuous challenge in Switzerland (Wyss and Lorenz 2000). Yet decentralized health units rarely use their autonomy in decision-making fully, as they are typically regulated at national level through financing and increasingly on the basis of performance. The three case studies highlight the context of decentralization and equity, which in Finland has drawn attention to the levels at which decisions on rights, responsibilities and resources are made. Balancing equity and efficiency goals and the starting point of policy changes are important in the context of recent reforms in Portugal and the role of specific minority groups is illustrated in the case study of migrants in Switzerland.

Decentralization of responsibilities and Europeanization of rights

In Finland, responsibilities for basic health care services and their financing remain at the municipal level. State subsidies have been provided to ensure equity and cross-subsidization. These were initially directed to health and social services, but in the early 1990s the State Subsidies Act was changed and municipalities received block grants, giving them freedom to decide how they provide services. Equity in decentralized activities became of further importance in the economic difficulties in the early 1990s, resulting in a reduction in resources for service provision in municipalities. The share of financing of municipalities in comparison to the state increased substantially in the 1990s (KELA 2001). With the exception of pharmaceutical costs, the growth of Finland's overall health care costs was largely contained during the 1990s, and the share of health care costs of the GDP has been relatively low due to economic growth (Ministry of Social Affairs and Health 2005). While decentralization policies were not necessarily intended to increase regressivity in health care financing, it is likely that decreasing central allocations of resources and new incentives for increasing user cost-sharing at municipality level produced this result.

The steering of decentralized service provision is complex even when substantial information resources and capacities are available. In the Finnish context, mechanisms of cross-subsidization between municipalities exist and also maximum levels of user fees have been set by the government. However, during the 1990s, a substantial increase in legal cases by citizens claiming their rights to care indicated the existence of a problem and the importance of having a legal framework of social rights. Mental health care-related complaints comprised a substantial portion of the cases (Ylikylä-Leiva 2003). The experiences during and after Finland's economic crisis point to the need to ensure rights of less vocal groups, such as alcoholics and psychiatric patients (Kalland 1996).

This has also led to some recentralization in governance. For example, in 1999, the Parliament returned temporarily to more normative steering and earmarked annual grants in the field of child psychiatry and allocated specific funds for this purpose (Ministry of Social Affairs and Health 2001). Finnish experiences of political decentralization thus suggest that even if financial cross-subsidization occurs in general, measures are needed to ensure the rights of citizens, particularly of less vocal groups.

Decentralization may induce additional problems if the geographical areas and population covered become small, as has been the case in Finland. Local capacities to influence hospital care and pharmaceutical costs tend to be more limited and lead to adverse incentives towards rationing within primary care services or utilizing more inequitable financing mechanisms. Thus, the balance between levels of care and between different channels of financing needs to be addressed as part of decentralization. In a health system with mixed channels of financing and organization, it is important to ensure that problems are addressed at the level where crucial decisions take place. This is essential since the shift of responsibility to the municipal level also shifts blame to the local level and can indirectly facilitate the continuation of inequitable policies.

The decentralization of services provision is also occurring in a world with increasing trade and market interests in service provision. The European legal sphere is expected to matter more, in light of the Services Directive and work in the context of services of general interest (European Commission 2001, 2003, 2004a). The European developments are also closely associated with negotiations concerning trade in services, government procurement and domestic regulation (European Commission 2003; Fidler 2003; Luff 2003). Thus, while municipalities may in principle have freedom to choose how they provide health and social services, this will be increasingly subject to European and global commercial regulatory frameworks.

Implications of decentralization (deconcentration) for equity in Portugal

In Portugal, substantial improvements in health outcomes (e.g. declining infant mortality from 58 per thousand live births in 1970 to 4.1 in 2003) can be attributed to the combined interaction of health and social conditions induced by the municipalization process, after the political changes of 1974, and by increasing the accessibility and quality of health services (Santana et al. 2003). Health care accessibility and quality became highly correlated with the growing geographical spread of primary health care (PHC) and public hospitals (about 90% of population living less than 60 minutes from a district hospital), anchored in a centralized (planning, financing and evaluation) national health service (Santana et al. 2003). This apparent contradiction – decentralized improvement of environmental conditions through municipalities yet centrally oriented development of health care provision – is one important characteristic of health and social development in Portugal.

Some health inequities still persist, however. The Portuguese health system cannot solve them all, because they reflect specific circumstances of particular communities (e.g. location) and solutions would involve a large amount of resources that are not available.

The operation of the Portuguese health care system, particularly regarding accessibility and utilization of health services, is characterized by constraints arising from several circumstances.

Unequal access to health services for all citizens

- Excessive concentration of public and private resources (human and technologies) in urban areas (Santana 2005). Oliveira and Bevan (2003, p. 290) demonstrated "the inequitable concentration of resources for acute hospitals in three urban areas (Lisbon, Coimbra and Porto)".
- Resource allocation, especially hospitals, has been based on "historic budgeting" and not on social-demographic or epidemiological characteristics of the population, reinforcing inequities in the distribution of hospital resources (Oliveira and Bevan 2003). After 2001, PHC funding was based 50% on "historic budget", and 50% on capitation (age, gender and chronic disease adjustment), compulsory immunization (1–14 years old) and haemodialysis. Inequities between regions decreased (SD = 7%, 2001) but still persist (higher values of per capita public expenses in south; low values in north) (Tranquada et al. 2000).
- Inability of public services to respond to increasing demand. Although average waiting time fell dramatically from nine months in 2002 to 2.7 months in 2003, the number of individuals on the waiting lists grew from 110 994 to 128 662 (OPSS 2004).
- Predominance of the curative model (NHS financing structure: hospitals 52.5%; PHC 42.3%) (IGIF 2004). This is associated with poor referral mechanisms between primary and secondary care, creating negative impacts for equity in accessibility and utilization of health care services, especially old people living in inland rural municipalities (Santana 2000, 2002, 2005).

Political context

- Lack of continuity in policies across different political majorities. Ten years after the publication of the legal framework for the decentralization of health services, there are still limitations regarding its implementation. The five Regional Health Administrations do not carry out all their competencies; Local Health Systems were not implemented;[1] Regional Agencies for Monitoring and Regulating Health have little or no influence on the improvement of public resources.
- There is duplication of structures (both regional and central levels), an element that encourages the continuation of centralized planning, resources allocation, technical support and performance evaluation.
- The latest health care reforms (privatization and hospital companies) were more oriented to obtain gains in efficiency and cost containment than to obtain gains in equity.

Local participation

- The participation of local communities and decision-makers generated good results in promoting healthy conditions, but their participation in the management of health care provision units (PHC and hospitals) is modest.
- Centralized health planning and decision-making, even substantially reducing local discretion to meet the different needs in different areas of the country, can be, in some cases, contradicted by local pressures, resulting in the overlapping of resources.

Addressing needs of migrant workers in Switzerland

Increasing migration to Switzerland, both from Europe and from outside Europe, has made this a priority topic. Typically, there are two broad groups of migrants: (1) refugees (including asylum seekers); and (2) migrant workers, ranging from those who have the right to live in Switzerland for some months to resident migrant workers who have lived in the country for decades. While asylum seekers and migrant workers constitute around 0.5% and 20% of the population respectively and are covered by health insurance, it is estimated that an additional 1–4% of the population are living illegally and without health insurance protection in Switzerland.

A substantial proportion of migrants live in conditions of considerable risk. Migrants are exposed to poor working and living conditions, which are in their own right determinants of poor health, and they have reduced access to health care. This is due to a number of political, administrative and cultural reasons, which vary for different groups. For example, barriers in accessing health care may reflect administrative obstacles to receiving care, including residence conditions which need to be fulfilled before services can be provided. In other situations, racial, cultural and linguistic barriers may prevent migrants from making appropriate use of available services.

There are several reasons why migrants should receive specific consideration when planning, managing and administering health interventions. It can be argued that there exists state responsibility to ensure access to preventive and curative health care, especially for less advantaged groups.

In Switzerland, there have been various efforts to address the health of migrants at federal level. A national strategy and priority areas for action have been proposed by the Federal Office of Public Health and are currently being implemented (Swiss Federal Office of Public Health 2002). Top priorities include capacity building of physicians and nurses for inter-cultural communication and the training of personnel with interpretation skills, as well as health prevention and promotion in the areas of reproductive health and HIV/AIDS.

While at the national level there are efforts to deal with migrants as a distinctive area for action, the reactions of decentralized entities (the cantons and communes) have varied. Cantons enjoy sovereignty in defining principles and standards, creating large differences in the extent of specific assistance provided to migrant groups. Certain cantons have set up distinct programmes targeting migrants, whereas others do not see the reduction of inequalities between migrants and non-migrants as a priority area for action. Further, operational capacities of local governments are in most situations limited due to resource constraints and administrative, managerial and organizational weaknesses of local health personnel. In some situations, the unwillingness and/or incapacity of local governments to address the health improvement of migrants leads to a situation where associations and voluntary organizations have to fill the vacuum.

International studies and evidence

International experiences of decentralization appear to be strongly related to the context in which decentralization exists or has taken place, as in many countries federal or regional arrangements exist or have existed for a long time. The implementation of decentralization as part of broader reforms has, during the 1980s and 1990s, been a prominent component of reforms in developing countries and broader public sector reforms. While decentralization has been carried out with predominantly positive attributes geared towards local democracy, it is unclear to what extent the expected positive experiences of decentralization have been realized in practice. Collins and Green raise several fundamental concerns over decentralization processes and especially the politics of decentralization in developing countries (Collins 1989; Collins and Green 1994).

In Europe, decentralization has been discussed especially in the context of Scandinavian countries, Italy and Spain. Equity has been a concern in Sweden in the context of privatization of services on the basis of local level decisions of privatizing hospitals (Burgermeister 2004). Diderichsen has pointed out that privatization in the context of decentralization, and the lack of power at the level of county councils to deal with the commercial sector, imply a need for national legislation, which in turn will limit the freedom of local government (Diderichsen 1999). A similar tension between regional and national policies has been reported from Spain, since the shift to block grants in regional funding in 2001. Concerns were raised when contracting out to the private sector was implemented in regions in spite of the opposition of the central government. The Cohesion Act was passed by the Parliament in 2003, in which the responsibility for ensuring equity of access in different regional health systems remains at national level (Bankauskaite et al. 2004). However, while there are concerns over sustainability of financing of health care, the coordination of the pharmaceutical market as well as with respect to equity, there is so far no clear evidence that inequalities in access to health care or health have increased in Spain due to decentralization (Vinuela 2000; López Casasnovas 2002; Gomez and Nicolas 2004a, 2004b; López Casasnovas et al. 2004). In Italy, decentralization is associated with great social inequalities between regions, which have drawn attention to the ways in which cross-subsidization is implemented. Poorer regions will have less room to manoeuvre health care expenditure, low-income regions will have to raise tax rates more than high-income regions, and it seems that also increasing reliance on indirect taxes will make the overall system of health care financing more regressive (Donatini et al. 2002).

At the global level, assessments of the impact of decentralization as a whole are mixed (Rondinelli and Nellis 1986; Mills 1994; Kolehmainen-Aitken 1998; Litvack et al. 1998; Kolehmainen-Aitken 1998; Bach 2000; Tang and Bloom 2000; Arredondo and Parada 2001; Saide and Stewart 2001; Bossert and Beauvais 2002; Wyss and Lorenz 2000; Khaleghian 2004). It is also not always clear to what extent problems of decentralization are related to decentralization as such or to the more complex nature of contracting, public–private partnerships, cost-sharing, privatization, autonomous hospitals and central government regulatory requirements associated with the process of administrative reform and decentralization. These may relate to the overall level of resources and capacities, but do not necessarily do so since, counter-intuitively, in developing countries decentralization is associated with higher immunization coverage rates in low-income countries, but lower coverage in middle-income countries (Khaleghian 2004). There is no reason to expect that local governments in European countries will be particularly resistant to problems of elite and interest groups, capture of decision-making process, lack of attention to equity, inter-jurisdictional free-riding or neglect of health promotion and public health measures.

Conclusion

The impact of decentralization upon equity seems to be mixed, depending on the overall policy choices and political context. In a real world with variations between affluence, geographical areas and health, there is a need to maintain cross-subsidies between population groups and geographical areas. In addition, care should be taken to ensure that decentralization does not have adverse impacts on different levels of service or in relation to particular illnesses and health problems. In addition to financing, also decentralization of administration may become problematic if cross-subsidization of financing across geographical areas is made without earmarking funds for health.

While decentralization is generally expected to increase equity, there is little evidence of this. In contrast, it is more likely that an increase in local or regional autonomy will increase variation. This can be corrected through varying levels of recentralization of regulation, standard setting, performance criteria and cross-subsidization across areas and population groups. However, this also means limiting the scope of autonomy. That in turn implies that decentralization needs necessarily to be complemented by recentralization and improved coordination of activities.

The effect on decentralization can be positive if services better reflect citizens' needs and the local cultural context. On the other hand, this context can also be problematic for equity and health, for example, with respect to access to reproductive health services and abortion. Addressing equity is in principle a matter of political priority, but also results from the capacity, skills and information needs of national governments to actually regulate decentralized bodies in an appropriate way to ensure equity. In health systems, local democratic decision-making may not always be conducive to the social rights of minority groups. Health care costs tend to accumulate and selecting people is the most efficient way to save costs and improve performance in health services and also in many social services. It is also clear that all health problems are not equal in terms of how these are valued in a society. If inequities are to be removed, special action is necessary to ensure the social rights of deprived groups of population and tackle particular health problems, such as mental health.

Health policy and the politics of health are important in the context of decentralization. Pierson (1994) has emphasized the need to avoid blame in the politics of welfare retrenchment. Decentralization of social responsibilities with diminishing resources is likely to have negative implications for the capacity to maintain equity. This creates incentives for more regressive mechanisms of financing through local charging of users and additional mechanisms of financing, such as private voluntary insurance. Inequalities in access to care are related to overall social inequalities and rural and urban variation. The more freedom is allowed for providers to choose their patients and patients to choose their providers, the more likely is the rise of inequities in access to care for those who bear a higher risk and have less capacity to choose. This is of importance as choice becomes a more common policy issue within health systems.

Finally, in the globalizing world in which the rights and regulatory terms of commercial actors are becoming increasingly centralized, to think that decentralization of social responsibilities could take place without affecting equity is difficult. The increasingly international regulatory framework of commerce and trade can influence the way in which regulatory means can be applied at national, regional and local levels to maintain equity, especially when health services are provided by a mix of public and private actors. It is likely that this will be important also for the sustainability of resources and for cost containment and quality issues such as for pharmaceuticals and health technology. Equity aspects of decentralization thus imply the necessity to ensure that resources, capacities and the scope to regulate and cross-subsidize are maintained not only nationally at local, regional and national levels, but also that these are ensured internationally at regional and global levels, where commercial and economic regulatory measures increasingly are influential.

Acknowledgements

Financial support for the Swiss country case study was provided by the Swiss National Science Foundation (SNSF) through the Individual Project 4 of the NCCR North-South: Research Partnerships for Mitigating Syndromes of Global Change.

The Portuguese country case study was only possible with the contribution of Artur Vaz, António Correia de Campos and Ana Escoval.

Note

1 There is only the local health system of Matosinhos.

References

Arredondo, A. and Parada, I. (2001) Financing indicators for health care decentralisation in Latin America: information and suggestions for health planning. *International Journal of Health Planning and Management*, **16**: 259–76.

Bach, S. (2000) Decentralisation and privatisation in municipal services. The case of health services. International Labour Office, Sectoral Activities Programme. Working Paper No. 164. Geneva, International Labour Organization.

Bankauskaite, V., Saltman, R.B. and Vrangbæk, K. (2004). The role of decentralisation of European health care systems. Report to IPPR, London.

Benzeval, M., Judge, K. and Whitehead, M. (eds) (1995) *Tackling inequalities in health: an agenda for action*. London, King's Fund.

Bossert, T. and Beauvais, J.D. (2002) Decentralisation of health systems in Ghana, Zambia, Uganda and the Philippines: a comparative analysis of decision space. *Health Policy and Planning*, **17**(1): 14–31.

Burgermeister, J. (2004) Sweden bans privatisation of hospitals. *British Medical Journal*, **328**: 484.

Collins, C. (1989) Decentralisation and the need for political and critical analysis. *Health Policy and Planning*, **4**(2): 168–71.

Collins, C. and Green, A. (1994) Decentralisation and primary health care: some negative implications in developing countries. *International Journal of Health Services*, **24**: 459–75.

Culyer, A. (2001) Equity: some theory and its policy implications. *Journal of Medical Ethics*, **27**: 275–83.

Diderichsen, F. (1999) Devolution in Swedish health care. *British Medical Journal*, **318**: 1156–7.

Donatini, A., Rico, A., D'Ambrosio, M.G. et al. (2001) *Health care systems in transition: Italy*. Copenhagen, European Observatory on Health Care Systems.

European Commission (2001) *The internal market and health services: report of the High Level Committee on health*. 17 December. Brussels, European Commission.

European Commission (2003) *Green paper on services of general interest*. 21 May 2003. COM. Final. Brussels, European Commission.

European Commission (2004a) *Proposal for a Directive of the European Parliament and of the Council on Services in the Internal Market*. COM 2004.2. Final. 13 January 2004. Brussels, European Commission.

European Commission (2004b) *Modernising social protection for the development of high-quality, accessible and sustainable health care and long-term care: support for the national strategies using the "open method of coordination"*. COM 2003.304. Final. Brussels, European Commission.

Fidler, D. (2003) Legal review of the General Agreement on Trade in Services (GATS) from a health policy perspective. Draft Working Paper. Globalisation, Trade and Health Working Paper Series. Geneva, World Health Organisation.

Gilson, L. (1998) In defence and pursuit of equity. *Social Science and Medicine*, **47**(12): 1891–6.

Gomez, P.G. and Nicolas, A.L. (2004a) Regional differences in socio-economic health inequalities in Spain. CRES Working Paper No. 40. October 2004. Barcelona, CRES.

Gomez, P.G. and Nicolas, A.L. (2004b) The evolution of inequality in the access to health care in Spain: 1987–2001. CRES Working Paper No. 39. October 2004. Barcelona, CRES.

Hurley, J. (2001) Ethics, economics, and public financing of health care. *Journal of Medical Ethics*, **27**: 234–9.

IGIF (2004) *Relatório e contas do serviço nacional de saúde, Abril 2004*. Lisbon, Instituto de

Gestão Informática e Financeira da Saúde (Departamento de Consolidação e Controle de Gestão do Serviço Nacional de Saúde).

Jackson, P.M. and Price, C.M. (1994) *Privatisation and regulation: a review of the issues*. New York, Longman.

Kalland, M. (1996) *Hyvin leikattu – huonosti ommeltu: erityisryhmien palveluihin kohdistuneet säästöt valtionosuusuudistuksen jälkeen*. YTY Helsinki, Edita.

KELA (2001) *Cost and financing of health care in Finland, 1960–1999*. Helsinki, KELA (Social Insurance Institution of Finland).

Khaleghian, P. (2004) Decentralisation and public services: the case of immunization. *Social Science and Medicine*, **59**: 163–83.

Klein, R. (2003) The new localism: once more through the revolving door. *Journal of Health Services Research and Policy*, **8**(4): 19–20.

Koivusalo, M. and Ollila, E. (1997) *Making a healthy world: actors, agencies and policies in international health*. London, Zed Books.

Kolehmainen-Aitken, R. (1998) Decentralisation and human resources: implications and impact. *Human Resources for Health Development Journal*, **2**(1): 1–21.

Krajewski, M. (2003) Public services and trade liberalization: mapping the legal framework. *Journal of International Economic Law*, **6**(2): 341–67.

Litvack, J., Ahmad, J. and Bird, R. (1998) *Rethinking decentralisation in developing countries*. The World Bank Sector Studies Series, 21491. September 1998. Poverty Reduction and Economic Management. Washington, DC, World Bank.

López Casasnovas, G. (2002) *The development of new regional health policies and the need for coordination: the case of the pharmaceutical markets*. Barcelona, CRES.

López Casasnovas, G., Costa-Font, J. and Planas, I. (2004) Diversity and regional inequalities: Assessing the outcomes of the Spanish "system of health care services". CRES Working Paper 34. Barcelona, CRES. (http://www.econ.upf.edu/docs/papers/downloads/745.pdf, accessed 22 March 2005).

Luff, D. (2003) Regulation of health services and international trade law. In Mattoo, A. and Sauve, P., eds, *Domestic regulation and service trade liberalisation*. Washington, DC/Oxford, World Bank and Oxford University Press.

Mackenbach, J. and Bakker, M. (2002) *Reducing inequalities in health: a European perspective*. London, Routledge.

Mackenbach, J. and Bakker, M. (2003) Tackling socioeconomic inequalities in health: analysis of European experiences. *Lancet*, **362**: 1409–13.

Mackintosh, M. (2001) Do health care systems contribute to inequalities? In Leon, D. and Walt, G., eds, *Poverty, inequality and health: an international perspective*. Oxford, Oxford University Press.

Marmot, M. and Wilkinson, R. (1999) *Social determinants of health*. Oxford, Oxford University Press.

Mills, A. (1994) Decentralisation and accountability in the health sector from an international perspective: what are the choices? *Public Administration and Development*, **14**(3): 281–92.

Mills, A., Bennet, S. and Russel, S. (2001) *The challenge of health sector reform: what must governments do?* New York, Palgrave.

Ministry of Social Affairs and Health (2001) *Report on the use of state subsidy for child and adolescent psychiatry in the year 2000*. Helsinki, Ministry of Social Affairs and Health.

Ministry of Social Affairs and Health (2005) *Trends in social protection in Finland 2004*. Helsinki, Ministry of Social Affairs and Health.

Oliveira, M.D. and Bevan, G. (2003) Measuring geographic inequities in the Portuguese health care system: an estimation of hospital care needs. *Health Policy*, **66**(3): 277–93.

OPSS (2004) Relatório da Primavera 2004, ENSP/UNL. Lisbon, Observatório Português dos Sistemas de Saúde Portugueses (www.observaport.org, accessed 22 March 2005).

Pierson, P. (1994) *Dismantling the welfare state? Reagan, Thatcher and the politics of retrenchment*. Cambridge, Cambridge University Press.

Rice, N. and Smith, P.C. (2002) Ethics and geographical equity in health care. *Journal of Medical Ethics*, **27**: 256–61.

Rondinelli, D. and Nellis, J.R. (1986) Assessing decentralisation policies in developing countries: the case for cautious optimism. *Development Policy Review*, **4**: 3–23.

Saide, M.A.O. and Stewart, E. (2001) Decentralisation and human resource management in the health sector: a case study (1996–1998) from Nampula province, Mozambique. *International Journal of Health Planning and Management*, **16**: 155–68.

Santana, P. (2000) Ageing in Portugal: regional iniquities in health and health care. *Social Science and Medicine*, **50**: 1025–36.

Santana, P. (2002) Poverty, social exclusion and health. *Social Science and Medicine*, **55**: 132–45.

Santana, P. (2005) *Geografias da saúde e do desenvolvimento*. Coimbra, Almedina.

Santana, P., Vaz, A. and Fachada, M. (2003) Measuring health inequalities in Portugal in the 90s. Paper presented at International Conference Poverty, Food and Health in Welfare. Current issues, future perspectives, 1–4 July, Lisbon.

Sutton, M. and Lock, P. (2000) Regional differences in health care delivery: implications for a national resource allocation formula. *Health Economics*, **9**: 547–59.

Swiss Federal Office of Public Health (2002) *Migration und Gesundheit*. Bern: Bundesamt für Gesundheit (http://www.suchtundaids.bag.admin.ch/imperia/md/content/migration/ strategie/4.pdf, accessed 16 April 2006).

Tang, S. and Bloom, G. (2000) Decentralising rural health services: a case study in China. *International Journal of Health Planning and Management*, **15**: 189–200.

Taroni, F. (2003) Restructuring health services in Italy: the paradox of devolution. In Sen, K., ed., *Restructuring health services: changing contexts and comparative perspectives*. London, Zed Books.

Tranquada, S., Martins, M. and Sousa, M. (2000) Critérios de financiamento dos cuidados de saúde primários: O exemplo Português. Paper presented at VII Encontro Nacional de Economia da Saúde, Lisbon, 16, 17 November.

Vinuela, J. (2000) *Fiscal decentralisation in Spain*. Washington, DC, International Monetary Fund (http://www.imf.org/external/pubs/ft/seminar/2000/fiscal/vinuela.pdf, accessed 22 March 2005).

Wagstaff, A. and Van Doorslaer, E. (1993) Equity in the finance and delivery of health care: concepts and definitions. In van Doorslaer, E., Wagstaff, A. and Rutten, F., eds, *Equity in the finance and delivery of health care: an international perspective*. European Community Health Services Research Series No. 8. Oxford, Oxford University Press.

Whitehead, M. (1998) Diffusion of ideas on social inequalities in health: a European perspective. *The Millbank Quarterly*, **76**(3): 469–92.

Wilensky, H.L. (1975) *The welfare state and equality*. Berkeley, CA, University of California Press.

Wyss, K. and Lorenz, N. (2000) Decentralisation and central and regional coordination of health services: the case of Switzerland. *International Journal of Health Planning and Management*, **15**(2): 103–14.

Ylikylä-Leiva, H. (2003) *Sosiaali-ja terveydenhuollon asiakkaan oikeudellisesta asemasta: selvitys asiakkaan kohtaamista oikeudellisista ongelmista ensiasteen päätöksenteossa*. Helsinki, Edita.

chapter twelve

Information strategies for decentralization

Peter C. Smith and Unto Häkkinen

Introduction

Comparative information is a resource that is crucial to any health system. It has three broad roles: (1) to help determine whether specific organizations and individuals are operating as efficiently and effectively as possible; (2) to help identify which processes in general lead to good performance; and (3) to serve as a means of communication between citizens, politicians and actors in the health system. These can be thought of as respectively the managerial, research and accountability roles of information.

In its managerial role, information can help draw attention to aspects of local health systems that are performing poorly, and offer targets for improvement and exemplars, in the form of "beacon" organizations. The emerging practice of benchmarking offers an important example of the intelligent use of comparative information, in which managers are given the opportunity to explore reasons for variations in performance and mechanisms to improve it.

While the managerial interest in information is to explore the relative performance of *specific* organizations or individuals, the research interest is in determining *general* patterns of organization or activity that give rise to improvement. This requires an adequate number of observations, measured on a consistent basis, to be able to draw secure statistical inferences about "what works". Research findings are essential for policy-makers considering health system reform, and local practitioners seeking to redesign local organizations.

In its accountability role, information has a central role to play in informing the choices of voters, politicians and patients. Comparative information can help voters assess the quality of the stewardship of their health systems at both a local and national level. Where some sort of market mechanism exists, it can help patients exercise informed choice of provider. It can also help national policy-makers to pursue national objectives, such as "fair" financing of localities or reducing disparities in health and health care.

Although there is considerable scope for overlap in these three roles, they are in principle quite distinct.[1] Information systems are intimately related to the state regulation function and decentralization, and can have a profound impact on system effectiveness. Consideration of their multiple roles of information has particular relevance to countries that are changing from steering and management based on resources and standards towards "softer regulation" or "information guidance" of the system. The success of such reforms relies on the assumption that the provision of information to local governments, producers and professionals will support constructive behavioural or system change.

Information can take many forms, ranging from anecdotal "soft" intelligence, to "hard" quantitative tabulations. Furthermore, our concept of information extends well beyond the notion of raw data, to embrace methods of data synthesis (such as statistical analysis), and methods of dissemination (such as public reports of comparative performance). As noted below, information can serve numerous diverse constituencies, with widely varying preoccupations and analytic capacity. Modes of presentation can therefore be crucial to its impact. The revolution in information technology has led to an explosion in the potential for assembling and disseminating data, and its importance within the health system is increasing markedly. In our view, appropriate deployment of information systems is therefore a crucial element in promoting efficiency and effectiveness.

Hurley et al. (1995) offer a useful discussion of the role of information in a decentralized health system, and distinguish between what might be termed technical information (for example, on the effectiveness of health technologies), value-based information (for example, on local preferences), and contingent information (such as local provider cost structures). Much of the theoretical literature makes use of this distinction. A crucial advantage enjoyed by localities in any health system is that they can in principle incorporate soft, tacit knowledge into local decisions. By its nature, such knowledge cannot be codified or transmitted systematically to other institutions. From the point of view of this chapter, a key decision is: how much freedom are localities to be allowed in using this tacit knowledge? The extent of decentralization will to a large extent determine this freedom.

Indeed, one possible measure of decentralization could be the number of regulatory instructions passed from the centre to localities. In highly decentralized systems, the number of such instruments is very low, in the extreme amounting to no more than a choice of levels of financing. In highly centralized systems, there will, in contrast, be a plethora of central attempts to influence local decisions. However, although decentralization reduces the need to communicate from centre to locality, it will paradoxically be the case that the centre requires a wide range of high quality comparative data in order to make good regulatory decisions. And localities will similarly need such data to support their local decisions. This chapter explores the links between information strategy and decentralization.

The first section discusses the numerous users of information, and how it can affect their decisions. The next section examines from a mainly theoretical perspective the implications of a given information structure for decentralization policy. Conversely, the next section examines the implications of a given decentralization structure for information policy. Practical approaches are discussed in the last section, and then some conclusions are drawn.

Information users

Crucial to any discussion of health system information is its intended audience. Numerous potential consumers of information can be identified:

- Managers within the health system require information for many purposes, such as ensuring that their own resources are deployed efficiently, and that they negotiate effective contracts with outside providers.
- Clinicians and other health care personnel require information as a central resource for peer review and personal improvement.
- Public health authorities and researchers cannot function effectively without access to wide-ranging, timely, high quality information. Frequently this will be population-level data, not directly related to health care.
- The general public funds the health system, and expects to receive reports about the use to which its contributions are being put. All citizens are potential users of the system, and therefore require assurance that as a whole it is operating effectively.
- Patients are citizens with specific health needs. They require information about the range and effectiveness of services available for them, especially when they can exercise some degree of choice as to provider. The notion of the "expert patient" is gaining importance, implying an important new information requirement. In the future, the electronic health record may become a crucial resource for patients.
- Patient advocacy groups often play a central role in seeking out and interpreting information.
- The media have a role to play in seeking out, synthesizing and explaining information about local health services.
- Politicians are intimately concerned with the operation of the health system in their stewardship role, especially when national or local governments are directly responsible for running the health system. Information is a key resource for them in securing and promoting accountability and probity.
- Regulators, inspectorates and legal authorities, acting on behalf of many of the above, are often among the most skilled and intensive users of information.

The information needs of these diverse users vary markedly. We briefly discuss their use of information under the three broad headings noted above: managerial, research and accountability.

Information for management

Management is crucial to the internal operations of the health system and comprises two very broad roles: *prospective*, in the form of allocating resources and putting in place associated regulatory instruments; and *retrospective*, through verifying that those resources are used to good effect, and correcting inefficiencies. Thus, a wide range of personnel perform managerial functions within the health system. For example, the term manager might embrace national leaders, hospital chief executives, departmental heads, team leaders, and ward managers. The definition therefore covers a wide range of professional backgrounds, extending well beyond the notion of a professional manager, to include any clinician with significant control over health system resources.

In allocating resources, managers need information on the expenditure needs and effectiveness of the relevant functions, on the appropriate mix of personnel and other inputs, and on special circumstances that warrant a departure from usual practice. They also need verifiable measurement instruments that can act as the basis for targets, contracts and incentive mechanisms. Both time series and comparison with other institutions will form the basis of much quantifiable information. It will often be supplemented by local qualitative information. Clearly the information required for making effective decisions increases with the level of autonomy enjoyed by the manager. Therefore, one might expect to see higher demand for detailed local information in more decentralized systems.

Information for research

The research role seeks to identify "what works" in the health system. This role ranges from qualitative narratives on how best to introduce reforms, to quantitative information on the cost-effectiveness of drugs. The essence of the research role is the dissemination of evidence that is generically useful and transferable between institutions. In its purest form, research evidence is a classic "public good", in the sense that – once created – it is available to all, and an extra user of the evidence imposes no additional cost on the health system. As a result, institutions have an incentive to free-ride on the research undertaken by others. It must therefore often be provided at some collective level, through mediums such as a national government's research programme, or a collective benchmarking club.

Users of research information include national regulators seeking to disseminate best practice, hospital and departmental managers seeking to identify best practice, professionals interested in continuous improvement, and patients wanting to know the implications of different treatment options. These research needs should not change markedly with decentralization. However, the potential for free-riding, and therefore under-provision of research, becomes much more evident in decentralized systems, and so some element of collective funding must usually be arranged. Much research takes the form of identifying best clinical practice, which is likely to be valued by professionals and patients throughout the entire health system. A key task is then to identify effective dissemination methods, for example, in the form of clinical guidelines. However, it may be the case that some disagreements about research priorities become evident under decentralization – for example, regions with long waiting times may have different priorities to those (say) with chronic labour shortages.

Furthermore, detailed scrutiny may carry the potential for embarrassment for some devolved institutions, causing them to wish to discourage research in that domain. An agreed mechanism for establishing research priorities and dissemination rules therefore becomes another requirement in a decentralized system.

An important requirement of research information is that it conforms to appropriate levels of scientific quality, for example, in the form of common data definitions, adequate sample sizes, high ethical standards and best statistical practice. This requires a national coordination function. For example, the definitions and classifications used in registers should be the same all over the country. If research is based on linking registers, patient confidentiality and data security should be ensured, often requiring regulation by central government

Information for accountability

The essence of the accountability role of information is that it is directed at users who are external to the organization under scrutiny. These might be regulators auditing the performance of entire hospitals, professional bodies scrutinizing the performance of members, citizens or their elected representatives challenging the performance of their executives, or patients checking the performance of their providers. In order to illustrate the challenges for information policy, Figure 12.1 shows some of the more important accountability relationships that exist in most health care systems. An arrow indicates where an agent (say, a clinician) is responsible to a principal (say, a patient), and so an accountability relationship exists. A crucial role of information is to serve that relationship, by enabling the principal to render an account, and the agent to hold the principal to account.

Clearly not all the relationships shown in Figure 12.1 are important in all health systems, for example, the notion of "insurer" is synonymous with government in many health systems. Moreover, the demand for accountability information depends heavily on the nature of the sanctions available to the

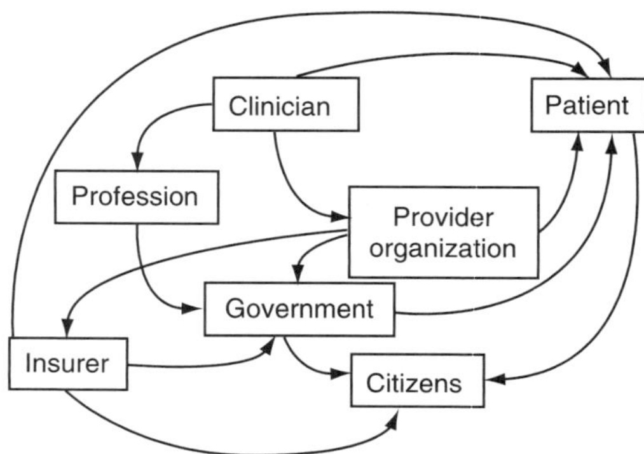

Figure 12.1 Some accountability relationships in health care

principal, in the form (say) of regulatory powers (for a government), professional accreditation (for the profession), voting (for the citizen), or choice of provider (for the patient). However, only when accountability information is aligned with the associated sanctions can it be used to best effect.

In a decentralized system, the requirements for accountability purposes also depend heavily on the precise institutional arrangements. If local government plays a major role in the decentralized structure, provision of relevant, timely information for voters on the general governance of their health care providers is one important requirement. In contrast, if the decentralization focuses mainly on patient empowerment and choice, then the emphasis may shift towards more detailed comparative information of direct use to patients. The media have an important role to play is disseminating and commenting on accountability information. And there is usually an important need for independent scrutiny and audit of accountability information.

The feature common to the diverse users and their information needs is a desire to compare performance across institutions or individual practitioners. The central theme of this chapter is that information weaknesses in this respect may be a key impediment to effective decentralization, and that cost-effective provision of appropriate information is therefore an important goal for policy-makers. Under decentralization, high quality comparative information acts as an important instrument for communication between localities and the centre (which has a continuing regulatory responsibility even under extreme decentralization). It helps the centre formulate policies necessarily coordinated at a national level, such as distributing central grants-in-aid, clinical education, public health, research and tackling disparities. Good comparative data also provide a crucial resource for decision-making by local managers and clinicians, which might otherwise be undertaken in isolation. It similarly helps shape the expectations and choices of individual voters and patients. We argue that the coordination of these information needs is a crucial function under decentralization, and it is on this issue that we shall focus.

Given the diverse constituency of accountability relationships and information users in health care, there are likely to be quite different needs regarding the level of detail, timeliness, mode of presentation and disaggregation of the data. At one extreme, a voter considering the performance of a national government may require only a very general national report on its stewardship of the health system, which documents year-on-year changes and international comparisons in a small number of key domains. At the other extreme, an individual patient may require very detailed information on the performance of specific physicians in relation to a particular condition, perhaps adjusted for case complexity, and taking proper account of uncertainty.

In many respects, the information needs of all constituencies are nevertheless complementary. For example, a good electronic patient record system should – as a low cost by-product of patient care – yield an enormous amount of information on system effectiveness that can be presented at a level of aggregation that is appropriate to the user's needs (see, for example, the Ontario Hospital Reports Project at http://wwwhospitalreport.ca). In a similar way, the US National Resident Assessment Instrument for Nursing Homes can be used at many levels, starting at the patient level to evaluate the needs and quality of care of individual patients, up to progressively more general benchmarking at ward, institution and regional levels (Morris et al. 1990). This approach has been piloted in Finland with very promising results (Noro et al. 2001).

However, there are also tensions between users in the priorities attached to different types of information, and some parties may wish to suppress certain types of information. For example, there are very strong accountability arguments for publicly releasing data on provider performance. Yet providers are often lukewarm about such public disclosure, and there is evidence that it can distort either provider behaviour or information sources, to the extent that disclosure may act against the interests of patients (Dranove et al. 2002). Under decentralization, the presumption of local autonomy may make the resolution of tensions between information users more complex than under central authority, and – because of its public good characteristic – there are likely to be persistent pressures to reduce the budget assigned to information resources.

Moreover, decentralization may in itself change the priorities within an information strategy. In general, we would hypothesize that increased decentralization will lead to more information needs, of higher quality, because of the increased diversity of the health system and the increased reliance on formal regulatory instruments. For example, decentralization encourages diversity, but the learning benefits of the associated experimentation may be lost if adequate data to evaluate the experiments, perhaps in the form of health technology assessments, are not collected. Also, decentralization may place greater emphasis on the accuracy and timeliness of a small number of regulatory instruments. The information underpinning these instruments may need to be of higher quality than under less formal bureaucratic control. Decentralization may also be associated with a greater use of explicit and legally binding contracts, and the associated information base on patient numbers, diagnoses and costs may therefore have to be strengthened.

The questions of concern for this chapter are first whether the nature of the existing (or potential) information structure should materially affect decentralization policy, and second, whether decentralization policy should materially affect information content and collection methods. These questions are given detailed consideration in the next two sections. In general terms, we argue that policies on decentralization and information are inextricably linked, and should be considered jointly rather than independently.

Implications of information structure for decentralization

Much research in public economics has focused on the role of information in determining the optimal level and nature of decentralization of public services (Oates 1999). In particular, formal analysis of the implications of the informational advantage enjoyed by localities for local demand and supply of public goods is beginning to emerge. In many respects, this literature implies that the extent and nature of information availability should drive decentralization policy, rather than vice versa. Although apparently remote from the messy reality of designing operational information systems, theoretical analyses of this sort emphasize the crucial role of information asymmetry in determining the optimal structure of health system governance.

Underlying the literature is the presumption that remote national governments cannot understand all the preferences, opportunities and constraints that affect the supply of local services, and localities cannot transmit that information to the centre. Therefore, a central authority may seek to impose managerial solutions that are inappropriate for local circumstances, and strike poor bargains with providers.

The decentralization literature mirrors parallel developments in the theory of industrial organization that seeks to assess the relative virtues of central and delegated decision-making in a firm. In a typical example, Melumad et al. (1997) show that the local freedom implicit in delegation entails an agency cost to the central authority, but this may be outweighed by allowing decisions to be more sensitive to the local manager's private information. Note that such models generally presume that the central authority's objectives are in some sense more legitimate than that of the devolved entity. This is of course questionable in the context of central-local governmental relations, and so associated results from the literature should be viewed with some caution.

In a governmental context, Gilbert and Picard (1996) assume that central governments are less well informed than local government about two crucial aspects of local services: local production costs and local preferences. They argue that – if central government had full information on production costs – then full centralization is optimal, while the reverse is the case if the central government had full information on local preferences (including the values attached to spillovers). Ambiguity arises when (as is usually the case) there is imperfect information on both costs and preferences. If information on costs improves, then the scope for exploitation by local providers decreases, so central government is in a good position to exercise its prime role of accommodating spillover effects. If, on the other hand, information on costs is poor (or spillovers are not important), then decentralization is preferred because local governments have better knowledge about the efficiency of local providers. In the same vein, decentralization may help the local coordination of services, particularly when the same local organization is responsible for a wide range of services such as primary and secondary health care, care of the elderly and personal social services.

One of the concerns often expressed in relation to decentralization is that it increases the probability of collusion between local purchasers and providers. This risk is especially important in health care, where there is an ever-present danger of local purchasers being "captured" by powerful providers. Laffont (2000) presents a model in which the centre has bounded rationality in capturing and processing information about localities. The information requirements of effective centralization are therefore costly or even impossible, and the informational advantages of delegation have to be weighed against the potential efficiency costs of collusion. The policy prescription depends on the relative importance of these two considerations.

Economic models often presume that the delegated authority is more vulnerable to provider capture than a central government. Bardhan and Mookherjee (2003) note that there are reasons to justify this claim, particularly arising from information asymmetry. However, they argue that there are also a number of factors that may create the opposite tendency for lower capture at the local level, most notably the increased costs and uncertainty associated with seeking to capture dispersed institutions. Oates (1999) notes that – in dispersing power and influence – decentralization can reduce the scope for government corruption. By introducing an element of inter-jurisdictional competition, the provision of reliable, validated comparative information can reinforce the resistance of decentralized systems to provider capture.

Implications of decentralization for information structure

Increased decentralization implies the use of a lower number of regulatory tools by the central authority. In the extreme, a health care regulator may resort merely to making a financial contribution to localities and leaving all other finance and policy matters to local choice. Yet in practice there will always be a need for regulatory supervision, even in highly decentralized systems. However extreme the decentralization, the centre will need to ensure that its regulatory decisions are based on good quality information. Part of the *quid pro quo* of decentralization should therefore be that the devolved entities are required to provide good quality information so that the centre can make fair, well-informed regulatory decisions.

Under decentralization, a heavy burden might be placed on a small number of instruments (such as financial allocations or minimum standards). If a central authority forces localities to provide information that cannot be independently verified to act as a basis for regulation, there is a danger that the information can be distorted, or that the locality misrepresents its true state of affairs. In particular, there may be an incentive for local purchasers and providers to mislead the centre about local spending needs. Localities might have an incentive to act strategically in an effort to secure more than their fair share of central resources, for example, by blaming high spending on high local needs rather than inefficiency.

For example, Levaggi and Smith (1994) model the case in which the locality increases its spending beyond its preferred level in order to attract higher government grant. Barrow (1986) shows how the competition between jurisdictions for a fixed central grant can induce spending in excess of efficient levels. Besley and Coate (2003) present a model of political economy in which localities have an incentive to overstate their spending needs. A policy implication of such results is that improved specification and audit of centrally collected information can reduce the scope for manipulation and – by enabling a central regulator to act fairly – can help support effective decentralization.

Comparative data are needed not only for central regulatory purposes. They also serve as a vital resource for local use, in the form of managerial benchmarking and public accountability. Economists have developed the notion of "yardstick competition" to describe the role of performance information in decentralized setting (Shleifer 1985). Through the process now usually known as benchmarking, devolved institutions can explore which of their peers are performing best, and seek out detailed qualitative and quantitative information on the context and processes contributing to good performance (Wait 2004). It can also help local managers set targets and rewards, and local electorates pass judgement on their local governments.

Furthermore, one of the putative benefits of decentralization is the innovation that it encourages. Local jurisdictions are free to experiment, say, with different modes of service delivery (Hurley et al. 1995). Yet the benefits of such natural experiments are seriously compromised if the comparative data necessary to evaluate them are absent. For example, since the devolution of responsibility for the health system to the countries of the United Kingdom, there have been several major divergences between England and Wales in the organization and delivery of health services. In principle, these natural experiments offer a rich source of comparative experience from which to infer "what works". In practice, a shortage of directly comparable data seriously reduces the ability to draw any meaningful inferences.

An example of the crucial importance assigned to comparative information in a regulated (as opposed to competitive) environment is the investigation of the UK Monopolies and Mergers Commission of the proposed merger of two of the ten major UK water companies. The proposed merger was rejected not on the direct grounds of reduced competition, but on the grounds that the reduction from ten to nine in the number of observed water companies represented a significant diminution of comparative performance data (Monopolies and Mergers Commission 1996). In other words, the comparative information secured from the ten water companies was too valuable a resource to dilute by allowing a merger.

Furthermore, because of its public good characteristics, there is a tendency for information to be underprovided in the absence of active cooperation or government intervention. In short, under decentralization, local organizations (such as health care providers or local jurisdictions) will be reluctant to provide as much information as society would ideally require because they are unable to recoup the full costs of data provision from potential users. There is therefore a compelling case for central intervention to optimize the provision of information. Although there are circumstances in which collaboration and consensus can be secured among all jurisdictions, it will usually be the case that only a central authority can specify and mandate the collection of the comparative data needed for informed decision-making at the local level.

The specification and coordination of information requirements are thus preeminently a national role. Whatever the level of decentralization in the health care system, it is difficult to envisage how the full benefits of information provision can be secured without a central coordination function. This role is taken for granted in many other fields of economic endeavour. Most especially, all governments in developed countries have centrally prescribed annual reporting requirements for private businesses. There are many serious debates about the best form of corporate reporting, and compliance costs are often large. However, the benefits of such reporting, in terms of accountability, probity and efficiency are manifest and rarely challenged. Whether this legitimate national role should be undertaken by a national *government* (rather than some independent agency) is a matter for debate that we consider later in the chapter.

Finally, it is important to keep in mind that, notwithstanding the need for central specification of information needs, an important rationale for decentralizing authority is that there exist important elements of the information base that are available only at a local level. For example, hospital managers often have to take realistic account of the personalities, skills and leadership qualities of their senior hospital physicians. By definition, these sorts of characteristics cannot be transmitted to the centre in a meaningful or efficient manner. Yet this softer, more contextual intelligence is vital to informing effective local decisions. Therefore, alongside centrally codified comparative data (which is largely quantitative), local managers will always need local intelligence (which is largely qualitative) if they are to secure the full benefits of decentralization.

Information strategies in practice

In the light of this discussion, it is not surprising that many health systems are seeking simultaneously to decentralize and to develop robust comparative information systems, both to enhance central regulation and to support local decision-making. Some national information strategies have been frankly opportunistic, seeking merely to assemble readily accessible data, often by-products of existing instruments, such as the financial reimbursement system. It is of course helpful to maximize the effectiveness of existing data resources. However, an increasing number of countries are seeking to develop a coherent conceptual framework within which future information collection, analysis and dissemination can be undertaken.

An example is the Canadian health indicator framework, which classifies information under four broad domains: (1) health status; (2) non-medical determinants of health; (3) health system performance; and (4) community and health system characteristics. The health system performance indicators are further divided into eight categories: acceptability, accessibility, appropriateness, competence, continuity, effectiveness, efficiency and safety. Both levels of performance and equity (distributional of performance within the population) are considered (Canadian Institute for Health Information 2003). Australia, the Netherlands and the United Kingdom have developed analogous frameworks. Although these are often intellectually coherent and comprehensive, there remain large data gaps. The enormity of the task of populating such frameworks with operational performance measures is evident once one considers the diverse areas of endeavour comprising the modern health system, and the difficulty of measuring many concepts of outcome.

The development of a conceptual framework is necessarily a "top-down", centralized approach to informing the design of a national information system to support decentralization. An alternative, "bottom-up" approach relies on individual professionals and provider organizations engaging in quality improvement initiatives. This has been a traditional feature of systems such as Sweden and the Netherlands (Rehnqvist 2002). Micro-level comparative data on clinical actions and outcomes are an essential element of such approaches, but the precise definition, collection and scrutiny of the data are left to professional groups to determine.

For example, Sweden has developed a set of voluntary "quality registers" for individual interventions. The aim of these is to disseminate good medical practice, to provide comparative performance data and to secure continuous quality improvement (Rehnqvist 2002). Each register is based on a clinical speciality and managed by a group based in one of the university hospitals. There are about 50 registers – examples include the cataract surgery register (covering 95% of all cataract surgery) and the hip arthroplasty register (the first register, initiated in 1979, which now covers 100% of hip replacements). The usual model is that a national register develops gradually from a local initiative. Funding is provided by the National Board for Health and Welfare and local government and medical organizations. About 70% of eligible clinicians participate in each register, and participants meet regularly to discuss comparative results aggregated to departments in participating institutions. The data collected vary from register to register, but might include patient data on diagnosis, treatment, patient experience and outcomes (Federation of Swedish County Councils 2000).

In our view, neither top-down nor bottom-up approach can be considered a panacea. The top-down philosophy ignores often profound differences in preoccupation between different specialities, and has great difficulty in providing useful information for patients or professionals interested in a specific condition. It also reduces the motivation for data collection if there is no direct feedback in terms of comparative (benchmarking) data. In contrast, the bottom-up approach provides valuable managerial and research information, and engages more successfully with patients and professionals, but does not necessarily answer concerns of accountability or ensure that all providers are properly scrutinized.

An example of a mixture of both approaches is a hospital benchmarking project in Finland, which is a collaboration between researchers at Stakes and hospitals (Järvelin et al. 2003). It uses a patient-level national register of discharges (for all somatic inpatient and outpatient admissions), costs data and mortality data as an outcome indicator. To measure output, a new measurement unit was developed. It is called the "care episode". An episode consists of all the admissions and outpatient visits for a patient due to one and the same illness. The indicators that are used to measure productivity can be assessed from two different viewpoints and at different levels: from the provider's viewpoint at the hospital level, speciality and patient group (diagnostic related groups level) and from the regional viewpoint at hospital-district and municipality levels. This permits, for example, the comparison of productivity in different hospitals and specialities disaggregated to comparison of episodes on each DRG group using indicators such as hospital admissions per episode, outpatient visits per episode, bed days per episode, and cost per episode.

In comparisons at the hospital-district or municipal level, the care episodes may cross over hospital and hospital-district boundaries, i.e. the episode is not restricted to any single provider. The regional measurement gives information on how much a hospital district's or a municipality's costs deviate from the national average, and on how much of this deviation depends on the inefficient delivery of services and the per capita use of services. Also this information can be disaggregated to patient group level. In addition, for some patient groups, outcome indicators have been developed. For example, acute myocardial infarction

(AMI) patients are followed one year with respect to costs, use of services and procedures (CABG, PTCA) and mortality.

More generally, the Nordic countries offer particularly good opportunities for constructing performance indicators based on utilization, cost and outcome of service, since each person has a unique identity designation (the personal identification number). Since registers cover the whole country, each individual can be followed over time. However, there are differences between the countries in the strategy of development of registers, which is partly related to the supervision role of central government. In Sweden, the National Board of Health and Welfare supervises, monitors and evaluates developments in all areas of social policy. The supervision focuses mainly on three areas: strict patient safety, patient's rights, and the care quality system.

In contrast, in Finland, there is no such national supervisory role, with the consequence that use of quality registers is not so developed. As a result, there exist many regional and local registers that are not coordinated, with a consequent loss of informational power. More generally the concern in Finland is that the quality of the national registers is not good. Historically, the motivation for collecting (top-down) data for national registers has been low, and has increased only gradually as the data have been used for benchmarking. This also underlines why the development of information systems should be done in close mutual cooperation with producers of services.

Modern IT developments offer huge possibilities for developing information systems. The electronic health record (EHR) is in many respects the cornerstone of real, effective decentralization. Most importantly, it has the potential to greatly improve the quality of patient care, and should ensure that patients can exercise choice of provider, but still secure continuity of care. However, it also carries the potential for great efficiency improvements and offers numerous other informational benefits in the managerial, research and accountability domains. We would argue that – while the patient focus must be the primary concern when developing the EHR – its broader potential for supporting decentralization should be an intrinsic part of the development programme. Some glimpses of the potential benefits can be seen from the quality improvements secured by the US Veterans' Health Administration through implementation of a rudimentary electronic record that can be shared across its institutions (Jha et al. 2003). However, there remain numerous technical questions to be resolved in the development of an effective EHR, and its implementation runs high risks of cost inflation and complex ethical concerns.

In Finland, the guiding principle is to gather performance data from the emerging electronic client and patient systems, which are increasingly available in the social and health care facilities. It is suggested that data gathering into national registers should be continuous and based on protected electronic on-line data collection. This reform is scheduled for 2010, as improved data security and changes in legislation may be needed before this kind of comprehensive reform can be undertaken. In the same vein, the British National Health Service is implementing an ambitious, centrally coordinated electronic health record, in contrast to its previous (failed) philosophy of encouraging local IT innovation.

The traditionally centralized health care systems of eastern Europe have an especially great challenge in decentralizing their health care systems and information resources. Although many CEE countries adopted Bismarckian health insurance with multiple insurers, in many cases, the centralized norms of the previous health care delivery system prevailed, making decentralized, independent decision-making difficult. In particular, the top-down manual statistical data collection systems have often survived. That system guaranteed standardized and comprehensive data in most CEE countries. However, the lack of computerization has led to continued high costs of data collection and poor data quality, while analytical capacity is often poor.

Gradually local involvement in health care provision and financing in eastern European countries is increasing and decentralization is gathering pace. However, the pressure to decentralize may perversely lead to a major new problem: there is little understanding of the important role of the central authorities in creating a uniform standard of content and quality for the emerging computerized information systems in health care. There is little evidence of the development of national information strategies, so the full benefits of computerization are unlikely to be secured.

The experience to date raises the question of who should take responsibility for information strategy, and how the different needs of users should be resolved. Much must depend on the institutions already in place within the health system. We have argued in loose terms that much of information strategy is a national function, but there is no reason why this should be a governmental responsibility. Nations with strong coordinating mechanisms within local government may take advantage of those institutional arrangements. Likewise, nations with strong presumptions against national government intervention may seek to put in place autonomous agencies to undertake the coordination function. Obviously the governance and accountability of such institutions is a key issue to be resolved. Whatever the institutional details, there will be a need to give resources and authority to the institution adequate to coordinate a system-wide information strategy.

The precise functions covered by the strategy should probably at a minimum include the nature and scope of mandatory data collection, who should collect the information, at what level of aggregation it is to be reported, arrangements for analysing and disseminating the information, links with quality improvement agencies, ethical policy, policy on public release, research priorities, mechanisms for evaluating and updating the strategy, and arrangements for audit and inspection. Furthermore, it is almost certainly the case that the specification of a core national EHR should form part of the strategy. Of course, none of this framework precludes voluntary collaboration between local agencies or professionals on additional information resources. The national strategy should refer merely to the mandatory core.

A discussion of information strategy raises the broader issue of the appropriate regulatory regime to apply to the health system. Ideally, one would want to introduce the most cost-effective regulatory structure, given the chosen type of health system. This would include arrangements for financing, setting minimum standards, assuring safety, audit and inspection, governance, lines of accountability and accreditation. This is clearly an enormous topic, well beyond the scope of this chapter (see e.g. Chapters 2 and 4). But, in principle, system design requires an overall view of the appropriate regulatory regime, of which decentralization policy and information policy form just a part.

Discussion

Comparative information has three broad, overlapping roles: managerial, research and accountability. These roles are important, whatever the level of decentralization. However, we have sought to demonstrate that health system decentralization offers special challenges for information strategy, particularly in the domains of regulation and management. The motivation for decentralization is to bring the organization and control of the health system closer to local people, and to take advantage of local intelligence. It might therefore suggest local freedom to choose what information should be collected and how it should be disseminated. Yet paradoxically a great deal of clinical performance, management and democratic debate within those localities requires high quality comparative information to function effectively. Failure to provide such information can be a serious negative effect of poorly managed decentralization. Therefore, along with decentralization of service organization and democratic control, there is a clear need for central coordination of information resources.

In the managerial domain, local managers need good quality comparative information to complement softer local intelligence when making their local resource allocation decisions. Local managers are the crucial interface between central regulatory decisions and local clinical decisions. They need to ensure that local decisions are sensitive to local preferences and constraints, but equally need to ensure that their providers are performing in line with their peers elsewhere, and respecting national regulations. In the research domain, comparative information can serve many purposes, such as health technology assessment, informing central regulatory decisions, evaluating local innovations, and understanding the causes of variations in outcomes. In the accountability domain, information in many comparative formats serves the many principal–agent relationships that exist in the health system.

We have argued that comparative information is a public good, and there is therefore likely to be a need for central coordination and mandatory provision if it is to be deployed in the most cost-effective fashion. In the context of decentralization, important specific purposes of such coordination are: (1) to support central regulatory decisions retained by the centre; (2) to support local decision-making; (3) to facilitate evaluation of local innovations; and (4) to enable citizens to pass informed judgement on local services.

In practice, the central specification of information requirements by a national government might be interpreted as an expression of power in its relationship with localities. There is therefore a case for delegating such specification to an organization independent of government. The precise content, specification and presentation of the information system will implicitly incorporate value judgements about what is important, with implications for the nature of democratic and managerial actions within localities. In short, what gets measured gets done, so care may be needed to ensure that data specification does not become a proxy for expression of undue influence on local choice. Moreover, IT capabilities, clinical practice and popular preoccupations change over time, so it will be important to ensure that the information system adapts to embrace new circumstances. Instigating a mechanism for accommodating these considerations is likely to be a major challenge.

Now that many systems have in place embryonic health information systems, attention is increasingly turning to the interpretation of data, in the form of the epidemiological, statistical and economic analysis. This often takes the form of some sort of risk adjustment that seeks to take account of variations in the environments in which providers or health systems must operate, variations in case mix and variations in resources. This is often a contentious and technically complex endeavour. Although there are manifest benefits for this to be a national function, it is probably best undertaken by an agency independent of any government. Canada (in the form of CIHI) has made the analysis function a particularly high priority.

More generally, a central issue in information policy is that data should be accurate and trusted. In a decentralized setting, information often serves as a fundamental resource for determining financial transfers, promoting comparison and accountability, and informing the decisions of patients, voters and other stakeholders. Yet many health system data are vulnerable to distortion and manipulation, and therefore an important issue is how to assure their credibility.

For example, reliable data are essential for calculating financial transfers between insurers or regions. Such transfers are central to the pursuit of establishing equity between payers, and therefore making operational the principle of national solidarity. If their reliability is called into question, then public and political trust in the fairness of the system may be undermined, threatening the viability of a decentralized health system. Indeed, one could argue that solidarity and decentralization are feasible only when comprehensive and trusted information sources are put in place. In the same way, payers will want to be assured that the data used to reimburse providers (such as DRG coding) are trustworthy.

In Europe, the issue of data integrity is most urgent in the health systems of eastern Europe, where there has been widespread politicization of data sources and lack of public trust. However, these problems are also present in many countries of western Europe seeking to reform their health systems. For example, in England, quarterly waiting time data have until recently been collected from hospitals for many decades without a great deal of public scrutiny or interest. However, since the national government set itself targets of dramatic reductions in waiting times in 2000, they have come under intense scrutiny, and a great deal of media and public scepticism about their veracity has developed. Thus, even if the system is improving in line with government intentions, it is becoming increasingly difficult to convince the public that this is the case.

There are therefore strong arguments for putting in place a reliable system of independent data audit. For example, in England, the independent Audit Commission has produced a series of influential reports on the reliability of health system data (Audit Commission 2004). This function becomes increasingly important as the health system becomes more decentralized, as financial flows become increasingly reliant on mechanistic reimbursement rules. Also in the United Kingdom, a commercial information provider known as Doctor Foster has established a market for detailed comparative information on health care providers. This is aimed at satisfying the needs of patients choosing providers, and is widely supported by patients' groups because of its perceived independence from government (web site at http://www.drfoster.co.uk/).

The experience outlined above indicates that – although most OECD nations acknowledge the need for an information strategy – they are at different stages of development and implementation, and little attention has been paid specifically to the crucial link between decentralization and information requirements. Several nations have sought to develop conceptual frameworks within which the performance measurement function must operate. The development of such frameworks reflects a top-down philosophy of seeking to impose some conceptual order on a complex system, and is likely to be appropriate for ensuring that the health system is clearly defined; that its objectives are made explicit; that data systems are developed with a clear rationale; and that under-measured aspects of the health system are not ignored. Under decentralization, it can serve as an important mechanism for agreeing uniform data standards.

However, we have highlighted the tensions between such "top-down" overarching frameworks and the more developmental, professionally led "bottom-up" approach to information systems. Our view is that both principles should be applied to information strategies. A top-down approach is needed to ensure that relevant aspects of system behaviour are measured on a comprehensive and uniform basis. It is particularly relevant to strategic decisions, such as voter choices, regulator choices, and managerial purchasing decisions. However, it is unlikely to be useful for detailed support of clinical processes. In contrast, the bottom-up approach is required where the data have direct relevance to front-line clinicians and their patients. It, in turn, is unlikely to be enough for issues more remote from front-line staff, such as resource use, disparities, research and population health.

The effectiveness of any information system must ultimately be judged by the extent to which it promotes (or compromises) the achievement of health system objectives, such as improving health and reducing disparities, and nurtures democratic debate. Information policy should therefore be evaluated in relation to these broad criteria. However, although technical design of information systems is advancing rapidly, there has been relatively little work on whether the systems are helping information users as intended. Do the data help citizens hold politicians to account? Do they help managers make better decisions? Do they enable regulators to devolve powers more effectively? Do they improve our understanding of how the health system works? There is therefore an important empirical research agenda that should determine, among other things:

- exactly what data are needed;
- how to present the data to their intended audience in a timely and understandable format (for example, to electorates);
- whether incentives are needed to encourage scrutiny and use of the data (for example, among clinicians);

- what resources and capacity are needed for users to use the data effectively;
- the role that professional bodies, inspectorates and the media have in nurturing improved use of the data.

The theoretical literature suggests great ambiguity about the appropriate level of decentralization, and its links with information strategy. Only with appropriate applied research of this sort can we begin to provide the evidence required by policy-makers wishing to make informed decisions.

Acknowledgements

We should like to thank the editors, the referees, the participants at the Venice workshop and Eero Linnakko for comments on this chapter.

Note

1 In health care there is a crucial fourth type of information, relating to the individual patient record, and the patient-level information available to (and created by) the clinician. The quality of such data is a critical determinant of patient outcome, but is only indirectly relevant to the decentralization debate.

References

Audit Commission (2004) *Information and data quality in the NHS*. London, The Stationery Office.

Bardhan, P. and Mookherjee, D. (2003) Relative capture of local and central governments: an essay in the political economy of decentralization. Working Paper Series C99–10. Berkeley, CA. Center for International and Development Economics Research, University of California Berkely.

Barrow, M.M. (1986) Central grants to local governments: a game theoretic approach. *Environment and planning C: government and policy*, **4**(2): 155–64.

Besley, T. and Coate, S. (2003) Centralized versus decentralized provision of local public goods: a political economy approach. *Journal of Public Economics*, **87**(12): 2611–37.

Canadian Institute for Health Information (2003) *Health care in Canada 2003: a fourth annual report*. Ottawa, Canadian Institute for Health Information.

Dranove, D., Kessler, D., McClellan, M. and Satterthwaite, M. (2002) Is more information better? The effects of "report cards" on health care providers. NBER Working Paper 8697. Cambridge: National Bureau of Economic Research.

Federation of Swedish County Councils (2000) *National health care quality registries in Sweden 1999*. Stockholm, Federation of Swedish County Councils.

Gilbert, G. and Picard, P. (1996) Incentives and optimal size of local jurisdictions. *European Economic Review*, **40**(1): 19–41.

Hurley, J., Birch, S. and Eyles, J. (1995) Geographically decentralized planning and management in health care: some informational issues and their implications for efficiency. *Social Science and Medicine*, **41**(1): 3–11.

Järvelin, J., Linna, M. and Häkkinen, U. (2003) The Hospital Benchmarking project: productivity information for hospital comparison. *Dialogi*, **1B**: 22–8.

Jha, A.K., Perlin, J.B., Kizer, K.W. and Dudley, R.A. (2003) Effect of the transformation of the veterans affairs health care system on the quality of care. *New England Journal of Medicine*, **348**: 2218–27.

Laffont, J-J. (2000) *Incentives and political economy*. Oxford, Oxford University Press.

Levaggi, R. and Smith, P. (1994) On the intergovernmental fiscal game. *Public Finance-Finances Publiques*, **49**(1): 72–86.

Melumad, N., Mookherjee, D. and Reichelstein, S. (1997) Contract complexity, incentives, and the value of delegation. *Journal of Economics and Management Strategy*, **6**(2): 257–89.

Monopolies and Mergers Commission (1996) *Severn Trent PLC and South West Water PLC: a report on the proposed merger*. London, Monopolies and Mergers Commission.

Morris, J., Hawes, C., Fries, B. et al. (1990) Designing the National Resident Assessment Instrument for Nursing Homes. *The Gerontologist*, **30**(3): 293–307.

Noro, A., Finne-Soveri, H., Björkgren, M. et al. (2001) *Implementation of RAI-instruments and benchmarking the care of the elderly*. Helsinki, Stakes Aiheita 17/2001 (in Finnish).

Oates, W.E. (1999) An essay on fiscal federalism. *Journal of Economic Literature*, **37**: 1120–49.

Rehnqvist, N. (2002) Improving accountability in a decentralised system. In Smith, P., ed., *Measuring up: improving health systems performance in OECD countries*. Paris, OECD.

Shleifer, A. (1985) A theory of yardstick competition. *Rand Journal of Economics* **16**(3): 319–27.

Wait, S. (2004) *Benchmarking: a policy analysis*. London, The Nuffield Trust.

chapter thirteen

Implementation of health care decentralization

Katarina Østergren, Silvia Boni, Kirill Danishevski and Oddvar Kaarbøe

Introduction

Decentralization is a central plank of many health sector reforms. It is believed to be an effective means to stimulate improvements in the delivery of services, to secure better allocation of resources according to needs, to involve the community in decisions about priorities, and to facilitate the reduction of inequities in health (Jacobsson 1994; Kaarbøe and Østergren 2001). However, while the rhetoric has been strong on the benefits of decentralization, knowledge of what factors influence the implementation of decentralization-related reforms is considerably weaker.

This chapter contributes to a more critical understanding of the problem involved in implementing a decentralized system in the health care sector. We explore the cultural-political processes surrounding the implementation process in three countries: Norway, the Russian Federation, and Italy. We explore: (1) how the interplay between various actors has shaped more overriding development of the decentralization process; and (2) how such developments become entwined with, and to some extent subsumed by, the broader discourses in the field concerned.

The theoretical lens through which these developments are examined is informed by a combined bottom-up and top-down perspective to implementation. Given our focus, such a combined perspective is appropriate as it is both concerned with analysis of the multitude of actors who interact at the operational (local) level on a particular problem or issue (Lipsky 1980; Hjern and Hull 1982) and at the same time with the rational aspects of the policy. There is a long debate in the literature about top-down versus bottom-up approaches. At one extreme is the ideal type of the perfectly pre-formed policy idea, which only requires execution, and the only problems it raises are those of control. At the other extreme, the policy idea is only an expression of basic principles and aspirations, a matter for philosophical reflection and political debate (Pressman and Wildavsky 1973). Our chapter is somewhere in between as we want to understand the cultural-political process and the interaction between central actors at all levels influencing the implementation process. Our position is thus to analyse developments in the health field, but to put particular emphasis on the effects of authoritative political restructuring initiatives aiming to decentralize functions in health care.

There are three important aspects in our approach. The first is the *aim and design* (or the rational idea) of decentralization. Simply put, which aspects of the health care system are decentralized and what is the aim of those changes? The second aspect is the *wider context* in which decentralization is introduced. What norms and values contribute to forming the process? The final aspect is the *actors* who are affected by, and influence, decentralization design, context and process.

The following section further elaborates on our theoretical point of departure. We then outline the different aspects for the three countries: design, wider context and actors. The concluding section summarizes the main findings and outlines the implications for implementing decentralization in the health care sector.

A conceptual framework: design, context and agency

Our approach focuses on the drivers behind the policy process. These drivers do not by themselves predict what type of result the implementation process will produce, but point to mechanisms through which change occurs. Knowledge about these mechanisms can form the basis for more precise statements about the implementation process. The basic idea is that actors involved in processes of policy change may be motivated by several key factors.

The first factor is the aim and design. The important questions are if and how political decisions are used in practice. It is a rational perspective where the outcome of the process is viewed as the result of a specific plan. The challenge for the implementer is to find better control and coordination mechanisms at the lower levels. In this sense, the perspective also is prescriptive.

Since this aim and design factor focuses on structure, it becomes important to classify which kinds of responsibility and power are transformed (Rondinelli 1981). What type of decentralization has occurred in the three countries?[1] Furthermore, we classify the reforms as: (1) comprehensive or narrow: is the whole health sector affected by the reform, or are only parts of the health sector decentralized?; (2) radical or cautious: to what extent does it break with the past?; and (3) well defined or with room for interpretation: how detailed is the blueprint and is the reform internally consistent?

In addition to the aim and design, there are two other factors we will focus on to understand the implementation process: the wider environment or context, and the agent. Both these are based on the bottom-up perspective. When using this perspective, we suppress the structural dimension and emphasize motives and incentives for the actors that execute the reform, and assess how these influence the overall implementation process (see, for example, Lipsky 1980; Barret and Fudge 1981; Hjern and Hull 1982).

This second factor considers norms and values in their *wider context*. This factor has a number of elements. First, in order to be implemented, policies have to be accepted as legitimate by the major actors and stakeholders involved. Second, legitimacy does not depend exclusively on the attractiveness of the policy content, but often as much on the procedures by which it is promoted. Similarly, legitimacy is not just a question of how resources are distributed, but also of the symbols and values in terms of which it is justified (Meyer and Rowan 1977). Third, policy change tends to be slow and piecemeal, since new proposals need to be accepted in terms of existing norms and symbols (Bleiklie et al. 2003).

In focusing on legitimacy, questions to answer include: (1) what is the degree of conflict, and how controversial is the initiative?; (2) does the policy represent a radical break from earlier logic or is it based on almost the same legitimacy base? For example, implementing private ideas in the public sector can be said to be a radical shift from previous logic; and (3) what is the pace of the implementation? Majone and Wildavsky (1978) argue that the implementation process is an ongoing process which has no resting point, no final realization and is endlessly evolving. Therefore, it is important to determine if implementation is an incremental process consisting of several decisions, or more of a big bang process where everything changes at once. Finally, what is the degree of completion compared to the initial plan? Is there a real shift in responsibilities/ power, and has the plan been changed along the way?

The third and final factor to consider is the *actors*. One of the main differences between the top-down and the bottom-up perspective is the level of analysis. The first perspective takes the formal organization as a starting point, while the later argues that in reality a political game is going on that makes it difficult to say in advance which actors will be important during the implementation process. A person playing this game seeks control over key organizational parameters. Control is obtained by bargaining, persuasion and manoeuvring under conditions of uncertainty (Bardach 1977).

It, therefore, becomes important to understand how actors try to acquire more resources, power or prestige. It is not sufficient to know policy contents in terms of policy aims and means, but in addition, one needs to know how actors perceive their interests to be affected by a policy, and what strategies they apply in order to promote their interests (Bleiklie et al. 2003).

Three case studies

The next part of the chapter explores three different country case studies: Norway, the Russian Federation and Italy. First, we describe aims and design in order to show decentralization ambitions of each country. Subsequently, we describe the decentralization process and the different actors' interpretations of the process. Finally, we describe lessons learned from the cases. The analysis is based on the theoretical points sketched out above, although empirical limitations make it necessary to focus on selected aspects. More detailed information on the details of decentralization in the case countries can be found in the Annexe.

Norway – aims and design

From January 2002, the central government in Norway took over responsibility for, and ownership of, all public hospitals. The reform represents a radical break with the past 30 years, when hospitals were owned and managed by 19 counties. The reform was the latest attempt by the central government to resolve the main problems confronting the Norwegian health care system: long waiting lists for elective treatment, lack of equity in the supply of hospital services, and a lack of financial responsibility and transparency. The reform was also presented as a solution to both the problem of lack of legitimacy of county governments, and to a political game where well-organized and resourceful actors permanently struggle for their interests.

There were four main elements in the 2001 Hospital Act (Ot.prp. nr. 66, 2000–01). It included elements of both centralization and decentralization. The first element of the hospital reform was that the central governments took over responsibility for all public hospitals and other parts of specialist care. Primary care was not affected by the reform so, in this respect, the reform was narrow. Second, the Minister of Health was given responsibility for the overall general management of specialist care. Hospitals continued to be publicly financed by general taxes, and, although the hospital organizations gained a semi-independent status by being organized as public enterprises with appointed boards, the Minister of Health was still the ultimate guarantee for solvency. Third, the central government kept the five health regions that were established in 1974 as the organizational unit for coordination and steering. This implied that the new organizations could start out with up-to-date descriptions of supply side and demand side factors, and based on existing plans.

The last element of the reform represents decentralization: both the health regions and hospitals are organized as health enterprises. These bodies are organized as independent legal subjects with their own responsibilities for personnel and capital. In this respect, the Norwegian hospital reform is similar to reforms in England, Sweden, Spain and Portugal that have focused on transforming hospitals into more autonomous actors (Busse et al. 2002). It is although important to remember that the Norwegian reform did not decentralize political power. The regional health enterprises have the statutory responsibility for providing health services to their inhabitants, and each regional health enterprise is the owner of most health care providers in its region. Within the regional health enterprises, the 70–80 hospitals and a number of smaller institutions were first (2002) organized as approximately 45 local health enterprises, and later (2003) reduced to approximately 25 health enterprises. The regional health enterprises were given freedom to organize the day-to-day running of the hospitals. In this respect, the reform gave room for interpretation.

In sum, the Norwegian reform can be defined as a narrow reform that represents a radical break with the past, and which gave the regional health enterprises a high degree of freedom to organize the specialist health services in their geographical areas.

The Russian Federation – aims and design

The process of decentralization started in the Russian Federation in the late 1980s and continued with the collapse of Soviet Union in the form of devolution of most responsibilities to regional and local levels where elected legislative and executive governments were developed. As noted earlier in Chapter 10, the health care financing system was changed and a partially decentralized system of compulsory medical insurance (CMI) was introduced in the early 1990s. This was a radical departure from the Soviet tradition in terms of shifting responsibility from central government. It was partial in reforming budgetary and labour legislation and in its involvement of lower levels of government in policy-making, which precluded change in social sectors. Being driven from outside health care, reforms did not lead to much change in health care indicators, such as doctor–patient relations or in the services provided. Nor did it create organizational diversity. Despite a radical shift of power, control and ownership of facilities from federal ministry and reforms of financial flows (Sheiman 1995; Chernichovsky and Potapchik 1997; Shishkin 1999; Twigg 1999; Sinuraya 2000), the infrastructure remained almost unchanged. In many instances years after the collapse of USSR, it is still the same Semashko system, emphasizing quantity over technology and over-using inpatient care.

Decentralization in the Russian Federation was viewed by ideologists and the public alike as part of democratization. It was a shift to a market economy and "westernization", with the goal of economic growth and a more effective state. No specific objectives were set in terms of health or health care. There was little involvement with representatives from the health system, who mostly saw decentralization as the chance to introduce various new opportunities to increase their own power and execute control. However, devolution was one of the most important processes affecting the health care system which, as with other elements of the Soviet system, had previously been highly centralized.

The lowest levels of the state system, localities, received ownership over the largest part of medical facilities. Localities were expected to nominate health administrators and to fund them out of their own budgets derived through local taxes and revenues. In 1994–1996, depending on the region, additional money was pumped in by the insurance system. Regional and federal levels were still responsible for referral and teaching hospitals and some other specialized functions such as surveillance, medical education and vertical target programmes. The main goal of the introduction of the health insurance system consisted of bringing additional funds into the health care system, as well as fostering competition, increasing accountability and quality of care. However, decentralization in health care can be viewed as a consequence of a global shift away from an administrative-command system in all the sectors of the economy, with no specific aim of introducing organizational change into the health system.

In sum, the Russian reform can be defined as a wide reform including the whole health care system. It represents a radical break with the past, from a centralized system to a decentralized system, both financially and managerially. The reform gave great room for interpretation while it did not have any specific goals concerning health care issues.

Italy – aims and design

The Reform Laws introducing decentralization during the 1990s in the Italian public administration and in the Italian National Health Service (INHS) stemmed from a common shared perspective which understood decentralization as a way to do the following:

- to attribute direct responsibilities (and relative powers) to local authorities (i.e. regions, provinces, municipalities, local health units) in order to programme, fund, organize and deliver services to citizens;
- to make public administrators and managers directly accountable, for the nature and quality of the services provided, to local communities;
- to reduce fiscal pressure through direct confrontation between administrators and citizens, and through horizontal competition among similar bodies (i.e. regions, local health units, municipalities).

This political, fiscal and organizational devolution implies the autonomous responsibility of the regions as far as funding, organization and delivery of health services in their own geographical areas. The decentralization process deeply modified both the role of the state and of the regional administrations. In this respect, the reform process has been wide and comprehensive.

The central government maintains the task of setting fundamental health principles and of addressing general guidelines to regions. The national level should act as a steward for the coherence of the overall system. The state should therefore monitor regional performance/outcomes, establish a new system of indicators, assess the Essential Health Care Levels (LEA) provided,[2] and identify key benchmarks such as quality of services provided. The state has made an effort, backed by the recently reorganized National Health Agency (ASRR), to build up a monitoring system to facilitate comparison among regional outcomes. Faced with a highly differentiated regional pattern, the state has experienced serious difficulties in setting the LEA standards and having them approved by the regions (Italian Ministry of Health and WHO 2003).

The decentralization process is not a break with the past, but rather a continuing process towards regional autonomy. This same process also changed the information needs of the regions. They need to explore local health problems in order to clarify, in the three-year regional health plan, their strategy regarding which services to guarantee to the local population. Therefore, regions need to be supported by systematically collected data about their current situation. A general effort to develop more effective regional health information systems can generally be noticed. This can be seen together with a new impulse to regional epidemiological observatories and the setting up of the regional health agencies as technical bodies in support of the regions.

All regions officially pursue a bottom-up programming approach, negotiating the regional health plan's objectives with the LHU and with the hospitals.

In this sense, the plan should be tailored to local needs and more easily achieved. This general attitude reflects a relatively new process for some regional administrations, and therefore it has to be implemented by empowering the different local institutions. In a few cases, it has already been fully developed.

Regions are also encouraged to promote innovative practices.[3] They may authorize local health units and hospitals can carry out experimental administrative projects, i.e. by accepting private participation in the management of health units, adopting co-payment charges for pharmaceutical assistance, or introducing new forms of funding such as Integrative Mutual Funds. These funds should cover the fees of those services which are not included in the INHS basic basket of services (Italian Ministry of Health and WHO 2003). Thus regions have a high degree of freedom in planning their own strategies and organizing their RHS. Some regions have taken legal action against the state regarding the "real interpretation" of the law, since the complex web of legal norms leaves room for different interpretations. Therefore, decentralization is developing as an ongoing process made of continuous adjustments on both sides.

Taken overall, looking at aims and design points out differences and similarities in the three cases. For both Norway and Italy, the aim of decentralization has been two-fold: to increase efficiency and to stop the existing blaming game between regions and central government. The regions were blamed for not taking enough financial responsibility. For the Russian Federation, the central aim seems to have been to replace the hierarchy left over from the former Soviet Union. Concerning design, we have identified two instances of radical change (in Italy and the Russian Federation) to a more moderate decentralization combined with centralization of ownership (in Norway).

The implementation process

According to our theoretical framework, a structural change like decentralization is not only about creating a new organizational structure, it is also about learning new ways of doing things, creating new routines and implementing new values (Meyer and Rowan 1977). Since we understand implementation as a continuous process, identifying key actors is essential to understanding how outcomes are related to the initial objectives. We now describe the implementation process and who we believe are the key actors in more detail.

Norway – implementation process

At first glance, the Norwegian hospital reform appears to have been approved without opposition, and implemented in a top-down, big bang fashion. However, a closer look at the picture reveals a more fragmented picture regarding key actors' view of the ingredients in the reform as well as the character of the start, the pace and the accomplishments of the implementation process. To understand why, one has to step back and describe the history leading up to the hospital reform.

In the past 15–20 years there has been growing tension between the regional (county level) and the central authorities concerning the performance of the Norwegian health care sector and its continued growing budget deficit. Central authorities often responded to the tension by introducing national standards (e.g. admission priorities, waiting time guarantees and other patient rights) or action plans (e.g. for heart, cancer and psychiatric patients) that often were associated with increased funding. As a result, the central authorities' expectations for health care results were raised. Furthermore, county councils became more financially dependent on the central government as the share of the county councils' own spending on somatic hospital services decreased from more than 72% in 1996 to less than 44% in 2001. The increased involvement of central authorities resulted in a blaming game between the county councils and the central government in which both parties tried to pin responsibility on the other for the sector's inability to attain central goals, e.g. reduced waiting time for elective patients, higher cost efficiency and cost control. This finger-pointing eroded the trust between central authorities and the county councils (Hagen and Kaarbøe 2006).

Three months after a minority Labour government came to power in March 2000, the Prime Minister hinted at a radical change in which ownership of hospitals would be an issue. With both the Conservatives and the Progressive Party backing the proposal in Parliament, the reform passed with an overwhelming majority and without consideration of other alternatives. Most central media favoured the proposal. The proposal was also supported by other important actors in the health care sector. Most patients' associations, medical labour unions and hospitals supported the transfer of ownership, so the degree of conflict was low. Most county councils opposed the transfer of ownership (Ot.prp. 66, 2000–01, ch.3).

The decision to organize hospitals as health enterprises was more disputed. Some patients' associations and labour unions e.g. the Nurses Association, were against this proposal. They argued that local political control and influence over specialized health care would be weakened since hospitals would no longer be a part of public administration. This led to a strong demand for open public hospital board meetings, a demand that was met from 2004 by order of the Health Minister. The Norwegian Medical Association and the hospitals did, however, support the concept that hospitals would be organized as health enterprises.

After the Labour Party decided to propose a central government takeover of hospitals, it also argued that it was critical that the reform be accomplished quickly. They believed that a long period of uncertainty on hospital ownership would be harmful for patients, counties and employees. Hence it was decided that the reform should be implemented quickly. One should also note that quick accomplishment was possible since the legal questions surrounding the 2002 Hospital Reform had been resolved in 1999 when the Norwegian Parliament approved organizing hospitals as municipal/county enterprises (Ot.prp. nr. 25, 1999–2000). Further, since the five health regions already existed (established in 1974), the new organizational unit for coordination and steering already was in place.

Taking these two facts into account, it is not clear that implementation occurred in a neat and distinguishable stage with a clear beginning and end.

This interpretation is supported by the fact that the process of transforming tasks from the counties and municipalities to the regional health enterprises continues. For example, the regional bodies took over the responsibility for, and ownership of, all public institutions that provide specialized drug and alcohol-related care from January 2004.

Hence it seems that the implementation process now is in the phase where different actors interpret and translate policies into new routines and practices. Since different stakeholders have different views on what is the correct and most legitimate translation, conflicts among different actors are now important elements of the implementation process.

According to our theoretical framework, this is what one should expect. The reform process is an extended one, even if the implementation strategy aims at a comprehensive, big push. The question is rather how the aims, the design and the implementation of decentralization can manage conflicts so that they play a positive role rather than becoming counterproductive.

When we take the wider context into account, we observe that parts of the initiative were controversial, especially the part that hospitals were organized as health enterprises. Furthermore, we observe that the policy content represents a radical break from the previous logic, since the regional health enterprises and hospitals are run by health managers and not by politicians. We have also shown that the implementation process is an extended one, and that the degree of completion is low since the central politicians are not willing to give up their power.

The Russian Federation – implementation process

The economic hardship of the late 1980s and early 1990s called for urgent action. Decentralization was viewed as a solution by many who wanted democracy and liberalization of the economy. As a result, decentralization covered the entire public sector, including health care, in a short period of time.

Major constitutional change in the post-communist period led a previously strong central government to cede extensive powers to lower levels. However, political decentralization in the form of devolving power, responsibility and ownership to subordinate organizations of the previously existing system (consisting of federal, regional and local levels) was not initiated within the health system. Instead, legislative and independently elected governments with significant authority were introduced at both regional and local levels, and they received a share of the health care system. It is important to state that the health sector, which traditionally is viewed as a non-productive burden in the Russian Federation, had almost nothing to say in the process. This lack of input helps explain why most health care functions were moved to the local level.

Regions set up health authorities, which were set as subordinates of both the elected governor of the *oblasts* and the Ministry of Health of the Russian Federation. Most of the local governments did not set up the local health authorities. Instead they gave all the management functions to the largest hospital in the district – the central *rayon* hospital, which hence received control over provision of most basic medical services.

In 2003, the status of central *rayon* hospitals was questioned and the court of one of the districts stated that this combination of functions contradicted anti-monopolistic legislation and created conflicts of interest. Subsequently the federal Ministry of Health released a new classification of facilities which abolished central *rayon* hospitals' status. Districts were suggested to set up health departments.

The regional health authorities were supposed to be partially subordinated to the national Ministry of Health as well as the local health system led by the regional health authorities. Despite decentralization, however, the old style of management through decrees was kept. It seems largely inefficient, given new realities, since all enforcement tools, such as funding or ability to hire and fire, were decentralized. Each level of the state nominates the head of its own tier of the health system, has its own budget and allocates a certain part of it to health care. In addition, the introduction of compulsory medical insurance meant that a significant portion of funds was not controlled by the system of health care administration. This further weakened the ability to enforce decisions.

In addition to the devolution of authority, delegation of financing was undertaken in the framework of introducing health insurance. The decline of already insufficient financing helped advocates of health reform push for implementation of a compulsory medical insurance system, which was legislated in 1991 and can be classified as quasi-privatization in nature.

The introduction of the CMI system, being a decentralization step itself, was set up in a decentralized manner. Regional funds tax 3.4% of payroll and a federal fund was set up to smooth regional inequalities and receives just 0.2% of payroll or 5% of total CMI funds (Sheiman 1985). Regional CMI funds were organized as non-budgetary semi-autonomous bodies run by executive directors appointed by the governor of the region and by a board. Although funds were set up as non-budgetary semi-autonomous juridical bodies, they actually failed to move away from the limitations and restrictions imposed by budgetary legislation and governmental rule. This means that the regional CMI funds still have to strictly obey the budget line-item principles of financing, as they fund budgetary governmental institutions and get their funds from a designated tax and (in most regions) from local budgets for the unemployed population.

As a result, regional CMI funds are obliged to follow unified salary scales and make all payments according to budget lines, which are calculated upon the resources of the health care facility (numbers of beds and staff), preventing development of innovative and creative incentive structures. However, regional funds are not supposed to finance or contract health care facilities directly. As stipulated in the law on health insurance, they must transfer the funds through a middle man, e.g. private insurance companies. However, no choice of insurance company was given to patients, also insurance companies have no discretion in terms of contracting certain facilities and not contracting others. In fact, insurance companies, although they are private, are only allowed to have contracts with governmental health facilities. The regional CMI fund decides which health insurance company can contract which facilities (Tulchinsky and Varavikova 2000).

The proclaimed rationale for developing health insurance in the Russian Federation was to bring complementary funds into health, but during an economically problematic period it rather became a substitute to decreasing budget funding. Still, the compulsory medical insurance system had many advocates when it was implemented. Probably one of the underlying factors for that was that new jobs for health administrators were set. Many medics and patients also saw a window of opportunity in setting up CMI as it was expected to improve the services and the incomes of physicians.

CMI does not pay for care for what are called socially important diseases, such as cancer, tuberculosis and sexually transmitted diseases, geriatric services, psychiatry, and emergency care, which are covered by the corresponding tier of government. As a result, health insurance funds account for only about a half of the total funding of central local hospitals (Goskomstat 2001). This precluded the health insurance system from meeting the expectations of reform ideologists, who believed it would raise efficiency, quality and access.

Overall, the powers of the Federal Health Ministry have been weakened considerably, with health care financing, regulation and delivery significantly decentralized. It is notable that CMI and devolution of administration systems did not meet much opposition. At the same time, one may ask whether it is real decentralization. The power to nominate health managers and to control funding was shifted to different levels of the state. No real power to reform was decentralized, as evidenced by the surprising monotony of health care throughout the regions of the Russian Federation. Structurally and in terms of incentives, the health sector is still very similar to the Semashko system of the former USSR. The scope for action by federal authorities is limited, but so is the power vested in the regions.

Instead, the localities or municipalities emerged as important bodies, as they own the facilities in which much of the routine health care is delivered and, both directly and indirectly, by virtue of their contributions of insurance premiums for the non-working, provide a substantial amount of health care financing. They, however, are tied up with the obsolete decrees of the Ministry of Health of the USSR (produced 1979–1980s) which are embedded in the system and can hardly be removed, as well as by common legislation, e.g. on taxation, labour and, most importantly, by budget law.

The failed health reforms in the Russian Federation are often viewed as a result of inertia and lack of local capacity. It is also important to mention that positive effects of decentralization in health care are mocked by slow speed and inefficiency of non-health care-specific legislation reforms, which are not aligned to the needs of the health sector, and which sustain Soviet patterns in all governmental sectors.

In sum, the Russian Federation reform can be described as a big bang implementation process. The Western ideas were desired by the public and it was almost impossible to slow down the decentralization. Thus, decentralization in the Russian Federation had a *high degree of legitimacy*, as it was seen as part of a desperately wanted democratization process. However, health care was a neglected sector and no objectives, besides a search for complementary funding from the new health insurance schemes, were set. In addition, no action in terms of improving policy was taken to meet the special needs of the health care sector. Therefore, the *degree of completion is low*.

Italy – implementation process

The previous Centre-Left Government (1996–2000) planned decentralization in a solidarity framework, according to the principle of subsidiarity (development of a partnership among regions and of a welfare community). After 2000, decentralization was managed by a Centre-Right coalition. The Prime Minister was the promoter of a liberal market approach, rooted in complete devolution and total autonomous self-regional determination.[4] These changes in government had a decisive influence in shaping decentralization in the health sector.

The government approved, on an experimental basis, the introduction of private not-for-profit foundations in the management of high quality public hospitals. Regions have full responsibility for the entire system and they have reorganized the services on a regional/local basis. Within this process, decentralization has been interpreted differently within different regional contexts, according to the values of the political ruling coalition and of the local historical tradition. For some regions, it was a way to adopt a purchaser–provider split and promote free patient choice, while for others it meant a chance to enhance programming and controlling services.

These two different approaches have contributed to cluster the various regions, with many different and complex forms of organization. Emilia Romagna, for example, has reorganized health and social services following two main strategies: hospitals' high specialization and reorganization (according to the Hub & Spoke model); and the empowerment of districts (part of LHUs) and municipalities in order to integrate and promote social and health services, and primary care with the involvement of GPs and paediatricians. Veneto, which has a strong tradition of social and health integration, has promoted concerted planning. To foster common programming, the region promoted cooperation between health districts (LHUs) and social municipal areas. Preliminary written agreements between municipalities and LHUs are becoming a common practice (also in other regions) as a way to integrate social and health services. The new regional health plan calls for the participation of various LHUs in a "Greater Area", to share some common services (pharmaceuticals, conventions with general physicians, etc.) and create a larger network. In the meantime, other experimental innovations include integrative private funds, to complete the basic package offered by the public service.

Tuscany is experimenting with the "Society for Health" public consortium (formed by LHUs and municipalities) for health and social well-being, which manages a common budget made up by funds from the two components. Lombardy is experimenting with project financing and private foundations for hospitals and new aggregations of public/private providers (such as associations among general practitioners, pediatricians, and other health professions) for primary care.

The innovations mentioned above share some general traits, but they differ in values, objectives, frameworks and organizational settings. To compare regional performances and general outcomes, using common monitoring and evaluation tools, the role of the state, and particularly of the National Health Agency, will be particularly significant.

The current situation offers several interesting issues for analysis. First, the main regional interest involves health costs. The General Directors of the local health units are rated on their ability to keep expenditure under control. Moreover, all regions (whether ruled by Central-Right or Central-Left governors) have asked the central government for more funding to manage devolution, arguing that hard budget constraints undermine the whole decentralization process.

Second, the process of devolution from the state to the regions is far from complete. The regions have not moved to decentralize their power to provinces and municipalities and local governmental structures. Regions so far have decentralized only the administrative-operative level while maintaining the strategic decision-making process.

The third consideration is that, while pursuing the devolution of power to the regions, the central government at the same time has proposed general rules that constrain regional autonomy, such as recent governmental cuts in the municipalities' social budget which undermine the integration of health and social services. Another example is the recent regularization of 750 000 immigrants, according to the Act n.189/2002, which requires their health assistance costs to be covered by the regions.

The fourth and final point is that regions in some cases demonstrate resistance to change, while local health units, pressed by citizens' control and continuous requests, are more dynamic. In fact, the local health units' adaptation to the new environment began long before. The decentralization process has strengthened the role played by the LHUs, particularly when specific guidelines from regions are partial or missing.

One further issue concerns the governance of the overall system. The complex relationship between the state and the regions (and their representative bodies such as the conference of the presidents of the regions), among the regions, and between regions and LHUs and municipalities, has formed an articulated system that has developed at different levels and in an incremental manner. In this differentiated structure, conflicts concerning health budgets arise not only between the state and the regions but also between regions.

Only a few regions can raise the resources needed to completely cover local health expenditure and to contribute to the Solidarity Fund. This accounts for the repeated tensions among regions about the mechanism for fiscal equalization, which is supposed to shift funds from wealthy regions to the more deprived ones.

Since the outcome of devolution depends on the strength of local governments (Saltman and Figueras 1997), regions with a strong tradition in managing services more often succeed in setting their priorities and developing their own strategies. On the other hand, traditionally weaker regions risk becoming even weaker. The existing historical gap between north and south has not been filled.[5] This highly differentiated situation generates worries about equity issues, however, it can also represent a positive chance to identify and resolve ancient problems.

The higher the degree of differentiation among the regions, the higher the need for coordination. Conflicts are an inherent element of the implementation process. The key issue is how to manage conflict in a positive and productive way. In a decentralized setting, managing conflicts can be more difficult, given the weaker role of the state and the interests of the different regions.

It can also be noted that the need to shift the attention/resources from acute care (hospitals) to long-term and preventive care (services), and the effort, made by the regions, to improve local programming, have contributed to give a new impulse to health and social integration.[6] Undoubtedly this is another result of the decentralization process.

Summary

In sum, we have identified different actors and different interpretations of what is going on in the health sector in the three cases. We have also detailed the degree of continual change that has occurred in the decentralization process. In both Norway and the Russian Federation, there have been difficulties moving power from central to regional level, and in both the Russian Federation and in Italy a considerable degree of power has devolved (or been seized) by local municipal-level entities.

Lessons learned

Lessons learned from the Norwegian case

As described earlier, the Norwegian reform includes elements of decentralization and of recentralization. A key argument for recentralizing the organizational unit for coordination and steering from 19 counties to five health regions was that it is easier for a larger unit to implement structural policy changes. Similarly, one of the main arguments behind organizing the health regions and hospitals as health enterprises was that hospitals should be organized as autonomous entities without local political control, but under the control of an executive board. The question is now whether the regional units that are outside direct political control are able to implement structural policy changes which are necessary to achieve the goals of the reform.

We now see an increasing number of decisions made on structural questions by these boards. It seems, however, that structural decisions made by the boards have low political legitimacy, and thus that national politicians can overturn some of the structural decisions the boards take. Decisions to shut down local hospitals, delivery rooms or emergency rooms in local hospitals already have been turned down by the Minister of Health. As a consequence of this political overruling, some members of the executive boards have resigned, arguing that the political control over the health enterprises is too strong.

The main lesson to be learned from this is that structural decisions made by non-political bodies in a Beveridge-type model seem to have low legitimacy and thus low probability of contributing to any real change. From this, it also follows that the proposition that it is easier to implement policy initiatives in health systems with more centralized power structures, is limited by the context in which the policy is implemented.

This lesson can be put into broader perspective by consulting the literature about fiscal federalism (Oates 1998; Rattsø 1998). According to this literature, the stability of a decentralized system is said to be contingent upon the balance and degree of overlap between the political, economic and administrative/operative dimensions of the system. The basic argument is that a system in which the responsibility for these dimensions is spread among actors at different hierarchical levels has built-in destabilizing features. In Norway, for example, prior to hospital reform, the regional level (i.e., the county councils) were responsible for running the hospitals, however, the central government provided more than 50% of the funding for these institutions. In this sense, there were already some destabilizing features built into the Norwegian model, thereby creating a drive for change. On the other hand, the fact that political actors and the bodies that are responsible for making structural decisions are still not aligned suggests that the current system also may be unstable.

Lessons learned from the Russian case

The Russian Federation began as a centralized country and underwent rapid decentralization. The process of devolution was facilitated by regional and local leaders who wanted more power and access to resources and by President Yeltsin. Mutual willingness of both central government and recipients of new responsibilities to decentralize meant that the process unfolded as a "big bang".

Economic hardship in the early 1990s led to implementation of a compulsory medical insurance system (CMI) legislated in 1991. Both devolution and the introduction of CMI were viewed as part of a shift towards a liberal democratic state and a market economy. In the first years, these changes brought about some innovations, for example, a system similar to the UK fund-holding in a number of regions. Later, decentralization resulted in the transition of control and power. However, the ability to change and implement reforms stagnated as it became clear that the general legislation regulating the "governmental sector" will not change.

The demand for change towards the Western way of life in the Russian Federation in the early 1990s was so powerful and the general situation in the country so explosive that the government simply could not resist. This meant that such barriers as a long tradition of overregulation and lack of managerial experience on regional and local levels were disregarded. However, as already mentioned, central government also did not have the skills needed in the new conditions. Moreover, the health system was a small coin in the trade-offs, and central government was willing to give away control over all but the largest national facilities. It can be argued that it was the Soviet tradition of top-down administration that allowed it to impose decentralization upon health care externally.

There are also lessons learned with regard to fiscal theory (Oates 1998). Decentralization being inconsistent in transferring different functions to different actors, with most financial responsibilities vested in the regional level, political power split between federal and regional government, yet with nearly all administrative functions given to local levels, meant that the system was instable and little agreement could be achieved as to the direction for change.

Lessons learned from the Italian case

In Italy, the deep changes created by political and fiscal reforms have ushered in a new, still highly uncertain, scenario. Implementation is an ongoing continuous process, a land of potentiality (Majone and Wildavsky 1984). In this land of potentiality, different interest groups together with governmental and non-governmental actors are redefining and negotiating their reciprocal roles and rules of interaction.

The state has been working to develop sound information, monitoring and communication systems. The state has been playing a significant role in supporting regions in experimental practices, in providing general guidelines and in enforcing equity. As different regional models are being developed, it is important to compare the practical tools and the solutions adopted.

The operating standards of regional staff are, in some cases, inadequate both as to programming a coherent strategy, and in offering guidelines to the LHUs. The same is true in terms of evaluation of facilities' performances and outcomes. From a federal perspective, these flaws must be amended through the creation and support of well-trained staff in general management (especially on programmes and evaluation of services, budgeting and control of the financial resources, monitoring services).

One important lesson learned from the Italian case is that a key role in the implementation of decentralization is played by the human variable. While the role of training in supporting change is crucial, it is surprising how rarely an adequate policy of investment in human resources, at the state or local level, is programmed (and therefore funded). The outcome of decentralization is highly dependent on the capacity of the managerial level to exert the appropriate knowledge and skills. This means that there is an urgent need to reinforce the process of programming, coordinating and evaluating (attributing them a new meaning in the changing setting), as well as enhancing the culture of negotiation and cooperation.

Conclusion

This chapter has explored the cultural and political processes surrounding the implementation of decentralization-based reforms in three countries. It suggests the need to extend the analysis of the decentralization process beyond belief in the perfectly pre-formed policy idea and its implementation (Yin 1980; Barrett and Fudge 1981). In fact, quite differently, one key conclusion here is that implementing decentralized structures in the health sector represents an arena of struggle between a local level wanting more autonomy and power and a central level either not providing adequate coordination (Italy, the Russian Federation), or re-asserting its own power (Norway).

In terms of "aim and design", the review above indicates that the reforms were designed quite differently in the three countries. Although the two Beveridge countries – Italy and Norway – had similar problems with political games and loose control over health expenditures, the two countries took very different approaches to the solution. In Italy, the reform design can be characterized as *comprehensive*, including the whole health sector. In addition, the Italian reforms were incrementally implemented in order to strengthen the regions: one reform decentralized the reimbursement system, while a second decentralized political power (devolution). Each reform measure can be described as *cautious* in the sense that it only created small step change. The state has a reduced role in the new system while the regions have *high discretion in the interpretation* of the reform.

The Norwegian reform design represents more of a *radical break* from previous traditions of regional ownership of health care. Both the administrative and management levels were decentralized in order to strengthen the regional level. This regionalization has led to a *large degree of interpretation* at the regional level. But at the same time, Norway strengthened the central government by centralizing political power, by keeping the central financing model and by creating state ownership. Compared to the other cases, the Norwegian reform also differs when it comes to its scope. It is more *narrow* then the reforms in Italy and the Russian Federation, since it only concerned specialized care and excluded primary care.

The Russian Federation, structured according to the Semashko model, had no problems with blaming games. Instead the problems were a bureaucratic and rigid health care sector that contributed to inefficient provision of health care. The solution was to strengthen the regions by decentralizing both administrative power and the reimbursement system. Central funding was replaced by a new insurance system (CMI) together with local taxes, with the idea of increasing the autonomy of local entities. The reform design can be characterized as *comprehensive, radical* and with a *high degree of interpretation* at the local level. Table 13.1 summarizes the design of the different reforms in the three countries.

The reform process can be further assessed in terms of three key dimensions: legitimacy, time and knowledge. One similarity among the three countries is that the decentralization reforms were supported and in that way *legitimized* by almost all stakeholders. In Norway, the reform was supported by both the political and the medical environment. Especially the transfer of ownership from the counties to the central government gained wide support, but also the proposal to establish hospitals as health enterprises was supported by the main political and medical actors. In the Russian Federation, the decentralization reforms were initiated outside health care but were broadly supported by all parties as part of the democratization process that followed the collapse of the Soviet Union. Also for Italy, the reforms were supported both by the regions and the central

Table 13.1 Differences in reform design

	Norway	*Russian Federation*	*Italy*
Extent	Narrow	Comprehensive	Comprehensive
Degree of newness	Radical	Radical	Cautious
Degree of interpretation	Large degree	Large degree	Large degree

government, based on a common agreement by which to resolve the severe problems the health sector faced.

The second dimension is *time*. In Norway, the reform was implemented and accomplished within a short period. This was possible both because the legal questions surrounding the reform were clear, and, since the health regions already had been established, an organizational unit for coordination and steering already existed. In addition, there was little resistance to the reform. The representatives from the hospitals hoped for both increased resources for the sector and increased autonomy with the state as the owner.

Also in the Russian Federation, the reform was implemented quickly in a top-down fashion. Once the central government began to default on its jurisdictional responsibilities toward the regions, in the face of severe economic difficulties, many of these regions began exercising autonomy beyond that provided for in the Constitution of 1993. This resulted in the *de facto* autonomy of the regions, although they rarely had either the legal authority, or financial or administrative ability to act effectively (Tragakes and Lessof 2003).

In Italy, in contrast to the other two cases, the decentralization process did not occur over a short period. It started in the 1970s and was reinforced in the 1990s, ushering in the constitutional reform (Law n.3/2000). In addition, Italy has a long tradition of great autonomy for regions on social issues.

How can we understand the differences in Table 13.2? In both Norway and the Russian Federation, the implementation process was made quickly and almost without resistance. Italy had the opposite situation, in which the decentralization process is a result of an incremental process and there was debate among the actors involved. One explanation for the differences is that regions in both Norway and the Russian Federation saw benefits in the new system. In Norway, even if the counties were against the new state-owned hospitals, the hospitals could see benefits in belonging to the wealthy state. In the Russian Federation, a history of extreme centralization pushed a disconnection from the state in a rapid way without understanding what it meant in practical or financial terms. Again, Italy differs from the other two cases in that regions already had substantial autonomy and were aware of the problems that decentralization could create on the financial side (a lack of resources and of managerial competence in some southern regions).

Finally, *knowledge* seems to be an important dimension in understanding the implementation process. By knowledge, we mean both competence to handle decentralization issues and problems at a local level, as well as good and valid

Table 13.2 Differences in reform implementation process

	Norway	*Russian Federation*	*Italy*
Legitimacy	Relatively high	High	Different in different regions
Pace	Big bang	Big bang	Incremental
Completion to initial plan	Medium	Low	Different in different regions

data to be able to manage the change process. For Norway, the quick implementation and accomplishment meant that some elements that affect the outcome of the health care sector were not adjusted from day one. Some of these elements have now developed and have been adjusted. Other elements are still going through learning processes and are, however, not in place yet. Most importantly, the central government still has to decide what role the regional health enterprises should take in the future. The relationship between the central government and the regions is still not fully formed.

For the Russian case, there is an obvious lack of knowledge at the local level to handle the decentralized health care system. The ensuing highly decentralized and fragmented structure has created a health care system resembling a multitude of loosely linked, semi-independent, territorial units. It has even been argued that the health care system today consists of multiple uncoordinated administrations. The result is a lack of governance for the health care system, as the Ministry of Health is no longer able to set policy and priorities in the form of recommendations.

The Italian case presents a general lack, especially in some regions, of managerial programmes addressed to regional/local administrators, though a special continuing education programme for health professionals was launched.

From a rational top-down perspective, the cases can be understood as demonstrating that the local level has insufficient competence to handle the new tasks, resource allocation, etc. Both in the Russian and the Italian (some regions) case, there was a need to negotiate increased resources, and to increase efficiency and effectiveness in the regions. From this perspective, a solution to the existing problems could be to increase the competence range at the local level.

On the other hand, when viewing decentralization at a broader system level, we can understand the decentralization process more as a new game that is played between the different actors in the sector. This means that the central problem is more about finding the new rules and roles for the actors. The rules of the game have to be established and agreed among all players. In the Norwegian case, it is a challenge to find out what role the central government and the regions should have. Also in the other cases, we can see how the regions try to position themselves in relation to other actors. In Italy, for example, some regions are allied together against the state.

Finally, we can understand the decentralization process as continuing to involve following the rules and bureaucratic structures. Institutional practice contributes to slowing down or diverting the reform process in all three cases. In the Russian Federation, the main bureaucratic obstacles to decentralization stem from the traditional way of managing the health care sector. The previous structure has disappeared only in some areas while at the same time no new system has been put in its place. In Norway, the main obstacles stem from the traditional way the new owner through the Health Ministry manages hospitals, through rule production and directives, and from rule production at multiple levels. Finally, in Italy, the major obstacle to decentralization derives from the difficulty in finding an appropriate balance between a national regulatory framework and regional autonomy.

Notes

1 See Chapter 3 for a developed discussion on the different types of decentralization.
2 Basic basket of services which should be assured in all the regions.
3 According to Act n. 405/2001, "Urgent Measures for Health Care Expenditure".
4 The anti-state revanchism of some northern regions also being consistently represented within the coalition.
5 Though also the situation among Southern Regions is highly differentiated, *Monitor* (2003) 5: 24–30.
6 According also to the Law n.328/00 on the reorganization of social services.

References

Bardach, E. (1977) *The implementation game*. Cambridge, MA, MIT Press.

Barrett, S. and Fudge, C. (1981) *Policy and action*. London, Methuen.

Bleiklie, I., Byrkjeflot, H. and Østergren, K. (2003) Taking power from knowledge: a theoretical framework for the study of two public sector reforms. Working paper 22–2003. Bergen, Stein Rokkan Centre to Social Studies.

Busse, R., van der Grinten, T. and Svennson, P-G. (2002) Regulating entrepreneurial behaviour in hospitals: theory and practice. In Saltman, R.B., Busse, R. and Mossialos, E., eds, *Regulating entrepreneural behaviour in European health care systems*. Buckingham, Open University Press.

Chernichovsky, D. and Potapchik, E. (1997) Health system reform under the Russian health insurance legislation, *International Journal of Health Planning Management*, **12**(4): 279–95.

Goskomstat (2001) *Russia in figures* (www.gks.ru, accessed 18 July 2006).

Hagen T.P. and Kaarbøe, O. (2006) The Norwegian hospital reform of 2002: central government takes over ownership of public hospitals. *Health Policy*, **76**(3): 320–33.

Hjern, B. and Hull, C. (1982) Implementation research as empirical constitutionalism. *European Journal of Political Research*, June: 105–16.

Italian Ministry of Health and WHO (2003) *Health facts and policies in Italy in the European context*. Rome: Italian Ministry of Health and WHO Regional Office for Europe.

Jacobsson, B. (1994) *Organisationsexperiment i kommuner och landsting*. Stockholm, Nerenius och Santerus.

Kaarbøe, O. and Østergren, K. (2001) Erfaringer fra ledelses- og organisasjonsreformer i den svenske helsesektoren på 1990-tallet. In Askildsen, J.E. and Haug, K., eds, *Helse, økonomi og politikk: Utfordringer for det norske helsevesenet*. Oslo, Cappelen.

Lipsky, M. (1980) *Street-level bureacuracy: dilemmas of the individual in public services*. New York, Russell Sage Foundation.

Majone, G. and Wildavsky, A. (1978) Implementation as evolution. In Freeman, E.H., ed., *Policy studies review annual*, vol. 2. Beverly Hills, CA, Sage.

Majone, G. and Wildavsky, A. (1984) Implementation as evolution. In Pressman, J.L., and Wildawsky, A., eds, *Implementation*. Berkeley, CA, University of California Press.

Meyer, J.W. and Rowan, B. (1977) Institutionalized organizations: formal structure as myth and ceremony. *American Journal of Sociology*, **83**(2): 340–63.

Oates, W.E. (1998) *The economics of fiscal federalism and local finance*. London, Edward Elgar.

Pressman, J.L. and Wildavsky, A.B. (1973) *Implementation*. Berkeley, CA, University of California Press.

Rattsø, J. (1998) *Fiscal federalism and state-local finance: the Scandinavian perspective*. Cheltenham, Edward Elgar.

Rondinelli, D. (1981) Government decentralization in comparative theory and practice in developing countries. *International Review of Administrative Sciences*, **47**: 133–45.

Saltman, R.B. and Figueras, J. (eds) (1997) *European health care reform: analysis of current strategies*. Copenhagen, WHO Regional Office for Europe.

Sheiman, I. (1995) New methods of financing and managing health care in the Russian Federation. *Health Policy*, **32**(1–3): 167–80.

Shishkin, S. (1999) Problems of transition from tax-based system of health care finance to mandatory health insurance model in Russia. *Croatian Medical Journal*, **40**: 195–201.

Sinuraya, T. (2000) Decentralisation of the health care system and territorial medical insurance coverage in Russia: friend or foe? *European Journal of Health Law*, **7**: 15–27.

Tragakes, E. and Lessof, S. (2003) *Health care systems in transition: Russian Federation*, Copenhagen, European Observatory on Health Systems and Policies.

Tulchinsky, T. and Varavikova, E. (2000) *The new public health: an introduction for the 21st century*. San Diego, Academic Press.

Twigg, J.L. (1999) Regional variation in Russian medical insurance: lessons from Moscow and Nizhny Novgorod. *Health Place*, **5**: 235–45.

Yin, R. (1980) *Studying the implementation of public programs*. Boundler, Solar Energy Research Institute.

chapter fourteen

Privatization as decentralization strategy

Rifat Atun

Introduction

This chapter examines privatization as a decentralization strategy in the health sector in Europe. The introductory section sets the scene while the second section explores decentralization and privatization as concepts and the link between the two. As decentralization is covered in detail in earlier chapters, the emphasis in this section is on privatization. The third section provides a summary of the empirical evidence on perceived benefits and risks of privatization in general and in the health sector in particular, followed by an analysis of the drivers of privatization in the public and health sectors such as neoclassical economics and New Public Management (NPM). The fourth section focuses on privatization experience to date in the health sector in Europe. Through case studies, this section explores major initiatives, examples and models of privatization in different countries of western, central and eastern Europe. In particular, this section analyses the experience of four modes of private sector involvement observed along the privatization continuum (Figure 14.1), namely: (1) full privatization with sale and transfer of assets; (2) outsourcing of services from the private sector; (3) creation of hybrid organizations such as public–private-partnerships; and (4) transforming or "modernizing" work practices in state organizations through the introduction of management practices from the private sector. This section also appraises available empirical evidence on the impact of privatization on the providers, consumers and the health system. The final section concludes by summarizing key findings and lessons learnt as well as identifying implications for policy-makers.

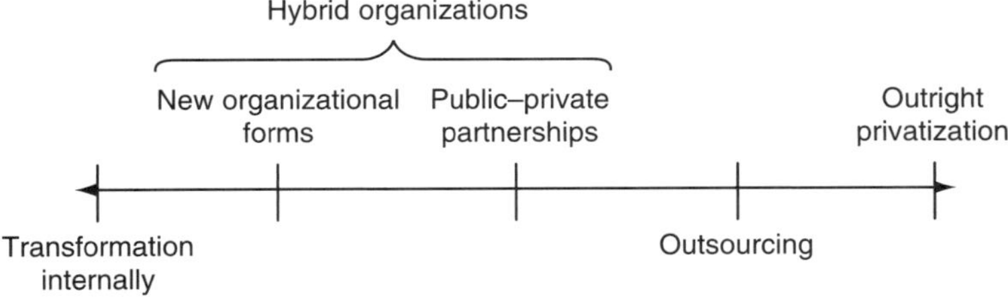

Figure 14.1 The privatization continuum

Decentralization and privatization: definitions and concepts

Decentralization is defined as the wide range of acts of transfer of power and authority from higher to lower levels of government for a number of functions, such as planning, human resource management, budgeting and performance management (Rondinelli 1981; Mills et al. 1990). Decentralization can be from national to sub-national levels, such as to regions, districts, municipalities, or to organizational levels, such as hospitals or primary care units. Administratively, powers and functions can be decentralized vertically within the same corporate entity (for instance, geographic decentralization from national to regional ministries of health with limited transfer of functions – deconcentration – or more extensive transfer of functions – delegation). Alternatively, with devolution, powers and functions can be decentralized to a different corporate entity within the public sector, such as the local government. There are varying views on what constitutes decentralization (Sherwood 1969; Rondinelli et al. 1983), or how the process should be analysed (Bossert 1998). Similarly, the views on the benefits or risks of decentralization (Collins and Green 1994; OECD 1997; World Bank 1997; World Bank 2001) and what the extent of decentralization or centralization should be also vary (Bjorkman 1985; Segall 2000). However, a discussion of these views is beyond the scope of this chapter.

Privatization involves the transfer of assets, responsibilities or functions from the government/public sector to a non-governmental organization which may be either a voluntary agency or a private company. Privatization is considered by some as the point for decentralization (Mills et al. 1990) but by others as being a distinctly different process (Collins 1989). Narrow definitions of privatization have focused on sale or transfer of assets from the public to the private sector (Saltman 2003). However, as in the privatization continuum described in Figure 14.1, broader definitions of privatization are more appropriate to include all mechanisms that encourage private sector participation or principles in financing and delivery of public services (Rondinelli and Iacona 1996).

The rationale for privatization

Proponents of privatization argue that the process helps a government to fulfil a number of objectives, for example, reduce administrative and financial burdens with respect to providing public services, increase efficiency and effectiveness of services to achieve value-for-money, encourage innovation, and develop more user-sensitive services appropriate for a particular community or context (Kikeri et al. 1992). This is because privatization aligns the interests of the principal (the government) and the agent (the manager) thereby improving performance (Vickers and Yarrow 1988). A further rationale for privatization is to give the purchasers and consumers a stronger voice through increased choice and competition (Beesley and Littlechild 1983). However, it is not clear to what extent these benefits, which are based on experience and economic analyses of non-health sectors, can be extrapolated to the health sector.

On the other hand, critics of privatization argue that privatization fails to meet the objectives defined above (Tittenbrun 1996). Especially in the health sector where there is market failure – due in part to externalities (where benefits of a health intervention accrue to an individual receiving it but also to the broader public, such as immunization), asymmetry of information (where consumers or patients are relatively ill informed about their health care needs), moral hazard (both on demand and supply side) and uninsurable risk. Therefore, there is a risk that inadequately regulated privatization will lead to market failure and inefficient allocation of resources. The USA, where there is widespread private involvement in health financing and provision, is often used as an example to show the risks of privatization: in spite of the highest per capita expenditure in the world, huge inequities in health access and outcomes exist. Others argue that privatization of health service provision does not hamper equity, but point to risks of privatizing health financing (Saltman et al. 2002).

Privatization in Europe: the evolving context

In the past 50 years, state policies in many European countries have oscillated between regulation and markets, and between measures that favoured the growth of the public sector or encouraged expansion of the private sector at the expense of the public sector. From the 1950s until the end of the 1970s, the pendulum swung in favour of state and public sector ownership. Many large national corporations, such as national health systems, were created. In the 1980s and 1990s, the pendulum swung in the opposite direction and the state gave way to markets. In this period, European countries adopted four major strategic directions of change to redefine the role of the state, profoundly changing the public sector by subjecting it to market forces and various modes of private sector involvement. These four directions were: (1) full privatization; (2) outsourcing services from the private sector; (3) creation of hybrid organizations, such as quasi-autonomous non-governmental but public bodies, subject to rigorous private sector management methods and managed at arm's-length through contracts and performance targets, as well as new ventures in the shape of public–private partnerships; and (4) transforming or "modernizing" work practices in those organizations that remained under state control (Figure 14.1).

First, in the period spanning the 1980s and 1990s, in several western European countries, many state assets, such as utilities, transport systems and public institutions, were privatized. Second, in a drive to achieve "value-for-money", internal markets and other mechanisms were introduced to increase contestability, when many services were outsourced from the private sector.

The third major change was the creation of "hybrid organizations". The assets and enterprises that could not be privatized were turned into new institutional forms. For example, some countries witnessed the introduction of non-governmental quasi-autonomous "agencies" that were not part of the civil service or mainstream public system but operated with a public sector ethos. These organizations had devolved management and own budgets. Accountability was maintained with contracts that had explicit performance targets (Efficiency Unit 1988). Other novel hybrid organizations were the public–private partnerships: joint ventures between the public and private sectors in financing, asset ownership and delivery of services.

The fourth major direction of change was to transform work practices in the organizations that remained within state control. Here, good practices from public and private sectors were adopted to encourage "modernization" of these organizations. For example, collective bargaining with employees was phased out and replaced by decentralized bargaining and individual contracts with development and performance targets. Political considerations were balanced with business (commercial) considerations. The managers in these organizations, which are subject to greater contestability, create business/strategic plans. These organizations formally assess their competences and resources; undertake sectoral reviews to assess the need of their clients; review their service portfolio to decide whether a service is needed; set performance targets; compare and benchmark the performance of own organization with their peers in the private and the public sector; consult more explicitly with citizens, clients, and especially local taxpayers; compete with private and public sector organizations to secure contracts from purchasers; and collaborate with private sector organizations as and when needed.

The drivers for privatization

Traditional models or organizations tend to see structures as relatively stable entities that adapt to internal and external forces. Systems assume that structures are stable simply because traditionally we have always assumed them to be so. Anthony Giddens' "Structuration Theory" challenges this way of thinking and views structures as fluid entities. Structures themselves can constrain activity but can also encourage activity that creates new structures (Giddens 1979). Hence, large systems and structures have their own trajectory, with restructuring, such as greater involvement of the private sector, public–private partnerships and privatization, being part of this broad process.

In Europe, in the period 1980 to 2005, one can observe an attempt to "reinvent the government" (Osborne and Gaebler 1992), e.g. downsize the state to a set of core activities and tasks, introduce "market-type mechanisms" (OECD 1992) with greater competition (especially on the provider side), and to encourage greater involvement of the private sector. A number of contextual factors influenced these changes, such as globalization, new public management, managerialization using information technology (IT), changes in views of organizational roles, and changing societal expectations, and these substantially affected the health sector.

Globalization

Globalization has created increased competition between countries and increased consumerism. This is compelling governments to work better and cost less. There is now more emphasis on enhancing effectiveness and efficiency of the public services, increased quality, becoming more client-oriented and adopting more market-like mechanisms with increased competition and a public–private mix in traditionally public sectors, such as education and health. Restructuring of the public sector, with increased privatization in health and other traditional public sector organizations, is a response to globalization as governments try to enhance efficiency and effectiveness to remain competitive. Further, the World Trade Organization (WTO), through the General Agreement on Trade in Services (GATS), encourages privatization of public services including health care (Pollock and Price 2000).

Neo-liberal economics

In the 1980s, some economists, notably from the USA, argued that neo-liberal economic models could be applied to health care, and stressed the beneficial effects of markets and strong incentives (Enthoven 1985). These arguments were influential in shaping health reforms in the United Kingdom, then subsequently in central and eastern Europe.

New Public Management (NPM)

The profound structural changes observed in many public and health sectors are, in part, attributed to the rise of the New Public Management (NPM) (Hood 1991, 1995; Dunleavy and Hood 1994). Globally, NPM has spread widely to replace traditional public administration. This change is most visible in the "high-impact" countries of the United Kingdom (Pollitt 1990; Ferlie et al. 1996), Australia (Campbell and Halligan 1992; Zifcak 1994), and New Zealand (Boston et al. 1996) but can also be observed in Brazil, Canada (Aucoin 1995), the United States of America (Barzelay 1992) and many European countries.

New Public Management marks a fundamental shift from "administering" towards "managing", with the roles of the "centre" and the "periphery" being redefined. The centre increasingly assumes a corporate stewardship role, centralizing or strengthening regulatory functions with decentralization of operational management (Figure 14.2). In particular, NPM encourages replacement of hierarchical bureaucracies with managed networks and emphasizes performance management (Ferlie 2001). A "command and control" mode of management gives way to managing through empowerment and motivation.

With NPM, there is more "market-like" orientation and increased convergence

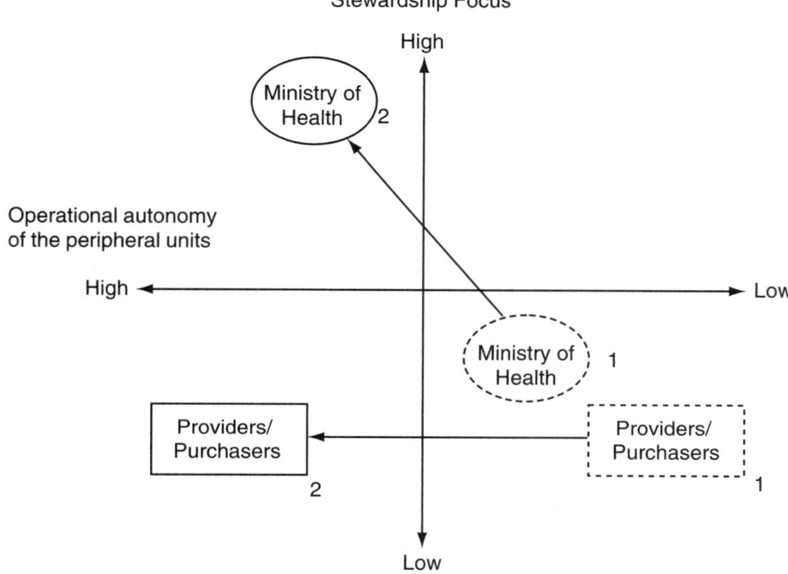

Figure 14.2 The changing roles of the centre and the periphery

with private sector models of organization. In countries which have moved to NPM mode, one can observe the emergence of quasi-markets or the introduction of market mechanisms within regulated environments. There is increased use of contracting, outsourcing, competitive tendering, and privatization in place of long-term salaried employment. New organizational forms – such as autonomous providers – are created. It should be noted that NPM is not without its critics, who claim it erodes public sector notions of due process, equity and probity at the expense of performance and efficiency, and that it reduces democratic accountability (Du Gay 1993).

Managerial changes

Availability of modern management instruments (such as performance management) and robust information systems have created greater transparency, forcing politicians and managers in the public sector to more explicitly set strategic goals and priorities (Flynn and Strehl 1996). In particular, the growth of IT has led to major managerial and societal transformation, with increased user expectations (Castells 1996). In the health sector, IT has enhanced accounting, performance management and benchmarking. This has encouraged more strict accounting practices and increased audit in health care organizations and has enabled comparison and benchmarking with public and private organizations, which in turn helped identify poor performers (Laughlin et al. 1992; Power 1997). When faced with such poor performers, the managers now had options to change practices in these organizations, outsourcing these activities, or privatizing the enterprise.

Resource-based view of the organization

In the private sector, in the past 20 years, there has been a significant growth in strategic management approaches that view resources and competences as the key drivers of organizational strategy (Barney 1991; Mahoney and Pandian 1992). At the heart of this "resource-based" approach, adopted by public sector organizations (Pettigrew and Whipp 1991), is the belief that in order to develop a sustainable strategy an organization must develop a deep understanding of its own (tangible and intangible) resources as well as current and potential future capabilities (Grant 1998). This understanding informs organizational strategy, which in turn reflects the "unique resources", "core competences" and the "capability" of the organization needed to deliver a particular service (or produce a product) better than its peers or competitors (Hamel and Prahalad 1990). For example, resource-based models applied to health care organizations in the public sector show that ability to manage strategic change was a key competence needed for comparative success (Pettigrew et al. 1992). Large public sector organizations have used this approach to define unique resources and the core competences needed to add value. Delayering and downsizing of corporate staff and outsourcing of non-core activities from the private sector have been used as strategies to focus and maintain core competences. The resource-based model of the organization has also encouraged the adoption of different management styles (strategic planning, strategic control, and financial control) when managing the core of the corporation compared to subsidiary units. Decentralization of subsidiary units has created strategic cost/revenue centres. These centres, which have been transformed internally, have been managed through strategic planning or control approaches, using contracts or strategic plans as the tools of control (for instance, Strategic Health Authorities in the British NHS). Units which have not been retained within the broader corporate structure have been outsourced or privatized (for instance, day surgery units in England). The relationship with these organizations is through contracts or service level agreements, allowing strategic and financial control.

Electoral pressure to lower taxation levels

One key driver of change in the 1980s was the unwillingness of the electorate to pay higher taxes, yet without a reduction in demand for health services. This forced many European governments to explore ways to achieve "better value for money" by downsizing, outsourcing or privatizing certain activities in their health systems and the public sector. Germany, through the "Leaner State" programme, encouraged contracting out, outsourcing and the growth of private finance (OECD 1998a). Sweden aimed to reduce expenditure by increased outsourcing (OECD 1998b). France increased privatization, began public sector restructuring, downsized public sector staff and encouraged private sources of finance for capital investment in health organizations, such as hospitals (OECD 1999). Similar changes were observed in the United Kingdom with widespread privatization, restructuring, outsourcing and public–private partnerships.

Privatization experience in the European health sector

Full privatization

In Europe, the extent of full privatization and the success of these policies vary. Central European countries such as Hungary, Poland, and the Czech Republic have privatized dentistry and pharmacy services. A similar trend can be observed in eastern Europe. There have been limited evaluations of the impact of privatizing dental or community pharmacy services. A study from the United Kingdom has found that dentists in privatized dental practices that provided both private and public services spent significantly more time in private consultations compared with NHS consultations, with consequent adverse affects on equity of access and quality of NHS dental care (Lynch and Calnan 2003).

In several central and eastern European countries such as Croatia, the Czech Republic, Georgia, Estonia, Hungary, Poland, Slovenia and The former Yugoslav Republic of Macedonia, primary health care (PHC) and hospital services have been privatized to varied levels.

In Estonia, there has been full privatization of family medicine (FM), which has been fully scaled up to cover the whole country (Atun 2005; Atun et al. 2005a). Since the reforms and privatization of FM, PHC effectiveness has been enhanced, as evidenced by improved management of key chronic conditions by family practitioners (FPs) in PHC settings and reduced hospital admissions for these conditions (Atun 2005). PHC efficiency (Koppel et al. 2003), equity (Kunst et al. 2002) and service quality (Kalda et al. 2004) have improved, as has user satisfaction (Polluste et al. 2000; Kalda et al. 2003) (see Box 14.1).

In Croatia, privatization of PHC providers was a key objective of the health reforms introduced in the 1990s. PHC doctors became individual business entities who contracted with the Croatian Health Insurance Institute. Those people who were insured through the compulsory health insurance were entitled to an essential package of services. Those with supplementary voluntary insurance or private insurance had access to a broader range of services. The now independent PHC physicians could work in privately owned facilities or in rented offices of public health institutions (Mastilica and Kubec 2005). Following privatization, at first, accessibility to services increased (Hebrang et al. 2003), but this increase was not even or sustained. In contrast to Estonia, privatization of health services has adversely affected equity – with increased out-of-pocket expenditure and reduced access for vulnerable groups (Mastilica and Chen 1998; Mastilica and Bozikov 1999) – as well as efficiency and user satisfaction (Chen and Mastilica 1998; Mastilica and Babic'-Bosanac 2002; Mastilica and Kubec 2005). There was an increase in the number of diagnostic procedures and referrals for specialist consultations, but a decline in continuity of care for patients with chronic illness, prevention and health promotion (Katic et al. 2004) (see Box 14.2).

Box 14.1 Privatization of family medicine services in Estonia

Prior to independence, the Estonian PHC system was based on the Soviet Semashko model with services provided in polyclinics and health centres owned by the municipalities. Family medicine as a specialty did not exist. Instead, the health centres were staffed by medical graduates without postgraduate or specialist training. Polyclinics were staffed by therapeutists, paediatricians, gynaecologists and sub-specialists such as ophthalmologists and ENT surgeons. The doctors who worked at PHC level had low status and pay compared to specialists. The PHC level did not effectively perform a gate-keeping function but instead acted as a referral point to specialists.

Following independence in 1991, waves of multifaceted PHC reforms were introduced, aimed at developing a family medicine-centred PHC system. The changes included new organizational structures, user choice of FPs, new payment methods, specialist training for family medicine, service contracts for FPs, broadened scope of services and evidence-based guidelines. Estonian citizens were required to register with a family physician of their choice and the law entitled family physicians to become independent contractors – either as sole private proprietors, partnerships or as a company. Family physicians practise either from centres which they own or which they privately rent. Initial findings point to the considerable success of these reforms.

Box 14.2 Privatizing PHC services in Croatia

The objectives of the Health Care Act and Health Insurance Act in 1993 were to improve the efficiency of health services, address shortages of pharmaceuticals, increase user satisfaction and increase the income of health professionals. Compulsory health insurance was introduced, with a Croatian Health Insurance Institute established to manage health financing, contracting and quality assurance of health services. A restricted range of services and pharmaceuticals are covered by the compulsory health insurance (Hebrang 1994). Those with higher incomes are able to purchase voluntary insurance – either as supplementary insurance to compulsory health insurance or as private insurance instead of compulsory health insurance for the highest income group. Citizens now purchase health care from public or private providers.

The perceptions of the health professionals, researchers and the users are that the privatization of health services has created a two-tiered health system. Low-income groups have been particularly badly hit. They report increased out-of-pocket expenditure, compromised access to health services, and greater dissatisfaction with health services. In contrast, citizens in the high-income groups have good access to higher quality services and experience lower out-of-pocket payments.

In the 1990s, Slovenia introduced privatization to the PHC sector, whereby family physicians, who were salaried employees, were allowed to become independent practitioners, have contracts with the National Health Insurance organization and practise privately. Initially, around 10% of the practices opted to become independent practitioners and since then this number has slowly risen. Doctors who chose to become independent reported increased satisfaction levels, improved doctor–patient relationship, enhanced accessibility and improved efficiency in service delivery due to the introduction of appointment systems (Švab et al. 2001).

In 1991, The former Yugoslav Republic of Macedonia created a Health Insurance Fund (HIF) and through the Health Care Law legalized delivery of PHC services by private providers. Many publicly employed PHC physicians opted to become private practitioners. Around 90% of those working in PHC had contracts with the HIF and were paid according to a fee for service (Nordyke and Peabody 2002). Studies of this early experience suggest that physician productivity was higher in the private sector, as compared with the public sector, and provided more intensive care (by greater use of equipment). The effects on outcomes or equity were not explored (Nordyke 2002).

Similarly, in the 1990s, Poland introduced economic and public sector reforms to move from a centrally planned to a market economy. In the health sector, purchaser–provider separation was achieved with the creation of health insurance and sickness funds, which became the purchasers and contracted with public and private providers. Primary health care services were gradually privatized, with the establishment of private individual and group practices. Structural and financing reforms created an even playing field for public and private providers and led to the emergence of structurally smaller health care provider entities (Chawla et al. 2004).

Faced with economic crisis and the collapse of government tax revenues in the transition period, from 1996, Georgia radically privatized its health sector (Gamkrelidze et al. 2002). This led to the almost total collapse of the public health services with a massive increase in out-of-pocket payments, which, in 1999, accounted for 87% of the total health expenditure. This catastrophic financial risk could not be absorbed by many households, and consequently many families slipped into poverty (World Bank 1999) (see Box 14.3).

Since 1983, there has been systematic privatization of the National Health Service (NHS) in the United Kingdom. The NHS began life as a mixed system, with personal medical services in primary care provided by independent family physicians who operated as solo practitioners or worked in groups. Since the 1980s, there has been further privatization of primary care facilities as well as dental, ophthalmic optician and out-of-hours services (Atun 1998). Most recently, to fill vacant practices, open tenders of family medicine services have been organized. However, to date, the most significant privatization has been witnessed in the long-term care sector. Following the NHS and Community Care Act in 1990, the responsibility for long-term care was devolved to local authorities and user charges introduced for those with a certain level of assets (Secretary of State for Health 1990). The Act was followed by further guidance from the Department of Health on "continuing care criteria" which defined the eligibility of elderly patients to "free" NHS care as opposed to

Box 14.3 Privatization of health services in Georgia

In the early 1990s, the fiscal crisis adversely affected the health system. In 1994, the government expenditure on health declined from 3–4.5% of the GDP to 0.3%, or US$0.8 per person. Faced with the catastrophic collapse in health finances, in 1995, Georgia introduced health insurance and separated purchasing and provision functions. Almost all the pharmacies and dentists were privatized in 1996. From 1999, all health service providers (with the exception of those in a few remote and mountainous areas) were incorporated under commercial law and became independent of the Ministry of Health. Some of these new corporations were fully privatized while others became private entities but with an obligation to continue to provide health services according to contracts with the State Medical Insurance Company, the municipalities, and the Ministry of Health. A basic benefits package was introduced but proved to be too complex for providers and users alike to understand. This created a perverse opportunity for many health care providers to flexibly interpret the rules on prices of interventions and cost sharing and engage in unethical rent-seeking behaviour. This furthered increased out-of-pocket payments, which in 1999 comprised 87% of total health expenditure.

"paid-for" long-term care in the social services sector. This led to a dramatic reduction in the number of long-term care beds, with downsizing of over 100 000 NHS beds. In contrast, in the period 1990–1999, the private sector beds for continuing care increased from 33 000 to 360 000 (Gaffney et al. 1999c). By the late 1990s, this market was worth over £10 billion per year (Atun 1998).

In Norway, despite its strong public sector traditions, 66% of primary care services in 2001 were provided by private, contracted doctors, as opposed to 19% which were delivered by salaried doctors (Sorensen and Grytten 2002). In Sweden, the operation of three hospitals were sold to the private sector in 2000. However, this decision was later reversed for all but one hospital (St. Görans in Stockholm County) and legislation introduced to prevent any further privatizations (Burgermeister 2004).

Outsourcing and contracting out

In European countries where privatization was not acceptable politically, services and responsibilities have been outsourced to private sector providers so as to enhance competition (Hermans 1998). For example, in the NHS in the United Kingdom, in an attempt to reduce waiting lists, a considerable volume of elective surgery has been outsourced to private providers (NHS 2000). Outsourcing from the private sector has since been expanded for diagnostic and other health services to enhance choice for patients. In its Patient Choice initiative, the UK

Government's objective is to ensure that by 2008, patients referred by their general practitioner for a specialist outpatient consultation will have the choice of any NHS, private or hybrid public–private organization (Secretary of State for Health 2004). All organizations providing services will be paid the same price according to the fixed national tariff for services (Department of Health 2004). Although this marks a further step in private sector participation in the NHS, it is not clear whether this initiative will enhance health outcomes, equity, efficiency, or indeed expand user choice (Appleby and Dixon 2004).

Sweden experimented with outsourcing in the 1990s. In 1994, Stockholm County created a limited company to manage a central county hospital with 200 beds (Sveman and Essinger 2001). In 1999, the hospital's operations were sold to Capio AB, a private company listed on the Swedish Stock Exchange, to run it on behalf of the county. Similarly, the management of a number of PHC centres was also outsourced to private companies (Saltman 2003).

In Spain, Catalonia, the first region to introduce a purchaser–provider split, outsourced management and other hospital functions to novel entities (consortia) created as part reforms and governed by a mixture of public and private laws (Busse et al. 2002). Similarly, Portugal has used a number of initiatives to introduce private sector practices into its health system. These included a purchaser–provider split with the creation of internal markets, the establishment of autonomous hospitals and the outsourcing of management and service provision in health care institutions, as well as public–private partnerships. As early as 1995, management of large public hospitals was contracted out to private institutions. Further, to address waiting lists for elective procedures, special programmes enabling outsourcing of elective surgery to the private sector were established (Campos 2004).

New organizational forms

Hybrid organizations

Hybrid organizations are not fully privatized and remain in the public sector but have many characteristics of private sector organizations. Various forms exist including autonomous trusts in the United Kingdom, state-owned joint stock companies, and public–private partnerships such as those created through private finance initiatives. Saltman has developed a typology to describe four major forms of private and public organizational forms: (1) private for profit; (2) private not-for-profit; (3) public but not state; and (4) public and state. To illustrate "public but non-state" organizations, Saltman describes regional and local government-run institutions – such as the autonomous provinces in Spain; the *Ländern* in Germany; county councils in Sweden or Denmark; municipal governments in Finland – as well the managerially independent but publicly accountable public entities: such as hospital trusts in the United Kingdom; independently managed hospitals in Norway, Sweden, and Spain, as well as primary health centres in Sweden (Saltman 2003).

Many of the hybrid organizations described below are adequately captured by Saltman's third category. However, the NHS Trusts, Foundation Trusts, and PHC Trusts in the United Kingdom and the public–private partnerships do not fit comfortably into the typology and can be considered to be new social organizations whose structure, scope and accountability frameworks are continually evolving. Although Harding and Preker define the creation of autonomous trusts and other arrangements as "corporatization" or "autonomization" (Harding and Preker 2000), in our analytical framework – the "privatization continuum" – the transformation of these hospitals into hybrid entities is regarded as a means for introducing private sector practices into public firms.

Autonomous trusts

Prior to the health reforms in 1991, hospitals in the United Kingdom were state owned and directly managed by district health authorities. In 1991, NHS hospital trusts were created and their management devolved to a board comprising a chair, a chief executive officer, executive and non-executive board members. In 2000, Primary Care Trusts were established. These trusts have management autonomy and devolved budgets, controlling up to 80% of the health system funds, which they use to purchase primary care and hospital services. They oversee the independent general practitioners. The Health and Social Care Bill of 2003 has, to a great extent, abolished government control of NHS trusts by establishing Foundation Trusts – independent health care corporations with the responsibility to provide services to the NHS but with the freedom to carry out any type of business. The Foundation Trusts compete with each other to gain NHS business from Primary Care Trusts, and generate income from private patients and raise funding from private sources, including capital markets (House of Commons 2003). Both NHS and private sector companies can apply to become Foundation Trusts that are regulated by an independent regulator and not the government. Some critics view the establishment of the Foundation Trusts as further privatization of the NHS, with concerns about adverse affect on equity (Pollock et al. 2003).

Similar changes have been introduced in Denmark, Italy, Germany, Portugal, Spain and Sweden, where independently managed novel hospital organizations have been created (Saltman 2003).

In 1995, Denmark established a purchaser–provider split by creating Copenhagen Hospital Trust – an independent consortium of several hospitals – and by establishing regional purchasers (Ministry of Health 1999). In Italy, especially in Lombardy Region, around 100 hospitals have been converted to autonomous trusts. In Germany, where a purchaser–private split already existed, in some *Ländern* public hospitals are required by law to become independent and be responsible for own financial management. In Spain, where regions have considerable autonomy in managing their local health economies, in the 1990s the purchaser–provider split was introduced and various forms of autonomous hospitals were created. For example, the Basque Country created a novel corporatized entity by transforming its regional health service into a "public entity under private law". Similarly, the central government, which controlled hospitals through INSALUD, and also Galicia Region, created autonomous hospitals (Busse et al. 2002).

In Portugal, transformation of public institutions into autonomous enterprises began in 1999 (Government of Portugal 1999). This was extended to the health sector in 2002 where autonomous primary health centres and hospitals were established (Government of Portugal 2002). Creation of autonomous hospitals took two forms. In the first, the public hospitals were "corporatized" as autonomous public institutions (hospitais SPA), and, in the second, established as private hospitals, but with the property remaining in the public domain (hospitais SA) (Campos 2004).

In central and eastern Europe, creation of autonomous hospitals has lagged behind western Europe. However, Estonia has been successful in achieving a planned and orderly downsizing of its hospital sector. The optimization of the hospital capacity was implemented according to the "Hospital Masterplan 2015" which enabled the incorporation of hospitals, under private law, as foundations (trusts) or joint stock companies. This allowed hospitals to merge and independently contract with the Estonian Health Insurance Fund (Atun 2005).

Statutory sickness funds in Germany

Statutory sickness funds in Germany are another example of hybrid organizations that have private ownership but operate according to public sector rules and regulations. These receive funding from both the private (industry sources) and public (guilds, regional *Länder* government, or the state) sources and are managed by an autonomous board composed of employees and employers, but are subject to laws that govern the public sector (Saltman 2003).

Hybrid organizations in the Swedish hospital sector

The Swedish experience of creating hybrid organizations is interesting. In 2000, the health care organization, Capio, was floated as an independent company on the Swedish stock exchange. Capio was owned by Bure, which was established by taxes raised by the state. Capio, then Bure, bought the operations of a Swedish public hospital, although the hospital remained in public ownership. Since then Capio has expanded its operations beyond Sweden to Norway, Denmark, the United Kingdom, Switzerland and Poland (Capio 2001, 2002, 2003).

Joint stock companies in Armenia

Despite a highly resource-constrained environment, Armenia has introduced structural changes with the separation of purchasing and provider functions and the creation of hybrid organizations in form of "state-owned closed joint stock companies", with managerial and budgetary autonomy and rights to establish contracts with public or private organizations (Atun et al. 2005b) (see Box 14.4).

Box 14.4 Hybrid organizations in Armenia

In 1996, the Medical Care Act created an environment where a public–private mix of financing was possible (Republic of Armenia 1996). This law stipulated that the public budget was no longer the sole authorized financing source and legalized alternative financing mechanisms to increase those obtained from public sources. Out-of-pocket payments were introduced in 1997 for the majority of health care services beyond the basic package and payable by all non-vulnerable and non-targeted groups of the population. Consequently, health providers were allowed to mobilize funds from various sources, including local budgets, external aid, health insurance payments, and private out-of-pocket payments.

The State Health Agency, which was created in 1997, assumed a strategic purchasing role. In the same year, all state health care establishments were granted the status of "state enterprises" and in 2000 were transformed into "state-owned closed joint stock companies", enabling the creation of new PHC and hospital provider organizations with managerial and budgetary autonomy. These provider organizations are able to contract with the State Health Agency to provide services included in the State Guaranteed Basic Benefits Package, but are unable to decide on the volume or the price of these services. These providers can also negotiate and sign contracts with private enterprises to provide health services. In 2000, the "Concept on the Strategy of Privatization of Health Care Facilities" was approved by the government, paving the way for privatization of health care facilities (Republic of Armenia 2001).

Public–private partnerships

Public–private partnership (PPP) is a term used to describe a variety of relationships between the private sector and public bodies. These range from informal and strategic partnerships to schemes that entail designing, building, financing and operating assets (with or without transfer) which were previously in the public domain. In effect, the private sector develops and builds assets and provides services which are financed or coordinated by the public sector (European Commission 1997a). PPP has been widely used for infrastructure development, facilities management and for service development and delivery. In these arrangements, there is shared capitalization and risk. The European Commission has actively encouraged the use of public–private partnerships and has provided grants to encourage their establishment (European Commission 1998). In the EU context, the aim of PPPs is to enhance efficiency and reduce expenditure in the public sector and create opportunities for the private sector (European Commission 1997b).

Public–private partnerships have been introduced in numerous European countries, including Austria, Finland, France, Ireland, Italy, Portugal, Spain and the United Kingdom, to varying extent (PriceWaterhouseCoopers 2003). In the

United Kingdom, which has the longest and most extensive experience of PPP, the Private Finance Initiative (PFI) has been the main vehicle for introducing PPPs and is used for infrastructure projects in the hospital and PHC sectors, for funding capital investments for IT and diagnostics (laboratories, diagnostic radiology), and even for service delivery (renal dialysis units) (see Box 14.5). To date, planned private sector investment in the health sector through PPPs amount to around £3.1 billion (Gaffney et al. 1999c).

Portugal has also actively promoted PPPs and has 14 projects with a net present value of 1.3 billion euro. France currently has some 11 active PPP projects with a further 20 under negotiation.

Transformation internally

In the 1990s, many European countries introduced internal markets to increase competition in the health sector, with a view to improving choice, diversity of

Box 14.5 The Private Finance Initiative in the United Kingdom

PFI is a financing mechanism to provide off-balance sheet (i.e. non-governmental) funding for major capital investments. In the UK model, private consortia are contracted to design, build and, in many cases, manage new infrastructure projects. Contracts typically last up to 30 years, during which assets are leased by the public institution. The appropriateness of PFI and its benefits have been called into question. Pollock et al. (1997) have demonstrated that the new facilities almost invariably provided less capacity than those they were intended to replace (Gaffney et al. 1999a), that the contracts were expensive, to the extent that this could be ascertained, given that they were shrouded in commercial secrecy (Pollock et al. 1997), and the economic arguments were questionable (Gaffney et al. 1999b). Green and Propper, who examined the impact of PFI on the efficiency of the UK public sector in conjunction with empirical evidence from OECD countries, concluded that the evidence of benefit is finely balanced. However, they concluded that there is little to support the notion that increased PFI would improve the efficiency of the NHS (Green and Propper 2001). Others have questioned the sustainability of PFI (Atun and McKee 2005), given possible changes in the way PFI financing is treated. Currently, PFI funding is treated as "off-balance sheet financing", and as such, not included in the net debt calculations for the United Kingdom. However, there are indications that the Office of National Statistics may change the rules so that a significant component of capital spending under PFI contracts could be reclassified as debt. This would have consequences for the United Kingdom (as for other EU members that use PFI-like instruments) whose ability to borrow is constrained by EU agreements on fiscal stability.

provision, performance and accountability (OECD 1992; Saltman et al. 1998). Financing and purchasing were separated from provision (Maynard 1991). Contracts, which stipulated service volumes, delivery targets and a budget, were introduced between purchasers and the providers to achieve better performance and accountability. Evidence for contracting for health service delivery is patchy. A recent review identifies potential benefits such as enhancing focus on outputs and results, overcoming absorptive capacity constraints in governments by enabling them to use resources made available to them, utilizing flexible approaches that prevail in the private sector, enhancing managerial autonomy, increasing competition, and releasing governments from operational responsibilities, so as to allow them to concentrate on more strategic functions. However, the evidence presented to support these assertions is limited (Loevinsohn and Harding 2005).

In Sweden, internal markets were introduced in 1994, where the purchasing and provision roles of the county councils were separated. The county councils became purchasers and developed contracts with hospitals based on diagnostic related groups (DRGs). Studies that examined the Swedish experience show that the internal market had a positive impact on efficiency, productivity and user focus (Hakansson 1994; Whitehead et al. 1997; Bergman 1998; Harrison and Calltrop 2000; Quaye 2001).

In Germany, where an internal market already existed, competition was enhanced by increasing the freedom of the sickness funds to use contracts and with the introduction of DRG-based provider payment systems. Although this led to substantial savings, the sickness funds were unable to influence the provision and structure of services, as they could not enter into selective contracts with providers (Riemer-Hommel 2002).

In the United Kingdom, internal markets were introduced in 1991 with the separation of purchasing and provision when health authorities and general practitioner fundholders became purchasers, while hospitals and GP practices became providers (Department of Health 1989a). Service contracts were introduced for hospitals and PHC units, based on volume of services and performance targets, to improve the efficiency and effectiveness of the services provided and to broaden the scope of services in PHC (Secretary of State 1987; Department of Health 1989b). The results achieved by the reforms were mixed. According to Le Grand, competition within the market was limited and the essential conditions for a market to operate were not fulfilled (Le Grand et al. 1998). Allen argued that the contracts did not enhance the accountability of health care providers and that the specification of the services and their quality were deficient in many health authority and GP fundholder contracts (Allen 2002). There was an increase in productivity in the hospital sector, widened scope of services in PHC with improved productivity but an adverse effect on equity (Robinson and Le Grand 1994; Silcock and Ratcliffe 1996; Le Grand et al. 1998).

Contracting, within internal markets or organizational changes which entailed purchaser–provider separation, has also been used in central and eastern Europe, although competition in these settings remains very limited. Croatia, Estonia, The former Yugoslav Republic of Macedonia and Slovenia, as described above, have examples of contracting with privatized providers. In

Box 14.6 Purchaser–provider separation and contracting in Bosnia and Herzegovina

Organizationally, there is a separation of purchasing and provision, with purchasing devolved to the Health Insurance Fund (HIF) in Republika Srpska (RS) and Cantonal Health Insurance Institutes (CHIIs) in the Federation of Bosnia and Herzegovina (FBIH). Family medicine teams have been established as the basic building block for PHC provider units in both entities. In the pilot regions, the HIF and CHII have established service contracts directly with primary health care centres or through these with the family medicine teams.

The contracts specify in detail the services to be provided by the FM teams as well as the equipment they need to use when delivering services. The scope of services and the equipment used are broader than those specified for non-specialist general practitioners. Contracts have increased transparency and meritocracy by clearly linking rewards to outputs.

other countries, contracts were developed with family medicine teams, family practitioners or primary care organizations that were not private. For example, in Bosnia and Herzegovina purchasing and provision were separated and contracts established with family medicine teams (Atun et al. 2005c) (see Box 14.6).

Similarly, in the Republic of Moldova, an embryonic internal market has been created. Purchasing and provision have been separated and contracts introduced between the Health Insurance Company and hospitals and PHC providers. Changes in the law also make it possible for individuals or legal entities to establish "medical institutions" to contract with the Health Insurance Company or its territorial branches (Atun et al. 2005e) (see Box 14.7).

In eastern Europe, Kyrgyzstan stands out as a success story in the creation of purchaser–provider split and use of contracts to enhance equity, efficiency and effectiveness of health services. Contracts with PHC providers and hospitals have led to improvements in the scope, quality, efficiency and equity of service delivery (Atun et al. 2005d) (see Box 14.8).

Conclusion

In Europe, there is considerable movement towards various forms of privatization of the health sector. There is evidence of heterogeneity of approaches adopted along the privatization continuum. The experience is characterized by the varied mechanisms and instruments used.

There is a growing degree of convergence in the environments within which the public and private sectors organizations operate. The term "Third Way" (Giddens 1998) has been coined to describe the transition from the strict separation of the public and private sectors to a situation where these organizations operate within a unified context and are subject to similar regulatory and

Box 14.7 Beginnings of internal markets and contracting in the Republic of Moldova

In 1998, the Law on Mandatory Health Insurance introduced financing from social insurance and established a mixed system of financing in Moldova. Government resolutions in 2002 enabled the creation of 11 territorial branches of the Health Insurance Company (HIC) and defined the scope of contracts between the HIC and health care providers. The contracts were based on the volume of activities for Basic Benefit Package of Health Care Services under the Mandatory Health Insurance and prices were based on tariffs set by the Ministry of Health.

In 2003, a government regulation defined the services covered by the Mandatory Health Insurance available only for the insured population. In addition, 21 national programmes, specified in the State Guaranteed Minimum Package, were available to all Moldovan citizens, regardless of insurance status.

The HIC agrees to an annual contract with the rayon (district) administration with a pre-specified price and volume of services to be provided by PHC providers, which are paid according to a per capita contract, and hospitals, which are paid per discharged patient and per case for emergencies. Since the introduction of the MHI, in the first three months of 2004 the number of PHC visits increased by 20% as compared with the same period in 2003.

Box 14.8 Purchaser–provider split and contracting in the Kyrgyzstan Republic

Following independence in 1991, Kyrgyzstan inherited a health system based on the Soviet Semashko model, characterized by hierarchical administrative organization, a large provider network dominated by hospitals and a poorly developed PHC level with poor gate-keeping. The system also had an inequitable resource allocation system based on historic activities which favoured large hospitals in urban centres at the expense of rural areas. Line-item budgeting of provider units and salary-based payment systems for staff encouraged inefficiency and discouraged improved performance.

Prior to independence, Kyrgyzstan devoted 3.5% of its GDP to health. Rapid economic decline further compromised the low level of funding to the health sector and led to underinvestment – creating a substantial funding gap between the level of financing needed by the health system and the resources available. Health reforms were introduced in the 1990s to address structural and financing inefficiencies and enhance equity.

A key achievement was the single payer system, which enabled pooling of all sub-national budget funds for health care in the Territorial Department of the Mandatory Health Insurance Fund into "single-pipe funding" to finance the State Guaranteed Benefits Package.

New PHC and hospital provider organizations have been established with autonomy to manage budgets and contract with the Mandatory Health Insurance Fund. Contracts and new provider payment methods have been successfully introduced: for PHC providers based on simple per capita mechanism, including partial fundholding for pharmaceuticals and for hospitals based on fee-for-service.

In PHC, the scope, content and the quality of services have expanded significantly. Unnecessary hospital referrals have diminished. There is evidence of enhanced equity. In hospitals, the average length of stay has declined.

managerial disciplines. With the Third Way, "hands-on management" practices by the government are replaced by "corporate stewardship", where the government aims to enhance local operational flexibility at the organizational level, but within the context of the reintroduction of stronger national regulatory frameworks. The roles and relationships of the centre and the periphery are being redefined, with more "arm's-length" rather than "hands-on" management styles prevailing. Hence, in this model, one witnesses simultaneous decentralization and recentralization: decentralization of operational flexibility with budgets and managerial autonomy and recentralization of regulatory powers, with stronger frameworks which specify process and performance criteria. In effect, the Third Way embodies an idealized hybrid between central and local control, to combine the benefits of both: decentralization to encourage innovation and responsiveness while maintaining arm's-length control to maintain performance and reduce risk – what Hoggett (1996) describes as "decentralization downwards, but accountability upwards". Therefore, narrow definitions of decentralization and centralization break down when dealing with new organizational forms and practices.

As regards managerial practices, the public sector is now less secluded from private sector methods. For example, in personnel, structure and business methods, private sector practices have been adopted. Further, the rules and regulations, which in the past limited the freedom of public officials in managing planning, budgets, human resources and contracts, have decreased due to decentralization. Wilson and Doig comment that in the public sector there is a clear move from an administrative culture operating in a bureaucratic environment – which they call "the enclosed bureaucratic" approach – towards managerial practices in a market environment – which they name "the responsive market" mode (Wilson and Doig 2000).

In western and central Europe there is rich experience of change along the privatization continuum. In eastern Europe, privatization experience is more limited, although in most countries oral health and pharmacy services have been fully privatized. Estonia, Armenia and Kyrgyzstan stand out as examples where elements of privatization have been successfully introduced with benefits to end users, as against Georgia where privatization attempts may have led to widening inequities.

There are a number of discourses on the theory and conceptual approaches to privatization as well as descriptive and analytical pieces that describe the privatization experience in Europe. However, in spite of the rich experience of privatization in the health sector, there are few studies that evaluate the impact of privatization practices on equity, efficiency, and effectiveness and user satisfaction. This is of major concern, as this knowledge gap can encourage "technical autism" at the expense of evidence-based policy – an alarming prospect for health systems and the citizens who stand to gain or lose from the privatization initiatives.

Acknowledgements

Akiko Maeda and António Correia de Campos contributed to an earlier version of this chapter.

References

Allen, P. (2002) A socio-legal and economic analysis of contracting in the NHS internal market using a case study of contracting for district nursing. *Social Science and Medicine*, **54**: 255–66.

Appleby, J. and Dixon, J. (2004) Patient choice in the NHS: having choice may not improve health outcome. *British Medical Journal*, **329**: 61–2.

Atun, R.A. (1998) *Opportunities in the UK health care market: a strategic analysis*. London, The Financial Times.

Atun, R.A. (2005) *Evaluation of the primary health care reforms in Estonia*. Report to the World Health Organization Regional Office for Europe. Copenhagen, World Health Organization Regional Office for Europe.

Atun, R.A. and McKee, M. (2005) Is the private finance initiative dead? *British Medical Journal*, **331**: 792–3.

Atun, R., Berdaga, V., Turcan, L. and Stefanetz, S. (2005a) The World Bank report no. 32354-ECA. Review of experience of family medicine in Europe and Central Asia: executive summary (in five volumes). Vol. I. Human development sector unit, Europe and Central Asia region. Washington, DC, World Bank.

Atun, R., Berdaga, V., Turcan, L. and Stefanetz, S. (2005b) The World Bank report no. 32354-ECA. Review of experience of family medicine in Europe and Central Asia: Armenia case study (in five volumes). Vol. II. Human Development sector unit, Europe and Central Asia region. Washington, DC, World Bank.

Atun, R., Berdaga, V., Turcan, L. and Stefanetz, S. (2005c) The World Bank report no. 32354-ECA. Review of experience of family medicine in Europe and Central Asia: Bosnia and Herzegovina case study (in five volumes). Vol. III. Human Development sector unit, Europe and Central Asia region. Washington, DC, World Bank.

Atun, R., Berdaga, V., Turcan, L. and Stefanetz, S. (2005d) The World Bank report no. 32354-ECA. Review of experience of family medicine in Europe and Central Asia:

Kyrgyz Republic case study (in five volumes). Vol. IV. Human Development sector unit, Europe and Central Asia region. Washington, DC, World Bank.

Atun, R., Berdaga, V., Turcan, L. and Stefanetz, S. (2005e) The World Bank report no. 32354-ECA. Review of experience of family medicine in Europe and Central Asia: Moldova case study (in five volumes). Vol. V. Human Development sector unit, Europe and Central Asia region, May 2005. Washington, DC, World Bank.

Aucoin, P. (1995) *The new public management: Canada in comparative perspective*. Montreal, IRPP.

Barney, J.B. (1991) Firm resources and sustained competitive advantage. *Journal of Management*, **17**: 99–120.

Barzelay, M. (1992) *Breaking through bureaucracy*. Berkeley, CA, University of California Press.

Beesley, M. and Littlechild, S. (1983) Privatisation: principles, problems and priorities. *Lloyds Bank Review*, **149**: 1–20.

Bergman, S. (1998) Swedish models of health care reform: a review and assessment. *International Journal of Health Planning and Management*, **13**: 91–106.

Bjorkman, J.W. (1985) Who governs the health sector? Comparative European and American experiences with representation, participation, and decentralization. *Comparative Politics*, **17**: 399–420.

Bossert, T. (1998) Analysing the decentralization of health systems in developing countries: decision space, innovation and performance. *Social Science and Medicine*, **47**: 1513–27.

Boston, J., Martin, J., Pallot, J. and Walsh, P. (1996) *Public management: the New Zealand model*. Auckland, Oxford University Press.

Burgermeister, V.J. (2004) Sweden bans privatisation of hospitals. *British Medical Journal*, **328**: 484.

Busse, R., van der Grinten, T. and Svensson, P.G. (2002) Regulating entrepreneurial behaviour in hospitals: theory and practice. In Saltman, R.B., Busse, R. and Mossialos, E., eds, *Regulating entrepreneurial behaviour in European health systems*. Buckingham, Open University Press.

Campbell, C. and Halligan, J. (1992) *Political leadership in an age of constraint*. Pittsburgh, PA, University of Pittsburgh Press.

Campos, A.C. (2004) Decentralization and privatization in Portuguese health reform. *Revista Portuguesa de Saúde Pública*, **4**: 7.

Capio (2001) *Annual report 2001*. Göteborg, Capio (http://www.capio.com//, accessed 19 April 2006).

Capio (2002) *Annual report 2002*. Göteborg, Capio (http://www.capio.com/, accessed 19 April 2006).

Capio (2003) *Annual report 2003*. Göteborg, Capio (http://www.capio.com/, accessed 19 April 2006).

Castells, M. (1996) *The rise of the network society*. Oxford, Basil Blackwell.

Chawla, M., Berman, P., Windak, A. and Kulis, M. (2004) Provision of ambulatory care services in Poland: a case study from Krakow. *Social Science and Medicine*, **58**: 227–35.

Chen, M-S. and Mastilica, M. (1998) Health care reform in Croatia: for better or for worse? *American Journal of Public Health*, **88**: 1156–60.

Collins, C. (1989) Decentralization and the need for political and critical analysis. *Health Policy and Planning*, **4**: 168–71.

Collins, C. and Green, A. (1994) Decentralization and primary health care: some negative implications in developing countries. *International Journal of Health Services*, **24**: 459–75.

Department of Health (1989a) *Working for patients: the health service in the 1990s*. Cm 555. London, HMSO.

Department of Health (1989b) *General practice in the National Health Service: the 1990 contract: the government's programme for changes to GPs' terms of service and renmuneration system*. London, Department of Health.

Department of Health (2004) *NHS reference costs 2003 and national tariffs 2004 (payment by results)*. London, Department of Health.

Du Gay, P. (1993) Entrepreneurial management in the public sector. *Work, Employment and Society*, **7**(4): 643–8.

Dunleavy, P. and Hood, C. (1994) From old public administration to new public management. *Public Money and Management*, **14**(3): 9–16.

Efficiency Unit (1988) *Improving management in government: the next steps* (the Ibbs Report). London, HMSO

Enthoven, A. (1985) Reflections on the management of the NHS, Occasional Paper 5, London, Nuffield Provincial Hospitals Trust

European Commission (1997a) *Public procurement in the European Union: exploring the way forward*. Brussels, European Commission Directorate General.

European Commission (1997b) *Making the most of the opening of public procurement*. Brussels, European Commission Directorate General.

European Commission (1998) *Government investment in the framework of economic strategy*. Brussels, European Commission.

Ferlie, E. (2001) Quasi strategy: strategic management in the contemporary public sector. In Pettigrew, A.M., Thomas, H. and Whittington, R., eds, *Handbook of strategy and management*. London, Sage.

Ferlie, E., Ashburner, L., Fitzgerald, L. and Pettigrew, A. (1996) *The new public management in action*. Oxford, Oxford University Press.

Flynn, N. and Strehl, F. (eds) (1996) *Public sector management in Europe*. London, Prentice Hall.

Gaffney, D., Pollock, A.M., Price, D., and Shaoul, J. (1999a) NHS capital expenditure and the private finance initiative: expansion or contraction? *British Medical Journal*, **319**: 48–51.

Gaffney, D., Pollock, A.M., Price, D. and Shaoul, J. (1999b) PFI in the NHS: is there an economic case? *British Medical Journal*, **319**: 116–19.

Gaffney, D., Pollock, A.M., Price, D. and Shaoul, J. (1999c) The politics of the private finance initiative and the new NHS. *British Medical Journal*, **319**: 249–53.

Gamkrelidze, A., Atun, R.A., Gotsadze, G. and Maclehouse, L. (2002) *Health systems in transition: Georgia*. Copenhagen, WHO Regional Office.

Giddens, A. (1979) *Central problems in social theory: action, structure and contradiction in social analysis*. Berkeley, CA University of California Press.

Giddens, A. (1998) *The third way*. London, Polity Press.

Government of Portugal (1999) Lei n° 159/99, de 14 de Setembro, Quadro de Transferências de Atribuições e Competências para as Autarquias Locais. Lisbon, Government of Portugal.

Government of Portugal (2002) Resolução do Conselho de Ministros n° 41/2002, de 20 de Agosto. Estabelece medidas para permitir a transformação de estabelecimentos públicos prestadores de cuidados hospitalares em entidades públicas empresariais (EPE). Lisbon, Government of Portugal.

Grant, R.M. (1998) *Contemporary strategy analysis*. 3rd edn. Oxford, Basil Blackwell.

Green, K. and Propper, C. (2001) A larger role for the private sector in financing UK health care: the arguments and the evidence. *Journal of Social Policy*, **4**: 685–704.

Hakansson, S. (1994) New ways of financing and organizing health care in Sweden. *International Journal of Health Services*, **24**(2): 231–51.

Hamel, G. and Pralahad, C.K. (1990) The core competences of the corporation. *Harvard Business Review*, **May/June**: 79–91.

Harding, A. and Preker, A.S. (2000) Organizational reform in the hospital sector: a conceptual framework. In Preker, A.S. and Harding, A., eds, *Innovations in health care reform: the corporatisation of public hospitals*. Baltimore, MD, Johns Hopkins University Press.

Harrison, M.I. and Calltrop, J. (2000) The reorientation of market-oriented reforms in Swedish health care. *Health Policy*, **50**(3): 219–40.

Hebrang, A. (1994) Reorganization of the Croatian health care system. *Croatian Medical Journal*, **35**: 130–6.

Hebrang, A., Henisburg, N., Erdeljic, V. et al. (2003) Privatisation in the health care system of Croatia: effects on general practice accessibility. *Health Policy and Planning*, **18**(4): 421–8.

Hermans, H. (1998) Contracting and the purchaser-provider split in Western Europe: a legal-organizational analysis. *Medicine and Law*, **17**(2): 167–88.

Hoggett, P. (1996) New modes of control in the public sector. *Public Administration*, **74**(1): 9–32.

Hood, C. (1991) A new public management for all seasons? *Public Administration*, **69**(1): 3–19.

Hood, C. (1995) The new public management in the 1980s – variations on a theme. *Accounting, Organisation and Society*, **20**(2/3): 93–110.

House of Commons (2003) Health and Social Care (Community Health and Standards) Bill. London, Stationery Office.

Kalda, R., Polluste, K. and Lember, M. (2003) Patient satisfaction with care is associated with personal choice of physician. *Health Policy*, **64**(1): 55–62.

Kalda, R., Sarapuu, H., Lember, M., Sontak, G. and Hapunova, M. (2004) Family physicians and pediatricians vaccinate children with same quality. *Family Medicine*, **34**(10): 714–15.

Katic, M., Juresa, V. and Oreskovic, S. (2004) Family medicine in Croatia. *Croatian Medical Journal*, **45**: 543–9.

Kikeri, S., Nellis, J. and Shirley, M. (1992) *Privatization: the lessons of experience*. Washington, DC, World Bank.

Koppel, A., Meiesaar, K., Valtonen, H., Metsa, A. and Lember, M. (2003) Evaluation of primary health care reform in Estonia. *Social Science and Medicine*, **56**: 2461–6.

Kunst, A.E., Leinsalu, M., Kasmel, A. and Habicht, J. (2002) *Social inequalities in health in Estonia*. Tallinn, Ministry of Social Affairs.

Laughlin, R., Broadbent, J. and Shearn, D. (1992) Recent financial and accountability changes in general practice: an unhealthy intrusion into medical autonomy? *Financial Accountability and Management*, **8**(2): 129–48.

Le Grand, J., Mays, N. and Mulligan, J. (eds) (1998) *Learning from the NHS internal market: a review of the evidence*. London, The King's Fund.

Loevinsohn, B. and Harding, A. (2005) Buying results: contracting for health service delivery in developing countries. *Lancet*, **366**: 676–81.

Lynch, M. and Calnan, M. (2003) The changing public/private mix in dentistry in the UK: a supply-side perspective. *Health Economics*, **12**: 309–21.

Mahoney, J. and Pandian, R. (1992) The resource-based view within the conversation of strategic management. *Strategic Management Journal*, **13**: 363–80.

Mastilica, M. and Babic'-Bosanac, S. (2002) Citizens' views on health insurance in Croatia. *Croatian Medical Journal*, **43**: 417–24.

Mastilica, M. and Bozikov, J. (1999) Out-of-pocket payments for health care in Croatia: implications for equity. *Croatian Medical Journal*, **40**: 152–9.

Mastilica, M. and Chen M-S. (1998) Health care reform in Croatia: the consumers' perspective. *Croatian Medical Journal*, **39**: 256–66.

Mastilica, M. and Kubec, S. (2005) Croatian healthcare system in transition, from the perspective of users. *British Medical Journal*, **331**: 223–6.

Maynard, A. (1991) Developing the health care market. *The Economic Journal*, **101**: 1277–86.

Mills, A., Vaughan, P.J., Smith, D.L. and Tabibzadeh, I. (eds) (1990) *Health system decentralization: concepts, issues and country experience*. Geneva, World Health Organization.

Ministry of Health (1999) *The Danish health care sector*. Copenhagen, Ministry of Health.

NHS (2000) *The NHS national plan* (http://www.nhs.uk/nationalplan/contents.htm (accessed 5 August 2005).

Nordyke, R.J. (2002) Determinants of PHC productivity and resource utilization: a comparison of public and private physicians in Macedonia. *Health Policy*, **60**(1): 67–96.

Nordyke, R.J. and Peabody, J.W. (2002) Market reforms and public incentive: finding a balance in the Republic of Macedonia. *Social Science and Medicine*, **54**: 939–53.

OECD (1992) *The reform of health care: a comparative analysis of seven OECD countries*. Paris, OECD.

OECD (1995) *Internal markets in the making*. Paris, OECD.

OECD (1997) *Managing across levels of government*. Paris, OECD.

OECD (1998a) *Economic survey – Germany*. Paris, OECD.

OECD (1998b) *Economic survey – Sweden*. Paris, OECD.

OECD (1999) *Economic survey – France*. Paris, OECD.

Osborne, D. and Gaebler, T. (1992) *Reinventing government: how the entrepreneurial spirit is transforming the public sector*. Reading, MA, Addison-Wesley.

Pettigrew, A. and Whipp, R. (1991) *Managing change for competitive success*. Oxford, Basil Blackwell.

Pettigrew, A., Ferlie, E. and McKee, L. (1992) *Shaping strategic change*. London, Sage.

Pollitt, C. (1990) *The new managerialism and the public services: the Anglo-American experience*. Oxford, Basil Blackwell.

Pollock, A.M. and Price, D. (2000) Rewriting the regulations: how the World Trade Organisation could accelerate privatisation in health-care systems. *Lancet*, **356**: 1995–2000.

Pollock, A.M., Dunnigan, M., Gaffney, D., Macfarlane, A. and Majeed, F.A. (1997) on behalf of the NHS Consultants' Association, Radical Statistics Health Group, and the NHS Support Federation. What happens when the private sector plans hospital services for the NHS: three case studies under the private finance initiative. *British Medical Journal*, **314**: 1266–71.

Pollock, A.M., Price, D., Talbot-Smith, A. and Mohan, J. (2003) NHS and the Health and Social Care Bill: end of Bevan's vision? *British Medical Journal*, **327**: 982–5.

Polluste, K., Kalda, R. and Lember, M. (2000) Primary health care system in transition: the patient's experience. *International Journal of Quality Health Care*, **12**(6): 503–9.

Power, M. (1997) *The audit society*. Oxford, Oxford University Press.

PriceWaterhouseCoopers (2003) *Developing public private partnerships in new Europe*. London, PriceWaterhouseCoopers.

Quaye, R.K. (2001) Internal market systems in Sweden: seven years after the Stockholm model. *European Journal of Public Health*, **11**: 380–5.

Republic of Armenia (1996) Law: "On medical aid and medical services for the population". Yerevan, Armenia.

Republic of Armenia (2001) Decree Number 80: "Concept paper of optimization in the health system of the Republic of Armenia".

Riemer-Hommel, P. (2002) The changing nature of contracts in German health care. *Social Science and Medicine*, **55**: 1447–55.

Robinson, R. and Le Grand, J. (1994) *Evaluating the NHS reforms*. London, The King's Fund.

Rondinelli, D. (1981) Government decentralization in comparative theory and practice in developing countries. *International Review of Administrative Sciences*, **47**: 133–45.

Rondinelli, D. and Iacona, M. (1996) *Policies and institutions for managing privatization*. Geneva, International Labour Organization.

Rondinelli, D.A., Nellis, J.R. and Cheema, G.S. (1983) Decentralization in developing countries. Staff Working Paper 581. Washington, DC, World Bank.

Saltman, R.B. (2003) Melting public-private boundaries in European health systems. *European Journal of Public Health*, **13**: 24–9.

Saltman R.B., Figueras, J. and Skellarides, C.S. (eds) (1998) *Critical challenges for health care reform in Europe*. Buckingham, Open University Press.

Saltman, R.B., Busses, R. and Mossialos, E. (eds) (2002) *Regulating entrepreneurial behaviour in European health care systems*. Buckingham, Open University Press.

Secretary of State (1987) *Promoting better health: the government's programme for improving primary health care*. London, HMSO.

Secretary of State for Health (1990) *National Health Service and Community Care Act 1990*. London, Her Majesty's Stationery Office.

Secretary of State for Health (2004) *The NHS improvement plan: putting people at the heart of public services*. London, Stationery Office.

Segall, M. (2000) From cooperation to competition in national health systems – and back? Impact on professional ethics and quality of care. *International Journal of Health Planning and Management*, **15**: 61–79.

Sherwood, F.P. (1969) Devolution as a problem of organization strategy. In Dalan, R.T., ed., *Comparative urban research*. Beverly Hills, CA, Sage.

Silcock, J. and Ratcliffe, J. (1996) The 1990 GP contract – meeting needs? *Health Policy*, **36**(2): 199–207.

Sorensen, R. and Grytten, J. (2002) Service production and contract choice of primary physician. *Health Policy*, **66**: 73–93.

Švab, I., Progar, I.V. and Vegnuti, M. (2001) Private practice in Slovenia after the health care reform. *European Journal of Public Health*, **11**: 407–12.

Sveman, E. and Essinger, K. (2001) Procurement of health care services in Sweden in general, and the example of procurement of acute care in the Stockholm region. In *European integration and health care systems: a challenge for social policy*. Stockholm, Swedish Federation of County Councils.

Tittenbrun, J. (1996) *Private versus public enterprise: in search of the economic rationale for privatisation*. London, Janus.

Vickers, J. and Yarrow, G. (1988) *Privatisation: an economic analysis*. Cambridge, MA, The MIT Press.

Whitehead, M., Varde, E. and Diderichsen, F. (1997) Resource allocation to health authorities: the quest for an equitable formula in Britain and Sweden. *British Medical Journal*, **315**: 875–8.

Wilson, J. and Doig, A. (2000) Local government management: a model for the future? *Public Management*, **2**(1): 57–83.

World Bank (1997) *World development report 1997: the state in a changing world*. Oxford, Oxford University Press/World Bank.

World Bank (1999) *Georgia: World Bank poverty assessment survey*. Washington, DC, World Bank.

World Bank (2001) *Decentralization and governance: does decentralization improve public service delivery?* Washington, DC, World Bank.

Zifcak, S. (1994) *New managerialism: administrative reform in Whitehall and Canberra*. Buckingham, Open University Press.

Annex

Description of the structure and development of decentralization in health care in selected countries in Europe and Canada[1]

Decentralization in Italy (2004)

Levels of government: current status

In Italy, planning of health care expenditure is undertaken by the 20 regions (one of which, Trentino Alto Adige, is divided into two highly autonomous provinces). The population of these regions varies largely, from 120 589 inhabitants for Valle d'Aosta to 9 121 714 for Lombardia. The Ministry allocates funds to Regional Health Authorities (RHA) according to a procedure based on a complex formula involving population size, average age, mortality rates and other regional characteristics. RHA are responsible for funding, organization and delivery of health services in their own area. They are free to develop the Regional Health Plans, the strategies and the political choices to meet local health needs and expectations. Regions are free on the revenue side of the regional budget and on the allocation of the resources. They can rely on regional Value Added Tax revenue, co-payments, in addition to the personal income tax and regional petrol tax sharing. Regions have full autonomy in establishing the amount of the overall budget invested in health. RHAs are also allowed to increase co-payment rates and to widen the range of services to which co-payments apply, and they can reimburse listed drugs and health care services not included in the nationally defined benefit package.

There were a total of 197 Local Health Enterprises (LHE) in 2002. Local Health Enterprises (*Aziende Sanitarie Locali*, or LHEs) operate with funds disbursed to them by the respective region to provide care directly through facilities or through services rendered by public hospital trusts (*Aziende Ospedaliere*) with financial and technical autonomy, research hospitals and accredited private providers. The regional health departments appoint the general manager of each LHE. LHEs are divided into a total of 960 health districts (2002). The number of health districts that a region has varies widely. Health districts are responsible for coordinating and providing primary care, non-hospital-based specialist medicine and residential care to their assigned populations, and they ensure accessibility, continuity and timeliness of care. They also encourage an inter-sector approach to health promotion and ensure integration between health services and social services.

Italian Hospital Trusts are administered by general managers and are independent from LHEs. These Hospital Trusts have to operate with balanced budgets: budgetary surplus can be used for investments and staff incentives while unjustified deficits result in the loss of the status of autonomy.

The Ministry of Health (*Ministero della Salute*) is responsible for general administration and health standards. National health planning is done through the formulation of health targets in the periodical National Health Plan, issued by the Ministry of Health, but negotiated and approved by the regions. As far as finances are concerned, the Ministry of Health sets the overall budget, raises taxes and redistributes funds. Contributions by the regions to the National Solidarity Fund are allocated to regions with narrower tax bases according to a complex formula, based on population, age structure, morbidity rate, interregional mobility, perinatal and infant mortality, and historical expenditure. Furthermore, the Ministry of Health is concerned with circulating common indicators and maintaining a homogeneous approach to data collection among the regions, and it defines the criteria for the accreditation of health services. The state has exclusive power to set the essential levels of care (*Livelli essenziali di assistenza* – LEA), which must be available to all residents throughout the country.

Historical process

In Italy the process of regional devolution with regard to health care started in the early 1970s. In 1978, health insurance funds were abolished and a national tax-based system (based on general taxation and payroll taxes) was established.[2] Regional governments did not have any tax-raising and collection powers. Municipalities were in charge of governing the Local Health Units (LHUs) that were created by the 1978 law. A series of reforms that started in the late 1980s progressively shifted municipal powers to the regional level.

Within health care, regional autonomy was limited to restricted administrative and organizational powers over hospital planning and management until the 1992 health reform, which broadened this autonomy considerably. Legislative enforcement during the 1990s made a strong impact in terms of instigating and accelerating a process of decentralization of the Italian health care system.

Starting in 1992, a network of public and private health care structures and providers was operating at the local level, among them a reduced number of LHUs,[3] turned into autonomous self-governing firms (LHEs) and major university teaching hospitals were turned into Hospital Trusts (*Aziende Ospedaliere*). Since 1992 an increased number of hospitals have been given the trust status. A 1999 reform bill[4] expanded the importance of Hospital Trusts and introduced managerial tasks. Law 502/92 introduced a new system of funding for the LHAs by the regions on a capitation basis with different system of compensation for the treatment of patients from other LHAs. Laws 502/92 and 517/93 transformed the LHAs and the main hospitals into public enterprises with their own budgets.

The gradual devolution of political power during the 1990s is now running parallel to fiscal reform which will grant regions significant autonomy over how they manage revenue in the regional budget, as well as allowing them complete autonomy over the allocation of funds. In January 1998, the Regional Production Tax (IRAP) was introduced. IRAP is not deductable from income tax, and is payable each tax period according to the net value produced in the given regional authority's territory. The percentage payable differs for capital stock companies and partnerships. The ordinary rate is 425%. From 1 January 2000, regional authorities will be able to increase the rate by a maximum of 1% and may introduce percentage differentiations according to sector and category of liability.

Recently, the November 2001 constitutional reform ruled that the state would guarantee exclusively the determination of the essential levels of health care provision as regards civic and social rights, whereas areas pertaining to human health would fall within the legislative and concurrent authorities of the regions. At the November 2001 conference of regional presidents, a model of fund allocation to regional health care was defined and outlined as follows: 5% for health prevention, 50% for district health care, and 45% for hospital health care. A series of stability agreements stipulated that at every level of government (central, regional and municipal) there would be direct accountability for direct and indirect debts. In particular, the August 2002 stability agreement between the state and the regions included unequivocal rules for health system management: most importantly, a platform was set up for ongoing political and technical negotiations between the state and the regions. Nevertheless, some recent decisions indicate a move towards recentralization policies: the setting of a national cap on drug expenditure by the national government, attempts to define regulations of health care manager contracts at national level and to impose a resource allocation formula, and blocking, through a provision of the 2003 budget law, the possibility of increasing local taxation to cover public spending.

Decentralization in Portugal (2004)

Levels of government: current status

The Portuguese health care system is characterized by three concurrent systems: (1) the national health service, with 100% of virtual and 75% real coverage; (2) special public and private insurance schemes for certain professions, such as civil servants, military personnel and dependants as well as bank workers (health subsystems); and (3) a growing voluntary private health insurance.

Through the Ministry of Health the central government is responsible for developing health policy and overseeing and evaluating its implementation. The health system is a tax-based centrally financed system covering the whole population and has been divided into five Regional Health Administrations (RHAs) since 1993. Their management responsibilities are a mix of strategic management of population health, supervision and control of hospitals and centralized direct management responsibilities for primary care/national health centres. RHAs are responsible for the regional implementation of national health policy objectives. RHA autonomy over budget setting and spending has been limited to primary health care, since hospital budgets continued to be defined and allocated by the Ministry of Health. Budgets for hospitals had been based on the previous year's funding updated for inflation, but since 1997, a growing portion is based on DRG information as well as on non-adjusted out-patient volume. The Ministry of Health allocates funds to the RHA, which in turn funds the global activity of each health centre, which is responsible for primary health care.

The five RHAs are subdivided into 18 sub-regions, each with a sub-regional coordinator. Below the region and sub-region in the administrative hierarchy are the municipalities. For the purpose of health care provision, boundaries are based on geographical proximity rather than administrative areas, so some communities may be included in neighbouring municipalities. Municipalities successfully implement various initiatives in public health area, but their overall role is limited.

The autonomous regions of Açores and Madeira have their own administration and regulation with regard to organization, management, funding and operation of health services, their policy being defined and executed by the regional government agencies.

Historical process

Health care provision before the 1979 NHS law[5] followed the social health insurance model that provided cover to the employed population and their dependants through compulsory contributions by employers and employees to sickness funds. The explicit case for a strong public component in health care financing was first made in 1971.[6] After the revolution of 25 April 1974, there was the first political-administrative decentralization movement at the regional level. At the same time district and central hospitals owned by the religious charities were taken over by the government, their staff becoming civil servants. Local hospitals were integrated with existing primary health care services in 1975. Over 2000 medical units or health posts, belonging to the social health insurance system, situated throughout the country were integrated into the health service in 1977. The NHS law in 1979 laid down the principles of centralized control, but with decentralized management. In fact, the Constitution (1976), the Law on the Fundamental Principles of Health (1990) and the Statute of the NHS (1993) provide political and normative support to the decentralization of the health service. The 1990 Law on the Fundamental Principles of Health comprised the decentralization of the system's operation and management at the regional level, integration of health centres and hospitals in health units and the contracting out of health services funded by national taxation.

There have been attempts to implement financial and administrative decentralization in the Portuguese health sector. In 1997 a capitation-based budgeting for resource allocation to the RHAs and a case-mix adjusted budgeting for hospitals were implemented. Furthermore, contracting agencies were created in each RHA in 1997, however, the uncertainties about the roles of these entities have hampered their effectiveness. Legislation was enacted in 1999 to set up the framework for the establishment of Responsibility Centres, however, this project has not been implemented to date on a national basis. Five regional public health centres were established in 1999.

Administrative decentralization of hospitals management has been on the political agenda since 1995. The most recent effort of this type includes the transformation of 34 hospitals, representing approximately 40% of all health service hospitals, into public enterprises ("hospital-companies") in 2002.

Decentralization in Poland (2004)

Levels of government: current status

Management of health care services takes place at subnational levels of government. The administrative regions in Poland are called voivodships (or *województwa*). Poland consists of 16 regions that are divided into 373 districts (or *powiaty*), 308 land districts and 65 urban districts. Districts are an intermediate administrative level between regions and the local communities. The most local level of government is formed by the 2489 counties (*gminy*). There are two actors operating in each voivodship: a voivoda and a marshal. The voivoda represents central government interests. Responsibility of a voivoda in the health care sector is limited to public health. Marshals own secondary care hospitals, allocate funds for some capital investments and plan health services to be financed by the National Health Fund (NHF). District authorities own several health care organizations within their territory (i.e., district hospitals and some outpatient clinics). Local communities are largely responsible for primary care (some large city *gminy* also manage secondary health care services). Private providers deliver most primary care services. All local forms of government (regions, districts and local communities) are governed by their elected councils and receive grants from the central government and they also raise their own taxes.

The Polish Minister of Health is responsible for national health policy, the establishment of legal regulations to implement legal acts of the Polish Parliament, as well as the financing of major capital investments, public health programmes and selected highly specialized health services (e.g. organ transplants). The ministry also has administrative responsibility for some health care institutions that it finances. Other responsibilities of the ministry include implementing health programmes, training health care personnel, funding medical equipment, and monitoring of health care provision (including health care standards). The Finance Ministry allocates health care budgets to the Ministry of Health and to other ministers responsible for some tasks in health care (Minister of Defence, Minister of Internal Affairs and Minister of Justice) as well as to the public administrative organs acting at regional level.

The Polish health care system is financed mainly through general (universal) health insurance contributions, managed by the NHF. Decisions on contracting are made at the regional level. However, most aspects of health insurance are arranged at the central level: the Polish parliament regulates the organization and functioning of universal health insurance (e.g. it decides the level of contribution paid by insured). The prime minister nominates the council members of the NHF, the Ministry of Health monitors and controls legal aspects of the NHF activities as well as health care provision financed by public money, and the Ministry of Finance deals with financial aspects of NHF functioning.

Historical process

Poland has moved from a highly centralized system towards the devolution of responsibility for health care. All tax income used to go to the central government. The Communist Party and later the parliament and the Ministry of Health debated how to spend these funds and notified clinics and hospitals accordingly. Between 1945 and 1975, the country was subdivided into 17 voivodships. In 1975, 49 smaller ones replaced these regions and the administrative districts were dissolved. The *Zespoly Opieki Zdrowotnej* (ZOZs) provided the main bases for primary and secondary care at the beginning of the 1990s. Since the early 1990s the role of the voivodas in the administration of health care has increased, and these in turn passed management responsibilities to the ZOZ, public health care providers delivering outpatient or inpatient care. In total, there were more than 500 ZOZs. They received funds from the budgets of voivodas to which they belonged.

In Poland, private health care has existed for some time. Prior to 1989, requirements for private practice were to obtain a permit (administrative decision) and that the physician should also work for public health care institution. The private health care was developed in ambulatory care. In the 1960s and later, private health delivery was more and more visible in ambulatory specialist care, though it never dominated. All services of this type of care were paid out of pocket.

In 1989, Poland underwent a dramatic system transformation. The 1991 Health Care Institutions Act allowed different types of ownership of health care organizations including central, provincial and local authorities, the voluntary (non-government, non-profit sector) and also private for-profit ownership. Privatization has been proceeding with pharmacies, dental practices and medical practices. Since then, each person willing to establish private health care unit can do so if proper technical requirements are met.

In 1992, the financing of health care was taken over by the Ministry of Finance. Since 1995, when new legislation enabled local communities to take over health services previously run by voivodas, many local communities, mostly in cities, have done so. In the late 1990s ZOZs were replaced by non-budgetary autonomous health care institutions known as SP ZOZ. The *powiaty*, abolished in 1975, were re-established prior to 1998 elections when the district authorities became owners of some health care institutions (e.g. secondary care hospitals) within their territory. The number of voivodships was reduced in January 1999 from 49 to 16.

In May 1995, the Ministry of Health issued a regulation on the conditions of the transfer of budgetary resources to self-managing institutions. This gave health care institutions the power to become responsible for managing their budgets. Before 1999, contracting of services took place only as an experiment in some parts of Poland. Contracts were signed mostly with public health care providers. The 6 February 1997[7] General Health Insurance Act mandated a transfer of health sector financing and administration to the regional sickness funds as of 1 January 1999. In the same year, financing of the parallel system of health services (provided by several ministries) was transferred to the national level branch health insurance fund. Since 1999, 17 sickness funds (16 regional and one fund for armed services covering the whole country) have been in charge of managing the financial contributions of employees. General social insurance institutions were responsible for collecting contributions.

Lately there has been some movement towards recentralization: in April 2003, the NHF took over this role from the sickness funds. The autonomous sickness funds were transformed into regional branches of the NHF. Nevertheless, in January 2004, the Constitutional Court decided that several elements of the law that established the NHF violated the Polish Constitution. On 27 August 2004, it was replaced by a new law. Since 1 October 2004, a new act has been implemented that partly re-centralized the health insurance system, increasing NHF regional branches' autonomy.

Decentralization in Spain (2004)

Levels of government: current status

Spain is divided into 17 autonomous communities (*Comunidades autónomas*) and two small autonomous cities in Northern Africa[8] (Ceuta and Melilla). The least populous community is La Rioja (287 390 in 2003), while Andalucía has the largest population (7 606 848 in 2003). The 1978 Constitution establishes that autonomous communities will manage a range of public services, among them health care, while the central government will establish the basic legislation and will coordinate the regions.

In 2001, the resource allocation formula was revised after a process of negotiation between the central government and the autonomous communities. Regions receive funds from a basket of taxes including a percentage of the VAT and income tax and other sources of taxes. Regions have full authority over the allocation of funds for health care and other activities. This model differs from the one applied to País Vasco and Navarra, two autonomous communities which are under a special regime (*Régimen Foral de Financiación*).

The General Health Law passed in 1986 established the National Health System as the Spanish organizational model for health care. The national government is entitled to enact "basic" legislation, and to coordinate the health care system, but it does not have the power to determine how regions organize or provide different services, including health services. In practical terms, this is rather problematic and usually conflicts are negotiated in the interterritorial council (*Consejo Interterritorial del Sistema Nacional de Salud*, or CISNS),[9] where national and regional representatives formalize mutual adjustments. In 2003, the Cohesion and Quality Law strengthened the functions of the interterritorial council that comprises coordination, cooperation, planning and evaluation.

The Spanish Ministry of Health and Consumer Affairs has exclusive authority in several fields. It establishes norms that define the minimum standards and requirements for health care provision. The ministry also has legislative power (e.g. in the area of pharmaceuticals). The regional resource allocation system was reformed in 1994. The new model partially rationalized the previous one, where each region's share was decided through bilateral negotiations subject to political discretion. In 2001, the resource allocation formula was again revised after a process of negotiation between the central government and the autonomous communities. Funds composed of national, regional and local taxes and grants from the central state and are distributed to finance health care, education and social services. In regard to health system coordination, the ministry is responsible for the establishment of systems facilitating reciprocal information and homogeneity of techniques, and for assuring cooperation between national health authorities and the autonomous communities. It is also responsible for interterritorial and international health issues and publicizes comparative reports (benchmarking and highlighting "best practice").

Historical process

During the Franco period, the social security branch for health care collected separate social payments from workers and employers and in turn ran hospitals and clinics in many parts of Spain. In 1977, this social security branch was redesignated the National Institute of Health (*Instituto Nacional de la Salud*, or INSALUD). The main health reform that took place in Spain during the 1980s was the transformation from a "Bismarckian" health care system to a national health service model (gradually replacing social health insurance with tax-based funding for health services), mainly by the 1986 General Health Act[10] (*Ley General de Sanidad*, or LGS). Apart from the major changes linked to that transformation, the General Health Act allowed the integration of the previous dispersed services into a single network. It also promoted a new model of primary health care and altered the territorial organization of health care delivery by creating health areas (catchments districts organized around a general hospital) and basic zones with each served by a neighbourhood primary health care centre. While this can be perceived as a centralization movement, there was a parallel movement towards decentralization. Also, the integration of

INSALUD into the tax-based system prepared the administration for further decentralization.

The 1978 Constitution designated a new territorial organization of the state and broadly defined the basis of the respective responsibilities of the state and autonomous communities. It created the possibility for the autonomous communities to obtain powers in general coordination and regulation of health care provision. The process of decentralization began by permitting some autonomy over service delivery in the 1980s in the autonomous communities of the País Vasco and Cataluña, swiftly followed by Andalucía and the Comunidad Valenciana. From 1981 to 1994, health powers were devolved to, in total, seven regions. The 1986 LGS further developed the constitutional provisions that governed this process of devolution. It established the fundamental principles that form the basis of the current decentralized system. It created the interterritorial CISNS as a coordinating body between the general state administration and the autonomous communities. The LGS more specifically defined the respective responsibilities of the state and the autonomous communities. The LGS also allocated the power to determine minimum health care requirements to the state. The 1990 Pharmaceutical Law[11] assigned the responsibility for legislation and implementation to the state and to the autonomous communities respectively.

Spain also has focused on transforming hospitals into more autonomous actors. In the 1990s a model of contractual management was introduced. New hospitals and some pilot projects also experimented with new management models of limited self-governing for hospitals, health care services and primary health care teams (e.g., hospital foundations or public enterprises). However, as the governing boards of these institutions are directly controlled by the regional public authorities, there is limited room for real strategic self-governing.

Recently, in January 2002, health care provision was devolved to the remaining ten autonomous communities. Simultaneously the health care financial model was replaced by a new agreement that increased fiscal decentralization and that incorporated health care funds into the block grants that the central state transfers to the autonomous communities. A 2001 law[12] provided further regulatory structure to fiscal and administrative issues now facing the autonomous communities' financing systems. In August 2002, INSALUD, the national institute that had been responsible for the administration and management of health care services, was dismantled.[13] In May 2003, the Cohesion and Quality Law[14] was approved. This law set up some common rules that guarantee certain minimum standards for health services in all the autonomous communities, seeking to avoid undesirable regional inequalities. It also changes the Ministry's role, which now is more orientated towards supervising the health service, to designing global strategies of quality, equity and efficiency and serving as an instrument of cooperation to facilitate regional initiatives. Nevertheless, the prospect of a more active role for the national government is controversial, unless it can mobilize substantial allocation of resources to back their initiatives and proposals. Furthermore, the Cohesion and Quality Law attributed additional functions to the CISNS and changed its composition, by reducing the power of representation of the central state.

Decentralization in the Russian Federation (2005)

Levels of government: current status

The Ministry of Health is the central policy formulating body for the Russian Federation and retains nominal rights to oversee the work and decisions devolved to the regions. Its responsibilities include developing and implementing state health care policy and federal health programmes, developing legislation, governance of federal medical facilities, medical education, epidemiological and environmental health monitoring and health statistics, control of infectious diseases, development of health regulations, control and licensing of drugs, and development of federal standards and recommendations for quality assurance. Federal health institutions are subordinated to different federal agencies and account for 6% of all inpatient facilities in the Russian Federation and 15% of other institutions (public health institutions and outpatient facilities).

In the Russian Federation, there are 89 regions (21 republics, 6 *krais*, 49 *oblasts*, 11 autonomous entities and the cities of Moscow and St. Petersburg) with a population ranging from 500 000 to a few million. Regional health bodies are accountable to the ministry only in the implementation of federal target programmes financed from the federal budget. But the regional level and, in particular, regional health care authorities have significant possibilities to manage the regional health care system, as the regional level has the relatively powerful financial instrument of the Regional Mandatory Health Insurance (MHI) Funds. The municipal (local) level consists of regions (rayons), cities, towns, villages and rural settlements. Depending on their size, cities may be divided into rayons or constitute a single rayon. The major part (58% in 2003) of public health care spending comes from regional and local tax revenue budgets. The remaining part is funded by the federal budget (10%), employers' MHI contributions for working residents and other incomes of MHI Funds (32%). According to the law, regional and local health care governing bodies are administratively accountable only to regional government and municipal authority correspondingly.

The Russian MHI collects funds through 2.8% (3.4% before 2005) payroll contributions to Regional MHI Funds. Executive directors appointed by the regional governor run these funds. The Federal MHI Fund levels out financial contributions for Regional MHI Funds, receiving 29% (6% before 2005) of the contributions paid to these funds. Regional MHI Funds are not supposed to contract and finance health care facilities directly, but they do this in 48 regions (2003). The private insurers (348 in 2003) act in MHI system in 64 regions.

The MHI does not cover health care services related to severe conditions such as cancer, tuberculosis, sexually transmitted diseases, geriatric services, psychiatry and emergency care. The corresponding tier of the government covers these conditions. The regional governments and municipalities provide contributions of insurance premiums for the non-employed to MHI Funds but the amount of contributions provided is not enough to reimburse all items of expenses for health services delivery to the insured. The regional governments and municipalities still allocate budget funds among public facilities. As a result, the same activity of public inpatient and outpatient clinics is co-financed from budgets and MHI Funds.

Historical process

Until 1991, the Russian health care system was under the central control of the state, which financed services through government revenues as part of the national social and economic development plans. In 1933, social health insurance funds were abolished. Hospitals, pharmacies and other health facilities were nationalized and brought under district health management. All health care personnel were employees of the central state, which paid salaries and provided supplies to all medical institutions. While the Supreme Soviet held the ultimate authority, responsibility for health care provision was delegated to the Ministry of Health of the USSR, which regulated management and resource allocation through the 15 Soviet Socialist Republics, including that of the Russian Federation. The mainstream health service delivery was mediated through a series of local government structures, all incorporated within the formal local government organization, which provided accountability through the elected nature of local assemblies. City health authorities managed city hospitals and polyclinics for adults, women and children. Regional (*oblast*), autonomous republic or *krai* governments provided both tertiary and secondary hospitals, and outpatient services at a state level. They also monitored rayon bodies that oversaw smaller territories or districts and provided a central hospital and outpatient service (polyclinic). There were further rural councils providing *uchastok* (micro-district) hospitals and in remote areas either doctor-led ambulatory clinics or feldsher-midwife stations.

Since 1992, the powers of the Federal Health Ministry have been weakened considerably as health care financing, regulation and delivery were significantly decentralized. But structurally and in terms of incentives, it is still very similar to the Semashko system of the USSR. Decentralization took place in the form of devolution of most responsibilities to regional and local levels where legislative and executive elected governments were formed and part of funding to health insurance was privatized. There were 73 oblast-level administrative territories until 1991, after which the addition of five republics and 11 autonomous entities raised the total to 89. In November 1991, the All-Union Ministry of Health ceased to exist and was re-established as the new Ministry of Health and Medical Industry of the Russian Federation. This involved what was in fact a merger of the all-Soviet ministry and the Russian republican ministry. The lowest level of the state system (municipalities) took ownership of the major part of medical facilities and was expected to fund them through their own budgets derived from local taxes and revenues, as well as nominating health administrators. Regional and federal levels kept referral and teaching hospitals and some other specialized functions such as surveillance, medical education and vertical target programmes. Following the 1995 law, "On general principles of organization of local self-government in the Russian Federation", municipal level governments do not have to report to the federal or *oblast* level governments, though they do have to comply with the ministry orders.

Legislation entitled, "Fundamentals of the Russian Federation legislation on citizens' health protection" from 1993 defined the responsibilities of the federal government and the regions respectively. The law on health insurance was adopted in 1991 and the MHI was created in 1993. The MHI system, being a step towards decentralization by itself, was set up in a decentralized manner. Regional MHI Funds were created in each Russian region to collect payments. They are subordinated to the top of regional government but not to the regional health care governing body. Prior to the implementation, regional health care governing bodies had full control of regional funds for health care. Nevertheless, through implementation of the MHI, they lost a portion of this control to the newly established territorial MHI Funds.

Decentralization in Sweden (2004)

Levels of government: current status

The Swedish 18 county councils (*Landsting*), two regional bodies (*Skåne* and *Västra Götaland*)[15] and one municipality without a county council (*Gotland*) are in charge of the health care delivery system from primary care to hospital care, including public health and preventive care. The county councils have overall authority over the hospital structure and responsibility for all health care services delivered. In 1999, 66% of their total income was generated through county taxes, 21% through state grants, 3.3% from user fees and 9.7% from other sources.

About half of the county councils are divided into 3–12 health care districts, each with the overall responsibility for the health of the population in its area. A health care district usually consists of one hospital and several primary care units, where the latter are further separated into primary health care districts. A primary health care district is usually the same geographical area as the local municipality, although larger cities have more than one health care district. In 2000, there were about 370 primary health care districts.

The 290 Swedish municipalities (*Kommuner*) are responsible for most other welfare services, including the care of the elderly and children. Each municipality has an elected assembly, the municipal council, which makes decisions on municipal matters. The municipal council appoints the municipal executive board, which leads and coordinates municipality work.

The central Swedish government has overriding political responsibility for the health of the population, and can institute national laws governing certain aspects of the health care system, such as basic patient rights or regulations regarding contagious diseases. Through the National Board of Health and Social Welfare, the government can also issue guidelines regarding medical practice and evaluate developments at county council level.

Historical process

The decentralized organization of the Swedish health care system dates back to 1862, when the regional political units (county councils) were created and given the responsibility of operating the hospitals in the country, which had been state-owned since the eighteenth century. After that, a number of responsibilities for planning, provision and financing of health care were gradually decentralized from the central government to the county councils. The 1928 Hospital Act made the county councils legally responsible for providing inpatient hospital care to their residents. In the 1930s, the county councils were gradually given responsibility for various health care services, such as maternity and paediatric health care, child dental care, etc. Ambulatory care was offered primarily by private practitioners in their own offices or at the hospital.

In 1955, national public health insurance was introduced, obliging the counties to provide care to all citizens at heavily subsidized costs, financed primarily through income tax levied by the counties. In this process, most of the remaining private providers in the outpatient sector disappeared, as their financial conditions deteriorated. By the late 1960s, roughly 80% of all physicians were employed at hospitals. During the 1960s, the national system of general practitioners and district nurses was transferred to the county councils, along with the state-owned mental hospitals. Different branches of health care were brought together into district health authorities. Since 1967, the county councils have been responsible for the administration and financing of all different branches of care.

Thus, until recently, Swedish health care could be described as a system of virtually all-publicly provided services, managed directly by elected county council politicians and their staff of civil servants. In the 1980s, a number of management responsibilities related to financial and personnel administration were decentralized to individual clinical departments, health centres and other basic units within the organization. The county councils decentralized financial responsibility for health care activities by introducing global budgets. It was stated that the role of the county council politicians should be to set goals for administrators and professionals within the system but leave its actual management to these groups. This meant that the previous emphasis of detailed local planning within the system was partly abandoned, while provider units (hospitals, clinics, primary care health care centres) became more self-governing. Health care districts became responsible for resource allocation within their geographical area. The board of county councils managed the districts by allocating the budget among the districts. In the late 1980s, reimbursement of providers through activity budgets replaced per-case payments.

The system of regional integration of health services was dissolved in 1992, when the responsibility for elderly care was further decentralized from the county councils to the municipalities. Health service provision has been increasingly privatized since the early 1990s, mainly in primary health care, but there are still no more than 5–10% private providers and most of them are publicly financed. At the beginning of the 1990s, about half of the county councils introduced an internal market with separate organizations for purchasers and providers of health care. Gradually the competition on the internal markets has been replaced by increasing cooperation between purchasers and providers, and between different providers within the councils. In recent years, this development has been combined with mergers of hospitals and county councils into larger regional councils, which have greater impact on regional policy goals than the traditional municipal associations.

Decentralization in Switzerland (2004)

Levels of government: current status

Switzerland has a federal structure with three different levels: the confederation (or, federal government), the cantons and the communes (or, municipalities). There are 26 cantons[16] with a population of between 15 000 (Appenzell Innerrhoden) and 947 100 (Berne).[17] Each canton has its own constitution, parliament, government and courts. These cantons are divided in 2 873 communes in total. Around one-fifth of these communes have their own parliament; in the other four-fifths, a process of direct democracy takes decisions in the local assembly. Citizens have the right to initiate laws and referendums at municipal, cantonal and federal level.

At the federal level there is no Ministry of Health. Several government offices share the responsibility for health and matters related to health services. They are all accountable to the federal parliament. Three of the executive offices are part of the Federal Department of Home Affairs: the Federal Office of Public Health, the Federal Social Insurance Office and the Federal Statistical Office. Another, the State Secretariat for Economic Affairs depends on the Federal Department of Economic Affairs. The role of the Federal Office of Public Health is limited to regulation and supervision of functions in the field of narcotics, serums and vaccines, poisons, food quality and radiation protection. Its activities in combating disease are directed towards epidemics, tuberculosis, rheumatism and HIV/AIDS. The Federal Social Insurance Office has the function of officially recognizing health insurance companies, of monitoring and controlling their activities, and of approving health insurance premiums every year. The Federal Office of Trade and Industry financially protects people who receive welfare payments from the federal disability or accident insurance. Income taxes are mainly levied by municipalities and cantons, and rates vary from place to place.

Health care providers are mostly financed by payments from health insurance companies or by direct payments by patients. In 2002, there were 93 private, non-profit sickness funds that have to offer the same, basic, compulsory health insurance. The services covered by the compulsory health insurance are defined in federal law. Insurance companies are free to set the premiums, which are allowed to vary among cantons, but not within one canton. Of public expenditures for health, the major part is borne by cantons and, less, by municipalities.

Cantons are constitutionally independent of the federal government. They have the responsibility for planning, monitoring and partly providing health care within a defined geographical area. The cantonal responsibilities encompass the elaboration of health and hygiene policy, the planning, operation and construction of hospitals, the regulation of hospital external care, the management of medical and paramedical schools, activities in the field of health prevention and promotion, and the regulation of patient rights. Cantons enjoy sovereignty to define principles and standards on which premium subsidies for low-income households are based and can choose, within some limits given by the federal level, to fix the cantonal budget available for premium subsidy. The federal level then matches the cantonal expenditures. With regard to the provision of health services, private and public providers co-exist, but private providers have a large area of responsibility, mainly for outpatient care and to a minor degree for hospital care. Ambulatory (outpatient) services and short inpatient stays are usually paid through fee-for-service payment. Point values are agreed upon annually and appear in a national fee schedule which has to be approved by the Federal Council. The price attached to the point value is negotiated at a cantonal level for compulsory health insurance, but at the federal level for other types of insurance. If health care providers and insurance companies cannot agree on the fee schedule, the government of the canton in which the provider is located fixes the level of fees. Federal and cantonal authorities have no direct planning controls over ambulatory services but have significant control over hospitals and residential nursing homes. Hospitals and nursing homes can only be reimbursed for services under compulsory health insurance if they are included in the canton's official list of hospitals and nursing homes. Cantons are responsible for the planning of these health care facilities. The cantons' decisions on hospital planning and lists can be challenged by submission to the Federal Council. At the cantonal level, the public and publicly subsidised hospitals have formed hospital associations that negotiate fees with the health insurance companies. To complement inpatient hospital care at the cantonal level, it is the task of the municipalities to arrange professional support for home care, which is often covered by voluntary organizations.

Municipalities have the task of organizing health promotion programmes and medical care in schools, as well as assistance for home deliveries. In the field of home and hospital external care, municipalities either employ municipal nurses or contract with private organizations depending on the needs and the political, demographic and economic situation of the locality.

Historical process

At the inception of the Swiss Federal state in 1848, there were practically no legislative powers in health care. Cantons, municipalities, private health care providers and private insurers were highly autonomous, but this situation gradually changed. Referendums proposing reforms and transfer of powers to the state often failed, but were usually adapted, repeated and finally approved. The administrative structure has remained rather constant. Since the creation of the canton Jura in 1978, Switzerland has consisted of 26 cantons. The number of communes declined slightly over the last few years due to amalgamations. Nevertheless, concentration did take place in the sickness fund sector: the number of sickness funds decreased from 207 in 1993 to 93 in 2002.

In 1877, qualifying examinations for doctors, pharmacists and veterinarians were standardized. Soon after, in 1886, a federal law to combat epidemic diseases came into force. At the end of the nineteenth century, the federal government was given a constitutional mandate to implement legislation on food and consumer safety; legislation based on this mandate came into force in 1909. A federal law on narcotic substances was implemented in 1925 and a law on tuberculosis in 1928. The federal government has been responsible for monitoring serums and vaccines since 1931. The new federal constitution, adopted on 18 April 1999, laid down the responsibility of the federal government for the training of health-related professionals other than doctors.

The area of sickness insurance clearly shows the gradual transfer of powers to the federal government. In 1890, the federal government was given a constitutional mandate to legislate on sickness and accidental insurance. The 1911 Federal Law on Sickness and Accident Insurance required health insurance funds that wished to take advantage of federal subsidies to register with the Federal Office for Social Insurance and abide by its rules. The law left it to the cantons to declare whether the insurance was compulsory. A 1964 law revised the system of subsidies to the funds, based on age and gender, and introduced user charges in the statutory health insurance system. In 1993, a within-canton risk-compensation scheme was started based on age and sex to compensate insurers for people with higher than average risks among their members; the sickness fund association became responsible for making the transfer between the companies. The Federal Law on Sickness Insurance (*Krankenversicherung-gesetz*, or KVG), implemented on 1 January 1996, contributed largely to the increase of power of the federal government and was in itself a manifestation of it. It replaced the 1911 Federal Law on Sickness and Accident Insurance, and introduced compulsory health insurance. The KVG compelled the cantons to plan hospital provision and to limit the range of providers who will be reimbursed. It also defined the general conditions by which all services will be assessed for reimbursement. The KVG allows cantons to impose fixed budgets for subsidies paid to public and publicly subsidised hospitals and nursing homes. Global budgets were introduced in five cantons in 1994 and have since, in varying configurations, been implemented in other cantons. The KVG also legalized a broad spectrum of HMO-like provider networks.

Decentralization in the United Kingdom (2004)

Levels of government: current status

The United Kingdom has devolved health care responsibilities to its constituent countries: England (49 138 831 inhabitants in 2001), Scotland (5 062 011), Wales (2 903 085) and Northern Ireland (1 685 267). But not all countries have the same extent of autonomy: Scotland has relatively large autonomy, while autonomy for Wales is much more limited. All countries mainly fund health care through national taxation, deliver services through public providers and have devolved purchasing responsibilities to local bodies (Primary Care Trusts in England, Health Boards in Scotland, local health groups in Wales and Health and Social Services Boards in Northern Ireland). The central government controls public expenditure and taxation. Public funds are redistributed to the countries. The Barnett formula provides that, where comparable, changes to programmes in England (Great Britain in the case of Northern Ireland) result in equivalent changes in the budgets of the territorial departments calculated on the basis of population shares. Only Scotland has the discretion to use its (marginal) tax-varying powers to raise additional revenue, though all administrations can choose to reallocate resources to health. In England, the Department of Health's policies determine how all areas of the National Health Service (NHS) and social care are structured, financed and managed. While hospitals are generally public in the United Kingdom, several hospitals are managed by private companies which are reimbursed by the government on an activity basis.[18] Each country has its own comparative information bases.

In England, Primary Care Trusts (PCTs) are local organizations (with population catchment areas of around 80 000–300 000) responsible for managing health services in the community and for commissioning all but highly specialist services. They are also responsible for the integration of health and social care, ensuring that local health organizations work together with local authorities. PCT chief executives are responsible for ensuring local clinical quality and financial control within a nationally agreed framework. NHS Trusts manage acute hospitals, responsible for providing medical and surgical treatment and care. The Trusts employ NHS staff including medical personnel, such as doctors and nurses, and non-medical personnel. Both PCTs and acute hospital NHS Trusts are accountable to 28 Strategic Health Authorities. They are both responsible for developing working relationships by means of service level agreements.

In Scotland, the NHS is divided into NHS Boards. NHS Boards directly manage hospitals. Primary care is managed through a system of localities, Community Health Partnerships, within each NHS Board. Acute Hospital Trusts are responsible for acute hospital services, and operate within the geographical boundaries of individual health boards. The role of these Health Boards is the protection and improvement of the health of their respective residents through implementation of Health Improvement Programmes. This is intended to improve cooperation not only between Trusts but also with the local authorities.

In Wales, there are 22 local health boards which coincide with the areas covered by the 22 local authorities. Local health boards are responsible for needs assessment, commissioning of specialist care from NHS trusts and the management of primary care. There are 14 NHS Trusts, covering broadly the same responsibilities as their equivalents in England except that trusts in Wales provide both acute hospital and community services, including mental health, to the local population.

In Northern Ireland, health and personal social services are provided as one integrated service. The four Health and Social Services Boards are agents of the Department of Health, Social Services and Public Safety in planning, commissioning, monitoring and purchasing services for the residents in their areas. The 19 Health and Social Services Trusts are the providers of health and social services. They manage staff and services and control their own budgets.

Historical process

There have always been some differences in the organization and administration of health policy in each part of the United Kingdom. There were territorial

Secretaries of State, and separate health departments with their own ministers in each country. Furthermore, Scotland has a separate legal system, requiring separate legislation. And the Barnett formula has been in existence for more than two decades, but instead of determining the budgets of the devolved administrations, it first determined budgets of three territorial departments (Scottish Office, Welsh Office and Northern Ireland Office). Nevertheless, until recently, health care policy has been largely determined by the central UK government.

Between 1979 and 1997, when the Conservative Party was in power, a quasi-market was introduced into health care. A whole range of health care services were removed from the NHS to be provided by the private sector, and cost sharing was introduced and increased. Furthermore, Health Authorities would commission and pay health care providers such as hospitals and general practitioners for health care treatments on behalf of the population in their area. Hospitals were required to charge for individual treatments on a full cost basis, including the cost of capital. Cross-subsidies were not permitted. More recently, there has been a turn to the Private Finance Initiative (PFI): the financing of new investment in hospitals, clinics and doctors' surgeries by the private sector which would design, build, finance and operate the facilities for the public sector in return for annual payments over 30 years. This was introduced in 1992 but did not take off until the Labour Party took office (1997). For some projects the process began already in 1994/5, but the first deal was closed only in July 1997.

Since the 1980s, various reforms have laid the groundwork for primary care purchasing. Preliminary reforms in 1985 and 1990 increased local GP, and thus primary care, accountability before purchasing was devolved. Primary Care Groups (PCGs) replaced fundholding and commissioning groups between 1999 and 2002. Some 481 PCGs were established in local communities. The average population served was 100 000 people, but ranged from 50 000 to over 250 000. Unlike fundholding, PCG membership was compulsory. PCGs were health authority subcommittees with a multi-agency governing body, although GPs formed the majority. The four levels of PCG differed in the range and scope of their purchasing. At Level 1, PCGs were commissioning advisers to health authorities. Budgetary responsibility and independence increased up to level 4. Here, PCGs commissioned care for the PCG population and provided community health services. In April 2002, England established PCTs as independent organizations across England and district health authorities were abolished. PCGs at levels 3 and 4 became Primary Care Trusts (PCTs). Furthermore, early in 2000, legislation was approved allowing GPs and the health authorities to form commercial ventures with private health care organizations, with GPs being able to charge for some services.

While the changes during the 1980s and 1990s increase the importance of market mechanisms, recently power has been devolved largely to the country level. The 1999 Health Act transferred power from the central government to the countries, while the central government remained responsible for health policy in England. In May 1999, Scotland and Wales elected their new assemblies, with health being one of their main responsibilities. Formal powers were devolved from the central government to Wales and Scotland until July 1999.

In Northern Ireland, the Belfast Agreement was signed on Good Friday 1998, establishing a Northern Irish Legislative Assembly, but power was not transferred until December 1999. But there has also been some centralization at the country level, for example, in Scotland, acute hospital trusts were merged into new, larger organizations, and the number of Trusts in Wales was reduced from 25 to 16 by April 1999. In July 2000, the English government's NHS Plan implied a shift in power towards principal health care professionals and patients. Old health authorities were disbanded and replaced by 28 Strategic Health Authorities.

Decentralization in Canada (2004)

Levels of government: current status

Although Canada's constitution vests jurisdiction over most health care activities at the sub-national (provincial) level, the Canadian Federal Government nonetheless exercises some broad direction over the provincial health insurance programmes by attaching conditions to its intergovernmental transfers. In addition to its regulatory responsibilities in terms of drug patents and food and drug safety, the federal government is also responsible for providing health care services and benefits to designated groups,[19] although it increasingly purchases such services rather than providing them directly. It also funds most health research, and may choose to take on a coordinating role for health-related functions such as health protection, disease prevention, and health promotion. The Canadian Institute of Health Information (CIHI) gathers Canadian health information which can be used to stimulate health policy, management of the health care system and public awareness of health affecting factors.

Canada's ten provinces and three territories are primarily responsible for financing certain "insured" health services – about 70% of Canadian health expenditures comes from public sector sources. This is accomplished through universal insurance programmes in each province/territory. To receive full federal funds, these plans must provide full coverage, without co-payments, to all insured persons for all "medically required" inpatient and outpatient services. Health care services are mostly delivered by private providers, with varying degrees of provincial control. Provinces also may be involved in planning, financing, regulating, and (on occasion) delivering additional services, including public health (surveillance, illness prevention and health promotion), mental health, rehabilitation, long-term care and home care services, and prescription drugs coverage. The precise arrangements can vary considerable from province to province and from community to community.

During the 1990s, nine of the ten provinces and one of the three territories restructured health care delivery by setting up Regional Health Authorities (RHAs). The province of Ontario, with a population of 12 million people (about 38% of Canada's total population), was the one exception; it instead regionalized on a sector-specific basis (e.g., such services as public health and home care were managed by decentralized regional bodies). RHAs were envisioned as intermediate bodies between the provincial government, on the one hand, and individual health institutions and providers, on the other. The health mandate of the RHAs varies in scope among the provinces and territories, as does the autonomy given to their managers. All of them included hospitals and none included physicians or drugs. Provinces varied in the extent to which other sub-sectors such as public health, home care, addiction services or mental health were assigned to RHAs, retained as provincial programmes, or left to private providers. RHA funding comes entirely from the provincial budgets. Unlike municipal governments or administrative units such as school boards, RHAs do not directly raise any revenues through taxation. The budget allocation varies according to provinces/territory: some adopted population-based funding formulas that take into consideration various factors including the age/gender and socio-economic composition of the population and its health needs, while others combine historical funding levels with business plans submitted by the RHAs. RHAs also vary in their freedom to allocate resources within their assigned budgets; some provincial governments have set up accountability arrangements, designated certain programmes as "protected" and otherwise restricted the extent of variability which they will permit across regions, while others have not.

Hospitals in Canada are officially not-for-profit organizations, owned by non-governmental organizations or sometimes by municipal governments. RHAs thus constituted a major centralization (rather than decentralization) of hospital services, moving operational control from formerly self-sufficient organizations to nominally private, quasi-public RHA boards. Physicians were not incorporated into regional reforms and remain largely self-employed. Many health care professionals, including physicians, are self-regulated. The majority of physicians are in private practice and paid on a fee-for-service basis by provincial government health insurance plans. However, most provinces are attempting to encourage "primary care reform" and move general practitioners away from solo practice arrangements. Long-term care, home care, rehabilitation, mental health, and the other services falling outside the federal terms and conditions, in contrast, are largely privately delivered. Public health tends to be publicly delivered, often through RHAs or (in Ontario) local public health units.

Historical process

In general, after the Second World War, when the Canadian health care system gradually took shape, it became largely the responsibility of the provinces and mostly publicly financed. As the costs of provincial and territorial health plans escalated through the 1980s, the sponsoring governments initiated a variety of studies, advisory committees and independent commissions of inquiries. Their task was to provide advice on how to constrain costs and improve the continuum of health services provided, paid for, or subsidised by the provinces and territories. The majority of the reports recommended the creation of geographically based RHAs, as it was argued that the province was too big a unit to be able to do this. In 1989, the first province (Quebec) transferred powers to RHAs. Later eight of the nine other provinces and one of the territories followed this example.

While the creation of RHAs is sometimes portrayed as decentralization, governance and decision-making were taken out of the hands of individual hospitals, nursing homes and similar institutions, thus representing a centralizing element as well. Numerous hospital (and elderly home, home care, etc.) boards were replaced by a more limited number of RHA boards. On several occasions, the number of RHAs decreased: e.g. Alberta collapsed its 17 RHAs into nine in April 2003, Saskatchewan collapsed 32 district boards into 12 RHAs in August 2002, Prince Edward Island amalgamated two RHAs and British Columbia reduced the number of RHAs to five in 2001 and Prince Edward Island abolished RHAs altogether in the 2005 budget.[20] Furthermore, some provinces changed their governance model. For example, in 2001, Alberta became the second province (after Saskatchewan) to have two-thirds of its board members elected by popular vote. In 2005, Ontario abolished its District Health Councils (which had been given responsibility for planning on a regional basis) and is setting up Local Health Integration Networks (LHINs), which could have the potential to develop into regional funding and management models.

Notes

1 The section is largely based on the Health Systems in Transition (HiT) country profiles (www.euro.who.int/observatory), comments by the authors of this volume and the websites of the respective countries' national and regional health care authorities.
2 Law 833/1978.
3 From 659 before the 1992 reforms to 197 in 1999.
4 Legislative Decree 229/1999.
5 *Lei do Serviço Nacional de Saúde* (56/79).
6 Decree 413/71 of 27 September 1971 already mentions the regional and local levels.
7 Amended on 18 August 1998.
8 On 1 January 2003 Ceuta had a population of 74 931 and Melilla of 68 463.
9 The Autonomous Communities Ceuta and Melilla were invited to attend the meetings of the CISNS as observers only in February 1997. Since 1999, Ceuta has member status.
10 25 April 1986: *Ley General de Sanidad* (14/1986).
11 20 December 1990: *Ley del Medicamento* (25/1990), modified by Law 24/2001.
12 27 December 2001: *Ley de Medidas Fiscales, Administrativas y del Orden Social* (24/2001).
13 2 August 2002: *Real Decreto 840/2002 de 2 de agosto*. It was renamed National Institute of Health Management and remained responsible for health care delivery in Ceuta and Melilla.
14 28 May 2003: *Ley de cohesión y calidad del Sistema Nacional de Salud* (16/2003).
15 *Skåne* was formed in 1999 through the merger of two county councils, while *Västra Götaland* was formed in 1998 through merger of three country councils.
16 Six of these 26 cantons are actually three cantons (Unterwalden, Appenzell and Basel), divided into two half-cantons each, for historical reasons.
17 On 31 December 2001.
18 On 1 September 2001, the Department of Health had signed 105 contracts with a total value of 2.5 billion GBP.
19 These groups include the Armed Forces, the Royal Canadian Mounted Police, and First Nations and Inuit peoples throughout Canada.
20 Nova Scotia seems to be an exception as it increased the number of regions from four to nine in 2002.

Index

Page numbers in *italics* refer to boxes and tables; *passim* indicates scattered mentions between page range.

PURCHASING TO IMPROVE HEALTH SYSTEMS PERFORMANCE

Edited by Josep Figueras, Ray Robinson and Elke Jakubowski

Purchasing is championed as key to improving health systems performance. However, despite the central role the purchasing function plays in many health system reforms, there is very little evidence about its development or its real impact on societal objectives. This book addresses this gap and provides:

- A comprehensive account of the theory and practice of purchasing for health services across Europe
- An up-to-date analysis of the evidence on different approaches to purchasing
- Support for policy-makers and practitioners as they formulate purchasing strategies so that they can increase effectiveness and improve performance in their own national context
- An assessment of the intersecting roles of citizens, the government and the providers

Written by leading health policy analysts, this book is essential reading for health policy makers, planners and managers as well as researchers and students in the field of health studies.

Contributors
Toni Ashton, Philip Berman, Michael Borowitz, Helmut Brand, Reinhard Busse, Andrea Donatini, Martin Dlouhy, Antonio Duran, Tamás Evetovits, André P. van den Exter, Josep Figueras, Nick Freemantle, Julian Forder, Péter Gaál, Chris Ham, Brian Hardy, Petr Hava, David Hunter, Danguole Jankauskiene, Maris Jesse, Ninel Kadyrova, Joe Kutzin, John Langenbrunner, Donald W. Light, Hans Maarse, Nicholas Mays, Martin McKee, Eva Orosz, John Øvretveit, Dominique Polton, Alexander S. Preker, Thomas A. Rathwell, Sabine Richard, Ray Robinson, Andrei Rys, Constantino Sakellarides, Sergey Shishkin, Peter C. Smith, Markus Schneider, Francesco Taroni, Marcial Velasco-Garrido, Miriam Wiley.

Contents

320pp   0 335 21367 7 (Paperback)   0 335 21368 5 (Hardback)